AF732349

LEGAL WRITING SOURCEBOOK

By

Executive Editor

Professor J. Lyn Entrikin

William H. Bowen School of Law,

University of Arkansas Little Rock

Copy Editor

Professor Mary Trevor

Mitchell | Hamline School of Law

Professor Heather Baxter

Nova Southeastern University Shepard Broad College of Law

Professor Deborah L. Borman

William H. Bowen School of Law,

University of Arkansas Little Rock

Professor Mary Bowman

Arizona State University Sandra Day O'Connor College of Law

Dean and Professor David R. Cleveland

Valparaiso University Law School

Visiting Professor Lurene Contento

Chicago-Kent College of Law,

Illinois Institute of Technology

Professor Olympia Duhart

Nova Southeastern University Shepard Broad College of Law

Professor J. Lyn Entrikin

William H. Bowen School of Law,

University of Arkansas Little Rock

Professor Emily Grant

Washburn University School of Law

Professor Tonya Kowalski
Washburn University School of Law

Professor Jan M. Levine
Duquesne University School of Law

Professor Sue Liemer
Elon University School of Law

Dean and Professor Anthony Niedwiecki
Golden Gate University School of Law

Professor Sara Rankin
Seattle University School of Law

Professor Kim D. Ricardo
UIC John Marshall Law School

Professor Suzanne E. Rowe
University of Oregon School of Law

Professor Michael R. Smith
University of Wyoming College of Law

Professor Kristen Konrad Tiscione
Georgetown University Law Center

Professor Catherine J. Wasson
Elon University School of Law

Professor Melissa H. Weresh
Drake University Law School

Professor Mark E. Wojcik
UIC John Marshall Law School

THE PUBLICATIONS COMMITTEE OF THE SECTION OF LEGAL EDUCATION AND ADMISSIONS TO THE BAR

THE AMERICAN BAR ASSOCIATION

ISBN 978-1-64105-080-7

AMERICAN BAR ASSOCIATION

Section of Legal Education and Admissions to the Bar

LEGAL WRITING SOURCEBOOK EXECUTIVE STEERING COMMITTEE MEMBERS

SUMMARY OF CONTENTS

TABLE OF CONTENTS

PREFACE

The ABA Section of Legal Education and Admissions to the Bar is proud to publish the *Legal Writing Sourcebook* and particularly pleased to offer this new, third edition of the book.

One of the most significant developments in legal education over the arc of my professional career has been the increased attention given by law schools to developing and improving students' communication skills. Key to this development has been the rise of a group of talented and dedicated faculty who focus their work on the teaching of these skills and scholarship about how to do it well.

We believe that the first edition of this book, published in 1997 by the Communication Skills Committee of the ABA Section of Legal Education and Admissions to the Bar, served the legal writing community well and played a significant role in the evolution of the teaching of legal writing, and communication skills more broadly. Approximately a decade later, the then current members of the Communication Skills Committee concluded that it was time to update, revise, and expand the *Sourcebook*. The resulting second edition of this *Sourcebook* continued to be an excellent source of ideas and guidance about legal writing programs.

Given the changes in legal education and the legal profession that have taken place since the second edition was published more than a decade ago, and with considerable further change on the horizon, it was certainly time to revise and update the *Sourcebook*.

Many members of the legal writing community lent a hand in the work needed to make this new edition a reality. Thanks to each of them. Thanks, too, to the members of the Section's Publications Committee that supported this effort; and to our Section Director, Erin Ruehrwein, whose hard work and persistence were central to the completion of the project. Special thanks to Professor J. Lyn

Entrikin of the Bowen School of Law at the University of Arkansas, Little Rock, and to Mary Trevor from Mitchell | Hamline School of Law for their excellent work.

We hope that this new edition will continue to serve well the needs of legal writing faculty and the legal education community.

Barry A. Currier
Managing Director
Accreditation and Legal Education
American Bar Association

PREAMBLE

What a difference a decade makes.

The last edition of the ABA *Sourcebook on Legal Writing Programs* – published more than a decade ago in 2006 – was an important update to the original book meant to serve as a resource for people designing, directing, and teaching in legal writing programs around the country. Over the past 14 years, both the demands and direction of programs have changed dramatically. And the evolution of Legal Writing programs since the very first edition of the *Sourcebook* in 1997 is even more remarkable. This newest edition of the *Sourcebook* aims to continue the important tradition paved by its earlier editions; it is also responsive to ever-evolving Legal Research & Writing (LRW) programs.

First, many programs have moved to an "autonomous" model – these programs have no director and instead give full autonomy to professors to set their own curriculum and pedagogical goals. Further, the LRW discipline has become increasingly professionalized. There is a critical movement to correct the professional status challenges that have long marked the discipline, and that positive movement has brought expansive opportunities and responsibilities for Legal Research and Writing programs. The gains in faculty status and governance translate to increased space for innovation and leadership; without a doubt, there is much more experimentation in the LRW classroom. Moreover, increased service and scholarship duties require intentional support for these additional threads.

In addition, the increased law school emphasis on formative assessment demanded by new ABA Accreditation Standards has opened the door for LRW Professors to lead the academy in teaching methods. The Legal Writing classroom has long been at the forefront of formative assessment, and the formal recognition of the value of feedback and assessment has given brand new opportunities for LRW professors and programs to contribute in important ways to a healthy law school culture committed to law student success.

Most importantly, the creativity and innovation of programs – whether led by a director, managed by a coordinator, or autonomous – has been truly boundless. This text examines platforms to explore the power of narrative and rhetoric, support for real client work, guidelines for teaching students with special needs, and ideas to boost wellness and student outreach initiatives. The new material also explores important considerations around implicit bias and inclusivity. In addition, it highlights the integration of skills and discipline-building through professional engagement. There is, we hope, something for everyone.

The new edition was only possible because of the hard work of Legal Writing professors who volunteered their energy and expertise to contribute to this project. We are incredibly thankful to the following professors for making time between memo-grading, student conferences, classes, and institutional committee work to contribute to this text:

- Professor Heather Baxter, Nova Southeastern University Shepard Broad College of Law
- Professor Deborah L. Borman, William H. Bowen School of Law, University of Arkansas Little Rock
- Professor Mary Bowman, Arizona State University Sandra Day O'Connor College of Law
- Dean and Professor David R. Cleveland, Valparaiso University Law School
- Visiting Professor Lurene Contento, Chicago-Kent College of Law, Illinois Institute of Technology
- Professor Olympia Duhart, Nova Southeastern University Shepard Broad College of Law
- Professor J. Lyn Entrikin, William H. Bowen School of Law, University of Arkansas Little Rock
- Professor Emily Grant, Washburn University School of Law

- Professor Tonya Kowalski, Washburn University School of Law
- Professor Jan M. Levine, Duquesne University School of Law
- Professor Sue Liemer, Elon University School of Law
- Dean and Professor Anthony Niedwiecki, Golden Gate University School of Law
- Professor Sara Rankin, Seattle University School of Law
- Professor Kim D. Ricardo, UIC John Marshall Law School
- Professor Suzanne E. Rowe, University of Oregon School of Law
- Professor Michael R. Smith, University of Wyoming College of Law
- Professor Kristen Konrad Tiscione, Georgetown University Law Center
- Professor Catherine J. Wasson, Elon University School of Law
- Professor Melissa H. Weresh, Drake University Law School
- Professor Mark E. Wojcik, UIC John Marshall Law School

We are especially grateful to our Executive Editor, Professor J. Lyn Entrikin of William H. Bowen School of Law, University of Arkansas Little Rock, for the countless hours she dedicated to this project. Another huge debt of gratitude is owed to our Copy Editor, Professor Mary Trevor of Mitchell | Hamline School of Law. Her thoughtful edits are sincerely appreciated. We also thank everyone who organized and contributed to the ALWD/LWI survey. The information captured in these annual surveys provided critical context throughout the text.

Finally, we thank Erin Ruehrwein, Section Director for the ABA Section of Legal Education and Admissions to the Bar. Her leadership, support, and dedication have been vital to our publication success. Further, the Section's Publications Committee gave us much-needed guidance in the nascent stages of our newest edition. We also want to thank the writers and editors of earlier editions, which formed the basis of this edition. We, of course, appreciate the support of the entire team at the ABA Section of Legal Education and Admissions to the Bar for investing in this important publication.

Despite the numerous differences in scope and coverage from its predecessors, the goals of the *Legal Writing Sourcebook* remain the same. This book is intended to highlight the common features of successful legal writing programs, offer practical guidance for program leaders, and inspire those committed to the discipline of Legal Writing to create and sustain their own successful models.

Ultimately, all of the *Sourcebooks* have focused on promoting student success. We are proud to start the new decade with our newest contribution to this goal. We hope this new edition inspires Legal Writing experts throughout the country to make their own Legal Writing programs the best they can be.

Olympia Duhart
Anthony Niedwiecki
Executive Steering Committee
ABA Legal Writing Sourcebook, 3d Edition

I. OVERVIEW OF LEGAL WRITING IN LAW SCHOOLS

A. Definition of "Legal Writing" and "Legal Writing Program"

The first step in understanding the nature of legal writing and legal writing programs in law schools is understanding the general meaning of these terms. Unfortunately, that is more complicated than it sounds. The terms *Legal Writing* and *Legal Writing Program* have various meanings depending on the context in which they are used. Not surprisingly, the flexible use of these terms has led to significant confusion over the years, especially among non-legal writing faculty. This section is designed to clear up much of that confusion.

1. Definition of "Legal Writing"

a. Introduction

The term *Legal Writing* does not refer to a single type of writing, but rather refers to several distinct types or categories of writing commonly practiced by lawyers, judges, paralegals, and law students. These categories differ in terms of purpose, intended audience, skills involved, and paradigmatic structure. Each of the categories of legal writing has its own collection of textbooks designed to teach that type of writing. What's more, proficiency in one category or type of legal writing does not necessarily assure proficiency in another category or type without additional instruction. Adding to the confusion is the fact that the term *Legal Writing* is often loosely used to include several non-writing skills that are customarily taught and practiced in conjunction with legal writing. For example, the term *Legal Writing* is often used as a shorthand moniker for a course that teaches both legal writing and legal research. To be sure, the skills of legal research—using research tools to locate sources relevant to a legal issue—are distinct from the skills of legal writing. Yet, the term *Legal Writing* often is used idiomatically to mean both legal writing and legal research. Other non-writing skills that are often incorporated into the term *Legal Writing* are discussed below.

b. Categories of Legal Writing[1]

i. Application Analysis Writing

The first and most common category of legal writing is Application Analysis Writing (also called Law Application Writing). In this type of writing, the writer communicates, either objectively or persuasively, how the law *applies* to a specific set of facts. Application Analysis Writing generally follows one of the popular paradigmatic structures for communicating legal analysis such as IRAC[2] or CREAC.[3] The types of documents included within this category are legal memoranda, pre-trial briefs, trial briefs, appellate briefs, bench briefs, judicial opinions, and traditional law school exam essay answers. All of these documents have one foundational characteristic in common: they all communicate how the relevant law applies to given facts.

Most law schools introduce their law students to legal writing by covering Application Analysis Writing in the first year, often through required courses that cover legal memoranda, court briefs, and essay exams. Because Application Analysis Writing is so pervasive in the required first-year curriculum of most law schools, many legal writing faculty and non-legal writing faculty are actually referring to this sub-category of legal writing when they use the general

---

[1]These categories are based on Michael R. Smith, *Alternative Substantive Approaches to Advanced Legal Writing Courses*, 54 J. LEGAL EDUC. 119, 122-26 (2004).

[2]IRAC stands for Issue, Rule, Application, and Conclusion.

[3]CREAC stands for Conclusion, Rule, Explanation of Rule, Application, and Conclusion.

term *Legal Writing*. The use of the term *Legal Writing* to refer to this single sub-category of legal writing, however, has contributed to confusion over the scope of the discipline.

ii. Legal Drafting

The second category of legal writing is Legal Drafting. Legal Drafting refers to writing that "produces a document that both reflects and yields a client's desired results in connection with some event that is meaningful under the law."[4] Legal Drafting is often broken down into three sub-categories: Transactional Drafting, Litigation Drafting, and Statutory Drafting. Transactional Drafting refers to writing documents that memorialize and effectuate business transactions. Examples include contracts, estate planning documents (such as wills and trusts), real estate documents (such as deeds, mortgages, leases, and easements), financial documents (such as promissory notes and bills of sale), and business-entity documents (such as partnership agreements and articles of incorporation). Litigation Drafting refers to writing the formal documents associated with litigation, such as pleadings, motions, interrogatories, and jury instructions. Statutory Drafting refers to writing state and federal statutes and local government ordinances.

iii. Critical Analysis Writing

The third category of legal writing is Critical Analysis Writing (also called Scholarly Legal Writing or Academic Legal Writing). Critical Analysis Writing is writing that critically analyzes a specific area of the law or legal phenomenon in terms of broader legal principles, public policy considerations, or concepts from other disciplines such as economics, history, philosophy, medicine, finance, science, psychology, sociology, political science, critical race theory, rhetoric, and literary theory. Critical Analysis Writing is typically associated with law school seminar courses and student

---

[4] Smith, *supra* note 1, at 124.

participation on law review. Examples of this type of legal writing are seminar papers and law review articles, notes, and comments.

iv. Legal Correspondence Writing

The fourth category of legal writing is Legal Correspondence Writing. As the name suggests, this type of legal writing refers to writing correspondence in connection with law practice. The documents included within this category are client letters, demand letters, letters to opposing counsel, opinion letters, and official email correspondence.

c. Other Lawyering Skills Often Included Within "Legal Writing"

As noted earlier, the term *Legal Writing* is sometimes used idiomatically as a catch-all or generic term for other non-writing skills that are customarily taught in conjunction with legal writing. These other lawyering skills include legal research, legal analysis, client interviewing, fact investigation, client counseling, negotiation, general oral communication, and oral advocacy, as well as others. The use of the term *Legal Writing* to mean not only legal writing per se but also its attendant skills has further contributed to the confusion over the discipline.

2. *Definition of "Legal Writing Program"*

The term *Legal Writing Program* also has various meanings depending on the context. Generally, it refers to the resources a law school devotes to the teaching of legal research and legal writing. More specifically, the term *Legal Writing Program* refers to a combination of three sets of resources at a law school: (1) the law school's legal research and legal writing *curriculum*, (2) the law school's *co-curricular activities and resources* regarding legal research and legal writing, and (3) the *people* hired to administer and teach legal research and legal writing courses at the law school.

As a first matter, the term *Legal Writing Program* customarily refers to a law school's legal research and legal writing curriculum, which would include both the required curriculum and upper-level electives in the area. The term also often encompasses a law school's co-curricular opportunities and resources for legal research and writing, such as writing competitions, co-curricular presentations on legal research or legal writing topics, and training sessions for law review editors. Finally, the term *Legal Writing Program* typically includes the human resources hired to administer and teach legal research and legal writing at a law school. These human resources can include legal writing administrators (such as Assistant Deans, Directors, and Assistant Directors), full-time faculty, full-time and part-time writing specialists, teaching librarians, administrative assistants, visiting faculty, teaching fellows, adjunct faculty, and student teaching assistants.

3. Terminology Used in This Sourcebook

Throughout this *Sourcebook*, we will refer to the basic required course in legal research and writing as the "LRW" course, and the faculty who teach the course as LRW faculty. While we sometimes refer to the LRW course as a "first-year" course, we mean the term to include any basic required courses, even if they extend beyond the first two semesters of the law school curriculum.

As the chapters in this *Sourcebook* show, although the LRW course primarily focuses on the Application Analysis Writing sub-category of legal writing described above, it often covers various other sub-categories as well. Further, the faculty who teach the LRW course often possess expertise and experience encompassing not only a number of those sub-categories, but also other areas of legal practice, doctrine, and scholarship.

B. ABA Standards That Guide LRW Instruction

1. The ABA and Law School Accreditation

a. Introduction

Support for university-based legal education has been an essential part of the ABA's mission since the organization was established. At its first meeting in August 1878, the ABA created the Committee on Legal Education and Admissions to the Bar, and adopted a resolution requiring the Committee to report back at the ABA's annual meeting "'some plan for assimilating throughout the Union, the requirements of candidates for admission to the bar.'"[5] At the annual meeting in 1879, the Committee reported that it favored university-based law schools over the apprenticeship model of legal training. At this meeting and over a period of years, the Committee presented resolutions in support of law schools.[6] The Committee evolved into the ABA's first section, the Section of Legal Education and Admissions to the Bar, in 1893.[7]

In 1921, the Section adopted resolutions stating that, in its opinion, admission to the bar required a candidate to complete at least two years of undergraduate work, complete three years of law school studies (more for part-time students), "and pass an examination 'by public authority.'"[8] Additionally, a law school had to provide an

---

[5] James P. White, *History of the Administration of the American Law School Process*, 51 J. LEGAL EDUC. 438, 439 (2001). *See generally ABA Timeline*, ABA: AM. BAR ASS'N, https://www.americanbar.org/about_the_aba/timeline/ (last visited Jan. 9, 2020) for a historical overview of the mission, structure, membership, and initiatives of the ABA.

[6] *See* White, *supra* note 5, at 440 (recounting in depth the various resolutions leading to the ABA becoming the central accrediting body of the profession); *see also* ROBERT STEVENS, LAW SCHOOL: LEGAL EDUCATION IN AMERICA FROM THE 1850S TO THE 1980S, at 27, 95-102 (1983).

[7] *ABA Timeline*, *supra* note 5.

[8] *Id.*

adequate library and a sufficient number of full-time faculty.[9] The ABA endorsed publication of the names of law schools that complied with these standards. The first list of law schools meeting these standards was published in the *ABA Journal* in 1923.[10]

These standards have evolved considerably over time, as have the Section itself and the accreditation process, creating a national and unified approach to legal education and law school accreditation. The first major revision of the 1921 standards was completed in 1973. The next comprehensive review was completed in 1996, with substantial additional revisions in academic years 2000/2001 and 2003/2005. The most recent comprehensive review was undertaken in 2008 and completed in 2014. The current standards comprise seven chapters. The chapters are organized by topic and include standards covering, among other things, the program of legal education and the faculty.

b. About the Section of Legal Education & Admissions to the Bar

The Section is governed by a Council, which has ultimate authority over approval of standards and the accreditation process. The Council is recognized as the national accrediting body for law schools by the U.S. Department of Education.[11] "In this function, the Council and the Section are independent of the ABA, as required by DOE regulations."[12] The Council comprises law school deans and

---

[9]White, *supra* note 5, at 440.

[10]*ABA Timeline*, *supra* note 5.

[11]*See* The Secretary's Recognition of Accrediting Agencies, 34 C.F.R. pt. 602 (2005); *see also Accreditation in the United States: Programmatic Accrediting Agencies*, U.S. DEPT. OF EDUC., https://www2.ed.gov/admins/finaid/accred/accreditation_pg7.html#law (last visited Jan. 9, 2020).

[12]ABA Section of Legal Educ. & Admission to the Bar, *About Us*, ABA: AM. BAR ASS'N, https://www.americanbar.org/groups/legal_education/about_us.html (last visited Jan. 8, 2020).

professors, practicing lawyers, judges, university administrators, and bar examiners. The Council is headed by a Chair of the Section. Each year, a new chair is elected, and the position rotates among deans, judges, and practicing attorneys. The work of the Section and its governing Council is administered through the office of the Managing Director of Accreditation and Legal Education, located in Chicago.

For many years, two Section committees played a critical role in the law school approval process. The Standards Review Committee (SRC) was "charged with reviewing proposed changes in or additions to Standards, Interpretations, Rules, Policies, Procedures, and Criteria."[13] An Accreditation Committee was charged with administering the law school accreditation process. Representative membership on these two committees was similar to that of the Council.

At its May 2018 meeting, the Council approved a restructuring plan designed to streamline the standards review process by eliminating the Standards Review and Accreditation Committees and having all work completed by the Council.[14] Related changes to the Council's bylaws and rules of procedure were also approved. The restructuring plan became effective when the ABA House of Delegates concurred in the plan at its August 2018 meeting.[15]

---

[13]ABA Section of Legal Educ. & Admission to the Bar, *Standards Review Process*, ABA: AM. BAR ASS'N, https://www.americanbar.org/groups/legal_education/committees/standards_review.html (last visited Nov. 6, 2019).

[14]*Summary of Actions of the Section's Council at its Meeting* (May 10-12, 2018), https://www.americanbar.org/content/dam/aba/administrative/legal_education_and_admissions_to_the_bar/2018_may_legal_ed_dc_summary_of_meeting.pdf (last visited Jan. 9, 2020).

[15]Despite the approval of these changes, the ABA website continues to refer to "the committee" when describing the standards review process. *See Standards Review Process*, *supra* note 13.

c. Promulgation of Standards

To promulgate new standards and revise current standards, the Council has historically used a "consensus validation model."[16] Until 2018/2019, it delegated to the SRC the role of reviewing proposed changes in or additions to the Standards, Interpretations, and Rules of Procedure for the approval of law schools [collectively, Standards]. Pursuant to the restructuring plan effective in 2018/2019, the Council is now primarily responsible for reviewing the Standards, but it may "appoint ad hoc committees, task forces, or working groups on accreditation-related matters."[17] Section 9 of the Council's Internal Operating Practices describes the process to be followed when reviewing and amending the Standards, as detailed in the following two paragraphs.[18]

The Council is required to engage in ongoing review of the Standards. The Council must give public notice of the sections that will be considered for revision each year and invite suggestions for other changes that should be considered. It may also engage in a comprehensive review of the Standards "whenever the Council determines that a more comprehensive review would serve the interests of legal education." When the Council determines that changes to the Standards should be made, "action to make those changes must

---

[16] Robert K. Walsh, *The ABA's Standards for the Accreditation of Law Schools*, 51 J. LEGAL EDUC. 427, 427 (2001). The process for promulgating and amending the Standards, Interpretations, and Rules of Procedure for the approval of law schools is described in Rule 8 of the Section's Internal Operating Procedures. *See 2019-2020 Internal Operating Practices*, https://www.americanbar.org/content/dam/aba/administrative/legal_education_and_admissions_to_the_bar/standards/2019-2020/2019-2020-aba-standards-internal-operating-practices.pdf (last visited Jan. 9, 2020).

[17] *2019-2020 Internal Operating Practices, supra* note 16, § 2.

[18] *See generally id.* § 9.

be initiated within 12 months . . . and shall be completed within a reasonable period of time."

During this period the Council "shall seek public comment, as appropriate." The Council must post any proposed changes or amendments and seek public comment, which may be solicited in writing or received orally during a public hearing, for which at least fifteen days' notice must be given. Both written comments and a transcript of oral testimony must be posted on the Section's website. A written report must be made available to the public when the Council acts on final revisions to the Standards. The Council's decision to "adopt, revise, amend, or repeal the [Standards]" must then be reviewed by the ABA House of Delegates.

If the House of Delegates concurs with the Council's proposed revisions, they become effective at the conclusion of the House of Delegates' meeting.[19] If the House does not concur, it may refer the matter back to the Council for further consideration.[20] After two referrals by the Council, "then the decision of the Council following the second referral will be final and will not be subject to further review by the House."[21]

i. The Importance of the Public Comment Phase

The public hearings and solicitations for written comment are important avenues that allow those with particular expertise and knowledge to communicate directly with the Council about proposed Standards. For example, whenever public hearings have been held on proposed changes to the standards that affect legal writing,

---

[19] *Rules of Procedure for Approval of Law Schools* Rule 52.c, https://www.americanbar.org/content/dam/aba/administrative/legal_education_and_admissions_to_the_bar/standards/2019-2020/2019-2020-aba-standards-rules-of-procedure.pdf (last visited Jan. 9, 2020).

[20] *Id.*

[21] *Id.*

members of the Association of Legal Writing Directors (ALWD) and the Legal Writing Institute (LWI) have testified about the need for the Standards to address issues relating to the quality of legal writing programs and the role of legal writing faculty in the academy. Additionally, both organizations have submitted extensive reports with recommendations on the quality of legal writing instruction.[22] Similarly, members of the Clinical Legal Education Association (CLEA) and the Society of American Law Teachers (SALT) have testified on a variety of proposed changes to the Standards, as have deans, both individually and through the American Law Deans Association (ALDA).

ii. The Role of Affiliated Groups

Various affiliated organizations within the legal academy have been granted "sibling" status, which allows these organizations to send representatives to the Council's meetings. These representatives may attend all public meetings of the Council, but they do not attend the highly confidential executive sessions when the Council discusses accreditation issues related to specific schools.

Several years ago, ALWD was granted affiliate status. It has routinely sent representatives to Council meetings to report on ALWD activities. These interactions promote better communication between the Council, ALWD, and other affiliated groups. Better communication in turn promotes a deeper understanding of the many issues the Council addresses.

---

[22] *See, e.g.*, Ass'n of Legal Writing Dirs. & The Legal Writing Inst., *Quality Legal Writing Instruction and ABA Accreditation Standard 405: Report & Recommendations* (Aug. 23, 2004) [hereinafter *Report & Recommendations*], https://www.alwd.org/images/resources/Standard%20405%20-%20ALWD%20_%20LWI%20Report%20_%20Recommendations%20-%20August%202004.pdf. See the website of the Association of Legal Writing Directors (ALWD), https://www.alwd.org/aba-engagement, for links to more than 20 reports and written comments regarding proposed changes to the Standards submitted by the organization since 2000.

2. *Standards Affecting LRW Instruction*

Several Standards and their Interpretations[23] affect LRW courses and LRW faculty. These standards have evolved over time, as will be explained in the sections below. Generally speaking, standards affecting course content and delivery have been strengthened and expanded since the first *Sourcebook* was published in 1997. Standards affecting the terms and conditions of employment for LRW faculty have evolved more slowly. LRW teachers—who are predominantly female—continue to work for lower salaries and with less job security than most legal academics.[24]

a. Evolution of the Standards from 1996 – 2008

The 1996, 2000/2001, and 2003/2005 reviews of the Standards added important requirements affecting LRW. The most relevant were the Preamble, Standard 302, Standard 402 and its Interpretations, and Standard 405 and its Interpretations.

i. Evolution of Standards Affecting LRW Courses

Chapter 3 of the Standards governs law schools' educational programs, covering such topics as curriculum requirements, the academic calendar, and clinical courses. Standard 302 governed the content of a law school's core educational program for many years. In 1996 the Standard 302 requirement that law schools offer all students "at least one rigorous writing requirement" was amended to include 302(a)(2), requiring a school to "offer to all students . . . an educational program designed to provide its graduates with basic competence in legal analysis and reasoning, legal research, problem

---

[23] Interpretations are the Council's explanations of the general principles embodied by the Standards.

[24] *See generally* survey data available at *Survey*, ALWD: ASS'N OF LEGAL WRITING DIRS., https://www.alwd.org/resources/survey (last visited Jan. 9, 2020).

solving, and oral and written communication." Similar language was added to the Standards' Preamble. This was the first time that the Standards specifically required law schools to provide a program designed to ensure that its graduates receive basic training in the skills taught in quality writing programs.

In 2001, Standard 302(a)(2) was amended to require schools to provide "substantial legal writing instruction, including at least one rigorous writing experience in the first year and at least one additional rigorous writing experience after the first year." Because many law schools already required students to complete both a first-year LRW course and an upper-level seminar course, this change was in some respects a codification of current practice. Nevertheless, the Section's further recognition of the importance of LRW instruction in the curriculum was a significant advancement.

Standard 302(a) was revised substantially during the 2003–2005 review of the Standards in connection with the Council's re-certification as the accrediting body for law schools. The revised Standard provided that

> [a] law school shall require that each student receive substantial instruction in: . . . (2) legal analysis and reasoning, legal research, problem solving, and oral communication; [and] (3) writing in a legal context, including at least one rigorous writing experience in the first year and at least one additional rigorous writing experience after the first year.

The prior version of these requirements simply stated that law students should "receive instruction" in these skills and lumped them together.

Interpretation 302-1 explained the revised Standard 302(a) by identifying specific factors that were to be considered in evaluating the "rigor" of writing instruction:

> the number and nature of writing projects assigned to students; the opportunities a student has to meet with a writing instructor for purposes of individualized assessment of the student's written products; the number of drafts that a student must produce of any writing project; and the form of assessment used by the writing instructor.

These factors allowed accreditation site teams (discussed more fully below) to inquire about the impact that class size and credit allocation for LRW courses might have on compliance with the Standard 302(a) requirement of "rigor" in legal writing instruction.

ii. Evolution of Standards Affecting LRW Faculty

Prior to 1996, LRW professors were almost invisible in the Standards. In that year, Interpretation 402-1 was added so that, for the first time, LRW professors who were not on tenure track could be counted in the student-faculty ratios that all law schools were required to report to the Section annually and during the Section's periodic re-accreditation processes. Previously, off-tenure-track clinicians and LRW faculty were not counted at all, even though most were full-time teachers. The new Interpretation 402-1 allowed a law school to count each full-time clinician and LRW faculty member as seven-tenths (0.7) of a faculty member if they were neither tenure-track nor afforded security of position "reasonably similar to tenure" under Standard 405(c). Tenure-track faculty and those with Standard 405(c) long-term, presumptively renewable contracts were each counted as a 1.0 full-time faculty member.

Also in 1996, Standard 405 was amended to include subsection (d), which required law schools that employed full-time LRW faculty to "provide conditions sufficient to attract well-qualified legal writing instructors or directors." Thus, for the first time, the Standards specifically recognized LRW faculty and directors as discrete categories within a law school faculty. Further, while not directly targeted at LRW faculty, Standard 405(c) was amended to require (rather than simply recommend) law schools to provide clinicians with a form of job security "reasonably similar to tenure."[25]

By 1999, when the Council began another comprehensive review of the Standards, LRW had emerged more fully as an academic discipline with an even more discernible pedagogy and a growing body of scholarship. The Council indicated a willingness to hear from various affiliated groups on how the Standards should be revised, so ALWD and LWI prepared a report to the Council and the SRC setting forth the reasons why LRW professors should be provided greater job security.[26] Additionally, members of the two organizations mobilized, attended SRC hearings, and testified about the importance of providing greater job security for full-time professors of LRW in ensuring quality LRW instruction. The LRW community focused on Standard 405, requesting an amendment to the clinical employment standard, 405(c), to include LRW faculty, and deletion of the separate LRW employment standard, 405(d).[27] This change would have provided LRW teachers with the same security of position as clinical teachers.

Instead, the SRC amended Standard 405(d) to require law schools to "afford legal writing teachers such security of position and other rights and privileges of faculty membership as may be necessary to (1) attract and retain a faculty that is well qualified to provide legal writing instruction as required by Standard 302(a)(2), and (2) safeguard academic freedom." While this change did not provide LRW teachers with the same security of position as clinical teachers, it did add important new language. Schools would now have

---

[25]This standard did not, however, preclude a school from having "a limited number of fixed, short-term" contracts if the clinical program was staffed predominantly with full-time faculty. Short-term contracts were also permitted in an "experimental program of limited duration."

[26]*See Report & Recommendations, supra* note 22.

[27]*Id.*

to "attract *and retain*" legal writing faculty and "safeguard [their] academic freedom." (Emphasis added.) To accompany this change, however, Interpretation 405-9 was added to clarify that 405(d) "[did] not preclude the use of short-term or non-renewable contracts for legal writing teachers." This interpretation permitted law schools to continue to "cap" an LRW teacher's employment at, for example, two years, but the Standard itself did require law schools to report to the Section on their ability to *retain* LRW faculty. This requirement permitted site teams to inquire whether short-term contracts and employment caps negatively affected a school's ability to provide the writing instruction required by Standard 302(a)(2).

The 2003-2005 revisions resulted in changes to Interpretation 405-9. This interpretation had stated that the "attract and retain" language in Standard 405(d) "[did] not preclude the use of short-term *or non-renewable* contracts for legal writing teachers." (Emphasis added.) The revised interpretation eliminated the explicit approval of non-renewable—i.e., "capped"—contracts, but stated that "[s]ubsection (d) of this Standard does not preclude the use of short-term contracts for legal writing teachers, nor does it preclude law schools from offering fellowship programs designed to produce candidates for full-time teaching by offering individuals supervised teaching experience."

The 2003-2005 revisions failed to correct many problematic job security aspects of the Standards, presaging the subsequent stalemate in the 2008-2014 review.[28] To summarize the situation that has resulted, the amendments recognized that non-renewable contracts are inconsistent with the text of Standard 405(d) that requires law schools to afford sufficient security of position to "retain" full-time LRW teachers. Although the prohibition of non-renewable contracts was a positive change, the continued explicit approval of short-term "fellowship" programs still allows law schools to staff LRW courses with relatively inexperienced, short-term professors who turn over

---

[28] *See infra* Section I(B)(2)(b)(ii).

frequently. The need to hire, train, and mentor these teachers places a significant administrative burden on LRW program directors and deprives students of experienced faculty.

b. Current Standards[29]

The SRC undertook another comprehensive review of the Standards from 2008 to 2014. The so-called "new standards" became effective in August 2014. Because of the sweeping nature of some of the changes to the Standards, particularly with regard to the law school curriculum and student assessment, law schools were given approximately two years to work toward compliance. During this transition period, ABA accreditation site teams were given guidance about how to evaluate "the seriousness of a law school's efforts" to comply with some of the new standards.[30]

The new standards marked a significant shift in focus from previous versions.[31] Among the many changes made, the new standards

---

[29] For the current standards as of the publication of this *Sourcebook*, see Section of Legal Educ. & Admissions to the Bar, *ABA Standards and Rules of Procedure for Approval of Law Schools (2019-2020)*, ABA: AM. BAR. ASS'N, https://www.americanbar.org/content/dam/aba/administrative/legal_education_and_admissions_to_the_bar/standards/2019-2020/2019-2020-aba-standards-and-rules-of-procedure.pdf. At least some revisions to the Standards are usually made every year. But the standards discussed in this section (I.B)—302, 302, 402, & 405—have not changed since 2014.

[30] *See* ABA Section of Legal Educ. & Admissions to the Bar, *Transition to and Implementation of the New Standards and Rules of Procedure for Approval of Law Schools* (Aug. 13, 2014), https://www.americanbar.org/content/dam/aba/administrative/legal_education_and_admissions_to_the_bar/governancedocuments/2014_august_transition_and_implementation_of_new_aba_standards_and_rules.pdf.

[31] *See* ABA Section of Legal Educ. & Admissions to the Bar Standards Review Committee, *Overview of Changes to the Standard for Approval of Law Schools*, https://www.americanbar.org/content/dam/aba/administrative/legal_education_and_admissions_to_the_bar/council_reports_and_resolutions/overview_of_changes.pdf (last visited Dec. 7, 2019).

are more objective, require greater transparency in a school's rules and policies, and adopt several new requirements for a law school's program of legal education. The overall impact of these changes has been felt throughout the legal academy; their direct impact on LRW courses and faculty, however, has been modest.

i. Current Standards Affecting LRW Courses

(1) Standards Specific to Writing

Former Standard 302 required law schools to "provide instruction" in five major areas, including "(2) legal analysis and reasoning, legal research, problem solving, and oral communication; [and] (3) writing in a legal context, including at least one rigorous writing experience in the first year and at least one additional rigorous writing experience after the first year." The new Standards break those provisions apart and place them in two different Standards.

Current Standard 302 requires law schools to "*establish learning outcomes* that shall . . . include competency in . . . (b) Legal analysis and reasoning, legal research, problem solving, and written and oral communication in the legal context." This standard thus combines former Standard 302(a)(2) with part of (a)(3). The remaining content of former Standard 302(a)(3) now appears in current Standard 303, but in a revised form. While the former Standard required "instruction" in legal writing that included at least two "rigorous" writing experiences, the current Standard 303(a)(2) provides that schools must only "offer a curriculum that requires each student to satisfactorily complete" two "writing experiences" that are "faculty supervised."

By exchanging "instruction" for "faculty supervis[ion]" and eliminating the requirement that student writing experiences be "rigorous," the current standards appear to require less of both teacher and student. Current Interpretation 303-2 seems to support this conclusion. While its predecessor, Interpretation 302-1, discussed the rigor of "writing instruction" partly in terms of meetings with and assessment by a "writing instructor," the current Interpretation 303-1 focuses on "a writing experience" rather than on "instruction," and eliminates all references to an "instructor." These changes permit site teams to inquire whether the new Standards inadvertently undermine students' opportunities to acquire the skills traditionally taught in LRW classrooms. On the other hand, co-curricular writing opportunities such as law review cannot meet the upper-level writing requirement unless a faculty member supervises the writing experience.

(2) Other Relevant Standards

Other revisions to Chapter 3 of the Standards intersect with the work traditionally done in LRW classrooms, although they do not expressly mention LRW as a subject area. For example, Standard 302(d) now requires schools to establish learning outcomes related to "competency in . . . (d) [o]ther professional skills needed for competent and ethical participation as a member of the legal profession." As explained in Interpretation 302-1, "other professional skills . . . may include skills such as[ ] interviewing, . . . fact development and analysis, . . . document drafting, . . . organization and management of legal work, collaboration, cultural competency, and self-evaluation." LRW programs and classes across the country have long given students an opportunity to develop some or all of these skills.

Similarly, the new curricular requirement for "experiential courses" incorporates course characteristics familiar to most LRW professors. Standard 303(a)(3) states that an "experiential" course must:

> (i) integrate doctrine, theory, skills, and legal ethics, and engage students in performance of one or more of the professional skills identified in Standard 302;
>
> (ii) develop the concepts underlying the professional skills being taught;
>
> (iii) provide multiple opportunities for performance; and
>
> (iv) provide opportunities for self-evaluation.

The defining characteristics of good LRW problem design and instruction include all of these requirements.[32]

Finally, Standard 314 requires a law school to perform both formative and summative student assessments, while Standard 315 requires a school to continually evaluate the effectiveness of its curriculum, student outcomes, and assessment methods. These kinds of assessment and reflection are perhaps *the* defining characteristics of LRW teaching and course design.[33] The reiterative writing process provides students with numerous opportunities for formative assessment through professor feedback, peer and self-evaluation, and self-reflection. Each project culminates in a summative assessment of a student's performance on a critical lawyering task—e.g., writing a memo or brief, arguing a motion, or delivering an appellate argument before a panel of judges. Moreover, as the law develops and the practice of law changes, LRW teachers constantly update their assignments to expose students to new legal issues and practice methods and to present them with opportunities to confront ethical issues and changing social norms.

ii. Current Standards Affecting LRW Faculty

While the 2014 revisions to Chapter 3 of the Standards (The Program of Legal Education) represented a major shift in focus for legal education, revisions to Chapter 4 (The Faculty) were far more modest. Standards 402 and 405 continue to be the most relevant to LRW faculty.

The current Standard 402, which governs the size of the full-time faculty, eliminates the requirement formerly found in subsection (b) to consider the student/faculty ratio when determining whether a law school complies with the Standards. That entire subsection has been deleted, and with it the requirement to count full-time clinical and LRW teachers not on tenure-track or its equivalent as only

---

[32] *See infra* Chapters II-III.

[33] *See infra* Chapters II-IV.

0.7 of a full-time faculty member. This change finally rids the Standards of the bias implied by designating a faculty cohort that is historically female as "less than" their colleagues who teach in other areas. At the same time, however, there is no longer an incentive to improve faculty status in order to improve a law school's student/faculty ratio.

Standard 405, which governs the professional environment for law school faculty, generated extensive discussion during the 2008-2014 comprehensive review of the Standards. Four alternatives to revise Standard 405 were proposed, but only two were circulated for notice and comment. One of the rejected proposals would have required *all* full-time faculty to have the same security of position. ALWD advocated for such a revision, noting that the Council had an opportunity to "eliminat[e] all forms of discrimination in ABA-accredited law schools, root and branch."[34]

One of the two proposals that were ultimately circulated for notice and comment would have simply required law schools to provide full-time faculty members with a form of security of position sufficient to attract and retain a competent faculty and ensure academic freedom. Although this proposal would have done away with the faculty hierarchies long embodied in Standards 405(b), (c), and (d) (concerning, respectively, tenure-track professors, clinical professors, and LRW professors), it would not have rectified the effects that the hierarchical approach had on legal writing faculty in the past. The second circulated proposal did not require any specific protection for security of position. Both proposals were the subject of intense debate.[35]

---

[34] Letter from ALWD President Kathleen Elliott Vinson et al. (Jan. 29, 2014), https://www.americanbar.org/content/dam/aba/administrative/legal_education_and_admissions_to_the_bar/council_reports_and_resolutions/comments/201401_comment_stds_205_206_303a3_ch_4_alwd.authcheckdam.pdf.

[35] Comments received from interested individuals, organizations, and institutions can be found in the *Notice and Comment Archive* on the ABA website. *See* https://www.americanbar.org/groups/legal_education/resources/notice_and_comment/notice_comment_archive.html (last visited Dec. 12, 2019).

Ultimately, although "[a] majority of the Council expressed dissatisfaction with current Standard 405,"[36] neither of the proposed alternatives that were circulated garnered majority support. As a result, Standard 405(d) remains unchanged, continuing to require that law schools offer LRW teachers only "such security of position and other rights and privileges of faculty membership as may be necessary to (1) attract and retain a faculty that is well-qualified to provide legal writing instruction as required by Standard 302(a)(2), and (2) safeguard academic freedom." With some small variations over the years, Interpretation 405-9 continues to explicitly allow law schools to use short-term contracts and limited-term fellowship programs for LRW teachers.

3. Why the Standards Do Not Refer to Salaries

As the result of an antitrust lawsuit, the ABA Standards do not require a law school to pay LRW professors the equivalent of other teachers' salaries. In 1995, the Antitrust Division of the U.S. Justice Department sued the ABA, alleging that, among other things, the ABA was using accreditation as a vehicle to pressure universities into paying higher salaries to law school faculties. The ABA signed a consent decree admitting no fault but agreeing, among other things, not to attempt to regulate law school salaries or even collect information on salaries.

For several years, ALWD and LWI have conducted annual surveys that collect data on salaries of LRW directors and faculty. While the data show that LRW faculty earn disproportionately less than tenure-track faculty, the ABA Standards do not require a law school to improve the compensation of LRW professors. An alternative way to challenge the disparity would be to allege salary

---

[36] ABA Section of Legal Educ. & Admissions to the Bar, *Explanation of Changes*, 14, https://www.americanbar.org/content/dam/aba/administrative/legal_education_and_admissions_to_the_bar/council_reports_and_resolutions/201408_explanation_changes.authcheckdam.pdf (last visited Dec. 12, 2019).

discrimination in violation of a statute such as 42 U.S.C. § 2000e, which prohibits employment discrimination.[37] Given such a claim, the ABA could investigate the complaint.[38]

A substantial body of scholarship explores the intersection of gender, status, and salary issues for LRW faculty.[39] As of this

---

[37]The Antitrust Division was concerned that collective industry standards on salary matters might tend to stabilize the "price" in the labor market for hiring full-time law professors. Of course, law schools as employers may not discriminate on prohibited bases such as the race or gender of faculty members in determining compensation.

[38]*See United States v. American Bar Ass'n*, No. 95-1211 CRR (D.D.C. June 25, 1996), https://www.justice.gov/atr/case-document/revised-final-judgment-0 (permitting the ABA, "upon receipt of a complaint concerning discrimination," to collect and consider "compensation information that is relevant to the allegations of discrimination in order to determine whether the school that is the subject of the complaint complies with Standards . . . or Interpretations . . . that prohibit discrimination.").

[39]*See, e.g.*, Lucille A. Jewell, *Oil and Water: How Legal Education's Doctrine and Skills Divide Reproduces Toxic Hierarchies*, 31 COLUM. J. GENDER & L. 111 (2015); Kathryn M. Stanchi, *Who Next, the Janitors? A Socio-Feminist Critique of the Status Hierarchy of Law Professors*, 73 UMKC L. REV. 467 (2005); Richard K. Neumann, Jr., *Women in Legal Education: A Statistical Update*, 73 UMKC L. REV. 419 (2004); Jo Anne Durako, *A Woman's Place: Employment Patterns in Legal Writing*, 6 EMP. RTS. & EMP. POL'Y J. 134 (2002); Jan M. Levine & Kathryn Stanchi, *Women, Writing & Wages: Breaking the Last Taboo*, 7 WM. & MARY J. WOMEN & L. 551 (2001) [hereinafter Levine & Stanchi, *Last Taboo]*; Hope Viner Samborn, *Legal Writing Instruction: The Pink Ghetto of Academe*, Persps. (Newsletter, ABA Comm'n. on Women in the Profession), Spring/Summer 2001, at 8; Kathryn Stanchi & Jan M. Levine, *Gender and Legal Writing: Law School's Dirty Little Secrets*, 16 BERKELEY WOMEN'S L.J. 3 (2001) [hereinafter Stanchi & Levine, *Dirty Little Secrets*]; Mary Beth Beazley, *"Riddikulus!": Tenure-Track Legal-Writing Faculty and the Boggart in the Wardrobe*, 7 SCRIBES J. LEGAL WRITING 79 (1998-2000); Jo Anne Durako, *Second-Class Citizens in the Pink Ghetto: Gender Bias in Legal Writing,* 50 J. LEGAL EDUC. 562 (2000); Richard K. Neumann, Jr., *Women in Legal Education: What the Statistics Show*, 50 J. LEGAL EDUC. 313 (2000); Jo Anne Durako, *Stop the Presses: Gender-Based Differences Discovered in the Legal-Writing Profession*, 7 SCRIBES J. LEGAL WRITING 87

writing, no complaints have been filed with the ABA specifically targeting the salary disparities for LRW professors. In 2013, however, a female professor at Denver University filed a discrimination complaint with the Equal Employment Opportunity Commission (EEOC) after discovering that female full professors earned almost $20,000 less than their male counterparts.[40] Six additional plaintiffs subsequently joined the suit, including a tenured professor who had directed Denver's LRW program from 2000-2007. In May 2018, a settlement was reached under which the plaintiffs will receive $2.66 million and pay increases.[41] The law school also must appoint an independent monitor to review employment decisions for six years and set up a secure website where faculty can review information about faculty pay.[42]

An increasing number of law schools are also moving towards some form of tenure—either programmatic tenure or unitary tenure—for all of their faculty.[43] Improvements in salary usually accompany such improvements in faculty status. In the current

---

(1998-2000) [hereinafter Durako, *Stop the Presses*]; Maureen J. Arrigo, *Hierarchy Maintained: Status and Gender Issues in Legal Writing Programs*, 70 Temp. L. Rev. 117 (1997); Pamela Edwards, *Teaching Legal Writing as Women's Work: Life on the Fringes of the Academy*, 4 Cardozo Women's L.J. 75 (1997).

[40] Press Release, U.S. Equal Emp't Opportunity Comm'n, University of Denver to Pay $2.66 Million and Increase Salaries to Settle EEOC Equal Pay Lawsuit (June 1, 2018), https://www.eeoc.gov/eeoc/newsroom/release/6-1-18.cfm.

[41] *Id.*

[42] *Id.*

[43] *See* J. Lyn Entrikin, Lucy Jewel, Susie Salmon, Craig T. Smith, Kristen K. Tiscione & Melissa H. Weresh, *Treating Professionals Professionally: Requiring Security of Position for All Skills-Focused Faculty Under ABA Accreditation Standard 405(c) and Eliminating 405(d),* 98 Or. L. Rev. 1, 38-39 (2020); Legal Writing Inst., Prof'l Status Comm. & Status-Related Advocacy, *Law School Tenure Status for LRW Faculty*, https://www.lwionline.org/sites/default/files/media-documents/School-Tenure%20Status%20List.April2019.pdf (last visited Oct. 13, 2019).

social and legal environment, it is likely that advancements at individual law schools and legal actions such as the one pursued at Denver University, rather than efforts to change the Standards, will inform and influence future revisions to the Standards, with positive benefits for LRW faculty.

4. Accreditation and Inspection Processes

In all but a few states, ABA accreditation is a prerequisite for a law school's graduates to take the state's bar examination and become licensed to practice law. The accreditation process is administered by the ABA Office of the Managing Director, which oversees the training and appointment of site evaluation teams, collects relevant law school data, and distributes site team reports and other accreditation materials to the Council.

A law school may apply for provisional accreditation no sooner than its second year of operation. The application must include a comprehensive feasibility study that addresses issues such as the school's goals, educational program, profile of potential students, and sufficiency of resources to sustain the law school. The school must also prepare a detailed self-study to establish that it is "in substantial compliance" with the Standards and has "a reliable plan" to bring the school into full compliance within three years of its provisional accreditation. The school is then inspected by a team of evaluators selected by the Section's Managing Director. After the inspection, the Council reviews the site team's written findings, holds a hearing with representatives of the law school, and prepares a report recommending approval or denial of the school's application. The Council's decision to grant provisional accreditation is final and effective immediately. A decision to deny is appealable to an Appeals Panel.

A law school must remain in provisional status for at least three years, during which it is subject to close monitoring and additional site evaluations. For full accreditation, the school must be re-inspected and once again receive approval from the Council.

Once fully accredited, a law school undergoes a full site evaluation in the third year after full approval. Thereafter, each accredited school, as with other accredited law schools, must be re-inspected every seven years.[44]

a. The Self-Study

The sabbatical inspection process involves three steps. First, a school about to be re-inspected must prepare a comprehensive self-study, as described in Standard 204. The self-study process has been streamlined in the new standards that took effect in 2014, but it still requires a law school to conduct a rigorous self-study, including, among other things, completing a detailed questionnaire, evaluating the educational quality of its program, and evaluating its effectiveness in achieving its educational objectives. Most law schools begin the self-study process one to two years before the next site visit. Although time-consuming, the self-study process is valuable because it forces a law school to refocus on its mission, identify its strengths and weaknesses, and develop a plan for improvement.

Service on a law school's self-study committee may offer LRW professors a unique opportunity to influence this important work. The LRW director or an experienced LRW professor should draft the section of the self-study that describes the LRW program, including factual information that is relevant to the governing standards. LRW professors may also bring their knowledge and experience to bear in sections of the self-study that discuss student learning outcomes and assessment. Finally, an LRW professor's organization and writing skills will improve the entire self-study,

---

[44]This re-inspection process is not a re-accreditation: A school's accreditation does not expire absent renewal by the ABA. Accreditation is continuing and ceases only if the ABA withdraws its approval, which rarely happens. The ABA often, however, requires a school to do specific things to remain in compliance with the Standards.

making it more reader-friendly for the site team members and decision-makers for whom it is written.

b. The Site Visit

The second step in the sabbatical inspection process is the site visit by a team selected by the Office of the Managing Director. Each team usually includes at least one dean, a doctrinal professor, a clinical or skills professor, a librarian, a university administrator, and a practicing lawyer.[45] Team members are volunteers who have an interest in legal education and the accreditation process, and each is required to attend training on the inspection process and Standards before being invited to serve on a site team. When a team is configured, each member of the team is asked to focus attention on specific portions of the standards—*e.g.*, the program of legal education, student services, or finance and administration. Approximately six weeks before the visit, team members receive copies of the self-study and questionnaire for review. The site visit usually lasts about three days, during which team members examine documents, read files, visit classes, and interview faculty, administrators, and students. During this visit, the team gets a very good sense of the school, including its strengths and weaknesses.

The LRW director and faculty should meet with at least one site team member, usually the clinical or skills professor. Often the site team member assigned to review the LRW program will contact the LRW director before the site visit to schedule a meeting. In the alternative, the LRW director may initiate the contact to ensure

---

[45]The Association of American Law Schools (AALS) also undertakes periodic inspection of its member schools. To reduce the burden on the schools being inspected, AALS normally coordinates these inspections with the ABA's sabbatical inspections. AALS appoints a representative known as the AALS reporter to serve on the ABA site team. The reporter then prepares a separate report to the AALS. *See* Am. Assoc. of Law Schools, *2019 AALS Site Evaluation Workshop* 3 (Jan. 5, 2019), https://www.aals.org/wp-content/uploads/2019/02/2019-Site-Evaluation-Handout-final.pdf.

that a member of the site team will meet with the LRW faculty. If time allows, the site team member may meet with the director and other LRW professors individually. If scheduling precludes separate meetings, the LRW faculty should meet as a group with the site team member.

LRW faculty should view the visit as an opportunity to receive credit for their program's strengths and assistance in improving its weaknesses. LRW faculty should review the relevant standards before a site team visit and be prepared to provide pertinent information.

c. The Site Report and Accreditation Decision

The final step in the sabbatical inspection process occurs after the site visit when the team writes a report that factually describes what the team learned from the self-study, questionnaire, and visit. The team is a factfinder; it is instructed to make no judgments as to whether the facts found during the inspection process demonstrate compliance or non-compliance with the Standards. The team's report is sent to the Council and the school. The school is entitled to submit written comments in response. The Council then meets, deliberates, and issues an action letter stating its conclusion.

If the Council concludes that the school is in compliance with the Standards, no further action on the part of the law school is required. If the Council concludes *either* that it lacks sufficient information to determine whether the school complies with the Standards *or* that the school does not appear to comply with one or more Standards, the action letter specifically describes the Standard(s) about which the Council needs further information or with which the school does not appear to comply. The law school is then given a deadline by which it must provide the necessary information or describe the steps it is taking to bring itself into compliance. This process may extend over two or more years while the school attempts to solve the problems identified in the action letter. The school must continue reporting to the Council until it sends the school a final approval letter.

5. *Conclusion*

The ongoing re-evaluation of the Standards for accrediting law schools in the United States has led to a growing realization that quality legal education requires quality legal writing instruction by qualified professionals. The most recent revisions to the Standards also reflect a new appreciation for the importance of accountability and transparency in legal education, as well as for the value of experiential learning. The Standards undoubtedly will continue to change, as they should, to ensure that lawyers of the future are well-prepared to serve their clients, their communities, and their profession. LRW professors, with their expertise in both doctrine and skills and their deep knowledge of teaching and learning theory, will continue to play a crucial role as advocates for high-quality teaching, sound curricula, and professional equality in the legal academy.

C. Legal Writing as a Discipline: Past, Present, and Future

Legal research and legal writing, particularly for persuasive purposes, have been a part of a lawyer's stock-in-trade at least as far back as ancient Greece and Rome.[46] But that history has not always been marked by laudable achievements. The written work of English lawyers was often ridiculed as obtuse, obfuscatory, and unintelligible.[47] Unfortunately, American lawyers, in their turn, have

---

[46]*See* MICHAEL R. SMITH, ADVANCED LEGAL WRITING: THEORIES AND STRATEGIES FOR PERSUASIVE WRITING 11-12 (3d ed. 2013).

[47]Judith D. Fischer, *Bareheaded and Barefaced Counsel: Courts React to Unprofessionalism in Lawyers' Papers*, 31 SUFFOLK U.L. REV. 1, 1 (1997) (citing 1 GEORGE SPENCE, THE EQUITABLE JURISDICTION OF THE COURT OF CHANCERY 376-77 n.h (1846) (reporting the 1595 case of *Mylward v. Weldon*)). The original

received much of the same ridicule.[48] Only in the past four decades has legal education in America devoted much attention to professional training in legal writing.

Serious scholarly attention to the history of legal education in America has long focused on the pervasive tension between training for law practice and the "scientific" graduate school model,[49] with the latter prevailing for many years. Even after Socratic dialogue and the case method became the normative model of delivering legal education, American law schools still relied in part on the oral tradition of advocacy and classical rhetoric techniques. Commentators noted the importance of the law review experience, particularly for the top students at elite law schools.[50] Law schools gave law librarians the responsibility for training students in legal research, with that training focused upon a bibliographic exploration of print-based sources of the law. Consequently, "the bar . . . expressed consistent dissatisfaction with the research and writing abilities of law school graduates."[51] Until the 1960s, scholarship about legal education simply did not pay attention to formal, school-wide training in

---

opinion of *Mylward*, which has garnered much attention over the centuries, is available at http://www.bailii.org/ew/cases/EWHC/Ch/1595/1.html (last visited Oct. 1, 2019).

48 Fischer, *supra* note 47, at 20-37.

49 *See* STEVENS, *supra* note 6.

50 *Id.* at 118.

51 Lucia A. Silecchia, *Designing and Teaching Advanced Legal Research and Writing Courses*, 33 DUQ. L. REV. 203, 206-07 (1995).

legal writing,[52] even when pressure from the bench and bar led to greater emphasis on clinical legal education.[53]

The early scholarly attention given to legal writing instruction instead focused on having full-time law faculty delegate the teaching of legal writing to part-time instructors appointed for only a year or two (most likely young, male, recent law school graduates) or to upper-level students (most likely with little or no instruction or training by experienced lawyers or teachers) with the goal of providing writing instruction at low cost.[54] Beginning in the 1970s,

---

[52] *See* STEVENS, *supra* note 6, at 232-63. Terms such as "legal writing," "legal research," and "library" are completely missing from the index to the Stevens book, although there are entries for "clinical law programs," *id.* at 318, and "curriculum" (which included a subentry for "skills teaching in"), *id.* at 319-20. Stevens did note the increasing attention paid in the 1950s and 1960s to "skills training," *id.* at 214-15, but pointed out the failures of such efforts because of the lack of materials, the unmet needs for small classes and attention to individual students, the lack of credit hours awarded for skills instruction, and the absence of good library facilities, *id.* at 215.

[53] *See, e.g.*, ABA SECTION OF LEGAL EDUC. & ADMISSIONS TO THE BAR, REPORT AND RECOMMENDATIONS OF THE TASK FORCE ON LAWYER COMPETENCY: THE ROLE OF THE LAW SCHOOLS 3-4 (1979) (commonly referred to as the Cramton Report); AM. BAR ASS'N, LEGAL EDUCATION AND PROFESSIONAL DEVELOPMENT – AN EDUCATIONAL REPORT OF THE TASK FORCE ON LAW SCHOOLS AND THE PROFESSION: NARROWING THE GAP (1990) (commonly referred to as the MacCrate Report); *see also* Peter A. Joy, *The Uneasy History of Experiential Education in U.S. Law Schools*, 122 DICK. L. REV. 551 (2018).

[54] *See, e.g.*, Stewart Macaulay & Henry G. Manne, *A Low-Cost Legal Writing Program – The Wisconsin Experience*, 11 J. LEGAL EDUC. 387, 388 (1959) (describing a program in which upper-division students taught legal writing under the supervision of faculty); Donald B. King, *A Survey Dealing with Legal Research and Writing Instructors*, 11 J. LEGAL EDUC. 406, 408-09 (1959) (describing instructors who had just graduated from law school or had only one or two years of experience); Jack Achtenberg, *Legal Writing and Research: The Neglected Orphan of the First Year*, 29 U. MIAMI L. REV. 241, 242-56 (1975).

however, things began to change, primarily in response to the pioneering efforts of Professor Marjorie Rombauer of the University of Washington School of Law. The late Professor Rombauer "is widely regarded as the founder of modern LRW programs and pedagogy."[55]

Over the ensuing half-century, the field of legal writing (LRW in *Sourcebook* terminology) has changed dramatically, and it continues to evolve. Those changes have come about because of advances in LRW pedagogy (including the impact of computer technology),[56] admission of increasingly diverse law students (including foreign students who are not native English speakers),[57] efforts to address perceived shortcomings in the pre-law-school academic training of law students,[58] increases in the raw numbers of law schools and

---

[55] Levine & Stanchi, *Last Taboo*, *supra* note 39, at 554*; see also* Mary S. Lawrence, *An Interview With Marjorie Rombauer*, 9 LEGAL WRITING 19, 19 (2003) ("Marjorie Dick Rombauer . . . founded the teaching of legal writing as a professional discipline. In the 1960s, when in most law schools writing instruction was haphazard, she created a rigorous, intellectually challenging program taught by full-time faculty.").

[56] *See, e.g.*, ERIC EASTON ET AL., ABA COMMC'NS SKILLS COMM., SOURCEBOOK ON LEGAL WRITING PROGRAMS 71-72 (2d ed. 2006) [hereinafter SOURCEBOOK 2d ed.]; W. Warren H. Binford, *Envisioning a Twenty-First Century Legal Education*, 43 WASH. U. J.L. & POL'Y 157 (2014); Suzanne Ehrenberg, *Legal Writing Unplugged: Evaluating the Role of Computer Technology in Legal Writing Pedagogy*, 4 LEGAL WRITING 1 (1998).

[57] *See, e.g.*, Johanna K. Dennis, *Ensuring a Multicultural Educational Experience in Legal Education: Start With the Legal Writing Classroom*, 16 TEX. WESLEYAN L. REV. 613 (2010); Mark E. Wojcik & Diane Penneys Edelman, *Overcoming Challenges in the Global Classroom: Teaching Legal Research and Writing to International Law Students and Law Graduates*, 3 LEGAL WRITING 127 (1997).

[58] *See, e.g.*, Susan Stuart & Ruth Vance, *Bringing a Knife to a Gunfight: The Academically Underprepared Law Student & Legal Education Reform*, 48 VAL. L. REV. 1 (2013); Symposium, *Teaching the Academically Underprepared Law*

law students throughout the 1980s and 1990s,[59] recognition of the gender discrimination present in law school hiring of—and salaries paid to—qualified teachers of LRW,[60] world-wide changes in law practice and the economics of law firms,[61] and increasing pressure from the bench and bar for law schools to invest more in teaching LRW.[62] The story of those changes can be summarized through an exploration of who teaches LRW (their qualifications, gender, and status),[63] the development of organizations addressing the teaching

---

Student, 53 DUQ. L. REV. NO. 1 (2015) (nine articles from a conference based upon the Stuart & Vance article).

[59] OFFICIAL AMERICAN BAR ASSOCIATION GUIDE TO APPROVED LAW SCHOOLS 454 (Rick L. Morgan & Kurt Snyder eds., 2001) (showing the rise in law school enrollment towards the end of the 20th century).

[60] *See, e.g.*, Ann C. McGinley, *Discrimination in Our Midst: Law Schools' Potential Liability for Employment Practices*, 14 UCLA WOMEN'S L.J. 1, 56-57 (2005); Stanchi & Levine, *Dirty Little Secrets, supra* note 39; Jo Anne Durako, *Stop the Presses*, *supra* note 39, at 87; Arrigo, *supra* note 39.

[61] *See, e.g.*, GEORGE R. BEATON & IMME KASCHNER, REMAKING LAW FIRMS: WHY AND HOW (2016); James G. Leipold & Judith N. Collins, *The Stories Behind the Numbers: Jobs for New Grads Over More Than Two Decades*, NALP BULLETIN (Dec. 2016), https://www.nalp.org/1216research.

[62] *See, e.g.*, Tony Mauro, *Kagan: Law Schools Must Do More to Boost Student Writing Skills*, NAT'L L. J., Aug. 27, 2015, at 1, https://advance.lexis.com/search?crid=ddffb015-0599-4028-b017-f90bbc9871ef&pdsearchterms=LNSDUID-ALM-NTLAWJ-1202735839548&pdbypasscitatordocs=False&pdmfid=1000516&pdisurlapi=true ("In an interview conducted last month by legal writing expert Bryan Garner, [U.S. Supreme Court Justice Elena] Kagan, who once taught at the University of Chicago Law School and was dean of Harvard Law School, said that for 'too many students,' even at the schools she worked at, 'nobody taught them' writing skills. She acknowledged that 'writing is one of the hardest things to teach.'").

[63] *See, e.g.*, Melissa H. Weresh, *Stars upon Thars: Evaluating the Discriminatory Impact of ABA Standard 405(c) "Tenure-Like" Security of Position*, 34 LAW & INEQ. 137 (2016) (addressing the gender discrimination inherent in the ABA Standards permitting different categories of job security, and the adverse

of LRW and the conditions under which LRW teachers labor, the modifications of the formal accreditation Standards governing LRW instruction,[64] the increases in the credit hours law schools have allocated to LRW courses,[65] and the phenomenal growth of schol-

---

consequences for future lawyers' perspectives on gender discrimination); Susan P. Liemer & Hollee S. Temple, *Did Your Legal Writing Professor Go to Harvard?: The Credentials of Legal Writing Faculty at Hiring Time,* 46 U. LOUISVILLE L. REV. 383 (2008) (comparing the qualifications of law school professors across subject areas); Susan P. Liemer & Jan M. Levine, *Legal Research and Writing: What Schools Are Doing and Who Is Doing the Teaching*, 9 SCRIBES J. LEGAL WRITING 113 (2003-2004) (describing LRW programs that cap the number of years teachers are permitted to stay at the institution and that force LRW teachers to leave their positions after a short duration); Levine & Stanchi, *Last Taboo*, *supra* note 39 (reporting on the low salaries paid to LRW teachers as compared to other law school faculty members); Peter Brandon Bayer, *A Plea for Rationality and Decency: The Disparate Treatment of Legal Writing Faculties as a Violation of Both Equal Protection and Professional Ethics*, 39 DUQ. L. REV. 329, 353 (2001) ("Among all full-time members of law school faculties, only legal writing teachers are subjected to systemic and persistent inequality ranging from remarkably disadvantageous terms of employment to disdain and segregation within their own law school societies.").

[64] *See supra* Part B of this chapter.

[65] *See* ABA SECTION OF LEGAL EDUC. & ADMISSIONS TO THE BAR, EXECUTIVE SUMMARY, A SURVEY OF LAW SCHOOL CURRICULA: 2002-2010, at 15 (Catherine L. Carpenter ed., 2012) ("Legal Research and Writing continues to grow in stature as law schools increased the number of [credit hour] units and expanded course coverage to include skills instruction beyond traditional advocacy."). Teachers of LRW courses know that student credit hours do not reflect faculty workload in creating and updating LRW assignments every year, critiquing student writing, and meeting with students for individual conferences. According to a summary found in a recent ALWD/LWI annual survey,

> [t]he average total number of pages of student work that LRW faculty members read in Fall 2014 also remained relatively constant from Fall 2013 (1520 pages in 2014; 1530 pages in 2013), and the average total number of pages of student work that LRW faculty members read in Spring 2015 decreased slightly (1520 pages in 2015; 1564 pages in 2014). . . . The average number of hours that LRW faculty members

arship about LRW specifically and legal writing generally (including, with this edition, the ABA's publication of three editions of the *Sourcebook*).[66]

Professor Rombauer was the first to conduct a survey of LRW instruction, in 1973.[67] This survey was intended to gather information about who was teaching LRW in American law schools.[68] That survey was followed by many more, leading to national surveys beginning in the 1990s conducted under the auspices of two legal writing organizations, the Legal Writing Institute and the Association of Legal Writing Directors.[69] The surveys reveal that over the past half-century, LRW instruction has become professionalized in both meanings of the word. Full-time LRW teachers have gone from

---

> spent preparing for class continued to increase slightly. Specifically, LRW faculty spent an average of 73.0 hours preparing for class in Fall 2014 (up from 71.6 hours in Fall 2013), and an average of 68.3 hours preparing for class in Spring 2015 (up from 66.9 hours in Spring 2014). The average number of hours that LRW faculty spent preparing major research and writing assignments increased slightly: 37.1 hours in Fall 2014 (compared with 36.5 hours in Fall 2013) and 38.0 hours in Spring 2015 (compared with 37.6 hours in Spring 2014).

Ass'n of Legal Writing Dirs. & The Legal Writing Inst., *Report of the 2015 Annual Survey* xviii (2016), https://www.alwd.org/images/resources/2015%20Survey%20Report%20(AY%202014-2015).pdf [hereinafter *2015 ALWD/LWI Survey*].

[66] For the earlier editions, see RALPH L. BRILL ET AL., ABA COMMC'NS SKILLS COMM., SOURCEBOOK ON LEGAL WRITING PROGRAMS (1st ed. 1997) [hereinafter SOURCEBOOK 1st ed.]; SOURCEBOOK 2d ed., *supra* note 56.

[67] Marjorie Dick Rombauer, *First-Year Legal Research and Writing: Then and Now*, 25 J. LEGAL EDUC. 538 (1973).

[68] *Id.* at 543-46.

[69] Extensive reports of the results of the annual surveys conducted by the Association of Legal Writing Directors and the Legal Writing Institute between 1999 and 2018 are available at https://www.alwd.org/resources/survey (last visited Jan. 9, 2020). In 2016-17 the survey was extensively expanded and split into two parts, one focused on schools and one addressing individual teachers, to be administered in alternating years.

being the exception to being the rule. Instead of holding full-time positions capped in duration with low faculty status, most LRW teachers now enjoy a measure of job security, for some including tenure, and higher pay than in the past.[70] However, salaries for

---

[70] *See 2015 ALWD/LWI Survey*, *supra* note 65, at viii-ix.

> As of 2015, continuing a trend that started in 2011, no school reported using law students or graduate students as LRW teachers. And, starting in 2012, no school reported using tenured or tenure track faculty teaching small sections of LRW when their main responsibility was to teach courses other than LRW and the small section was their only LRW responsibility. In responses to the 2015 Survey, only one school (less than 1%) assigned tenured or tenure-track faculty to teach LRW as part of their first-year doctrinal class. Similarly, in responses to the 2011 Survey and the 2014 Survey, only one school (also less than 1%) assigned tenured or tenure-track faculty to teach LRW as part of their first-year doctrinal class. In responses to the 2012 Survey and the 2013 Survey, none of the reporting schools taught LRW as part of a doctrinal first year course.
>
> The highest numbers of teachers in both unitary programs and hybrid ones were reported for schools using full time non-tenure track teachers with long-term or short-term contracts. The biggest differences between the hybrid and non-hybrid programs is that the hybrid programs used significantly more adjuncts (77%) than the non-hybrid programs (5%) and the hybrid programs used significantly more non-tenure track faculty with short or long term contracts (90%) than the non-hybrid ones (45%). The hybrid programs also used more law students, graduate students, and part-time faculty than non-hybrid programs. The least-used staffing models in hybrid programs were those relying on tenured or tenure track faculty to teach LRW as part of a doctrinal class or to a small section where the teacher had no other LRW responsibilities except the small section. The numbers for these two categories were equally small in unitary programs. However, as noted earlier, unitary programs also used no upper level students or graduate students, whereas hybrid programs used a few.

Id.

For a historical overview covering the period from 1973 to 2000, see Jo Anne Durako, *Snapshot of Writing Programs at the Millennium*, 6 LEGAL WRITING 95

most LRW faculty still lag significantly behind the salaries paid to tenure-track and tenured doctrinal law professors.[71] Increasingly, teachers of LRW are also able to boast credentials indistinguishable from those of other law professors, and they are often hired after a national search, following the same interview and selection process used for other faculty hiring.[72]

Although once dominant, programs of LRW instruction based exclusively on short-term faculty appointments, upper-level students, or adjuncts have all but vanished from American law schools, replaced by instruction offered by full-time faculty with security of employment, although hybrid programs still exist.[73] Law schools do not have departments like those found in undergraduate and graduate schools. But the closest analog involves LRW and clinical

---

(2000); Susan P. Liemer & Jan M. Levine, *Legal Research and Writing: What Schools Are Doing and Who Is Doing the Teaching (Three Years Later)*, 9 SCRIBES J. LEGAL WRITING 113 (2003-2004); Jill J. Ramsfield, *Legal Writing in the Twenty-First Century: A Sharper Image*, 2 LEGAL WRITING 1 (1996); Jill J. Ramsfield, *Legal Writing in the Twenty-First Century: The First Images: A Survey of Legal Research and Writing Programs*, 1 LEGAL WRITING 123 (1991); Rombauer, *supra* note 67.

[71] *See, e.g.*, Levine & Stanchi, *Last Taboo*, *supra* note 39, at 577 ("In dollars adjusted for the hypothetical location with 1998's average cost of living of 100, nation-wide LRW faculty were paid, on the average, fifty-seven percent of the median salary paid to assistant, tenure-track professors of doctrinal subjects. . . . In adjusted dollars, they are being paid fifty-one percent of the average median salary paid to associate professors . . . . They are paid, in adjusted dollars, forty percent of the average median salary paid to full professors . . . .").

[72] SOURCEBOOK 2d ed., *supra* note 56, at 140.

[73] *See id.*; *infra* Chapter V; *see also* Beazley, *supra* note 39, at 79; Jan M. Levine, *Voices in the Wilderness: Tenured and Tenure-Track Directors and Teachers in Legal Research and Writing Programs*, 45 J. LEGAL EDUC. 530 (1995); Linda Edwards & Martha Siegel, *Legal Writing Taught by Full-Time Teachers*, *in* THE POLITICS OF LEGAL WRITING: PROCEEDINGS OF A CONFERENCE FOR LEGAL RESEARCH AND WRITING PROGRAM DIRECTORS, 97 (Jan M. Levine et al. eds., 1995) [hereinafter THE POLITICS OF LEGAL WRITING].

instruction, where a program involving several faculty members is usually overseen or administered by a faculty director, often with tenure or other security of position. With the steady increase in the number of LRW programs in which all the faculty are tenure-track or tenured, or have some other form of security of position, schools have been moving to "directorless" programs with greater autonomy for individual teachers.[74]

The gender composition of those teaching LRW has historically been, and remains, predominantly female. Approximately 70-75% of full-time LRW professors are women.[75] Several explanations for this phenomenon have been offered, ranging from the type of teaching involved to the nature of the labor pool. But, as noted earlier,[76] close examination of the data and explanations leads scholars to only one conclusion: The disproportionate hiring of women into low-status, low-salary, and high-workload positions in law schools is fundamentally discriminatory.

Over the years, as the numbers, experience level, and status of LRW teachers continued to improve, they founded professional organizations to promote the growth of the field. The Association of American Law Schools (AALS) recognized the Section on Legal Writing, Reasoning, and Research in 1974.[77] The section offers yearly programs at the annual meeting of the AALS, often in conjunction with other

---

[74] *2015 ALWD/LWI Survey*, *supra* note 65, at vii.

[75] *Id.* at ix ("With respect to gender, nearly 3⁄4 of LRW faculty are female, while slightly over 1⁄4 are male.").

[76] *See* Levine & Stanchi, *Last Taboo*, *supra* note 39; *see also* McGinley, *supra* note 60.

[77] "The Section on Legal Writing, Reasoning, and Research promotes the communication of ideas, interests, and activities among the members of the Section; reports on the status of legal research and writing; and makes recommendations on matters concerning law school administration and matters of interest in the teaching and improvement of law school curriculum." *Section on Legal Writing, Reasoning, and Research*, Ass'n of Am. Law Schools, https://www.aals.org/sections/list/legal-writing-reasoning-and-research/ (last visited Oct. 1, 2019).

sections.[78] The American Bar Association established the Communication Skills Committee (CSC) in 1990, which offered sessions at the annual ABA meetings and proposed changes to the ABA Accreditation Standards. The CSC was also responsible for the preparation of the first and second editions of this *Sourcebook* in 1997 and 2006.[79]

Of the greatest importance in the development of the field of LRW, however, has been the creation of two national organizations: the Legal Writing Institute in 1985, following the first national conference of LRW teachers in 1984;[80] and the Association of Legal Writing Directors in 1996, following a national conference held in 1995.[81] These organizations continue to advance the field of LRW in many ways, including holding biennial national conferences in alternate years, supporting smaller regional conferences, publishing scholarly journals and other newsletters and books advancing the field, promoting changes in ABA Standards, and offering financial support for scholarship written by LRW teachers. Perhaps the most significant work of the two organizations to promote change has been the administration, analysis, and publication of a yearly survey of LRW teachers. The 2015 Survey boasted a response rate of 95%.[82] It gathered data about teachers (such as gender, status, salary,

---

[78] *See id.*

[79] *See supra* Preface to this *Sourcebook* edition; SOURCEBOOK 1st ed., *supra* note 66; SOURCEBOOK 2d ed., *supra* note 56. This third edition has been substantially revised and expanded under the leadership of the ABA Publications Committee, the successor to the former ABA Communication Skills Committee.

[80] *See* Mary S. Lawrence, *The Legal Writing Institute—The Beginning: Extraordinary Vision, Extraordinary Accomplishment*, 11 LEGAL WRITING 213 (2005) (focusing on the founding of the Legal Writing Institute, led by faculty from the University of Puget Sound (later Seattle University)).

[81] *See* Ralph L. Brill, *Introduction*, *in* THE POLITICS OF LEGAL WRITING, *supra* note 73 (explaining the 1995 conference that led to the formation of the Association of Legal Writing Directors); *id.* Appendix B, at 126-28 (reporting on the process of forming the Association of Legal Writing Directors as an independent organization and election of the first group of officers).

[82] *2015 ALWD/LWI Survey*, *supra* note 65, at vii.

and other support offered by law schools; teaching loads; other teaching and related activities; and experience level) and programs (including credit hours, required and elective courses, and program design).[83] Data from the surveys show in detail the evolving norms in pedagogy, curriculum, and faculty status and salary.

Scholarship about legal writing—covering both LRW and legal writing more broadly—over the past half-century has resulted in an explosion of available material of increasing depth and breadth. In the early 1980s, only a dozen or so LRW textbooks were available from which an LRW professor could choose. In 2018, however, myriad textbook options are available covering basic to advanced courses.[84] Recent law review articles about legal writing address pedagogy, rhetorical theory, learning theory, law and literature, computer technology, status and salary of teachers, history, advocacy techniques, and more.[85] Several dedicated journals are devoted to the scholarship of legal writing.[86] ALWD produces under its aus-

---

[83] *Id.* at vii-xx.

[84] For the 2018-19 academic year, the publisher Wolters Kluwer alone offered 50 coursebooks for first-year LRW courses, not including several categories of books for advanced courses. *See Wolters Kluwer Legal Education: 1-L Coursebooks, Legal Research and Writing*, https://www.wklegaledu.com/textbooks/law-school/legal-research-and-writing (last visited Oct. 1, 2019).

[85] A comprehensive bibliography for this ever-increasing body of legal scholarship is beyond the scope of this *Sourcebook*, but numerous references are scattered in footnotes throughout this publication. *See, e.g.*, citations *infra* in Part D of this chapter and Part F.4.c of Chapter V. For a more complete—but still not comprehensive—overview of legal writing scholarship, review the archives of the Legal Writing Institute and the Association of Legal Writing Directors, whose website addresses are included *infra* note 86.

[86] The Legal Writing Institute (LWI) has numerous publications; all have shifted from print to electronic format. *See Publications*, LEGAL WRITING INST., https://www.lwionline.org/publications (last visited Oct. 1, 2019). The organization publishes a journal, LEGAL WRITING: THE JOURNAL OF THE LEGAL WRITING INSTITUTE; a reprinted monograph series of important articles; a periodical newsletter, THE SECOND DRAFT; and another newsletter titled LWI LIVES about legal writing teachers (all available through links from the LWI *Publications* page,

pices a citation manual that focuses on instruction in practical legal citation skills, rather than footnote citation formats unique to scholarly legal writing.[87] The field has bootstrapped itself into a major academic discipline, and its production of scholarship has led to heightened status and job security for those teaching LRW.

The pedagogy underlying the teaching of LRW has also evolved over the past half-century and will be addressed in greater detail later in this *Sourcebook*. As LRW teachers remain in the field longer and gain more experience, they write and publish articles and books about what they teach, their methods of teaching, and curriculum design, leading to innovation and increasing sophistication. Modern LRW programs integrate legal research instruction with writing instruction,[88] focusing on finding relevant materials, analyzing

---

supra). LWI also has prepared LEGAL WRITING INST., JAMES DIMITRI, MELISSA GREIPP, & SUSIE SALMON, THE MOOT COURT ADVISOR'S HANDBOOK: A GUIDE FOR LAW STUDENTS, FACULTY, AND PRACTITIONERS (2015), and maintains an SSRN database of articles, the LEGAL WRITING EJOURNAL. These sources are also available through links from the LWI *Publications* page, *supra*.

The Association of Legal Writing Directors also has produced scholarly publications. Since 2000, ALWD has published a citation guide. *See, e.g.*, ASS'N OF LEGAL WRITING DIRS. & COLEEN M. BARGER, ALWD GUIDE TO LEGAL CITATION (6th ed. 2017). ALWD also publishes a journal, LEGAL COMMUNICATION & RHETORIC: THE JOURNAL OF THE ASSOCIATION OF LEGAL WRITING DIRECTORS. This publication also has moved from print to electronic form, and its archives and other materials are available at https://www.alwd.org/aboutlcr (last visited Oct. 1, 2019).

SCRIBES, the American Society of Legal Writers, publishes THE SCRIBES JOURNAL OF LEGAL WRITING (archives available at https://www.scribes.org/the-journal-of-legal-writing) (last visited Oct. 1, 2019); and a newsletter, THE SCRIVENER (partial archives available at https://www.scribes.org/the-scrivener) (last visited Oct. 1, 2019).

[87] *See* ASS'N OF LEGAL WRITING DIRS. & COLEEN M. BARGER, ALWD GUIDE TO LEGAL CITATION (6th ed. 2017).

[88] *2015 ALWD/LWI Survey Report*, *supra* note 65, at x ("Approximately 86% of LRW courses integrate the teaching of legal research with the teaching of legal writing.").

complex issues, and conveying written (and oral) legal analysis to lawyers (and others) in office memoranda (whether in print form or as email messages), appellate briefs and oral arguments, and other documents.[89] As the number of courses and credit hours devoted to instruction in LRW have increased, teachers have been able to explore other methods of providing feedback to students. Expanded or new courses now address other lawyering skills (such as client interviewing and counseling) and have added many types of

---

[89] *Id.* at xi. More specifically, the 2015 survey noted:

> All 194 of the LRW programs responding to the 2015 Survey reported that they use the office memorandum as one of the writing assignments required by the program. The office memorandum has always been the writing assignment used most by writing programs, but the 2014-2015 academic year appears to be the first year that 100% of programs indicated that they used an office memorandum. Other writing assignments used by more than 50% of responding programs include email memos (65%), client letters (63%), pretrial briefs (61%), and appellate briefs (72%). The only other specific assignment used by a significant number of programs was a drafting assignment, used by approximately 35% of responding schools. However, 126 schools (65%) reported using "other writing assignments."

documents (ranging from client letters to legislation).[90] Assignments involving oral presentations have also proliferated.[91]

Common to all LRW instruction, however, is the huge workload commensurate with teaching writing well.[92] Teaching writing

---

[90] *Id.* at x. More specifically, the 2015 survey noted:

> Almost all schools (97%) offer elective upper level writing courses. While only 8% of the courses are taught exclusively by LRW faculty, an additional 75% are taught by either LRW faculty or non-LRW faculty. That means that only 14% of the schools that report offering upper level writing, do not use any faculty from the writing program to teach the upper level writing courses. With respect to a requirement that before graduation students take an upper-level writing course, beyond the required first year course, 91% of the responding schools now have such a requirement. Traditionally, schools with an upper level writing requirement allowed students to satisfy that requirement only by doing some sort of scholarly writing, such as a journal article or seminar paper. However, the data, going back to 2011, show a significant increase in the percentage of schools that now allow students to satisfy the upper-level writing requirement by taking some type of legal writing course. The increase has been most noticeable in general advanced writing courses, advanced advocacy courses, transactional drafting courses, and especially in judicial opinion writing courses.

[91] *Id.* More specifically, the 2015 survey noted:

> The most common speaking skills taught included appellate arguments (73%), oral reports to senior partners (53%), pre-trial motion arguments (49%), and in-class presentations (47%). The trend over the past several years toward increasing numbers of schools using non-traditional speaking assignments, such as oral reports to senior partners and in-class presentations, has continued.).

[92] Jan M. Levine, *Leveling the Hill of Sisyphus: Becoming a Professor of Legal Writing*, 26 FLA. ST. U. L. REV. 1067, 1081 n.50 (1999) ("Every single article about legal writing programs and faculty – regardless of any other point the authors make – reports on the overwhelming physical and mental demands of the teaching involved . . . ."); Susan P. Liemer, *The Quest for Scholarship: The Legal Writing Professor's Paradox*, 80 OR. L. REV. 1007, 1015 (2001) ("During the

requires providing individualized critiques of student work, meeting with individual students to address those critiques, and guiding and reviewing student revisions. In recognition, previous editions of this *Sourcebook* recommended limiting the number of students assigned to each LRW teacher.[93] As law school deans and faculties became more aware of the field's "heavy lifting," as well as its increasing professionalization, many realized the need to limit teaching loads. Compounding the workload problem is the need for even more individualized attention to remediate the educational shortcomings of recent law school admittees. Many lack adequate preparation in critical thinking, close reading, and analytical writing.[94]

By the close of the twentieth century, the field of LRW had progressed as law schools realized that it was counterproductive to repeatedly overload poorly-paid, short-term teachers—however dedicated—and replace them as they burned out or reached the end of their term, and then start all over again. As we move through the twenty-first century, we may well be seeing yet another time for change due to the unfortunate confluence of financial pressures (resulting from the drop in law school applications and admissions)[95] and the admission of students who need greater assistance in order to have a chance of success in the legal profession.

---

academic year, in addition to time spent preparing for class and actually teaching in the classroom, a typical LRW professor invests up to an extra hour per student each week proving individualized feedback and instruction.").

[93] *See, e.g.,* SOURCEBOOK 1st ed., *supra* note 66, at 62 (recommending "no more than 40 to 45 students" for each full-time writing professor); SOURCEBOOK 2d ed., *supra* note 56, at 95 (recommending "no more than 30 to 45 students per semester, assuming the professor is not teaching another course"); *see also infra* Ch. V, Part A.2 (recommending 30 to 35 students per semester for each full-time professor teaching exclusively LRW courses).

[94] Stuart & Vance, *supra* note 58.

[95] *See, e.g.*, Deborah M. Hussey Freeland, *The Demand for Legal Education: The Long View*, 65 J. LEGAL EDUC. 164 (2015).

Since 2006, LRW has been included as a "Specialty Category" in the law school rankings published yearly by *U.S. News & World Report*.[96] This recognition has likely helped to influence some deans and law schools to realize that providing excellent LRW instruction can attract students and distinguish schools in the rough-and-tumble of increasingly competitive admission and job placement environments.

The next several decades in the development of LRW should show continuing improvements in the status, salary, and job security of those teaching LRW, recognizing the ever-increasing quality of their credentials, more and more scholarship about LRW and legal writing generally, and the resulting ever-improving instruction of law students. While all legal educators will have to confront many challenges—those already mentioned as well as continuing changes in law practice, continuing development of technology and artificial intelligence, and others we cannot yet foresee—the fourth edition of this *Sourcebook* will undoubtedly show that LRW educators rose to meet those challenges and prospered, teaching their students more effectively than ever.

---

[96] *See Best Law Schools, Best Legal Writing Programs*, U.S. NEWS & WORLD REPORT, https://www.usnews.com/best-graduate-schools/top-law-schools/legal-writing-rankings?int=9d0608&int=acf809 (last visited Oct. 1, 2019). As explained by the *Report*, the methodology was changed for the 2018 rankings:

> This year for the first time, law school faculty members who teach in each specialty area rated the other law schools in that specialty area on a 5-point scale. Those schools with the highest average scores among those raters who rated them appear in the rankings and are ranked in descending order based on their average peer score they received in that specialty area. In all the previous law school specialty rankings, the law school raters chose their top 15 in a specialty area. This new methodology produced a significantly larger number of schools that were ranked in each specialty area – in some cases five or six times more.

Best Law Schools, Methodology: 2019 Best Law Schools Rankings, U.S. NEWS & WORLD REPORT, https://www.usnews.com/education/best-graduate-schools/articles/law-schools-methodology (last visited Oct. 1, 2019).

D. Writing Across the Curriculum (WAC)

1. What Is WAC?

Writing Across the Curriculum (WAC) has been a pedagogical movement in higher education in the United States for many decades. WAC may encompass any curriculum-wide writing requirements and additional optional offerings in writing instruction. For undergraduates, it typically supplements the more traditional, required writing courses, such as freshman composition courses provided by English departments for all majors, or departmental senior capstone writing courses. Students in any major may experience WAC in their undergraduate departments at any type of college or university. Many WAC resources originally created for use by undergraduate professors and institutions may be equally useful for law professors and law schools. These resources include websites, books, blogs, conferences, newsletters, organizations, and the like.[97]

A small number of law schools in the United States have embraced Writing Across the Curriculum.[98] In the law school context, WAC usually refers to a requirement that (1) every course in the law school include some kind of written assignment in addition to

---

[97] A helpful starting point for information on all aspects of WAC is the WAC Clearinghouse, https://wac.colostate.edu/ (last visited Dec. 12, 2019).

[98] In 2018, the annual ALWD-LWI Survey asked whether law schools had "adopted a 'writing across the curriculum' program or required Legal Writing Assignments in any Non-LRW Courses other than seminars." Four law schools responded, "Yes, our school requires a writing assignment in all Non-LRW Courses." Another twenty law schools responded, "Yes, our school requires a writing assignment in some Non-LRW Courses that are not seminars." Ass'n of Legal Writing Dirs. & Legal Writing Inst., *Report of the 2017-2018 Institutional Survey* 211, Question 20.2 (2018), https://www.lwionline.org/sites/default/files/Final%20ALWD%20LWI%202017-18%20Institutional%20Survey%20Report.pdf (reporting responses from 182 ABA-accredited law schools).

any final exam,[99] and (2) the students receive some kind of feedback on the assignment.[100] Within this general concept, there is much room for customization. One law school's WAC rules may define in detail the written assignments and feedback that meet the requirement, while another law school may have more broadly stated rules. A law school WAC requirement may apply only to upper-level courses or required courses, or it may apply to all courses, including all first-year courses. A WAC requirement could include or exclude midterm essay exams, allow group feedback or not, or vary in terms of other particulars.

A WAC requirement does not mean every law professor must give long writing assignments and provide detailed critiques on huge stacks of papers. The requirement can be designed to allow short writing assignments and many forms of feedback. For instance, a WAC assignment could ask students to write a new provision for an existing document, one IRAC applying a statutory term to hypothetical facts, or a summary of a challenging reading assignment.

---

[99] A major reason why the qualifying WAC assignment should not be a final examination is that "many doctrinal faculty members only marginally consider the quality of student writing when grading law school examinations." J. Lyn Entrikin Goering, *A Vision for the Future: Integrating Legal Research and Writing Across the Law School Curriculum*, 18 SECOND DRAFT, June 2004, at 19. Another reason is that law school final examinations usually are not formative assessments, i.e., assessments designed as learning experiences to improve students' skills; rather, they tend to be summative assessments, designed to determine final course grades.

[100] While all writing practice helps students strengthen their writing skills, especially as the purpose and audience shift with each assignment, feedback on their writing is an important component for maximizing the learning that takes place. When the ABA evaluates the rigor of those writing experiences required by the accreditation Standards, one factor considered is "the form and extent of individualized assessment of a student's written products." Section of Legal Educ. & Admissions to the Bar, *ABA Standards and Rules of Procedure for Approval of Law Schools (2019-2020)* at 16, Interpretation 303-2, https://www.americanbar.org/content/dam/aba/administrative/legal_education_and_admissions_to_the_bar/standards/2019-2020/2019-2020-aba-standards-and-rules-of-procedure.pdf.

Not every course needs to include a full appellate brief or publishable law journal article to provide a useful opportunity for students to write and receive feedback. And while individualized feedback from the professor is ideal, students also benefit from a peer review exercise, a self-assessment assignment, a professor's in-class review of a model paper, or feedback from a course teaching assistant or an academic support department teaching assistant.

2. *Why WAC?*

There are multiple reasons for a law school in the United States today to consider adopting WAC.[101] Proficiency with the written word remains *the* key lawyering skill for lawyers and judges in our legal system. Employers of new law school graduates need and expect them to be able to write at a professional level.[102] Writing is a challenging skill to hone to a professional level, and it is a developmental skill, i.e., one that requires repeated instruction and practice to develop. For a number of reasons, today's students

---

[101] *See generally* Carol McCrehan Parker, *Writing Is Everybody's Business: Theoretical and Practical Justifications for Teaching Writing across the Law School Curriculum*, 12 Legal Writing 175 (2007); Pamela Lysaght & Cristina D. Lockwood, *Writing-Across-the-Law-School Curriculum: Theoretical Justifications, Curricular Implications*, 2 J. ALWD 73 (2004).

[102] *See* Alli Gerkman & Logan Cornett, *Foundations for Practice: The Whole Lawyer and the Character Quotient* 8 (Inst. for Advancement of Am. Legal Sys. 2016), https://iaals.du.edu/sites/default/files/documents/publications/foundations_for_practice_whole_lawyer_character_quotient.pdf (reporting that 98% of practicing attorneys agree that law graduates either should "be able to write in a manner that meets legal and professional standards" or must acquire that ability); Bryant G. Garth & Joanne Martin, *Law Schools and the Construction of Competence,* 43 J. Legal Educ. 469, 490 tbl.11 (1993) (reporting that 90% of hiring partners at major Chicago law firms expected new attorneys to arrive with written and oral communication skills, while only 30% expected new graduates to arrive with substantive law knowledge).

increasingly enter law school with weaknesses in their core writing skills.[103] Sadly, students with weaker writing skills—the ones who most need to do more writing—often shy away from writing-intensive courses and activities. Yet legal writing itself is now being tested directly on an increasing number of bar examinations as more states adopt the Uniform Bar Examination and its Multistate Performance Test.

Within the WAC community, the approaches used to develop strong writing skills are called, unsurprisingly, *learning to write*.[104] As the gap increases between the writing skills of entering students and the writing skills expected of law graduates, WAC can help a law school provide the repeated instruction and practice today's law students need. A law school can implement WAC without hiring additional faculty members, which is particularly helpful in times of lean law school budgets. If every course provides at least one opportunity for writing and feedback, every student will have many more opportunities to develop their writing skills over the course of two or three years.

Another reason for adopting WAC is to help law students learn the material covered in all of their law school courses.[105] Within the WAC community, when writing is used to enhance students' learning of the underlying subject matter, those approaches are called

---

[103] *See generally* Lindsey P. Gustafson, *Texting and the Friction of Writing*, 19 LEGAL WRITING 161 (2014); Jan Levine, *Forward, Fourth Colonial Frontier Legal Writing Conference: Teaching the Academically Underprepared Law Student*, 53 DUQ. L. REV. 1 (2015); Stuart & Vance, *supra* note 58.

[104] *See* Carol McCrehan Parker, *Writing Throughout the Curriculum: Why Law Schools Need It and How to Achieve It*, 76 NEB. L. REV. 561, 581-589 (1997); McArdle, *supra* note 59.

[105] *See* Parker, *supra* note 104, at 568-80; Laurel Currie Oates, *Beyond Communication: Writing as a Means of Learning*, 6 LEGAL WRITING 1 (2000).

writing to learn. Gaps in analysis, confusion about doctrine, or poor understanding of theory all become visible to both the student and the professor when the student writes about course topics. Once errors are made visible, the professor can address them and identify how best to help the student. In addition, if a professor does not teach students how to write in that professor's area of specialty, who will?[106] For instance, if the professor teaching Trusts and Estates does not teach students how to write a will or a trust, the students likely will not gain that knowledge and experience elsewhere in the curriculum.[107] Thus, WAC helps law students learn the subject matter covered throughout the curriculum.[108] Typically, law professors who have not taught LRW will gravitate more toward assignments that provide *writing to learn* opportunities.

---

[106] *See* KATHERINE GOTTSCHALK & KEITH HJORTSHOJ, THE ELEMENTS OF TEACHING WRITING: A RESOURCE FOR INSTRUCTORS IN ALL DISCIPLINES (2003); Molly Warner Lien, *Breach of Trust: Legal Education's Failure to Prepare Law Students for the Practice of Law*, 1 J. ALWD 118, 121 (2002) ("[W]hat could be more logical than having a contracts professor who has completed the materials on offer, acceptance, and consideration assigning a contract drafting assignment?").

[107] *See* Alice M. Noble-Allgire, *Desegregating the Law School Curriculum: How to Integrate More of the Skills and Values Identified by the MacCrate Report into a Doctrinal Course*, 5 NEV. L.J. 32, 49-53 (2002) (describing multiple Trusts & Estates course drafting exercises).

[108] *See, e.g.*, Michael J. Madison, *Writing to Learn and Writing in Law: An Intellectual Property Illustration*, 52 ST. LOUIS L.J. 823 (2008); Eric Goldman, *Integrating Contract Drafting Skills and Doctrine*, 12 LEGAL WRITING 209 (2006); Robert E. Keeton, *Teaching Torts Through Exercises on Drafting Verdict Forms*, 45 ST. LOUIS U. L.J. 779 (2001); Barbara J. Busharis & Suzanne E. Rowe, *The Gordian Knot: Uniting Skills and Substance in Employment Discrimination and Federal Taxation Courses*, 33 J. MARSHALL L. REV. 303 (2000); Susan L. DeJarnatt, *In Re MacCrate: Using Consumer Bankruptcy as a Context for Learning in Advanced Legal Writing*, 50 J. LEGAL EDUC. 50 (2000); Robert M. Jarvis, *Using Entertainment Law to Teach Legal Writing*, 3 ENTM'T L. & SPORTS J. 243 (1986).

3. *How to Create a WAC Requirement*

As with other curricular requirements that may bind the entire law faculty, it is prudent to start work on creating a WAC requirement in the curriculum committee. And it is prudent for the committee to focus first on educating itself and the rest of the faculty. Then the committee can draft an appropriate WAC requirement for the school and its culture, submit the draft to the faculty for discussion, revise it accordingly, and eventually bring it to the faculty for a full vote.

Useful information for a law school curriculum committee (or some subset of it) to compile at the outset includes:

- a list of courses that already have writing assignments other than a final exam, including the names of the professors teaching the courses and the type of feedback provided to students;
- a list of cocurricular activities in which the students complete writing assignments, including the names of faculty advisors, if any, and the type of feedback provided to students, if any; and
- a list of the types of writing experiences that the students of that particular law school typically have while working in law jobs during the school year or the summer, including the names of supervisors and the type of feedback received on on-the-job writing during law school.

Collecting information about law students' on-the-job writing may require surveying students and their employers. The career services and alumni affairs offices can provide employers' contact information. Practicing attorneys and sitting judges often express concern about the writing skills of recent law school graduates[109]

---

[109]This concern is not new. *See, e.g.*, Justice Elizabeth Lacy et al., *Law School Curriculum, Training Law Students, and the Vitality of the Profession: The Judicial Perspective*, 1 J. ALWD 297 (2002) (conference closing plenary discussion giving the judiciary's view of inadequate writing and other skills of law school

and thus will have a natural interest in assisting a law school in collecting this information.

The information collected will help a curriculum committee determine whether the law schools' students would benefit from a WAC requirement or whether some other approach might be better.[110] If a WAC requirement seems promising, the information collected will help the committee identify the specific needs that the WAC requirement should address.[111] For example, if the information shows that some students are receiving multiple opportunities for rigorous writing experiences with detailed feedback, but other students are not, a WAC requirement could be drafted to ensure all students receive a certain number of rigorous writing experiences with detailed feedback.

4. *How to Implement WAC*

A law school curriculum committee should prepare for predictable reactions from the faculty to a WAC proposal. The information collected will be helpful for explaining the identified student needs to the rest of the law faculty and for explaining how WAC will meet those needs.[112] The committee should anticipate that colleagues will want assurances about the nature and amount of change to expect

---

graduates); Stuart A. Handmaker, *The Law School Product from the Buyer's Point of View,* 29 VAL. U. L. REV. 897 (1995) (giving a practitioner's perspective on law graduates' inadequate writing and other skills).

[110]For a discussion of other aspects of upper-level legal writing, see *infra* Chapter II, Part C.

[111]For a less traditional view of WAC in the law school context, see Susan E. Thrower, *Teaching Legal Writing Through Subject-Matter Specialties: A Reconception of Writing Across the Curriculum*, 13 LEGAL WRITING 3 (2007).

[112]*See* Pamela Lysaght, *Writing across the Law School Curriculum: Considerations for Casebook Faculty*, 12 LEGAL WRITING 191 (2007); Toni M. Fine, *Do Best Pedagogical Practices in Legal Education Include a Curriculum that Integrates Theory, Skill, and Doctrine?*, 1 J. ALWD 65 (2001).

in their teaching work, as well as assurances that they will receive guidance and assistance in implementing changes.

Some faculty members' first reactions will simply be to resist any change.[113] The information on courses already providing writing experiences likely will reassure colleagues that much of the curriculum will not change at all. A list of law school courses with writing assignments that are not a final examination typically includes more than half of the school's course offerings. In the upper-level curriculum in particular, advanced skills courses, experiential courses, simulation courses, problem-based courses, clinics, externships, seminars, independent study, and the like already have writing assignments, instead of or in addition to any final examination. Cocurricular activities for which academic credit is granted—such as moot court, mock trial team, and law journals—also already require writing that is not a final examination.

Drafting a WAC rule that does not require professors to make large changes in their courses also will tend to minimize resistance.[114] For example, one professor may want reassurance that her traditional midterm essay examination will fulfill the requirement, until she sees how a new WAC rule plays out for other colleagues. Others may simply need illustrations of what may be expected. A typical law school WAC requirement can be met with shorter assignments than some professors may at first realize. And some professors may need assurance that they will receive guidance on how to create writing assignments or where to find existing assignments.

Many case book professors will want reassurance about the workload created by providing feedback on writing assignments. Some professors may simply need assurance that they will receive

---

[113] *See* Michael R. Koval & R. Michael Garner, *I Don't Do Writing: A Model for Overcoming Faculty Resistance to Using Writing Assignments in the Classroom*, 15 ATLANTIC L.J. 120 (2013).

[114] *See* Susan J. Hankin, *Bridging Gaps and Blurring Lines: Integrating Analysis, Writing, Doctrine, and Theory*, 17 LEGAL WRITING 325 (2011).

guidance on how to provide feedback efficiently or that they can seek assistance from others. Thus, the committee should be prepared to offer conveniently scheduled opportunities for faculty to discuss the rule, to learn how to create writing assignments, and to explore ways to provide feedback effectively and efficiently.

Fortunately, each law school already has in-house experts to tap as a resource: its LRW professors.[115] These experts can provide specific assistance on creating assignments and giving feedback. They also have teaching materials to share—such as checklists, rubrics, templates, and samples—and know where to find others. Also, the teaching assistants hired by casebook professors or by the academic support professors may be a useful resource.[116] For example, a TA could grade pass/fail assignments with the aid of a checklist and identify students whose written work suggests they need to have individual meetings with the professor. A curriculum committee proposing a WAC requirement would do well to consult the LRW professors and the academic support professors ahead of time. These professors can provide expertise relevant to the final form of the rule and also support the casebook faculty in determining how to comply with the new rule.

When a law faculty considers a WAC requirement, inevitably someone will raise academic freedom as an issue. Of course, law professors do not have unbridled freedom in all aspects of their teaching. The ABA Standards regulate matters like the number of hours of instruction required for an academic credit. And law faculties choose to bind themselves by adopting other rules related to teaching, such as grading curves and prohibitions on additional assignments during reading day. Similarly, a faculty may choose collectively to require WAC.

---

[115] *See* Lisa Eichhorn, *The Role of Legal Writing Faculty in an Integrated Curriculum*, 1 J. ALWD 85 (2002).

[116] *See* BETH FINCH HEDENGREN, A TA'S GUIDE TO TEACHING WRITING IN ALL DISCIPLINES (2004).

The committee should ensure support for WAC from the dean's office, too. Depending on the culture of the school, securing the dean's support may need to take place even before introducing the faculty to the idea. Some deans have provided guidebooks on how to incorporate writing assignments into a course as gifts to each faculty member. A shelf in the faculty lounge filled with books on WAC and related materials would be a helpful resource. The dean might also provide lunch for faculty members during forums at which the faculty discusses the proposed WAC rule or receives assistance in learning how to implement it.

One other consideration when implementing a WAC rule is its impact on student workload. Faculty members who teach first-year and upper-level required courses may want to consider coordinating the timing of their writing assignments so that students do not have multiple written assignments due on the same day.[117] Another possible approach is for the faculty to designate a certain midterm period for the WAC assignment due dates for all first-year or upper-level required courses. This approach allows the faculty to space out the due dates in much the same way final examinations are spaced out over a designated time period.

As with many new initiatives for a law faculty, the vote in favor of a WAC requirement does not need to be unanimous for the initiative to be successful in the long term. If most of the faculty implements WAC with enthusiasm—or at least some willingness to innovate—the students will receive the benefits of repeated instruction and practice in writing.

---

[117] *See* Suzanne J. Schmitz & Alice M. Noble-Allgire, *Reinvigorating the 1L Curriculum: Sequenced "Writing Across the Curriculum" Assignments as the Foundation for Producing Practice-Ready Law Graduates*, 26 S. Ill. U. L.J. 287 (2012).

5. *How to Maintain a WAC Requirement*

Having a WAC requirement can change the culture at a law school in many positive ways. It can encourage faculty members to explore active learning approaches, to assist each other and collaborate, and to erase unproductive lines between casebook, clinic, and LRW faculty. Maintaining that culture in the long term does require some continued work. Year by year, as faculty members retire or leave, newly hired faculty members may need information about the goals of WAC, its history at the law school, and where to find assistance for complying with the WAC requirement. Without understanding this aspect of the law school's academic culture, new faculty members, particularly those on the tenure track who face pressure to publish, might perceive WAC assignments merely as a box to check, rather than a rich teaching opportunity.

One way to maintain a culture that values WAC is to have faculty members regularly share their experiences with each other. At an annual event, such as a faculty forum at lunchtime, colleagues can describe their WAC assignments and their students' learning and challenges. Participants may want to brainstorm new ideas for assignments, ask questions, and explore responses. In addition, it is helpful to keep faculty members informed about upcoming WAC events elsewhere on campus, as well as regional, national, and international WAC conferences. Periodic reminders to the faculty about sources of related teaching materials are also helpful.

Having the dean's office provide support for maintaining WAC may be crucial for its ongoing success. To monitor compliance with a WAC requirement, the original rule should include a monitoring mechanism. The simplest approach is to have the dean add a question to the annual faculty activity report, asking how each faculty member complied. Then faculty members will describe annually their WAC assignments for each course taught. Knowing that the dean is monitoring this aspect of their teaching tends to encourage faculty members to comply with the requirement. In addition, faculty members will know that their WAC assignments will be described in the activity reports that the tenure and promotion committee reads during reviews for retention, promotion, and tenure.

To monitor the overall impact of a WAC requirement, some mechanism for periodic evaluation and assessment should be included in the original rule. The curriculum committee may want to require a review of the initiative's effects four years after it is implemented. At a law school with a traditional three-year course of study to obtain a J.D. degree, after four years every student who matriculated before the WAC rule took effect likely will have graduated or otherwise moved on. Thus, four years is a reasonable time period over which to evaluate a cultural change at a law school. The committee could decide to survey any number of affected constituents, including professors, students, administrators, externship supervisors, and other employers. Creating a comprehensive list of the entire faculty's WAC assignments, for example, by copying them from the faculty annual activity reports year by year, is an easy way to demonstrate to all constituencies that WAC enriches the law school curriculum.

II. DEVELOPING A COMPREHENSIVE LEGAL WRITING CURRICULUM

A. Foundational Required Courses

The American Bar Association's law school Accreditation Standards establish the basic foundation for a law school's required legal research, writing, and analysis (LRW) program.[1] The standards were substantially revised in 2014 to focus primarily on student learning outcomes.[2] At minimum, an accredited law school must

> establish learning outcomes that . . . include competency in . . . : (b) [l]egal analysis and reasoning, legal research, problem-solving, and written and oral communication in the legal context; (c) [e]xercise of proper professional and ethical responsibilities to clients and the legal system; and (d) [o]ther professional skills needed for competent and ethical participation as a member of the legal profession.[3]

---

[1]See *supra* Chapter I, Part B, for a detailed discussion of these foundational standards, their history, and their impact on LRW faculty and programs.

[2]*See* Steven C. Bahls, *Adoption of Student Learning Outcomes: Lessons for Systemic Change in Legal Education*, 67 J. LEGAL EDUC. 376, 376 (2018) (noting that the ABA's revision of its law school accreditation standards "to focus on student learning outcomes is the most significant change in law school accreditation standards in decades"). Dean Bahls was an instrumental member of the ABA Standards Review Committee during its multi-year consideration of the revised standards that were ultimately adopted in 2014. *See also* Susan Hanley Duncan, *They're Back! The New Accreditation Standards Coming to A Law School Near You—A 2018 Update, Guide to Compliance, and Dean's Role in Implementing*, 67 J. LEGAL EDUC. 462 (2018) (discussing how law schools can effectively implement the new ABA Standards with faculty involvement); *supra* Chapter I, Part B.2.b (discussing significant revisions pertaining to LRW instruction adopted in 2014).

[3]Section of Legal Educ. & Admissions to the Bar, *ABA Standards and Rules of Procedure for Approval of Law Schools (2019-2020)*, ABA: AM. BAR. ASS'N, Standard 302 [hereinafter *ABA Standards (2019–2020)*], https://www.americanbar

To achieve these learning outcomes, a law school must "maintain a rigorous program of legal education that prepares its students, upon graduation, for admission to the bar and for effective, ethical, and responsible participation as members of the legal profession."[4] To that end, "each student [must] satisfactorily complete at least . . . one writing experience in the first year and at least one additional writing experience after the first year," and each required writing experience must be faculty supervised.[5]

More than three decades before the 2014 comprehensive revision, the ABA's *MacCrate Report*[6] had admonished law schools to emphasize and, as appropriate, expand instruction in legal analysis, research, and writing skills. These themes were echoed even more emphatically in the 2007 Carnegie Report, *Educating Lawyers: Preparation for the Practice of Law*.[7] The Carnegie Report explicitly recognized a deficiency in modern legal education, noting that

---

.org/content/dam/aba/administrative/legal_education_and_admissions_to_the_bar/standards/2019-2020/2019-2020-aba-standards-and-rules-of-procedure.pdf (last visited Dec. 12, 2019).

[4] *Id.*, Standard 301(a).

[5] *Id.*, Standard 303(a)(2). Interpretation 303-2 enumerates the "[f]actors to be considered in evaluating the rigor of a writing experience," including "the number and nature of writing projects assigned to students, the form and extent of individualized assessment of a student's written products, and the number of drafts that a student must produce for any writing experience."

[6] ABA SECTION OF LEGAL EDUC. & ADMISSIONS TO THE BAR, LEGAL EDUCATION AND PROFESSIONAL DEVELOPMENT—AN EDUCATIONAL CONTINUUM: REPORT OF THE TASK FORCE ON LAW SCHOOLS AND THE PROFESSION: NARROWING THE GAP 331-32, ¶¶ 12-14 (1992) [hereinafter *MacCrate Report*], https://www.americanbar.org/content/dam/aba/publications/misc/legal_education/2013_legal_education_and_professional_development_maccrate_report).authcheckdam.pdf. While considerable progress has been made since 1992 with respect to LRW programs, the admonitions of the *MacCrate Report* continue to provide useful guidance on the fundamental importance of professional skills instruction in law schools.

[7] For a summary of the report, see WILLIAM M. SULLIVAN ET AL., EDUCATING LAWYERS: PREPARATION FOR THE PRACTICE OF LAW: SUMMARY (Carnegie Found.

"[m]ost law schools give only casual attention to teaching students how to use legal thinking in the complexity of actual law practice, . . . conveying the impression that lawyers are more like competitive scholars than attorneys engaged with the problems of clients."[8] Among its many recommendations, the Carnegie Report called for "[g]reater coherence and integration in the law school experience,"[9] with increasing attention on student learning outcomes and teaching methods incorporating formative assessment.[10]

Also in 2007, the Clinical Legal Education Association (CLEA) published *Best Practices for Legal Education.*[11] The Executive Summary captured the authors' recommendations succinctly by "call[ing] on law schools to make a commitment to improve the preparation of their students for practice, clarify and expand their educational objectives, improve and diversify methods for delivering instruction, and give more attention to evaluating the success of their programs of instruction."[12]

Both the *Carnegie Report* and *Best Practices* underscored the need for innovation in the traditional law school curriculum. Both

---

for Advancement of Teaching 2007), http://archive.carnegiefoundation.org/pdfs/elibrary/elibrary_pdf_632.pdf.

[8] *Id.* at 6.

[9] *Id.* at 8. "Students need a dynamic curriculum that moves them back and forth between understanding and enactment, experience and analysis. Law schools face an increasingly urgent need to bridge the gap between analytical and practical knowledge, and a demand for more robust professional integrity." *Id.*; *see* Susan J. Hankin, *Bridging Gaps and Blurring Lines: Integrating Analysis, Writing, Doctrine, and Theory*, 17 LEGAL WRITING 325, 326 (2011) (discussing "two models for integrating skills with doctrine in the first-year curriculum" and recommending other ways to integrate the law school curriculum).

[10] SULLIVAN ET AL., *supra* note 7, at 7.

[11] ROY STUCKEY ET AL., BEST PRACTICES FOR LEGAL EDUCATION: A VISION AND A ROADMAP (2007), https://www.cleaweb.org/Resources/Documents/best_practices-full.pdf.

[12] *Id.* at 5.

emphasized the need to prepare students for law practice[13] by integrating the law school curriculum[14] and enhancing formative and institutional assessment strategies.[15] To some extent, the ABA's substantial revisions to law school Accreditation Standards beginning in August 2014 reflected those recommendations, building upon those embodied in the 1992 *MacCrate Report*.[16]

1. Learning Outcomes

While the ABA Accreditation Standards provide the foundational requirements for any law school curriculum, the goals of a particular law school for its first-year LRW course ultimately depend on a variety of institution-specific factors. Achieving those goals depends on the number of credits allocated to the course, the course content, program staffing, upper-level writing requirements and electives, and other program-related factors. Other important influences include the law school's institutional history, culture, and

---

[13] *See* Sherri Lee Keene, *One Small Step for Legal Writing, One Giant Leap for Legal Education: Making the Case for More Writing Opportunities in the "Practice-Ready" Law School Curriculum*, 65 MERCER L. REV. 467, 471 (2014) (explaining that "legal writing practice helps legal novices not only to improve their basic writing abilities, but also to develop their professional expertise").

[14] *See* Suzanne E. Rowe & Susan P. Liemer, *One Small Step: Beginning the Process of Institutional Change to Integrate the Law School Curriculum*, 1 J. ALWD 218 (2002).

[15] *See, e.g.*, Larry Cunningham, *Building a Culture of Assessment in Law Schools*, 69 CASE W. RES. L. REV. 395 (2018); *see also* Deborah L. Borman, *De-Grading Assessment: Rejecting Rubrics in Favor of Authentic Analysis*, 41 SEATTLE U. L. REV. 713, 714 (2018); Marie Summerlin Hamm et al., *The Rubric Meets the Road in Law Schools: Program Assessment of Student Learning as a Fundamental Way for Law Schools to Improve and Fulfill Their Respective Missions*, 95 U. DET. MERCY L. REV. 343 (2018).

[16] *See, e.g.*, Mary Beth Beazley, *Finishing the Job of Legal Education Reform*, 51 WAKE FOREST L. REV. 275, 278 (2016) ("Consistent with the new ABA Standards, forward-looking law schools must embrace experiential learning techniques, educational outcomes, and formative assessment methods.").

mission. The support of the law school administration and faculty is essential to the success of any LRW program.

All LRW programs fundamentally endeavor to teach students to think and communicate like lawyers. This broad goal suggests at least seven specific student learning outcomes that all effective LRW programs should seek to achieve. Specifically, upon completing a first-year LRW program, a student should be able to

a. understand the U.S. legal system and the interrelationships among its components;

b. analyze facts, legal issues, and relevant legal authorities;

c. conduct legal research efficiently in both print and electronic sources;

d. communicate effectively to a legal audience in written and oral expression;

e. recognize and address professional responsibility and other ethical issues;

f. understand the lawyer's various professional roles; and

g. apply legal knowledge and skills to solve novel legal problems.

Achieving even these fundamental learning outcomes in a two-semester LRW program is a major challenge indeed, even for the most experienced LRW professor. Over the last four decades, several authors have urged law schools to expand LRW curricula to require legal writing experiences in all three years of legal education.[17] Since the early 2000s, when the ABA Standards

---

[17]The 1979 ABA Task Force on Lawyer Competency, chaired by Dean Roger Cramton, urged the ABA to require legal writing courses in all three years of law school. ABA SECTION OF LEGAL EDUC. & ADMISSION TO THE BAR, REPORT AND RECOMMENDATIONS OF THE TASK FORCE ON LAWYER COMPETENCY: THE ROLE

began requiring every law student to engage in a minimum of two faculty-supervised, rigorous legal writing experiences, an increasing number of law schools have expanded their required LRW programs to span three or more semesters.[18]

Although students sometimes complain about the amount of work in the LRW course, the various assignments provide opportunities for students to develop efficient legal analysis, research, and writing skills so they can respond to the demands of legal practice to produce quality work in a short time frame. Long before the end of the course, most students, even those who complain about the workload, recognize the value of learning these skills with the guidance and support of an engaged professor.

A well-executed LRW course integrates legal doctrine, skills, and professional identity in a way that helps students achieve a sense of competence, if not mastery, by the end of the required foundational course.

OF THE LAW SCHOOLS 15 (1979) (better known as the *Cramton Report*); Roger Cramton, *Lawyer Competence and the Law Schools,* 4 U. ARK. LITTLE ROCK L.J. 1, 13 (1981); *see also, e.g.,* George D. Gopen, *The State of Legal Writing:* Res Ipsa Loquitur, 86 MICH. L. REV. 333, 357-58 (1987) (describing Professor Ralph Brill's pioneering three-year legal writing program at Chicago-Kent and calling on other law schools to "do what logic and sound pedagogy demand—to implement a three-year writing requirement for all law students"); Adam Lamparello & Charles E. MacLean, *A Proposal to the ABA: Integrating Legal Writing and Experiential Learning into a Required Six-Semester Curriculum That Trains Students in Core Competencies, "Soft" Skills, and Real-World Judgment*, 43 CAP. U. L. REV. 59 (2015); John C. Weistart, *The Law School Curriculum: The Process of Reform*, 1987 DUKE L.J. 317, 328 ("Roger Cramton has perhaps done the most to call attention to the disarray in the present curriculum and to propose a comprehensive alternative.").

[18] *E.g.,* Johanna K.P. Dennis, *The Renaissance Road: Redesigning the Legal Writing Instructional Model*, 38 S.U. L. REV. 111, 146 (2010) (noting that 47 of 181 responding law schools in 2008 reportedly required LRW credits beyond the second year of law school (citing Ass'n of Legal Writing Dirs. & Legal Writing Inst., *2008 Survey Report*)).

a. Understanding the U.S. Legal System and the Interrelationships Among Its Components

Students should acquire a foundational knowledge of the United States legal system and how it works. This basic knowledge includes the three branches of government, the various sources of primary law, the concept of federalism, and the interrelationships among the dual state and federal legal systems. Students need a basic understanding of how the different sources of law relate to each other, how the law is applied and enforced, and how three branches of government interact and overlap in many respects.

Many first-year students have never been exposed to the common-law process and judge-made law, and most have only a vague understanding of the legislative process and statutory law. While all first-year courses should emphasize the forms of legal reasoning involved in each of these features of the American legal system, an essential focus of the LRW course is the interrelationship among the various sources of law and lawmaking processes. Moreover, although students learn how to interpret and apply court rules in other courses, most do not learn elsewhere how court rules are proposed and adopted (generally subject to legislative approval).[19] In addition to legislation and litigation, an LRW course should introduce students to administrative rulemaking[20] and alternative

---

[19] *See, e.g.*, Rules Enabling Act, 28 U.S.C. §§ 2071-77 (2018); *see also* United States Courts, *About the Rulemaking Process: How the Rulemaking Process Works: Overview for the Bench, Bar, and Public*, http://www.uscourts.gov/rules-policies/about-rulemaking-process/how-rulemaking-process-works/overview-bench-bar-and-public (last visited Dec. 13, 2019).

[20] *See* Paul Beneke, *Start with Enacted Law, Not Common Law*, 10 PERSPS. 76 (2002); Mary Nicol Bowman & Lisa Brodoff, *Cracking Student Silos: Linking Legal Writing and Clinical Learning Through Transference*, 25 CLINICAL L. REV. 269 (2019); Sarah J. Morath, *Stand Out from the Crowd: Making Your Voice Heard in an Era of "Notice and Spam,"* 43 RUTGERS L. REC. 133 (2016); Sarah J. Morath, *The E-Comment: A Simple Exercise for Public Law Courses*, 24 PERSPS. 8 (2016).

dispute resolution.[21] Some LRW courses also include basic instruction in negotiation.[22]

Over the last decade, several prominent law schools have added a first-year foundational course in legislation and regulation (often known informally as "LegReg").[23] But most law schools still do not require students to take courses in Legislation or Administrative Law. In those law schools, students may not have another opportunity beyond LRW courses to learn how each branch of government engages in lawmaking. Legislatures enact statutes and propose constitutional provisions; the executive branch issues executive orders, and its agencies adopt regulations; and the courts adopt court rules and issue published opinions. Students in the first-year LRW course should be introduced to each of these foundational components of the United States legal system, particularly if the law school does not require first-year students to take a basic LegReg course.

---

[21] *See, e.g.*, Mary Dunnewold & Mary Trevor, *Escaping the Appellate Litigation Straitjacket: Incorporating an Alternative Dispute Resolution Simulation into a First-Year Legal Writing Class*, 18 LEGAL WRITING 209 (2012); Kate O'Neill, *Adding an Alternative Dispute Resolution (ADR) Perspective to a Traditional Legal Writing Course*, 50 FLA. L. REV. 709 (1998).

[22] *E.g.*, Nancy Schultz, *The Integrated Curriculum of the Future: Integrating First-Year Legal Writing with Other Lawyering Skills*, 7 ELON L. REV. 405, 408 (2015).

[23] *E.g.*, James J. Brudney, *Legislation and Regulation in the Core Curriculum: A Virtue or a Necessity?*, 65 J. LEGAL EDUC. 3 (2015); J. Lyn Entrikin, *The Death of Common Law*, 42 HARV. J.L. & PUB. POL'Y 351, 480-81 & nn. 521-22 (2019); John F. Manning & Matthew Stephenson, *Legislation & Regulation and Reform of the First Year*, 65 J. LEGAL EDUC. 45, 45 (2015); Peter L. Strauss, *Christopher Columbus Langdell and the Public Law Curriculum*, 66 J. LEGAL EDUC. 157, 168 (2016); Chris Walker, *The Rise of the 1L Leg-Reg Course*, 36 YALE J. ON REG.: NOTICE & COMMENT (Oct. 21, 2014), http://yalejreg.com/nc/the-rise-of-the-1l-leg-reg-course-by-chris-walker/.

b. Analyzing Facts, Legal Issues, and Relevant Legal Authorities

The practice of law requires accurate and precise analysis of facts, legal issues, and authorities, as well as effective communication of that analysis. LRW professors must therefore instruct students in the fundamental skill of legal analysis—"thinking like a lawyer"—as they teach the conventions of legal communication and expression. These analytical skills are taught in the LRW classroom using a hands-on, problem-solving method that complements the traditional doctrinal approach of other courses in the required first-year curriculum.[24]

In the LRW course, students learn to "think like a lawyer" by working through problems set in specific jurisdictions.[25] By its nature, this problem-based method requires students to use analytical skills as if they were lawyers operating within the constraints of practice. In that sense, LRW is a simulation course. Students may identify a range of reasonable interpretations of the law and accordingly reach varying results for the client's problem. But students also learn that legal analysis reaches the wrong conclusion if based on a misunderstanding of the relevant facts, or if students fail to identify and synthesize mandatory authority. Working within these

---

[24] The following articles compare traditional approaches taken by LRW and doctrinal faculty to teaching legal analysis: Mary Ellen Gale, *Legal Writing: The Impossible Takes a Little Longer*, 44 ALB. L. REV. 298, 311-17 (1979-80); Richard K. Greenstein, *Teaching Case Synthesis*, 2 GA. ST. U. L. REV. 1, 7-17 (1985-86); Carol M. Parker, *Writing Throughout the Curriculum: Why Law Schools Need It and How to Achieve It*, 76 NEB. L. REV. 561, 568 (1997); David S. Romantz, *The Truth About Cats and Dogs: Legal Writing Courses and the Law School Curriculum*, 52 KAN. L. REV. 105, 136-45 (2003); Marjorie Dick Rombauer, *Regular Faculty Staffing for an Expanded First-Year Research and Writing Course: A Post Mortem*, 44 ALB. L. REV. 392, 393-94 (1979-80).

[25] *See* Suzanne E. Rowe, *Legal Research, Legal Writing, and Legal Analysis: Putting Law School into Practice* 2 (July 11, 2015), https://ssrn.com/abstract=1223682 or http://dx.doi.org/10.2139/ssrn.1223682.

boundaries, students gradually internalize the critical skills of accurate and precise legal thinking.[26]

The analytical teaching approach in LRW classes complements the approach generally followed in other first-year courses, but in a more rigorous, practice-oriented fashion. In courses like torts or contracts without the constraints of simulated law practice, students learn the same analytical skills from a different perspective. Casebook professors typically work through a series of individual cases from various jurisdictions, each testing the limits of a legal principle using hypotheticals with ever-changing facts. Students and professors have more flexibility to question the validity of different doctrinal approaches, to test the reasonable limits of doctrine, and to explore policy themes underlying each primary area of law.

Ideally, first-year law students should experience and learn to appreciate the critical synergy of these two complementary approaches to teaching legal analysis. Integrating the two approaches—one primarily theoretical, the other primarily focused on skills and practice—helps students become sophisticated legal thinkers in ways they will draw upon as practicing lawyers.

c. *Conducting Legal Research in Print and Electronic Sources*

Students in a first-year LRW course should learn to conduct legal research thoroughly and efficiently in all commonly available sources and media. The first-year research curriculum must introduce students to basic primary sources of law including constitutions, judicial opinions, statutes, court rules, and administrative regulations; secondary sources that comment on the law such as legal treatises, legal periodicals, encyclopedias, and legal

---

[26] *See* Jane Kent Gionfriddo, *"The Reasonable Zone of Right Answers": Analytical Feedback on Student Work*, 40 Gonz. L. Rev. 427, 430-33 (2005).

dictionaries; and finding tools such as annotations, digests, citators, and online research services.

In addition, students must understand and demonstrate how to plan and execute a systematic strategy for conducting comprehensive legal research to resolve a legal problem or dispute based on a specific set of facts.[27] An important aspect of research instruction is learning to use various primary and secondary authorities in combination to solve a specific legal issue. Another essential aspect of legal research instruction is the need to update authorities using online citators. Students should be taught that online citators largely rely on judicial opinions, and that they are much less reliable for updating statutes and administrative rules. While online citators are both useful and efficient, they are certainly not fool-proof, and students must understand how to research comprehensively to overcome their deficiencies.[28]

Given the increasing prominence of electronic research in the students' previous academic experience and in law practice, the LRW curriculum should emphasize the importance of both print and electronic research. Today's students tend to rely far too heavily

---

[27] *See, e.g.*, Caroline L. Osborne, *The Legal Research Plan and the Research Log: An Examination of the Role of the Research Plan and Research Log in the Research Process*, 35 LEGAL REF. SERVS. Q. 179 (2016).

[28] *See, e.g.*, Paul Hellyer, *Evaluating Shepard's, Keycite, and Bcite for Case Validation Accuracy*, 110 LAW LIBR. J. 449, 476 (2018) ("[R]esearchers need to be aware of the citators' shortcomings. Relying only on a citator's treatment symbols is a risky strategy for case validation."); Aaron S. Kirschenfeld, *Yellow Flag Fever: Describing Negative Legal Precedent in Citators*, 108 LAW LIBR. J. 77, 78 (2016) ("[S]erious questions surround the citator's place in legal research."); Alan Wolf & Lynn Wishart, *Shepard's and KeyCite Are Flawed (or Maybe It's You)*, 75 N.Y. ST. B. J. 24 (Sept. 2003) (describing inherent deficiencies in both KeyCite and Shepard's).

on research strategies using online search and citator tools without recognizing their weaknesses.[29]

Over the last decade, many law libraries have allocated an increasing proportion of their acquisition budgets to computer databases, e-books, and other electronic services.[30] But students need to understand the relative value of various legal research methods, and many excellent sources are still not available online. Moreover, experience with print research offers students valuable insights concerning the structure and language of the law, experience using subject-matter indices as finding tools, and learning opportunities by browsing the books and making serendipitous discoveries.

Ideally, LRW programs should integrate legal research instruction with legal writing and analysis. Students learn to research more effectively—and more realistically—by using various research tools in combination to resolve a legal problem in the context of a well-designed legal writing assignment.[31]

---

[29] Dennis S. Sears, *The Pedagogical Value of an Integrated Approach to Legal Research Instruction: Overcoming Student Resistance to the Use of Print Sources and Striking a Balance That Instills an Appreciation of the Strengths and Weaknesses of Both Print and Online Sources*, 33 LEGAL REF. SERVS. Q. 38 (2014); *see also* sources cited in note 28, *supra*.

[30] *See, e.g.*, Amanda Watson, *Don't Burn the Books, Read Them!*, 46 INT'L J. LEGAL INFO. 79, 81 (2018) (noting that while digital library resources are leading the market largely due to budget considerations, they are not necessarily best for teaching research skills to law students); *see also* Ursula Gorham & Paul T. Jaeger, *The Law School Library or the Library at the Law School? How Lessons from Other Types of Libraries Can Inform the Evolution of the Academic Law Library in the Digital Age*, 109 LAW LIBR. J. 51, 55 (2017) (noting substantial budgetary and space constraints on contemporary law school libraries).

[31] *See, e.g.*, Liz McCurry Johnson, *Teaching Legal Research and Writing in a Fully Integrated Way*, 30 SECOND DRAFT 31, 35-36 (2017); *see also* Steven I. Friedland, *Adaptive Strategies for the Future of Legal Education*, 61 LOY. L. REV. 211, 221 (2015) ("Integration is justified now, more than ever, by the new job market reality."); Jan M. Levine, *"You Can't Please Everyone, So You'd Better Please Yourself": Directing (or Teaching in) A First-Year Legal Writing Program,*

d. Communicating Effectively to a Legal Audience in Written and Oral Expression

Law schools rely primarily on LRW programs to teach students to communicate effectively, both in writing and in oral advocacy. Traditional doctrinal courses using a Socratic or oral discussion method contribute to these goals. But only the LRW course offers systematic instruction in communicating legal analysis and advocacy in both written and oral expression.

LRW courses typically address both professional writing and legal writing.[32] Effective professional writing requires students to write succinctly and clearly with grammatical and syntactical precision, and to carefully revise and edit their own work. Effective legal writing goes beyond technical correctness and proficiency to deliver well-organized, clearly expressed legal analysis that meets the expectations of law-trained readers. Writing effectively in law practice requires a thorough understanding of legal analysis and how best to communicate that analysis to different audiences for different purposes.

Most law schools include instruction in oral communication as an integral part of the LRW curriculum, typically in the context of preparing and delivering an oral argument on a pretrial motion or an

---

29 Val. U. L. Rev. 611, 622–23 (1995) (opining that "first-year legal research and writing courses should focus on teaching the fundamentals of analysis in the context of research and writing[;] [l]egal research is best taught when integrated wholly with legal writing, as interconnected parts of legal discourse and analysis; all student writing assignments should be research-based"); Schultz, *supra* note 22, at 410 ("[T]he fundamental underlying principle is that integration is the key—integrating skills, context, research, and writing leads to a better-written product and a stronger understanding of the lawyer's work.").

[32] *See* Jonathan K. Van Patten, *Skills for Law Students*, 61 S.D. L. Rev. 165, 194 (2016) ("Writing continues to be an essential skill and law school is an excellent place to improve.").

appellate brief assignment.[33] These arguments may be the capstone of a school's LRW program and are sometimes linked to extra-curricular moot court programs.[34] Students learn how to structure a compelling oral argument based on an extensive written brief, how to present it to the court, and how to respond professionally to the court's questions.

Increasingly, LRW programs include drafting skills as an essential component of the law school curriculum.[35] The most recent ABA curriculum survey noted that among all ABA-accredited law schools, the most commonly reported curriculum innovation between 2002 and 2010 was expanded offerings in legal drafting courses.[36]

---

[33] Lucia Ann Silecchia, *Legal Skills Training in the First Year of Law School: Research? Writing? Analysis? Or More?*, 100 DICK. L. REV. 245, 257 (1996).

[34] Traditionally, moot court programs were the primary focus of legal communication instruction in American legal education. Jeffrey D. Jackson & David R. Cleveland, *Legal Writing: A History from the Colonial Era to the End of the Civil War*, 19 LEGAL WRITING 191, 195 (2014) (noting that "moot courts," in the form of mandatory exercises modeled after those conducted by the English Inns of Court, were the primary way early law schools taught legal writing). *See generally* John T. Gaubatz, *Moot Court in the Modern Law School*, 31 J. LEGAL EDUC. 87 (1981).

[35] *See, e.g.*, Louis N. Schulze, Jr., *Transactional Law in the Required Legal Writing Curriculum: An Empirical Study of the Forgotten Future Business Lawyer*, 55 CLEV. ST. L. REV. 59, 62 (2007) (considering whether the first-year writing course should be expanded to include transactional drafting); Silecchia, *Legal Skills Training*, *supra* note 33, at 280 (noting the value of teaching multiple professional skills, including legal drafting, as part of the LRW curriculum); *see also* J. Lyn Entrikin & Richard K. Neumann Jr., *Teaching the Art and Craft of Drafting Public Law: Statutes, Rules, and More*, 55 DUQ. L. REV. 9, 16–17 (2017) (promoting legal drafting as an "essential component of every lawyer's professional education").

[36] *See* CATHERINE L. CARPENTER, A SURVEY OF LAW SCHOOL CURRICULA: 2002-2010, at 78 & fig.64 (2012); *see id.* Exec. Summary 16 ("Transactional Drafting courses and upper division Legal Writing courses experienced the greatest growth in offerings.").

e. Recognizing and Addressing Professional Responsibility and Other Ethical Issues

A comprehensive first-year LRW course should introduce students to principles of professional responsibility and ethical professional behavior.[37] Ethical professional conduct can be taught in stand-alone class sessions or integrated throughout the course.[38] Either way, the goals are to help students recognize potential professional responsibility issues that regularly arise in law practice, and to help them realize that ethical decision-making is inseparable from professional conduct.

As students learn how to prepare various legal documents, they also learn about ethical standards of competent representation, regular and prompt communications with clients, and professional norms requiring candor to the tribunal, including truthful representations of law and fact.[39] The required LRW course is ideally suited to emphasize to students that the lawyer's role as an officer of the court, including the duty to protect the integrity of the

---

[37] *See, e.g.*, MELISSA H. WERESH, LEGAL WRITING: ETHICAL AND PROFESSIONAL CONSIDERATIONS (2d ed. 2009); Ben Bratman, *Toward A Deeper Understanding of Professionalism: Learning to Write and Writing to Learn During the First Two Weeks of Law School*, 32 J. LEGAL PROF. 115, 122 (2008) (explaining why LRW courses are an ideal venue for teaching ethics and professional responsibility); Beth D. Cohen, *Instilling an Appreciation of Legal Ethics and Professional Responsibility in First Year Legal Writing Courses*, 4 PERSPS. 5 (1995); Wayne Schiess, *Ethical Legal Writing*, 21 REV. LITIG. 527 (2002).

[38] *See* Deborah L. Rhode, *Legal Ethics in Legal Education*, 16 CLINICAL L. REV. 43 (2009) (promoting integration of professional ethics throughout the law school curriculum).

[39] *See* Frances C. DeLaurentis, *When Ethical Worlds Collide: Teaching Novice Legal Writers to Balance the Duties of Zealous Advocacy and Candor to the Tribunal*, 7 DREXEL L. REV. 1, 7 (2014) (noting the ethical issues that arise in teaching students how to prepare advocacy documents).

judicial system, outweighs even the lawyer's professional duty to the client.[40]

In addition to introducing students to expectations within the profession, LRW is often the course in which students are taught academic and professional expectations regarding plagiarism.[41] By associating academic integrity with professional responsibility, students learn that the professionalism and ethical behavior expected of them in law school are precursors to the standards of behavior expected within the legal profession.[42] The LRW classroom can also be used to teach students to perform at a high level of technical competence, including such professional requisites as meeting deadlines, maintaining civil discourse,[43] and complying with court rules for formatting and submitting legal documents.[44]

---

[40] *See* ABA Model Rules of Prof'l Conduct R. 3.3 cmt. 2 (noting special duties of lawyers as officers of court to avoid conduct undermining integrity of adjudicative process); Deborah M. Hussey Freeland, *What Is a Lawyer—A Reconstruction of the Lawyer as an Officer of the Court*, 31 St. Louis U. Pub. L. Rev. 425 (2012).

[41] *See* Robin F. Hansen & Alexandra Anderson, *Law Student Plagiarism: Contemporary Challenges and Responses,* 64 J. Legal Educ. 416 (2015); Teri LeClercq, *Failure to Teach: Due Process and Law School Plagiarism*, 49 J. Legal Educ. 236 (1999); Decarlous Y. Spearman, *Citing Sources or Mitigating Plagiarism: Teaching Law Students the Proper Use of Authority Attribution in the Digital Age*, 42 Int'l J. Legal Info. 177 (2014); Nancy A. Wanderer, *Legal Writing: Original Thinking or Patchwork Plagiarism*, 33 Me. B.J. 31, 35 (2018). Teaching materials on plagiarism are available on the website of the Legal Writing Institute, http://www.lwionline.org, at https://www.lwionline.org/plagiarism (last visited Dec. 13, 2019).

[42] *See, e.g.,* Douglas R. Richmond, *Why Legal Ethics Rules Are Relevant to Lawyer Liability*, 38 St. Mary's L.J. 929, 939 (2007) (noting that most jurisdictions consider ethics rules as relevant evidence in civil lawsuits against lawyers).

[43] *See* Sophie Sparrow, *Practicing Civility in the Legal Writing Course: Helping Law Students Learn Professionalism*, 13 Legal Writing 113 (2007).

[44] *See, e.g.,* Fed. R. App. P. 46(c) ("A court of appeals may discipline an attorney who practices before it for . . . failure to comply with any court rule.").

f. Understanding the Lawyer's Varying Professional Roles

A comprehensive LRW course should introduce students to the variety of ways lawyers serve their clients, the judiciary, the legal system, and the public.[45] Students should understand how to objectively analyze the law to competently advise a client, and how to develop a persuasive argument to advocate on behalf of a client. A course that covers skills beyond legal analysis, research, and writing[46] may also teach students how to effectively engage in client interviewing and counseling;[47] other skills may include how to interact with opposing counsel in negotiation, mediation, or other alternative dispute resolution strategies to resolve a client's legal problem.[48]

---

[45] *See, e.g.*, LINDA H. EDWARDS, LEGAL WRITING AND ANALYSIS 3-5 (5th ed. 2019); Jill J. Ramsfield & J. Christopher Rideout, *Using Legal Writing to Narrow the Gap: Socializing Students into Legal Education and Law Practice*, *in MacCrate Report*, *supra* note 6.

[46] *See* Debra Harris & Susan D. Susman, *Toward a More Perfect Union: Using Lawyering Pedagogy to Enhance Legal Writing Courses*, 49 J. LEGAL EDUC. 185 (1999).

[47] *See* Kirsten A. Dauphinais, *Using an Interviewing, Counseling, Negotiating, and Drafting Simulation in the First Year Legal Writing Program*, 15 TRANSACTIONS 105 (2013).

[48] *See* O'Neill, *supra* note 21; Melissa Shafer, *Shakespeare in Law: How the Theater Department Can Enhance Lawyering Skills Instruction,* 8 PERSPS. 108 (2000). For articles addressing the breadth of skills coverage in LRW courses, see Susan L. Brody, *Teaching Skills and Values During the Law School Years*, *in MacCrate Report*, *supra* note 6 ("There exists in every law school a required course or series of courses which . . . reflect the importance of oral and written communication. Usually labeled 'Legal Writing and Research,' these courses teach almost all of the other skills that the *MacCrate Report* identifies as fundamental."); *see also* Schultz, *supra* note 22, at 410 ("[I]ntegration is the key—integrating skills, context, research, and writing leads to a better-written product and a stronger understanding of the lawyer's work."); Silecchia, *supra* note 33, at 256 (describing more than a dozen fundamental lawyering skills other than research and writing covered in many first-year LRW courses).

g. *Applying Knowledge and Skills to Solve Novel Legal Problems*

Finally, students should leave their first year of LRW equipped to apply the knowledge and skills they have learned to solve real-world legal problems.[49] They should be able to analyze, research, and write about a legal issue, and they should be able to continue the process of learning about the law without the support of the LRW professor.

This last goal is perhaps the most challenging because it requires the professor to teach students how to teach themselves—to recognize and fill gaps in their own knowledge as they address new legal issues in the context of a client's unique circumstances.[50] In that sense, LRW courses qualify as foundational experiential learning in a simulated context.[51] By the end of a comprehensive LRW course, students should have developed the potential to become competent legal researchers, analysts, communicators, and advocates.

---

[49] *See* Van Patten, *supra* note 32, at 176.

[50] Soma R. Kedia, *Redirecting the Scope of First-Year Writing Courses: Toward a New Paradigm of Teaching Legal Writing*, 87 U. Det. Mercy L. Rev. 147, 154 (2010) (noting the importance of teaching students the ability to learn on their own).

[51] *See, e.g.*, Nantiya Ruan, *Student, Esquire?: The Practice of Law in the Collaborative Classroom*, 20 Clinical L. Rev. 429, 430 (2014) (describing how law school faculty "are leaving their silos and collaborating with one another to provide experiential learning opportunities that incorporate client work into the learning of the class . . . [including] legal research and writing (LRW), clinical, externship, doctrinal faculty, and non-profit lawyers working together in a variety of partnerships"); Sarah O. Schrup & Susan E. Provenzano, *The Conscious Curriculum: From Novice Towards Mastery in Written Legal Analysis and Advocacy*, 108 Nw. U.L. Rev. Colloquy 80, 81 (2013) (proposing a "blueprint for implementing the integrated apprenticeship for written legal analysis and advocacy in a realistic way"); *see also* Lamparello & MacLean, *supra* note 17, at 98-109 (proposing a comprehensive six-semester curriculum incorporating doctrinal, skills, and clinical courses). Part D of this chapter provides a more detailed overview of legal writing in conjunction with experiential learning and simulation courses.

2. *Instructional Content*

a. Legal Reasoning and Analysis

Legal reasoning and analysis skills are the foundation of any LRW course.[52] Students should understand legislative, judicial, and administrative institutions and processes that produce legal authority, the weight of each type of authority, and the way each type of authority relates to the others. LRW courses should also introduce students to administrative law, the rulemaking process, and quasi-judicial administrative tribunals.[53] Students should understand the concepts and interrelationships among primary, secondary, mandatory, and persuasive authority. And they must be able to identify and apply various rule structures, including conjunctive and disjunctive elements tests, factors tests, and combinations of each.

Students should understand the basic legislative process and the various judicial approaches to statutory interpretation. They should understand judicial opinions, precedent, and the concept of *stare decisis*. They should understand the primary jurisprudential approaches and forms of legal reasoning, including rule-based, analogical, policy-based, and narrative reasoning. They should understand how to select appropriate and effective forms of reasoning to use in various legal settings. For example, students should understand that policy arguments are generally less persuasive when presenting a case to a trial court dealing with established law, but they

---

[52] *See, e.g.*, Linda H. Edwards, *Legal Writing: A Doctrinal Course*, 1 SAVANNAH L. REV. 1 (2014). "The typical first-year Legal Writing course . . . is 'doctrinal' in all senses of the word. Legal Writing . . . teaches the body of law generally applicable to all legal issues (the principles of legal method). It teaches a particular body of law applicable to predictive and persuasive analysis . . . . Finally, it teaches a well-recognized body of ideas applicable to the subject of the course: the content and communication of written and oral legal analysis." *Id.* at 6.

[53] *Cf.* Sara K. Rankin, Lisa Brodoff & Mary Nicol Bowman, *We Have a Dream: Integrating Skills Courses and Public Interest Work in the First Year of Law School (and Beyond)*, 17 CHAP. L. REV. 89, 93 (2013) (describing innovative collaboration between legal writing and administrative law clinics).

might be very useful when addressing an appellate court on how to resolve a novel legal issue.

By the end of their first year, LRW students should understand the difference between legal analysis and legal synthesis, and they should be able to competently engage in both kinds of legal reasoning. Common law analysis often begins with exercises, such as case briefing, that require students to break a case into its component parts and label and understand the purpose and significance of each part. Next, students might be asked to identify the similarities and differences in the facts and holdings in a series of related cases. Finally, students might be challenged to synthesize and reconcile those similarities and differences into a legal rule to solve an analogous legal issue arising from a new set of facts.

Asking students to locate, identify, and assess patterns across cases is more challenging than it might initially appear. Students frequently start law school with little experience in manipulating information and in exercising creative, independent judgment about the appropriate meaning to attach to patterns they identify in judicial opinions. Some students may struggle with analogical reasoning by looking for cases involving identical facts, which will necessarily result in frustration when students discover that virtually every case can be distinguished on its facts to a greater or lesser degree. Even students who readily adapt to analogical reasoning might have difficulty recognizing how common law rules develop incrementally over time, how unarticulated factors in a series of cases might turn out to influence future courts in shaping or narrowing the rule, or how the identification of legally relevant facts should lead to a predictable outcome.

In addition to common law analysis and synthesis, students should learn to analyze and interpret complex statutes and regulations.[54] Contemporary law students need to understand that statutes

---

[54] *See* Harold Anthony Lloyd, *Why Legal Writing Is "Doctrinal" and More Importantly Profound*, 19 NEV. L.J. 729, 737 (2019). "If someone asks me what a statute means, I will flesh it out . . . by describing how it plays out in experience.

and regulations supersede common law in most instances.[55] Students who master common law reasoning may have difficulty with the close legal analysis and critical reading necessary for competent interpretation and application of statutes and other enacted law. Generally, first-year students do not readily appreciate these concepts from other first-year courses, which rely significantly on judicial decisions as primary teaching materials. Students must learn to deconstruct poorly drafted statutes, court rules, and administrative regulations by diagramming component rules, breaking them down into their subparts, and mentally reframing them in a way that helps them solve client problems.[56]

In summary, by the end of the first year, LRW students should understand how to critically read, analyze, and interpret the language of the law, how to isolate relevant facts in a novel set of circumstances, and how to effectively apply the law to those specific facts. For example, students might be asked to explain the meaning of the law, argue for an extension or adoption of a legal rule, or apply settled law to a novel or complex set of facts.

b. Integrating Legal Analysis, Research, and Writing Skills

Legal reasoning and analysis cannot be separated from legal research and writing without negatively affecting the students'

Such ‘fleshing out’ is at the heart of the skills taught in legal writing where students must produce actual objective and persuasive written and oral products required of practicing lawyers. Such ‘fleshing out’ is also at the heart of meaning.” *Id.*

[55] *See generally* Entrikin, *supra* note 23, at 351 (explaining that judge-made law is subordinate to enacted law, and American law schools place far too little emphasis on the latter, to the disadvantage of law students as prospective practicing lawyers).

[56] *See* Entrikin & Neumann Jr., *supra* note 35, at 58-73 (explaining how to analyze enacted statutes and rules to identify their working components and to reconstruct them to understand what they mean and how they function).

learning experience.[57] Those who view LRW courses as focusing solely on writing (in a grammar and sentence structure sense) fail to recognize that teaching reasoning and analytical skills is an essential aspect of teaching legal writing. In its broadest sense, legal writing is the written expression of legal analysis.[58] And legal analysis can be neither limited to the doctrinal classroom nor eliminated from the LRW classroom.

Although some elements of legal analysis can be taught in other ways, in LRW courses legal analysis is conveyed to students using a series of increasingly challenging written assignments that reflect as closely as possible the analytical processes students will apply in law practice.[59] For example, LRW students begin to understand legal analysis most effectively when they learn how the unique facts pertaining to a hypothetical client interact with the law to yield a solution to a legal issue. Early in the course, the professor might isolate the legal issue to reduce the complexity of the students' analytical task. As the course progresses, students should develop the ability to identify the relevant legal issues raised by the client's particular circumstances.

During the initial stages of analysis and research, as students work through the following types of questions, they gradually learn to understand the nature and relationship of different kinds of legal

---

[57] *See* Phillip C. Kissam, *Thinking (by Writing) about Legal Writing*, 40 VAND. L. REV. 135, 138-140 (1987) (explaining how legal writing instruction develops expertise in legal thinking); J. Christopher Rideout & Jill J. Ramsfield, *Legal Writing: The View from Within*, 61 MERCER L. REV. 705, 707 (2010) (observing that "legal writing [is] legal thinking itself").

[58] *See* Lynn N. Hughes, *The Metaphysics of Courses in Legal Writing*, 8 LEGAL WRITING 11, 13 (2002) ("Legal writing affords the student the ability to fuse culture and analysis in exposition. The facts of our heritage must be applied with the *force of reason* to old problems in new contexts . . . .") (emphasis original).

[59] For a typical sequence of assignments, see Rowe, *supra* note 25. *See also infra* Part 2.c of this chapter (describing written assignments in a standard first-year LRW course).

authority. Does the situation involve an issue of federal or state law? What forum will decide the legal issue, and how does that information influence the hierarchy of legal authority? Has the relevant jurisdiction's legislature enacted an applicable statute? If so, how, if at all, have courts in the controlling jurisdiction interpreted and applied the statute in precedential cases? If no statute applies, have the courts otherwise addressed the question? If so, which decisions are mandatory and which are persuasive authority given the hierarchy of courts in the forum jurisdiction? If neither a statute nor a mandatory precedent applies, what persuasive authorities might best predict the outcome? Will the court follow persuasive authorities from other jurisdictions? Have other courts established majority or minority rules that might inform the court in deciding an issue of first impression?

As the legal research process develops, students begin to recognize that legal analysis and research are intimately and unavoidably intertwined. By locating and analyzing relevant legal authority, students discover that they need to carefully review the unique facts of the case to identify analogies and distinctions. And they might need to reevaluate the initial research strategy to identify additional avenues of inquiry.

At the point when students begin an intensive legal analysis, many discover they need better skills in reading and re-reading critically to improve their comprehension of relevant facts and applicable legal authority. Because students tend to skim and vaguely paraphrase complex ideas, they may struggle to gain an accurate and nuanced understanding of statutes, rules, and judicial opinions. Various short exercises are often used in LRW courses to help students practice and master increasingly challenging legal analysis skills.[60] LRW professors commonly rely on comprehensive, ongoing feedback from reviewing students' progress on written and in-class

[60] *E.g.*, Terri L. Enns & Monte Smith, *Take a (Cognitive) Load Off: Creating Space to Allow First-Year Legal Writing Students to Focus on Analytical and Writing Processes*, 20 LEGAL WRITING 109, 131-39 (2015) (explaining how assessment rubrics help to scaffold student learning of legal writing and analysis skills).

exercises to assess whether the class as a whole is grasping the fundamentals of legal analysis.[61] In turn, students learn to focus on the actual text of the controlling authorities and, when applicable, the relevant facts provided in the assignment.

Once students gain more skill and confidence in reading legal authority, they begin to construct the analytical framework for the relevant law they need to solve the hypothetical client's problem.[62] Initially, students learn that this framework depends upon the applicable hierarchy of legal authority in the controlling jurisdiction. For instance, if Congress or the state legislature has enacted a relevant statute, that statute (assuming it is constitutional) is the starting point for analyzing the client's legal issue.

Next, students must engage in careful analysis to further develop a suitable legal framework to resolve the issue. In simple assignments, one or more authorities may explicitly articulate the overall analytical structure and sufficiently describe all rule components. For instance, a court might clearly set out the required elements to state a cause of action or describe an affirmative defense.

In other assignments, the legal authorities may articulate many important ideas but fail to sufficiently describe all components of the applicable legal analysis, fail to identify precisely the sequence and interrelationships of the various rule components, or fail to sufficiently explain the operation of each element or factor in the legal framework. In these situations, students must recognize the gap in

---

[61] *See, e.g.*, Leslie M. Rose, *Norm-Referenced Grading in the Age of Carnegie: Why Criteria-Referenced Grading Is More Consistent with Current Trends in Legal Education and How Legal Writing Can Lead the Way*, 17 LEGAL WRITING 123, 148–49 (2011) (explaining that LRW professors and clinicians regularly use formative assessment and therefore provide a model assessment strategy for other law faculty as they adapt to outcomes-based assessment requirements).

[62] *See id.* at 139 ("As the students became more familiar and practiced in providing written analysis using the structures outlined in the rubric, the need for that scaffold declines because the students have constructed appropriate schema.").

the law, demonstrate why the gap exists in the relevant jurisdiction, and then marshal more sophisticated analytical methods using persuasive authority to predict how a court in the relevant jurisdiction will fill the gap.

For example, students might work on a statutory issue in which the relevant term has not been defined or the statutory definition is ambiguous, but the term's meaning has not been explained in any binding judicial opinion. In this situation, students must learn how to use the basic canons of statutory interpretation to figure out whether the statute applies to the client's circumstances and, if it does, its likely effect. Students must also learn that some traditional canons of statutory interpretation might not apply because of a superseding statute in the relevant jurisdiction, or because the statute itself includes enacted rules governing its interpretation.[63]

In a common law problem, if the courts in the relevant jurisdiction have addressed the issue but without fully articulating the analysis, students must learn to synthesize concepts and policies from reading groups of relevant cases with analogous facts. Students initially learn to parse the courts' explicit language in each case and identify patterns in the holdings. They then proceed to infer judicial reasoning that is often only implicit to fill the gaps in the analytical framework.

In developing in-depth legal analysis, students learn about the relationships between legal doctrine and underlying judicial

---

[63] *See* James J. Brudney & Ethan J. Leib, *Statutory Interpretation as "Interbranch Dialogue"?*, 66 UCLA L. Rev. 346, 379 (2019) (noting that "legislated canons and judicial reliance on common law canons often appear like two ships passing in the night"); Abbe R. Gluck, *The States as Laboratories of Statutory Interpretation: Methodological Consensus and the New Modified Textualism*, 119 Yale L.J. 1750, 1824-29 (2010) (outlining the "new questions" and unresolved institutional power dynamics represented by enacted rules of statutory interpretation, which some state courts have resisted). *See generally* Jacob Scott, *Codified Canons and the Common Law of Interpretation*, 98 Geo. L.J. 341 (2010).

reasoning, including which social policy arguments the courts in a particular jurisdiction have found persuasive and which ones they have rejected.[64] As students eventually come to understand, determining which interpretations of a particular legal doctrine are reasonable ultimately depends on the motivating principles that led a court to embrace a specific legal theory when determining the outcome of a precedent case.

LRW students are also exposed to a range of different legal standards and tests —such as elements tests, factors tests, balancing tests, totality-of-the-circumstances tests, or a combination of any or all of these. Students who successfully complete the LRW course gain a comprehensive understanding about how different kinds of legal standards and tests govern the outcome of a client's fact-specific legal issue.

Because students must interpret the applicable "law" to figure out the most likely outcome for the client's problem, they must also engage in thorough fact analysis. In LRW, students learn the difference between pleaded facts, evidentiary facts, inferences from facts, and factual characterizations. They also learn how to distinguish issues of fact from issues of law and why the distinction is so important. In learning persuasive advocacy, students must understand how to present facts in a manner that both motivates the court

---

[64] *See* Ellie Margolis, *Closing the Floodgates: Making Persuasive Policy Arguments in Appellate Briefs*, 62 MONT. L. REV. 59, 61 (2001) ("Policy argumentation is an important skill which should be taught in law school legal writing programs."); Ellie Margolis, *Teaching Students to Make Effective Policy Arguments in Appellate Briefs*, 9 PERSPS. 73, 73 (2001) ("[S]tudents should be taught to understand the nature of different types of policy arguments and how an understanding of policy can affect the way a legal problem is viewed."). *See generally* Ellie Margolis, *Beyond Brandeis: Exploring the Uses of Non-Legal Materials in Appellate Briefs*, 34 U.S.F. L. REV. 197 (2000) (explaining how to use legislative facts to support policy arguments in appellate advocacy); Michael R. Smith, *The Sociological and Cognitive Dimensions of Policy-Based Persuasion*, 22 J.L. & POL'Y 35, 36 (2013) (building on Professor Margolis' scholarly work from a social science perspective).

to accept the client's legal argument and justifies the client's desired outcome. And students must learn to do so without misstating or mischaracterizing the relevant facts, and without misstating the applicable law or asking the court to adopt an unreasonable change or expansion of settled law.

c. *Written Assignments in the Standard First-Year LRW Course*

LRW writing assignments require students to use analytical skills in different but complementary ways. For example, all LRW courses require students to engage in objective analysis by preparing a predictive office memorandum addressed to a hypothetical supervising lawyer. In a predictive memo, students must figure out, organize, and clearly express legal analysis that objectively articulates and explains the relevant legal authorities. Students must then demonstrate how that legal analysis applies to the relevant, dispositive facts of the client's case and how it supports the probable outcome if presented to a court in the relevant jurisdiction.[65] This process requires students to understand how to reason by analogy by comparing the facts of the client's case to the facts of precedent cases to predict how the court will rule when applying the relevant law to the client's facts.

Virtually all LRW courses also require students to engage in persuasive legal analysis to support a litigation argument on behalf of a client. To learn persuasive legal analysis, students must learn to fashion an interpretation of the relevant law that provides the client's best chance for obtaining a favorable outcome, whether in the form of a trial court's ruling on a pretrial motion or an appellate

---

[65] *See* Mark K. Osbeck, *Lawyer As Soothsayer: Exploring the Important Role of Outcome Prediction in the Practice of Law*, 123 PENN ST. L. REV. 41, 43 (2018) ("One of the most important tasks lawyers undertake in furtherance of [their] advisory role is outcome prediction: that is, advising the client as to the likely outcome of various legal proceedings.").

court's decision based on a persuasive brief. Formulating a compelling legal argument requires students to engage in numerous complex analytical skills. These include identifying legally dispositive facts; developing a persuasive theme incorporating those facts; and marshaling relevant statutes, judicial precedent, and legal reasoning to support a suitable interpretation of relevant law that will convince the court to decide the issues favorably to the hypothetical client.

Many LRW courses also require students to report or explain some analytical aspect of the case to the client in writing. A client letter assignment requires students to understand the legal analysis so comprehensively that they can simplify it for a less knowledgeable audience in a way that captures the essential concepts without patronizing or overwhelming the client with legalese and unnecessary detail.

The value of assigning a client letter midway through the first-year LRW course is that students instantly recognize the extent to which legal language has become almost second nature to them in a relatively short period of time. A good deal of nuanced legal analysis is required for students to translate complex legal principles into "lay" language meaningful to a typical client. The client letter also offers an excellent opportunity for students to engage in the kind of real-world lawyering tasks they will regularly perform in practice. Because client communication requires a well-developed, sophisticated understanding of professional norms governing the lawyer-client relationship, some LRW programs reserve this kind of writing assignment for an upper-level LRW course.

Over the last two decades, e-mail communication has become almost ubiquitous in law practice. For that reason, many LRW courses instruct students how to appropriately use email in an ethical manner to communicate legal analysis to supervising attorneys and to clients. First-year law students are often surprised to learn that lawyers have a professional responsibility to maintain confidentiality in communicating sensitive information to clients. Students should understand the risks to client confidentiality of using email (and other electronic media) to communicate with clients.[66] Moreover, students should be cautioned that email invites a degree of informality that is generally unsuitable for conveying legal advice to clients.

3. Teaching Approaches

LRW professors use a variety of teaching methods, sequences, and strategies to ensure that students successfully develop the capability to demonstrate each of the learning outcomes discussed in Part A.1 of this chapter. Because each professor brings unique professional experiences and skills to the legal academy,[67] LRW programs should allow sufficient flexibility to allow each instructor to adapt standard pedagogical techniques to complement the professor's individual teaching style. Professors should be encouraged to develop innovative assignments, experiment with various teaching methods, and share their results with other law faculty at the local, regional, and national levels.

The following discussion provides a sampling of typical teaching approaches for each essential component of the LRW course.

---

[66] *See* ABA Standing Comm. on Ethics & Prof'l Responsibility, Formal Op. 14-006 (2017) (addressing ethical risks of using technology in law practice), https://www.americanbar.org/content/dam/aba/images/abanews/FormalOpinion477.pdf; *see also, e.g.,* Rebecca Bolin, *Risky Mail: Concerns in Confidential Attorney-Client Email*, 81 U. CIN. L. REV. 601 (2012); Vanessa S. Browne-Barbour, *"Why Can't We Be 'Friends'?": Ethical Concerns in the Use of Social Media*, 57 S. TEX. L. REV. 551 (2016); Steven C. Bennett, *Ethics of Lawyer Social Networking*, 73 ALB. L. REV. 113 (2009); Cheryl B. Preston, *Lawyers' Abuse of Technology*, 103 CORNELL L. REV. 879, 883 (2018) ("[T]he profession has made almost no effort to explicate for future guidance how technology may pose particular risks to civility, professionalism, and ethics and how the risks should be addressed.").

[67] *See* Susan P. Liemer, *Many Birds, One Stone: Teaching the Law You Love, in Legal Writing Class*, 53 J. LEGAL EDUC. 284, 285 (2003) (encouraging LRW professors draw from their favorite legal subject matter areas in creating engaging LRW assignments to their students' benefit).

a. Legal Analysis

For most law students, their first exposure to the foundational process of legal analysis occurs in the LRW course.[68] Accordingly, analytical skills should be taught comprehensively and intensively. LRW professors should devote significant class time to discussing these skills in the abstract, and then working through practice exercises. Exercises can be assigned in advance for students to discuss in class, or professors can use class time to allow students to work in small groups to practice legal analysis and then discuss their results with the entire class.

The LRW course offers excellent opportunities to teach students legal analysis by delivering personalized intensive critique on draft documents, together with one-on-one student conferences to discuss the professor's feedback and to guide students in the process of revising and improving their working drafts.[69] In the written and oral feedback, the professor should reinforce each student's ability to demonstrate fundamental analytical skills by refraining from giving the student the "correct" legal analysis or the "right" answer to a legal issue. Many beginning law students are frustrated to learn that in legal analysis, no single "right answer" exists; rather, successful law students must develop the capacity to follow an analytical *process* to reach a variety of plausible answers to a legal question.[70]

---

[68] Miriam E. Felsenburg & Laura P. Graham, *A Better Beginning: Why and How to Help Novice Legal Writers Build A Solid Foundation by Shifting Their Focus from Product to Process*, 24 REGENT U. L. REV. 83, 85–86 (2012).

[69] *See* Daniel L. Barnett, *Triage in the Trenches of the Legal Writing Course: The Theory and Methodology of Analytical Critique*, 38 U. TOL. L. REV. 651, 652 (2007) (discussing the challenges and demands of critiquing students' written work and noting that "[t]he average legal writing teacher provides feedback on 1,204 pages of student writing each year"); Robin S. Wellford-Slocum, *The Law School Student-Faculty Conference: Towards a Transformative Learning Experience*, 45 S. TEX. L. REV. 255, 260 (2004) (explaining that "the student conference can be one of the most important learning experiences of a law student's education").

[70] *See* Gionfriddo, *supra* note 26, at 428–29.

LRW students learn the mysterious process of "thinking like a lawyer" by developing and practicing legal analytical skills.[71] In the LRW classroom, students learn the fundamentals of legal analysis they will use in all other first-year law school courses and beyond as they progress through the rest of law school and into law practice.

b. Writing

While LRW professors use a variety of approaches to teach legal writing, the most effective writing instruction embodies the following four essential aspects.

Consider the Audience. As an initial step in writing any document, students must recognize and embrace the importance of audience, which guides the writer's decisions about content, coverage, and language choice. In a first-year LRW course, students should be taught that different audiences have different needs and expectations (*e.g.*, in-house counsel, clients, judges, and opposing counsel). Students should be given opportunities to write for various legal audiences so they understand how to vary the content, tone, and organization of each legal document to suit the unique needs of the reader. Assignments might include an objective office memo for another lawyer, a persuasive brief for a judge, a client advice letter, or even a demand letter or proposed settlement offer.

Understand the Primary Purpose of the Legal Document. Students should understand and be able to articulate the purpose of a particular legal document and how that purpose affects its content, organization, and tone. For an objective office memorandum, the document's primary purpose is to inform by providing balanced legal analysis, and its secondary purpose is to help the reader advise the client how best to resolve a legal issue. The primary purpose of a trial or appellate brief is to persuade the court, but a secondary

---

[71] For an excellent supplemental text reinforcing legal analysis instruction, see KEITH VANDEVELDE, THINKING LIKE A LAWYER (2d ed. 2010).

purpose is "raise the ante" by convincing the opposing party's counsel that the client has a compelling argument. And the purpose of a client letter is to answer a client's legal question or to advise the client on alternative strategies for resolving a legal dispute.

Follow a Systematic Writing Process. LRW students should understand and demonstrate each of the various stages of the writing process: planning, analyzing, researching, drafting, and revising. Students should also understand how such factors as personal experience and deadline pressure may affect the extent to which they follow that process.

Recognize the Various Legal Skills Required to Competently Prepare a Document. Students must learn to diagnose problems with their own writing and assess their progress as legal writers. In short, they must become their own best editors.[72] Only then can they continue to learn and grow even after completing the LRW course. The structure and teaching approach for the LRW course should be intellectually challenging but also supportive, diagnostic, and explanatory to give students a model they can later use as they become independent learners.

---

[72] Indeed, many experienced LRW professors recognize that teaching students to identify, correct, revise, and improve their own writing is among the most challenging aspects of teaching an LRW course. *See* Mary Beth Beazley, *The Self-Graded Draft: Teaching Students to Revise Using Guided Self-Critique*, 3 LEGAL WRITING 175, 175 (1997) [hereinafter Beazley, *Self-Graded Draft*]. "If there is anything more difficult than editing another person's writing, it is editing one's own writing. [T]he self-editor . . . often lacks the psychological distance necessary to distinguish between the information on the printed page and the information still inside the writer's head." *Id.; see also* Cassandra L. Hill, *Peer Editing: A Comprehensive Pedagogical Approach to Maximize Assessment Opportunities, Integrate Collaborative Learning, and Achieve Desired Outcomes*, 11 NEV. L.J. 667, 669 (2011) (explaining how professors can use collaborative peer editing as part of their assessment plans); Tonya Kowalski, *Toward A Pedagogy for Teaching Legal Writing in Law School Clinics*, 17 CLINICAL L. REV. 285, 341-44 (2010) (explaining the value of using self-critique and peer critique in teaching legal writing).

The variety of teaching approaches employed in LRW courses reflects changes in writing instruction over the past several decades in college composition and rhetoric, as well as the changing attitude within the legal academy and the legal profession in favor of professional skills development. The following teaching approaches represent those most commonly used in LRW programs. But the field is continually evolving by developing innovative teaching strategies, which is perhaps the hallmark of the LRW community.[73]

An important trend in teaching LRW incorporates theories and approaches first developed in college composition courses.[74] Especially prominent is the process-oriented approach to writing instruction, which emphasizes the process of researching and drafting in stages, and then revising—an inherently recursive rather than linear model.[75] The process-oriented approach is appropriate for novice writers who are unfamiliar with the assigned document and how to

---

[73] *See, e.g.*, Dennis, *supra* note 18 (discussing the pedagogical value of transitioning to a three-semester program and proposing various models); Rideout & Ramsfield, *supra* note 57, at 745 ("As teachers of legal writing, we are all positioned somewhere between the conventions of legal discourse, which we are obligated to teach, and our reformist sense of what lies both behind and beyond those conventions.").

[74] Nancy Soonpaa, *Using Composition Theory and Scholarship to Teach Legal Writing More Effectively*, 3 LEGAL WRITING 81 (1997); Adam Todd, *Neither Dead Nor Dangerous: Postmodernism and the Teaching of Legal Writing*, 58 BAYLOR L. REV. 893, 918 (2006) ("The changes in composition and rhetoric theory [in the mid-twentieth century] were mirrored in legal writing pedagogy.").

[75] *See, e.g.*, Ellie Margolis & Susan L. DeJarnatt, *Moving Beyond Product to Process: Building a Better LRW Program*, 46 SANTA CLARA L. REV. 93, 99 (2005); *see also* Cara Cunningham & Michelle Streicher, *The Methodology of Persuasion: A Process-Based Approach to Persuasive Writing*, 13 LEGAL WRITING 159 (2007); Teresa Godwin Phelps, *The New Legal Rhetoric*, 40 SW. L.J. 1089, 1093-96 (1986); *cf.* John A. Lynch, Jr., *The New Legal Writing Pedagogy: Is Our Pride and Joy a Hobble?*, 61 J. LEGAL EDUC. 231, 244 (2011) (critiquing the process approach as "a labor-intensive model for legal writing pedagogy [that] an ABA interpretation has foisted . . . on legal education").

prepare it. The prewriting stage emphasizes idea development and macro-organization; the drafting stage involves transferring ideas from the writer's mind to the paper; and the revision stage focuses on improving and refining the document.

The recursive sequence may be reflected in the LRW classroom. In class, students can discuss the document's analytical content, relevant legal authorities identified in the research process, and the overall organization of their arguments. Both inside and outside class, students can draft the assignment, either in sections or as a whole. Similarly, professors can use time inside and outside class to provide both individual and group feedback to enable students to revise their working drafts before submitting them to the LRW professor for final assessment.

Another teaching approach borrowed from college composition is the portfolio method.[76] This method expands on the process approach by giving students multiple opportunities to receive feedback and to revise a document. Students continue to work on individual assignments throughout the semester, turning in their collection of written work in portfolio form at the end of the semester. Only then are assignments evaluated for a final grade.

Still another approach draws inspiration from clinical legal education. The "law firm" approach teaches writing in a practice

---

[76] *See, e.g.*, Neil Hamilton, *Formation-of-an-Ethical-Professional-Identity (Professionalism) Learning Outcomes and E-Portfolio Formative Assessments*, 48 U. Pac. L. Rev. 847, 848 (2017) (analyzing how "an e-portfolio curricular strategy" can advance both student learning outcomes and institutional goals); Steven J. Johansen, *"What Were You Thinking?" Using Annotated Portfolios to Improve Student Assessment*, 4 Legal Writing 123 (1998); Victoria L. VanZandt, *Creating Assessment Plans for Introductory Legal Research and Writing Courses*, 16 Legal Writing 313, 344-45 (2010) (describing how portfolios can be used for legal writing assessment).

setting.[77] Students can be divided into law firms in which they work collaboratively as a team, perhaps following the procedural requirements of a "court" in formatting and submitting persuasive writing assignments.[78] This approach can be used in a basic LRW course, or an expanded "lawyering skills" course[79] in which students also learn other professional skills such as client interviewing and counseling,[80] alternative dispute resolution,[81] contract or statute drafting, and delivering oral reports to a hypothetical senior partner.

A recent variation on the law firm approach is team-based learning, which some legal educators have advocated as "an effective and transformative teaching strategy for law school courses."[82] In fact, a 2017 article co-authored by two Harvard professors urged that "[l]aw schools should encourage faculty to have at least one-third of law school courses, assignments, and assessments be team-based and should work with faculty members to help them adapt innovative new ways to teach team-based courses."[83]

---

[77] *See* James E. Moliterno, *Legal Education, Experiential Education, and Professional Responsibility*, 38 Wm. & Mary L. Rev. 71 (1996).

[78] *See* Daan Braveman, *Law Firm: A First-Year Course on Lawyering*, 39 J. Legal Educ. 501 (1989).

[79] *See* Harris & Susman, *supra* note 46; Silecchia, *supra* note 33.

[80] *See* Shafer, *supra* note 48.

[81] *See* O'Neill, *supra* note 21.

[82] Sophie M. Sparrow & Margaret Sova McCabe, *Team-Based Learning in Law*, 18 Legal Writing 153, 154 (2012); *see* Steven I. Friedland, *Adaptive Strategies for the Future of Legal Education*, 61 Loy. L. Rev. 211, 221 n.46 (2015) (citing Team-Based Learning: A Transformative Use of Small Groups in College Teaching (Larry K. Michaelsen et al. eds., 2004)).

[83] Scott A. Westfahl & David B. Wilkins, *The Leadership Imperative: A Collaborative Approach to Professional Development in the Global Age of More for Less*, 69 Stan. L. Rev. 1667, 1708 (2017).

i. Commonly Assigned Legal Documents

The most recent data available in published form confirms that the most commonly taught documents in a foundational LRW course are one or more objective office memoranda, a persuasive brief (trial or appellate), and a client letter.[84] An increasing number of LRW programs require students to prepare email memoranda,[85] reflecting their frequent use by practicing lawyers.

The objective office memorandum is the most frequently assigned document because it introduces basic analytical and organizational skills that all attorneys need to communicate their analysis effectively in writing. In addition, the office memo serves as a vehicle for introducing each of the primary goals of effective writing instruction outlined above. Subsequent assignments add new skills and reinforce the primary learning objectives of the course.

---

[84]The 2014-15 academic year was the last in which annual survey data was collected by gathering information from responding law schools on the kinds of legal documents assigned in the required LRW course. *See* Ass'n of Legal Writing Directors & Legal Writing Inst., *Report of the Annual Legal Writing Survey* vii (2015), https://www.alwd.org/images/resources/2015%20Survey%20Report%20(AY%202014-2015).pdf [hereinafter *2015 ALWD/LWI Survey*]; *see id.* at 13 (compiling data from respondents on the kinds of documents assigned in the required LRW course). The 2015 survey reported that among 194 responding law schools, 193 assigned the office memorandum, 139 schools assigned the appellate brief, 117 schools assigned the pretrial brief, 77 schools assigned the trial brief, and 122 schools assigned the client letter. *Id.* The 2015 survey reflected some notable changes in the nature of writing assignments compared to earlier years. *See id.* For example, 67 law schools reported giving unspecified drafting assignments in the required LRW course. *Id.*

[85]Electronic (e-mail) memoranda were assigned by 127 law schools in 2014-15. *Id.* For information on how to incorporate email assignments into LRW courses, see Joe Fore, *The Comparative Benefits of Standalone E-Mail Assignments in the First-Year Legal Writing Curriculum*, 22 LEGAL WRITING 151, 153 (2018) (recommending that "email assignments should be an integral part of the first-year legal writing curriculum").

The objective office memorandum requires a student to understand basic skills of objective legal analysis and how to communicate that analysis using effective organization; proper citation to authority; and clear, concise, error-free writing. The persuasive brief, whether the audience is a trial or appellate court, adds the skill of persuasive written advocacy. The brief often involves multiple, more complex issues compared to the office memo assignment and thus offers students more advanced practice with legal analysis. Client letters are typically advisory and may combine characteristics of both objective and persuasive communication. Because they also introduce the skill of translating sophisticated legal ideas and terms into written language for a lay audience, they should be assigned after students are already familiar with basic legal analysis.

ii. Characteristics of Good Writing Assignments

A well-thought-out LRW assignment challenges students without overwhelming them.[86] Appropriate assignments allow stronger students to grow as legal writers and analysts without abandoning

---

[86]Information on how to access ready-made assignments in the Legal Writing Institute's Idea Bank is available on the LWI's Resources page at https://www.lwionline.org/resources (last visited July 17, 2019). Members of the LWI listserv regularly exchange assignments pertaining to specific subject matter upon request. *See LRWPROF-L Guidelines* (May 2015), https://www.lwionline.org/sites/default/files/LRWPROF%20Guidelines%20May%202015%20Adoption-revised.pdf. For advice on how to create assignments from scratch, see Lorraine Bannai, Anne Enquist, Judith Maier & Susan McClellan, *Sailing Through Designing Memo Assignments,* 5 LEGAL WRITING 193 (1999); Grace Tonner & Diana Pratt, *Selecting and Designing Effective Legal Writing Problems*, 3 LEGAL WRITING 163 (1997); Jan M. Levine, *Designing Assignments for Teaching Legal Analysis, Research, and Writing*, 3 PERSPS. 58 (1995); James B. Levy, *Dead Bodies and Dueling: Be Creative in Developing Ideas for Open Universe Memoranda*, 2 PERSPS. 58 (1998); Kathleen A. Portuan Miller, *Creating an Appellate Brief Assignment: A Recipe for Success*, 16 PERSPS. 165 (2008); *see also* Nicholas W. Allard & Heidi K. Brown, *Training Powerful Legal Communicators*, 90 N.Y. ST. B.J. 10, 12 (Sept. 2018) (noting that "professors are developing new genres of legal research and writing assignments, such as blogs and op-eds, to teach students how

students who learn professional skills at a slower pace. In addition, the challenging-but-not-overwhelming approach allows students to gain additional confidence with each progressively complex assignment. An assignment should be tied to specific learning goals to help focus both the professor in developing the assignment and the students in executing it. An assignment should be consistent with the LRW course's programmatic structure, complementing earlier assignments and providing a bridge to future assignments.

Professors must also decide whether to set their assignments in real or hypothetical jurisdictions. While hypothetical jurisdictions may be appropriate in very limited circumstances (e.g., short, closed assignments early in the first year), setting assignments in a real jurisdiction provides a more realistic learning experience.[87] For example, in a "case of first impression," a real attorney would always find and cite some authorities from the controlling jurisdiction to show how the relevant law has been applied to cases with similar legal, factual, or policy issues. Overall, whether the assignment presents new or well-established issues, students benefit the most from conducting legal analysis in the context of a real rather than a hypothetical jurisdiction.

In addition, LRW professors generally strive to create balanced assignments in which each party has facts and authority to support strong arguments as well as counterarguments. This balance need not be perfect; one side might have stronger facts while the other has stronger law. Or one side may have stronger policy arguments while the other has stronger favorable precedent. This type of balance is particularly important for a persuasive writing assignment

---

to communicate with the general public and explain complex laws and legal concepts in terms non-lawyers can understand").

[87] *See, e.g.,* Elizabeth Inglehart & Martha Kanter, *Creating a Compelling Appellate Brief Assignment Based on a Real-World Case*, 17 PERSPS. 128 (2009).

if half the students are assigned to argue each side of the case.[88] Balanced assignments help students avoid cursory or incomplete analysis, which might result if only one outcome seems reasonable. If students are assigned to write for opposing parties in a persuasive assignment, a balanced problem provides a suitable learning experience for the entire class, with the added advantage of encouraging students to learn about persuasive legal analysis by discussing and debating the problem with one another outside class.

Balance may be unnecessary for an objective assignment, and it is not a significant concern if all students are assigned to the same side for a persuasive writing assignment. Some professors deliberately create early objective writing assignments to lead students to a fairly definite predictive outcome. These assignments can counter the impression — which arises in some doctrinal courses — that all legal issues are unsettled. For an "unbalanced" assignment, however, the LRW professor must take extra care to ensure that the assignment is sufficiently challenging to students.

Even for objective writing assignments, randomly assigning students to different sides offers several teaching opportunities. Students may find it difficult to fully articulate each side's arguments, which is a necessary aspect of learning legal analysis, so having students "represent" opposing sides can provide beneficial opportunities for debate and discussion. Also, students find it instructive if each side of a legal issue reaches the same conclusion. A student on the "losing" side may be tempted to misrepresent the strength of the client's case in an effort to present only "good news" to a senior attorney. This common problem offers an opportunity to teach

---

[88] Annual publications of balanced records provided for trial or appellate persuasive writing assignments include The Moot Court Casebook, published by NYU Law. For information about the book's annual availability, see https://phpprod.law.nyu.edu/jpp/journals/12 (last visited Dec. 13, 2019). *See also* Texas Young Lawyers' Ass'n, *State Moot Court Competition*, https://tyla.org/smc/ (providing links to current and past problems) (last visited Dec. 13, 2019).

students that objective analysis sometimes requires an attorney to deliver "bad news" to provide competent legal advice to a hypothetical client.

When designing each writing assignment, the LRW professor must choose among several equally valid features. For example, the professor selects the assignment's length and complexity, its analytical structure or organizational scheme (*e.g.*, elements-based, factors, or balancing tests), its jurisdictional basis (state or federal law), the relevant forum (state or federal court), and the predominant type of legal authority (statutes or case law). By mixing and matching the different features of each assignment, a professor can advance complementary learning goals with each increasingly challenging assignment.

iii. Incorporating Required Redrafts

Students must be given opportunities to revise their work after they have a reasonable amount of time to review individualized written or oral feedback from the LRW professor. Prompt feedback is essential to the students' process-oriented learning. Revising a document in response to that feedback gives students practice in refining the core skills of legal analysis and written communication. Early drafts should focus on legal analysis and appropriate organizational schemes to present that analysis. Later drafts should focus on issues such as presenting the analysis precisely, concisely, and clearly, including adhering to plain English.

In evaluating the rigor of legal writing assignments, the ABA Standards focus in part on the number of required drafts.[89] The num-

---

[89]ABA Standards, Interpretation 303-2. "Factors to be considered in evaluating the rigor of a writing experience include the number and nature of writing projects assigned to students, the form and extent of individualized assessment of a student's written products, and the number of drafts that a student must produce for any writing experience." *Id.*

ber of drafts the LRW professor can realistically require depends on a multitude of variables including class size, the number of credits allocated to the LRW course, the number and nature of assigned documents, and even the institution's expectations for the professor to engage in faculty service and scholarship.

iv. Learning Outcomes

After two or three semesters, all LRW students should have developed basic proficiency in each of the following skills of written communication:

Organization. LRW students should learn organization on all levels, ranging from the paragraph (micro- or small-scale organization) to the complete document (macro- or large-scale organization). Paragraph-level organization requires students to understand the need for topic and thesis sentences as well as paragraph coherence and unity. Because the overall organization of legal analysis typically follows the structure of the applicable legal rule, students should understand how to identify common rule structures and to develop appropriate corresponding organizational schemes.[90] Students should also understand how to vary the prescribed overall organization of a legal document for optimum persuasive effect.

In particular, many law students struggle to understand that a legal audience expects a thorough explanation and analysis of the

---

[90]For a detailed discussion of the pros and cons of the IRAC organizational scheme, see the comments from numerous legal writing educators in *Point/Counterpoint: Use of IRAC-type Formulas—Desirable or Dangerous?*, 10 SECOND DRAFT, Nov. 1995, at 1-20. Most first-year LRW textbooks teach students to use alternative organizational frameworks that are more suitable for written discourse, such as CREAC and its many variations. Students should be taught that IRAC is a template recommended for casebook course exams, not the professional legal documents they learn to prepare in an LRW course. *See, e.g.,* Tracy Turner, *Finding Consensus in Legal Writing Discourse Regarding Organizational Structure: A Review and Analysis of the Use of IRAC and Its Progenies*, 9 J. ALWD 351 (2012).

applicable law (rule explanation) before they apply the law to the client's specific facts to predict a legal conclusion (rule application). Before they understand this basic organizational feature of legal analysis, many students find it challenging to identify and focus on the relevant, dispositive facts. To learn how to carefully select from the available facts to isolate which ones to include in a written legal document, students must first master the basic skill of legal analysis. Many students instead want to "tell the client's story" first and then immediately explain how they think the law applies. Students must learn that the process of careful legal research and analysis reveals *which* specific facts in the narrative are relevant, either to predict the outcome or to persuade a judge to adopt the analysis that best favors the client's desired result.

Format. By the end of the required LRW course, students should understand the conventional formats for office memoranda and briefs. They should also understand that they might need to adapt the format of an assignment to meet the specific requirements of a law office or court. A more comprehensive LRW course—one that offers more course credits or extends beyond two semesters—should introduce students to other legal documents such as pleadings, contracts, or statutes so students comprehend the many ways they differ from office memos and litigation briefs.

Writing Style. Students should understand the conventions of written discourse in the legal profession. These features include appropriate tone and formality, as well as avoiding archaic legalese and other conventions that are no longer acceptable in a "Plain English" era.

Understandably, beginning law students often assume that the legalese, redundant phrases, and archaic wording so characteristic of the judicial opinions they read in casebook courses reflect how to "write like a lawyer." The LRW professor needs to explain, often repeatedly, that phrases like "instant case," "hereinafter," "whereas," and so forth instead mark law students as mere novices in the professional community.[91] As students gain confidence by mastering the appropriate legal concepts and terminology, they are generally less prone to rely on legal jargon.

Students should also learn how to adapt their writing style to meet the needs of various kinds of audiences and to accomplish a variety of purposes. Many students arrive at law school believing they are "good writers,"[92] but most need continual coaching on how to use clear, concise, error-free English in every document they prepare for a legal audience.

Citation Format. Students should understand the purpose, format, and proper placement of legal citations. They should be able to cite legal authority and litigation documents consistent with at least one set of formal citation guidelines: the *ALWD Citation Guide*,[93] the *Bluebook*,[94] or state-specific citation rules.[95] As one legal writing expert recently observed, "citation [is] part of legal style itself"; "writers should embrace [citations] as integral to the text as a whole."[96]

---

[91] *See, e.g.*, Ross Guberman, *Judges Speaking Softly: What They Long for When They Read*, 44 LITIG., Summer 2018, at 48, 50 (listing legalistic phrases and terms judges detest in legal briefs).

[92] *E.g.*, Gerald Lebovits, *How to Succeed in Legal Writing by Really Trying*, 90 N.Y. ST. B.J. 61, 62 (Sept. 2018) ("Students start law school confident in their own abilities as writers[; the] writing professor is the first to crush their confidence.").

[93] COLEEN M. BARGER & ASS'N OF LEGAL WRITING DIRECTORS, ALWD GUIDE TO LEGAL CITATION (6th ed. 2017).

[94] THE BLUEBOOK: A UNIFORM SYSTEM OF CITATION (Columbia Law Review Ass'n et al. eds., 20th ed. 2015).

[95] *E.g.*, UNIV. OF TEX. SCHOOL OF LAW, TEXAS RULES OF FORM: THE GREENBOOK (14th ed. 2018).

[96] Alexa Z. Chew, *Stylish Legal Citation*, 71 ARK. L. REV. 823, 828-29 (2019).

c. Research

As discussed above, competency in legal research is one of the fundamental learning outcomes that all LRW students must master.[97] While the ABA Standards require students to undertake one faculty-supervised legal writing experience in the first year and a second after the first year, a law school may offer legal research courses either in the first-year LRW program, in an upper-level course, or both.[98]

Most law schools incorporate basic legal research instruction early in the first-year LRW course.[99] Some law schools offer advanced legal research as an elective; others require students to enroll in an advanced or specialized legal research course after the first year that builds on the basic skills students learn in the first-year LRW course. While an increasing number of law schools integrate basic legal research into the foundational LRW course, some follow a more traditional model by offering research instruction in a

---

[97] *See* ABA Standards, Standard 302(b); *see also* text accompanying note 3, *supra* (quoting the standard); Ellie Margolis, *Surfin' Safari—Why Competent Lawyers Should Research on the Web*, 10 YALE J. L. & TECH. 82, 82 (2007) ("[L]ocating relevant legal authority and evaluating it are fundamental skills every lawyer should possess.").

[98] *See* ABA Standards, Standard 302(b).

[99] Ass'n of Legal Writing Directors & Legal Writing Inst., *Report of the 2017-2018 Institutional Survey* 34-35 (2019), https://www.lwionline.org/sites/default/files/Final%20ALWD%20LWI%202017-18%20Institutional%20Survey%20Report.pdf [hereinafter *2017-18 ALWD/LWI Institutional Survey*]; Ian Gallacher, *Forty-Two: The Hitchhiker's Guide to Teaching Legal Research to the Google Generation*, 39 AKRON L. REV. 151, 168 & n.82 (2006); Caroline L. Osborne, *The State of Legal Research Education: A Survey of First-Year Legal Research Programs, or "Why Johnny and Jane Cannot Research"*, 108 LAW LIBR. J. 403, 408 (2016) ("Eighty-two percent of [200 law school] respondents indicated that legal research was a required first-year class.").

separate course,[100] often taught by law librarians.[101] Other programs rely on law librarians to teach research within the overall structure of the LRW course taught by an LRW professor. A significant number of law schools rely in part on commercial legal research vendors to instruct students in basic legal research.[102]

i. Basic Legal Research Instruction

A variety of factors influence the design and staffing of legal research programs. Increasingly, law schools have integrated research, analysis, and writing instruction to help students understand that all of these skills are components of a holistic problem-solving experience.[103] An integrated approach is best suited to prepare students for the practice of law, in which research is never conducted in isolation.[104] Rather, an attorney uses a combination

---

[100] *2017-18 ALWD/LWI Institutional Survey*, *supra* note 99, at 21. Twenty-one percent (or 39) of the 182 law schools responding to the most recent survey reported that basic legal research was taught "independently" from other LRW courses. *Id.* Seven percent (12 law schools) reported that a required course in advanced legal research is taught independently. *Id.* In a 2014 survey conducted by Washington and Lee law library staff, just 16 percent of all responding institutions reported having a "stand-alone" legal research course. Osborne, *supra* note 99, at 408.

[101] *2017-18 ALWD/LWI Institutional Survey*, *supra* note 99, at 36.

[102] *See id.*

[103] Barbara Glesner Fines, *Out of the Shadows: What Legal Research Instruction Reveals About Incorporating Skills Throughout the Curriculum*, 2013 J. Disp. Resol. 159, 182 (noting that legal research has been integrated into LRW programs as they have grown in curricular significance, sometimes leading to tension between LRW faculty and law librarians as to the proper way to teach first-year legal research); *see, e.g.*, Osborne, *supra* note 99, at 409 (interpreting survey results to suggest that "writing and other skills development are the focus of the [LRW] class, with research as the orphan child").

[104] *See* Gallacher, *supra* note 99, at 171 ("Depriving [LRW] students of th[e] opportunity to integrate reading, analysis, and expression would be a significant disservice.").

of legal research and analysis in a recursive process to identify the legal authority that will resolve the client's problem or win the client's case.

Even if research and writing are taught separately, research instruction should be delivered in the context of realistic legal problems rather than library search exercises for raw information. A legal research curriculum must aim to teach students how to use both basic print and electronic sources and techniques.[105] It must also instruct students in

- recognizing the importance of research in comprehensively analyzing a legal problem and communicating that analysis in written form;
- appreciating the role of intuition, imagination, and serendipity throughout the research process;
- planning a research strategy at the outset, while maintaining flexibility to revise the plan if appropriate as the research process progresses; and
- determining when the research process is sufficiently exhaustive, given the time constraints and economic realities of law practice.

As with legal writing, legal research should be taught as a recursive process. In an era of internet research, most entering law students lack rigorous research experience using a variety of print and electronic authorities. Students must learn how to (a) plan an effective research strategy, (b) properly use print indexes and other finding aids, (c) carefully record the progress of research using logs or journals, (d) efficiently use various research tools, (e) update and validate their results, and (f) determine when the research process is

---

[105] *See* Patrick W. Spangler, *The New World Versus the Old World of Legal Research*, 20 CHI. B. ASS'N REC., Apr. 2006, at 48, 49.

sufficiently complete to meet professional expectations and satisfy the needs of clients.[106]

Choosing the legal research resources to cover in the foundational LRW course is difficult. Given the many other interrelated goals of the course and depending on the number of credits allocated, first-year students' ability to absorb and understand the material must be balanced against the likelihood that they might have little or no further research training in law school. The breadth and depth of legal research instruction must also take into consideration the LRW professor's teaching load, scholarship and service commitments, and the overall goals of the LRW course as a component of the law school curriculum. As with all professional skills, a student gains competence from first learning foundational legal research concepts and principles that in turn yield new insights as students gain experience by researching increasingly complex legal issues. Most LRW professors and law librarians alike would probably agree with educational experts that one year of legal research instruction is not enough.[107]

At a minimum, students should be exposed to a variety of primary sources and secondary sources. Students should learn to research, interpret, and analyze not only judicial opinions but also constitutions, statutes, court rules, and administrative regulations. Research instruction in the first-year LRW course should develop mastery in understanding the hierarchy of legal authority by introducing and distinguishing between the following kinds of authority:

---

[106] *See* Osbeck, *supra* note 65, at 67-68 (explaining why "determining exactly what 'the law' is that should be applied to a given factual scenario is often less straightforward than it might seem at first blush"). For general information on how technology is rapidly changing the nature and economics of law practice, see Nancy B. Rapoport & Joseph R. Tiano, Jr., *Legal Analytics, Social Science, and Legal Fees: Reimagining "Legal Spend" Decisions in an Evolving Industry*, 35 GA. ST. U. L. REV. 1269 (2019).

[107] *See, e.g.*, Fines, *supra* note 103, at 183.

- federal and state sources of law,
- primary and secondary authority,
- mandatory and persuasive authority,
- published and "unpublished" (nonprecedential) judicial opinions,
- official and unofficial authorities, and
- annotated and unannotated resources.

In addition, first-year students should learn how to use the wide variety of available secondary sources, including legal treatises and hornbooks, scholarly periodicals, annotations, restatements, uniform laws and model codes, legal encyclopedias, bar journals, and legal newspapers. As an essential component of basic legal research instruction, students must learn how to use legal digests, including the West key number system and other subject-matter finding tools.

Finally, every first-year student must understand how to use citators and other research tools to validate legal authority of all kinds. Students need to understand how citators work and how they are built; otherwise, students may fail to recognize their limitations and predictable gaps and inaccuracies. Most students assume that online Shepard's and KeyCite are infallible. Without understanding that citators of all kinds essentially rely on judicial opinions to identify cases and other primary authorities that are no longer "good law," students will assume (inaccurately) that all they need to do is press a couple of keys to verify that a legal authority has not been either overruled or superseded.[108]

Coverage should include the availability of each research tool in all formats and media. Along with exposure to Lexis Advance,[109]

---

[108] For resources explaining why citators are not fool-proof and have inherent deficiencies (whether in print or online), see *supra* note 28 and accompanying text.

[109] https://advance.lexis.com (last visited Dec. 13, 2019).

Westlaw Edge,[110] Bloomberg Law,[111] FastCase,[112] and other commercial products, students should learn about free online research resources such as FindLaw,[113] Cornell's Legal Information Institute,[114] and many others.

While contemporary law students are intimately familiar with internet "research,"[115] they generally have little or no formal training in how to research effectively. Most probably do not know how to use search engines beyond a basic plain-language search, or how to critically assess the information available on a particular website. Students are likely unaware of the substantial amount of legal and factual research that can be performed online, the limitations of free online research, or the true cost of commercial online legal research products.

Whether basic legal research instruction is provided by LRW professors or law librarians, the instructor should caution students that commercial research services are not "free," even to law students. Law schools annually pay six-figure subscription fees to major commercial firms to enable students and faculty to access those services, and that expense is built into student tuition. When it comes to commercial online legal research services, there is no such

---

[110] https://legal.thomsonreuters.com/en/products/westlaw (last visited Dec. 13, 2019).

[111] https://pro.bloomberglaw.com/ (last visited Dec. 13, 2019).

[112] https://www.fastcase.com/ (last visited Dec. 13, 2019). In 2015, FastCase acquired the legal research platform previously known as Loislaw. Victor Li, *Fastcase Acquires Rival Legal-research Company Loislaw*, ABA J. (Sept. 21, 2015), http://www.abajournal.com/news/article/fastcase_acquires_rival_legal_research_company_loislaw.

[113] https://www.findlaw.com/ (last visited Dec. 13, 2019).

[114] https://www.law.cornell.edu/ (last visited Dec. 13, 2019).

[115] Emily A. Benfer & Colleen F. Shanahan, *Educating the Invincibles: Strategies for Teaching the Millennial Generation in Law School*, 20 CLINICAL L. REV. 1, 10-11 (2013) (explaining that "[m]illennial students relate to the world through technology and are inseparable from the Internet," and they believe "themselves to be technologically savvy and efficient multi-taskers").

thing as a "free lunch." Students need to understand that the commercial research firms are in business to make a profit, and while most vendor representatives are well-meaning, they do not always have students' best interests at heart.

In addition, law students of today are generally unfamiliar with researching in books and other print materials, so many need to learn the fundamentals of conducting *offline* research. Many students may be surprised to learn that online research tools are limited in breadth and depth, and the most helpful secondary research authorities may be available only in print. All students should learn how to effectively integrate research results from both print and online sources and understand how to reconcile them.

ii. Advanced Legal Research Instruction

Covering more specialized research sources depends on the structure of a school's LRW program and the opportunities for research instruction beyond the foundational course. Ideally, students should learn the basics of researching state and federal legislative history, administrative regulations and quasi-judicial rulings, government documents, loose-leaf services and other specialty publications, practice manuals, and pattern jury instructions. Some of these authorities can be introduced in a first-year integrated LRW course that offers six or more course credits, or in a program requiring three semesters of required LRW coursework. Or students may learn about more sophisticated legal research resources in an advanced legal research course, whether required or elective.[116]

Students may have several opportunities in their second and third years to learn these and other advanced research skills. An increasing number of schools have extended the basic LRW curriculum to span three or more semesters. Many schools offer an advanced

---

[116] *See generally* Lucia Ann Silecchia, *Designing and Teaching Advanced Legal Research and Writing Courses*, 33 DUQ. L. REV. 203 (1995).

research course, while others offer research modules attached to doctrinal or clinical courses for additional credit. For instance, an Immigration Law course could include an optional module covering the specific sources and techniques most useful for researching this specialized area of law. Finally, upper-level students may gain experience researching a specialized area as a member of law review under the guidance of a professor, or as a student writing a paper in an independent study or seminar course.

d. Oral Advocacy

Compared to traditional law practice, in the modern era oral advocacy skills are less essential. For example, most federal trial courts have such busy dockets that oral arguments on pre-trial motions are rarely scheduled. While state trial courts in some regions may continue to rely on oral argument, many state and federal appellate courts no longer permit oral argument as a matter of course.[117]

While oral advocacy skills are less important today than they once were, most LRW programs continue to require oral argument on either a trial brief or an appellate brief as an important component of the course.[118] This tradition is especially entrenched in law

---

[117]Michael Vitiello, *Teaching Oral Advocacy: Creating More Opportunities for an Essential Skill*, 45 SETON HALL L. REV. 1031, 1044 (2015).

> [T]he chances that an attorney will present an appellate argument today have diminished over time. Since the 1980s, the trend towards limiting oral argument even in federal circuits where litigants have an appeal of right has continued. Currently, every federal circuit has curtailed oral argument; those courts grant oral argument in fewer than half of all appeals. Further, circuits have limited the amount of time available for oral argument: for example, in some cases in the Ninth Circuit, an advocate has ten minutes in which to make her case. In addition, the federal appellate docket, after years of expansion, has started to decline.

Id. (footnotes omitted).

[118]*See infra* note 119 for supporting data drawn from annual surveys of legal writing programs. The literature reflects a diversity of opinions about the value

schools that have traditionally devoted significant resources to moot court competitions as a cocurricular student activity.

i. Oral Argument

Most LRW programs include some oral advocacy instruction,[119] typically near the end of the first-year course. Students and faculty often perceive the oral argument as the capstone of the LRW course — a rite of passage for law students — even though the time devoted to oral advocacy is generally small compared to the primary focus on legal analysis, research, and writing skills.

If oral advocacy skills are included in the required LRW course, faculty should identify the student learning outcomes for the exercise, which should guide the nature and scope of oral advocacy instruction. These might include improving legal analysis, developing basic oral advocacy techniques, and increasing students'

---

of requiring a moot court experience. *Compare, e.g.,* Alex Kozinski, *In Praise of Moot Court—Not!,* 97 COLUM. L. REV. 178, 180 (1997) (criticizing the moot court tradition, noting that "moot court . . . counts for next to nothing when compared to law review membership, which is especially damning given how little relevance law review work has to practice") *with, e.g.,* Darby Dickerson, In re *Moot Court*, 29 STETSON L. REV. 1217 (2000) ("reporting" a hypothetical Supreme Court argument defending the merits of moot court in legal education); Richard E. Finneran, *Wherefore Moot Court?,* 53 WASH. U. J.L. & POL'Y 121, 133 (2017) (positing that effective oral argument "is of immense value both to courts and the litigants who practice before them"); Michael V. Hernandez, *In Defense of Moot Court: A Response to "In Praise of Moot Court—Not!"*, 17 REV. LITIG. 69, 70 (1998) (responding to Judge Kozinski's essay by outlining the benefits to law students of moot court programs).

[119]When this third edition of the *Sourcebook* went to press, 2015 was the most recent year for which annual survey information was available on oral advocacy program requirements. In that year, 140 of 194 responding law schools (about 75 percent) required an appellate brief argument, 95 (about 50 percent) required a pretrial motion argument, and 54 (slightly more than 25 percent) required a trial brief argument. *2015 ALWD/LWI Survey*, *supra* note 84, at 13, Question 20(k)-(m).

self-confidence in thinking and speaking contemporaneously in a professional setting. At minimum, oral advocacy instruction should address the purpose and relevance of oral argument, the relationship between the written brief and the oral argument, appropriate deference to the court, conventions of oral argument structure and presentation, and responding to questions from the bench.

If the LRW course includes instruction in oral advocacy, each professor must decide how and when to "shoehorn" it into an already very full course. Given the constraints of time and the number of credits allocated to the required course, oral advocacy instruction is generally limited to the basics. A valuable introduction might include attending a live oral argument in a nearby trial or appellate court, or watching an online video of an oral argument.[120] Assigning an online video offers a valuable teaching experience by

---

[120] An increasing number of state appellate courts offer online access to videos of oral arguments. *E.g.,* Arkansas Judiciary, *Supreme Court of Arkansas Streaming Media Archive*, https://www.arcourts.gov/courts/supreme-court/oral-argument-videos; California Courts, *Oral Argument Webcasts,* https://www.courts.ca.gov/35333.htm; Kansas Judicial Branch, *Kansas Supreme Court Archived Oral Arguments,* http://www.kscourts.org/kansas-courts/supreme-court/archived-arguments.asp; New York Court of Appeals, *Oral Argument Archives,* https://www.nycourts.gov/ctapps/OA-Archives.htm. *See generally* National Center for State Courts, *Appellate Procedure State Links: Appellate Court Oral Arguments Online,* https://www.ncsc.org/Topics/Appellate/Appellate-Procedure/State-Links.aspx?cat=Appellate%20Court%20Oral%20Arguments%20Online (providing links for access to state appellate court oral argument recordings) (last visited Dec. 13, 2019). Cameras are generally not permitted in federal appellate courts, but audio recordings of oral arguments are generally available online. *E.g.,* Supreme Court of the United States, *Argument Audio*, https://www.supremecourt.gov/oral_arguments/argument_audio/2018 (last visited Dec. 13, 2019); United States Court of Appeals for the Tenth Circuit, *Oral Argument Recording Archive,* https://www.ca10.uscourts.gov/clerk/oral-argument-recording-archive (last visited Dec. 13, 2019). *See generally* Court Listener, *Advanced Oral Argument Search,* https://www.courtlistener.com/audio/ (offering links to each federal appellate court's website) (last visited Dec. 13, 2019).

asking students to critique each attorney's presentation to the court, as well as to evaluate how each side responded to questions from the bench. Students might predict how the court ruled (or will rule) based solely on the oral argument. The LRW professor might then assign students to read the briefs, which are often available online, and then read the court's decision in the case. This kind of exercise is especially valuable to demonstrate to students how the professional skills covered in LRW are highly interrelated in the real world of legal practice.

Some law schools still "outsource" oral advocacy instruction to a student group — for example, as part of a separate moot court program or trial team competition. But delegating oral advocacy instruction to student-run moot court programs poses inherent instructional challenges.[121] A better way to teach oral advocacy is to collaborate with the school's moot court or other cocurricular advocacy program. The collaborative approach allows the LRW program to exercise some quality control over the instruction.

An additional challenge in teaching oral advocacy skills is that many students fear public speaking beyond the typical level of apprehension for any student learning a new skill.[122] Experienced law faculty, particularly those who were successful litigators before beginning their teaching careers, may fail to recognize that even the most diligent and academically talented law students often experience tremendous anxiety about the oral argument experience.

---

[121] First, the LRW program and the student group may not have similar goals. Student-supervised oral advocacy instruction invariably focuses on succeeding in moot court competitions, which differ significantly from real-world oral advocacy. Second, while using the same moot court fact pattern for all LRW students might appear expedient, uniformity may reduce the instructional autonomy of individual LRW professors. That said, many schools use the same fact pattern across all LRW sections for a variety of other reasons.

[122] *See* Heidi K. Brown, *The "Silent but Gifted" Law Student: Transforming Anxious Public Speakers into Well-Rounded Advocates*, 18 LEGAL WRITING 291 (2012).

Scheduling optional or mandatory practice rounds as part of the oral advocacy sequence will help allay student performance anxiety.

A final consideration in teaching oral advocacy is when to schedule oral arguments on the written brief. Many schools follow the traditional practice of holding oral arguments after students submit their final briefs. However, a number of schools require students to prepare and deliver oral arguments near the end of the drafting process. That alternative allows students to gain valuable insights from preparing the oral argument that in turn help them refine not only the written argument but also its organization. Students who might otherwise write around gaps in reasoning are pushed to recognize and grapple with those gaps in oral argument. Moreover, students who must distill their points to present a cogent oral argument learn to anticipate judges' questions about the case and focus the argument in a more logical and coherent way.

One way to have the best of both alternatives is to hold oral argument practice during the drafting process, and then use class time to discuss how to best to use the experience to strengthen the brief. Another is to require students to rewrite the brief after oral argument.

Ideally, students should have an opportunity to demonstrate oral advocacy skills in a realistic courtroom setting. The professor might consider videotaping the students' oral arguments for later review and critique by the professor and the student together. However, the professor should be particularly sensitive to students with performance anxiety, who may find it more stressful to have their arguments recorded. A related concern is whether to permit other students in the course to observe oral arguments. One way to address the issue is to permit observers only if all students participating in the oral argument agree to open the argument to others.

The oral argument is generally presented to a panel of "judges" that includes the LRW professor, practicing lawyers and local judges, or upper-level law students. While the LRW professor is in the best position to know the brief problem and therefore ask appropriately probing questions, the professor may find it challenging to serve as both judge and evaluator simultaneously. On the other hand, a LRW professor who serves as a "judge" has the opportunity to neutralize any unspoken agenda that guest judges might bring to the exercise, and to provide some degree of uniformity to the students' experiences if different outside judges participate for each oral argument team.

Practicing attorneys, law school alumni, and local judges may be invited to serve as judges for oral arguments. Asking attorneys and judges to participate can serve to strengthen ties between the law school and the bench and bar. It has the added advantage of exposing students to the expectations of law practice. One drawback is that practitioners may not have a sufficiently nuanced understanding of the assignment's legal or analytical foundation to give students high-level feedback on the substantive content of the argument. Other challenges include potential scheduling problems and the need for backup plans if a lawyer or judge is unexpectedly unavailable at the last minute.

At some schools, recruiting and scheduling judges are tasks delegated to experienced administrative assistants. In any event, asking others to serve as judges requires the LRW professor (or perhaps a teaching assistant) to prepare a bench brief to familiarize the panel of judges with the assignment in advance and to suggest questions they may want to ask the students during argument.[123] Some LRW professors ask students in the course to submit proposed questions to include in the bench brief, which helps them learn to anticipate the questions a judge might ask, strengthening their oral argument preparation.

---

[123] A teaching assistant, research assistant, or moot court board member can write the bench brief for a first-year problem.

Finally, the LRW professor must decide whether oral argument will be a graded experience or evaluated as a pass/fail requirement. Grading the argument acknowledges the skills of students who naturally excel at oral advocacy or who work diligently to acquire those skills, but who may be slow to develop skills in written advocacy. If the oral argument is a graded component, the LRW professor must also consider appropriate criteria to evaluate the oral argument.

Either way, the professor should give appropriate weight to the oral argument assessment in proportion to the many other skills students are expected to master in the course, while also considering the time and practice students are expected to devote to preparing for oral argument. As with any other graded component of the course, law students tend to focus more time and attention on learning activities that weigh more heavily in the grading calculation.[124]

Yet another assessment issue is whether the evaluation should be done by the LRW professor alone or with the participation of guest judges. Unless all students in a section are evaluated by the same set of judges, fair grading may be difficult to achieve. Recording the oral arguments on video allows the professor to complete the evaluation after reviewing the recorded argument, perhaps with student participation.

---

[124] Sophie M. Sparrow, *Teaching and Assessing Soft Skills*, 67 J. LEGAL EDUC. 553, 565 (2018).

> If we grade select lawyering foundation skills, we denote that these are important, much like other learning goals in the course. Students pay attention to how they earn their grades, and if we want our grades to reflect how well students meet our learning goals, then that performance must become part of their final course grade.

Id. (footnotes omitted). For a comprehensive empirical analysis of law student assessment preferences, see Emily Zimmerman, *What Do Law Students Want?: The Missing Piece of the Assessment Puzzle*, 42 RUTGERS L.J. 1, 59 (2010) (observing that the majority of first-year law students prefer multiple graded assignments).

ii. Other Oral Skills

Some LRW programs require other kinds of oral presentations. For instance, an increasing number of programs require students to deliver an oral "report to the senior partner," in which students describe their preliminary research and analysis and assess the predicted outcome in an individual meeting with the professor posing as the senior attorney.[125] Others require each student to make an oral presentation to the class, which might involve reporting information, presenting steps in legal analysis, or teaching a discrete skill such as a citation rule.[126] An LRW professor might also require students to make an oral presentation to a hypothetical client explaining alternative strategies for resolving the client's legal issue.

These other kinds of oral presentation experiences allow students to develop confidence and competence in presenting legal information orally without the formality, intensity, and scheduling issues involved with preparing, presenting, and assessing traditional moot court oral arguments.

e. Lawyering Skills

A lawyering skills approach integrates interviewing and counseling, negotiation, alternative dispute resolution (ADR), and legal drafting along with the foundational components of the LRW curriculum. This kind of multifaceted course is designed to help students achieve a basic level of competence in a full range of lawyering skills.

---

[125] In 2015, the most recent year for which aggregate data are available on required course content, 103 of 194 responding law schools reported requiring an "[o]ral report to senior partner" as part of the required LRW curriculum. *2015 ALWD/LWI Survey, supra* note 84, at 13, Question 20(o). The proportion of responding law schools reporting this requirement had steadily increased over the four previous survey years. *See id.*

[126] In 2015, 90 of the 194 responding law schools required an in-class presentation. *Id.* at 13, Question 20(n).

Over the last decade, with the increasing emphasis on preparing students for law practice, LRW programs have added many of these skills to the foundational course.[127] Some LRW courses selectively incorporate specific lawyering skills, such as client interviewing, to provide a realistic law practice context without expecting students to fully master these additional skills. Others require students to take a lawyering skills course in the third or fourth semester after completing the foundational LRW course in the first year.

A lawyering skills curriculum can incorporate a variety of exercises. For example, students might be asked to interview a "real" client to gain an appreciation for the importance of facts before beginning their initial research and analysis of the legal issues. Later on, as students write the first draft of a persuasive brief, they might engage in a settlement negotiation to test their respective analytical approaches. Throughout the course, the LRW professor might distribute the clients' facts through a series of emails, memoranda, or interview transcripts from the supervising attorney and paralegals working on the case to provide real-world examples of how lawyers learn and analyze client facts.

In a more comprehensive lawyering skills approach requiring students to achieve a level of competence in client interviewing, negotiation, or alternative dispute resolution (ADR) skills, the LRW program should consider a number of factors related to course coverage and depth.

- The greater the range of skills covered in the LRW course, the greater the likelihood that each skill can be merely introduced rather than developed to the level of competence. A lawyering

[127] *See 2015 ALWD/LWI Survey*, *supra* note 84, at 13 (noting the steady increase over the previous five years in the average number of different types of assignments and skills taught in LRW programs); *2017-18 ALWD/LWI Institutional Survey*, *supra* note 99, at 22-23 (listing the wide variety of other professional skills law schools reported requiring in the LRW course during the 2017-18 academic year).

skills approach is most appropriate in a curriculum that is assigned a relatively high number of credits or that spans three or more semesters.

- Teaching lawyering skills such as interviewing, negotiation, ADR, and legal drafting can be quite time-consuming, especially if the LRW professor is expected to assess student performance on each of these skills for the final course grade.
- Writing a fact pattern that works effectively for teaching basic analytical, research, and writing skills is especially challenging if the assignment is also designed to teach other lawyering skills.
- As adults, law students learn skills better in context than in isolation.[128] In addition, teaching skills in combination can have a synergistic effect. A student who interviews a client, uses the facts learned in that interview to make research decisions, and then uses that research to draft an objective office memorandum has learned more than just three discrete skills. The student has learned about the interrelationships among the various skills and how they are integrated in law practice.
- The *MacCrate Report* reflects the view of the practicing bar that graduates are ill-prepared for the actual practice of law due to insufficient skills training.[129]

---

[128] *E.g.*, STUCKEY ET AL., supra note 11, at 141-42; Camille Lamar Campbell, *How to Use a Tube Top and a Dress Code to Demystify the Predictive Writing Process and Build a Framework of Hope During the First Weeks of Class*, 48 DUQ. L. REV. 273, 288 (2010) ("[A]dult learners prefer active learning environments where professors make explicit connections between students' past experiences and prior learning, create respectful learning environments, and acknowledge the distinct generational preferences of adult learners.").

[129] *MacCrate Report*, *supra* note 6, Introduction; Stuart A. Handmaker, *The Law School Product from the Buyer's Point of View*, 29 VAL. U. L. REV. 897 (1995) (giving a practitioner's perspective); *see also* Elizabeth Lacy, Paul Michel & John R. Tunheim, *Law School Curriculum, Training Law Students and the Vitality of the Profession: The Judicial Perspective*, 1 J. ALWD 297 (2001) (giving the judiciary's view of the inadequacy of skills training in law school).

- Developing a relationship with a client—even a hypothetical one—often engages students more than a written set of facts. In meeting with a client face-to-face, students quickly learn that empathy and other "people skills" are assets in law practice.
- Incorporating additional lawyering skills into the required LRW course is yet another way to give students an opportunity to excel in essential professional skills beyond written legal analysis.

f. Professional and Ethical Norms

The LRW course should introduce students to the basic norms of the legal profession.[130] Students need a sense of how lawyers are expected to behave as officers of the court and as professionals in the legal system. They should understand their ethical obligations not only to clients, but also to courts and the legal profession.[131] They should understand the importance of civility and professionalism, as well as the power and influence they will assume in their communities as attorneys.

Several elements of professionalism are particularly relevant to the LRW course, including policies related to plagiarism and collaborative work. LRW courses also help students to develop a professional identity and to learn practical skills in time management and efficiency.

---

[130] *See, e.g.*, Melissa H. Weresh, *Fostering a Respect for Our Students, Our Specialty, and the Legal Profession: Introducing Ethics and Professionalism into the Legal Writing Curriculum*, 21 Touro L. Rev. 427, 428 (2005).

[131] *See id.* at 463 ("There is little doubt that the legal writing professional who teaches in the first year curriculum will influence how our students behave in practice, not only with regard to basic competency but also with regard to the ethical and professional character of their representation.").

i. Rules of Professional Conduct

All ABA-accredited law schools must provide instruction in professional responsibility.[132] Most require students to complete a stand-alone course in ethics and the legal profession, and many others include legal ethics in all courses in what has become known as the "pervasive" approach.[133] Some law schools offer both. The goal of professional responsibility instruction is to help students learn to identify ethical issues when they arise in practice and to resolve those issues consistent with the ethical requirements of the profession. Law students need to know both the substantive law of legal ethics and how to identify and analyze an ethics issue. Both goals can be advanced by including an introduction to legal ethics in the context of the LRW course.[134]

If the law school follows the pervasive approach to teaching professional responsibility, the LRW course must include an ethics component. In that case, the LRW professor should consider introducing students to relevant parts of the ABA Model Rules of

---

[132]ABA Standard 303(a)(1) requires all law students to successfully complete at least "one course of at least two credit hours in professional responsibility that includes substantial instruction in rules of professional conduct, and the values and responsibilities of the legal profession and its members."

[133]DEBORAH L. RHODE, PROFESSIONAL RESPONSIBILITY: ETHICS BY THE PERVASIVE METHOD (2d ed. 1998); Paula Schaefer, *Building on the Professionalism Foundation of* Best Practices for Legal Education, 14 U. ST. THOMAS L.J. 320, 322–23 (2018) ("Deborah Rhode . . . observed that if law schools do not address professionalism issues as they arise in courses, students will view professionalism as 'a digression from what is really important.'" (citing RHODE, *supra*)); *see also* STUCKEY ET AL., *supra* note 11, at 104-16 (urging law schools to use context-based teaching approaches throughout the curriculum).

[134]*See, e.g.,* Beth D. Cohen, *Instilling an Appreciation of Legal Ethics and Professional Responsibility in First-Year Legal Research and Writing Courses*, 4 PERSPS. 5 (1995).

Professional Conduct,[135] which most state supreme courts have adopted in some form. Because the comments accompanying the rules offer important explanations and elaborations, the LRW professor might consider asking students to read relevant portions of both the rules and the commentary.[136]

Several rules of professional conduct relate directly to the lawyering skills of legal analysis, research, and writing. At minimum, students need to understand these basic obligations of practicing lawyers as they learn other professional conventions in the LRW course.[137]

MRPC 1.1 – Competence.[138] This fundamental rule of professionalism requires lawyers to "provide competent representation," which "requires the legal knowledge, skill, thoroughness and preparation reasonably necessary for the representation" of a client. This rule is directly relevant to instruction in legal research, analysis, and writing, the core skills taught in every LRW course.

MRPC 1.3 – Diligence.[139] This rule requires lawyers to act diligently and promptly in representing a client. LRW courses can support this requirement by helping students develop time management skills to avoid procrastinating in their professional work. Disciplinary cases abound illustrating the dire consequences when

---

[135] Model R. Prof'l Conduct (Am. Bar Ass'n 2016) [hereinafter MRPC], https://www.americanbar.org/groups/professional_responsibility/publications/model_rules_of_professional_conduct/rule_1_1_competence/.

[136] *See, e.g., id.* R. 1.6(c) cmt. 18; *id.* R. 4.4(b) cmt. 2 (addressing ethical risks of email communications with clients and other attorneys).

[137] *See* Michele Bradley & Nancy Oliver, *The Complete Professional: How Our New Professional Ideals for Law Students Help Us in the Legal Research and Writing Classroom*, 26 Persps. 14, 14 (2018) ("It is incumbent on law schools to teach professionalism.").

[138] MRPC, *supra* note 135, R. 1.1.

[139] MRPC, *supra* note 135, R. 1.3.

lawyers delay working on a client's case.[140] Assigning some of these cases for outside reading can help students grasp the importance of these professional norms.

MRPC 1.4 – Communications.[141] This rule governs the communication aspects of the lawyer-client relationship and is particularly relevant if LRW students are asked to draft client advice letters. Rule 1.4 reinforces the principle that good legal writing considers the needs of the particular audience. Students may not fully appreciate that the needs of a client in written communication differ greatly from the expectations of a judge or opposing counsel.

The rule also requires lawyers to use clear, plain-language prose when writing to clients. Each ethical rule governing client communication requires the attorney to ensure that the client understands the substance of the message sufficiently to make informed decisions about the representation.[142]

MRPC 1.6 – Confidentiality of Information.[143] This rule protects the client's privilege to maintain the confidentiality of communications with the lawyer. Today's law students are so familiar with social media, email, and other forms of internet communication that they are often surprised to learn they have an ethical duty to use communication methods that minimize the risk of violating the client's privilege. As LRW professors increasingly add email memos as a component of the course, introducing this rule is especially

---

[140] *See* Judith D. Fischer, *The Role of Ethics in Legal Writing: The Forensic Embroider, the Minimalist Wizard, and Other Stories,* 9 SCRIBES J. LEGAL WRITING 77 (2003-2004); Judith D. Fischer, *Bareheaded and Barefaced Counsel: Courts React to Unprofessionalism in Lawyers' Papers*, 31 SUFFOLK UNIV. L.R. 1 (1997).

[141] MRPC, *supra* note 135, R. 1.4.

[142] *See, e.g., id.* R. 1.4(c) ("A lawyer shall explain a matter to the extent reasonably necessary to permit the client to make informed decisions regarding the representation.").

[143] *Id.* R. 1.6.

important to help students understand the inherent risks to the client of sending sensitive information by email.

MRPC 3.1 – Meritorious Claims and Contentions.[144] Before a lawyer initiates or defends a legal proceeding, this rule requires a "basis in law and fact . . . that is not frivolous, which includes a good faith argument for an extension, modification or reversal of existing law." LRW students must understand that a lawyer cannot misstate, create, or ignore relevant facts or applicable law when drafting legal documents. By implication, the lawyer has a duty to advocate creatively and in good faith to extend or modify current law if appropriate to meet the client's goals.

MRPC 3.3 – Candor Toward the Tribunal.[145] Among other things, this rule requires an attorney to disclose to the bench any "legal authority in the controlling jurisdiction known to the lawyer to be directly adverse to the position of the client," if opposing counsel fails to disclose it.[146] The rule also prohibits offering evidence or facts that the lawyer knows are false.[147] In an *ex parte* proceeding, the lawyer must also disclose any material facts known to the lawyer that would help the tribunal make an informed decision, even if those facts are adverse to the lawyer's client.[148]

While other professional conduct rules can be introduced, the rules listed above are most closely related to the content of required

---

[144] *Id.* R. 3.1.

[145] *Id.* R. 3.3.

[146] *Id.* R. 3.3(a)(2). This little-understood rule requires disclosure of *any* adverse authority in the *controlling jurisdiction,* even if the authority itself is not binding on the tribunal. *See* Hon. Steve Leben, *On the Duty of Candor to the Tribunal*, 76 J. KAN. B. ASS'N 19, 19 (Mar. 2007) ("The duty to disclose adverse law relates to 'legal authority in the controlling jurisdiction,' not to 'controlling authorities.'); *see also* David L. Hudson, Jr., *Even If It Hurts Your Case: Lawyers Have a Duty to Disclose Adverse Legal Authority*, 105 ABA J. 24 (June 2009).

[147] MRPC, *supra* note 135, R. 3.3(a)(1), (3).

[148] *Id.* R. 3.3(d).

LRW programs. All these rules are important in teaching students their duties as lawyers in written documents or in oral argument—the very skills covered in LRW courses.

ii. Civility Codes

An increasing number of state and federal jurisdictions have adopted civility codes, as distinguished from disciplinary rules of professional conduct.[149] These rules are generally aspirational rather than disciplinary in nature, akin to what were formerly known as "Ethical Rules" in the ABA Model Code of Professional Responsibility,[150] which predated today's Model Rules of Professional Conduct. Judges, especially in the state courts, have become increasingly concerned with the lack of civility in the legal profession.[151]

Introducing students to professional civility standards reinforces norms of professional conduct that all law students should embrace as prospective members of the legal community.

---

[149] *E.g., Standards for Professional Conduct Within the Seventh Federal Judicial Circuit,* http://www.ca7.uscourts.gov/rules-procedures/rules//rules.htm#standards (last visited Dec. 14, 2019); *Pennsylvania Code of Civility,* http://www.pacourts.us/assets/opinions/Supreme/out/258spct-attach.pdf#search=%22civility%20code%22 (last visited Dec. 14, 2019). *Utah Standards of Professionalism and Civility*, https://www.utcourts.gov/courts/sup/civility.htm (last visited Dec. 13, 2019). *See generally* Donald E. Campbell, *Raise Your Right Hand and Swear to Be Civil: Defining Civility as an Obligation of Professional Responsibility*, 47 GONZ. L. REV. 99 (2012) (discussing the development of civility codes as distinct from professional ethics rules).

[150] The ABA Model Code of Professional Responsibility, issued in 1969, was the precursor to the ABA Model Rules of Professional Conduct, issued in 1983. The 1969 Model Code comprised both aspirational Ethical Rules (designated ER) and mandatory Disciplinary Rules (designated DR). Many state professional responsibility codes continued to follow the Model Code pattern for several years after the ABA introduced the Model Rules.

[151] *See* DAVID F. HERR & ROGER S. HAYDOCK, MOTION PRACTICE § 7.04 (8th ed. 2019) (addressing the development of professional civility rules "to reduce perceived growing hostility and antagonism among litigators").

iii. Efficiency and Time Management

Among the most important skills students should learn in an LRW program are budgeting time, working efficiently, and managing professional work projects. First-year students have many demands on their time, and they must learn how to balance their many assignments and cocurricular activities with personal commitments.

To assist students in developing these skills, it may be useful to require students to develop a calendar or timeline for completing a major writing assignment, taking into account other assignments and responsibilities. Some LRW professors have students keep time sheets for an assignment so they can "bill" their time to the hypothetical client. This exercise can reinforce the ethical constraints on reasonable legal fees.[152]

iv. Other Professional Norms and Expectations

As the most prominent "skills" course in the first-year curriculum, the LRW course should expose students to the general norms and expectations of the legal profession. For example, many programs require students to role-play as lawyers and to abide by professional norms and typical court rules. The LRW professor might demonstrate the consequences of violating professional norms by assigning disciplinary opinions sanctioning lawyers for their written or oral work.[153] These cases encourage students to become good legal thinkers and writers by illustrating the importance of complying with professional standards.

Additionally, by creating assignments that require students to research, identify, and apply court rules, an LRW program reinforces

---

[152] *See* MRPC, *supra* note 135, R. 1.5(a). "A lawyer shall not make an agreement for, charge, or collect an unreasonable fee or an unreasonable amount for expenses." *Id.* (listing various factors in determining reasonableness).

[153] For cases useful for this purpose, see *supra* note 140 (citing articles by Professor Judith D. Fischer); *see also* WERESH, *supra* note 37.

standards of professionalism. LRW courses can begin teaching students to comply with deadlines by rigorously enforcing them in written and other assignments. Some LRW professors require students who request additional time for an assignment to draft their request in the form of a motion, explaining how the request satisfies the professor's criteria for granting an extension of time.

LRW programs often create standard course rules giving deadlines, length limits, typeface and font size, and citation requirements, much like court rules. This approach exposes students to rules of the profession and requires them to practice conforming to sometimes rigid court rules and expectations. From a practical perspective, taking a firm approach also makes it easier for the professor to fairly and efficiently apply course rules. The rules should be provided to students in writing, either in a syllabus at the beginning of the course or in memos describing the parameters of specific writing assignments. Students must learn to read the relevant rules and comply with them, just as they must do in legal practice.

v. Plagiarism and Other Academic Misconduct

One of the most difficult challenges for an LRW program is teaching students how to work collaboratively while ensuring academic honesty and fair assessment for all students. These challenges are all the greater in the academic setting, in which appropriate collaboration policies are often at odds with real-world law practice. Lawyers in the same firm frequently share one another's work and often recycle significant portions of court documents without attribution. Of course, plagiarism issues can still arise in practice if a lawyer fails to give proper attribution to outside sources, which may lead to serious sanctions for unethical professional conduct.[154]

---

[154] *See, e.g.*, Iowa Sup. Ct. Bd. of Prof'l Ethics & Conduct v. Lane, 642 N.W.2d 296, 302 (Iowa 2002) (denying attorney fees for preparing a substantially plagiarized brief, and suspending lawyer from practice for six months). The court explained, "Honesty is fundamental to the functioning of the legal profession, and

Some LRW programs are charged with explicitly discussing issues of plagiarism in law school settings. Excellent materials are available from the Legal Writing Institute, including a pamphlet describing and discussing plagiarism that a professor may copy and distribute to students. These materials also contain hypothetical examples for in-class discussion and a certificate students may be asked to sign to document that they understand the principles discussed in the materials.[155]

All students should understand that copying the work of another student is unacceptable. When law schools warn students about plagiarism, some students may interpret the rule to mean only that they must not copy from another student. Students may not realize that cutting and pasting from a judicial opinion or other legal authority without using quotation marks and proper attribution also qualifies as plagiarism.[156] Others may not understand that they must cite to the original source of an idea, even if they express the idea in different words. Still others may not understand that plagiarism includes

---

Lane's conduct . . . has compromised that honesty. Moreover, Lane has jeopardized the integrity of the Bar and the public's trust in the legal profession." *Id. See generally* Cooper J. Strickland, Recent Development, *The Dark Side of Unattributed Copying and the Ethical Implications of Plagiarism in the Legal Profession*, 90 N.C. L. Rev. 920, 921–22 (2012) (describing circumstances in legal practice in which plagiarism is considered a significant ethical issue).

[155] These and other resource materials are available on the LWI website, https://www.lwionline.org/plagiarism (last visited Dec. 14, 2019).

[156] *See, e.g.*, Liberty Towers Realty, LLC v. Richmond Liberty, LLC, 569 B.R. 534, 542 n.6 (E.D.N.Y. 2017) (chastising attorney whose brief plagiarized from an article by directly copying pages without attribution), *aff'd*, 734 F. App'x 68 (2d Cir. 2018); A.L. v. Chicago Pub. Sch. Dist. No. 299, No. 10 C 494, 2012 WL 3028337, at *6 (N.D. Ill. July 24, 2012) (reducing a bill for attorney fees by 90 percent after discovering that "counsel lifted verbatim large portions of Plaintiffs' briefs directly from judicial decisions, without appropriate attribution").

In one case, the Sixth Circuit discovered in preparing for oral argument that some 20 pages of an appellate brief were copied nearly verbatim from a published federal court decision without proper attribution:

lifting citations, with or without explanatory parentheticals, from another legal authority such as a treatise or law journal article.[157]

LRW professors may not fully appreciate the scope of the problem in law practice from the judicial perspective. But the extent to which courts continue to admonish practicing lawyers for plagiarizing in legal briefs suggests that law schools in general, and LRW faculty in particular, must do more to address the issue.[158]

Unfortunately, law schools have not identified an effective method for preventing or identifying academic plagiarism. Some

---

> When our discovery of this outright plagiarism was called to the attention of . . . counsel . . . at oral argument, he did little to explain it, stating only he did not cite the case because it does not constitute binding precedent in this circuit, and he copied from it verbatim because he would lose the essence of the argument if he changed even one word. While our legal system stands upon the building blocks of precedent, necessitating some amount of quotation or paraphrasing, citation to authority is absolutely required when language is borrowed.
>
> We made it very clear [to counsel] during oral argument this behavior is completely unacceptable and reiterate it here as an admonishment to all attorneys tempted to "cut and paste" helpful analysis into their briefs.

United States v. Bowen, 194 F. App'x 393, 402 n.3 (6th Cir. 2006).

[157] *See, e.g., In re* Burghoff, 374 B.R. 681, 685 (Bankr. N.D. Iowa 2007) ("By passing off [copied string] citations as his own, [counsel] plagiarized [the authors'] ideas and expressions just as surely as if he had copied an equivalent amount of text."); *see also* Iowa Sup. Ct. Atty. Disc. Bd. v. Cannon, 789 N.W.2d 756, 760 (Iowa 2010) (imposing public reprimand for acts of plagiarism identified in *Burghoff*).

[158] *See* Consolidated Paving, Inc. v. County of Peoria, No. 10-CV-1045, 2013 WL 916212, at *6 (C.D. Ill. Mar. 8, 2013) ("Plagiarism is a serious issue, and several courts have found such behavior unacceptable and a violation of the Rules of Professional Conduct that govern attorneys' behavior." (citing cases)); Lohan v. Perez, 924 F. Supp. 2d 447, 458 (E.D.N.Y. 2013) (granting defense motion for monetary sanctions against plaintiff's counsel for taking "the vast majority" of the motion brief from other sources without proper attribution).

schools use computer services to check the text of student papers against each other and against materials available on the internet.[159] However, these services were not developed to meet the specific needs of law faculty. An experienced professor can often spot suspicious wording or passages that stand out because the writing style contrasts with the rest of the paper. Checking these passages against relevant authorities, or running a search in an online research service, might reveal whether the student has failed to properly attribute the passage to the original source.

The best strategy is preventative. First, the LRW professor should establish and consistently enforce clear, written plagiarism policies. Second, the LRW professor should provide students with examples showing how to properly use quotation marks and block quotes, as well as ellipses to show omission of irrelevant portions of a quoted source. Students must be instructed on proper use of citations to credit each source, including materials found on the internet. Students should be explicitly cautioned about copying even a footnote from another source without proper attribution, which can result in a charge of plagiarism.[160]

The LRW professor must repeatedly explain to students that proper citations to legal authority do not diminish the value of the writer's work, but instead strengthen legal analysis and increase the writer's credibility from the perspective of the law-trained reader. Providing a proper citation allows readers to consult the original source to check the full context of a quotation, to obtain additional information about a particular point of law, and to locate secondary materials that may help them better understand the cited sources.[161]

---

[159] *See, e.g.*, Turnitin, https://www.turnitin.com/ (last visited Jan. 10, 2020).

[160] *See Burghoff*, 374 B.R. at 685.

[161] *See* MARK E. WOJCIK, INTRODUCTION TO LEGAL ENGLISH: AN INTRODUCTION TO LEGAL TERMINOLOGY, REASONING, AND WRITING IN PLAIN ENGLISH 280 (2d ed. 2001).

Students have difficulty understanding that legal citation conventions have other important purposes as well. Essentially, citations amount to a specialized code or shorthand that gives the legal reader a great deal of information about the authoritative value of the cited source, which in turn enables much more concise legal writing.

vi. Collaboration Skills

Many LRW programs have as one of their goals exposing students to collaborative work experiences.[162] For programs with a moot court component, collaboration is often an explicit requirement. This experience is certainly a legitimate goal because collaboration is a skill that lawyers will find useful in legal practice.[163] But assisting students to develop that skill can be a significant challenge. Students often resist collaborative work out of concerns about fairness, academic honesty, and assessment.

In developing collaboration policies, the LRW program must have a firm grip on the law school's policies related to plagiarism and other forms of academic dishonesty. Also relevant are institutional policies on sharing academic work, whether graded or ungraded. Program policies must be consistent with other academic rules that govern the law school community.

---

[162]Tom Cobb & Sarah Kaltsounis, *Real Collaborative Context: Opinion Writing and the Appellate Process*, 5 J. ALWD 156, 156 (2008) (reporting trend favoring use of collaborative learning in LRW courses); *see, e.g.*, Bari R. Burke, *Legal Writing (Groups) at the University of Montana: Professional Voice Lessons in a Communal Context*, 52 MONT. L. REV. 373 (1991); Elizabeth L. Inglehart, Kathleen Dillon Narko & Clifford S. Zimmerman, *From Cooperative Learning to Collaborative Writing in the Legal Writing Classroom*, 9 LEGAL WRITING 185 (2003).

[163]Gerald Lebovits, *Writing with Friends: Collaborative Legal Writing*, 90 N.Y. ST. B.J. 62 (July/Aug. 2018) (discussing effective collaborative writing in law practice); *see also* Julie Clement, *A Community of Writers: Building A Virtual Legal-Writing Center*, 16 T.M. COOLEY J. PRAC. & CLINICAL L. 1 (2013).

For assignments to be completed outside class, rules on permissible collaboration should be provided in writing. For example, are students permitted to research assignments together? Under what conditions and constraints? Must students file a notice of intent to research together? What are the limits of this collaboration? May students research and discuss legal authority but not share their written work? How many students may work together on any given assignment? May the same students work together throughout the year, or must students work with many different students throughout the course?

At some schools, LRW professors distribute a written collaboration policy and require each student to read and sign it. If questions or problems arise later, the signed statement documents what each student received, read, and presumably understood.

Collaborative work can be used effectively for in-class assignments or exercises. For example, LRW students might engage in peer-review or peer-editing exercises, which not only help students develop skills as editors but also expose them to different styles of writing and organization.[164] Or students may engage in brainstorming activities to develop theories relevant to a research and writing assignment, or work together to draft particular parts of an assignment.

As discussed above in more detail, LRW programs are in a unique position to expose students to professional norms and expectations, including the ethical requirements of lawyering. In doing so, LRW professors participate in the process of developing lawyers who will serve the highest aspirations of the profession. Additionally, requiring students to engage in these collaborative activities demonstrates the importance of the skills taught in LRW courses.

---

[164] *See, e.g.,* Kirsten K. Davis, *Designing and Using Peer Review in a First-Year Legal Research and Writing Course*, 9 LEGAL WRITING 1 (2003); Hill, *supra* note 72; Marilyn R. Walter, *"Writing As Conversation": Using Peer Review to Teach Legal Writing*, 16 LEGAL WRITING 411 (2010).

h. *Teaching Self-Reliance and the Ability to Educate Oneself*

An important but elusive goal of the LRW program is teaching students to become self-reliant once they complete the course and after they become practicing lawyers.[165]

While many students will practice in government offices, law firms, and judges' chambers, where they can consult colleagues, many others will work in solo practices or small firms with limited opportunities to consult more experienced lawyers. In any case, lawyers cannot constantly rely on others' reassurance and direction. Every law student must develop the capacity to become self-starters without depending on the guidance of others. LRW programs can develop self-reliance in two ways.

First, a program should be structured so that students learn to work more independently as the course progresses. Early writing assignments may be "closed universe" with the legal authorities provided to the students. Later assignments should require students to research independently. Early assignments may have more required drafts with more in-class discussion of organization and content; later assignments should give students more latitude to make independent decisions. Ultimately, the program should help students achieve competence by learning how to independently apply lawyering skills to produce an acceptable final work product with minimal direction from the professor.

Second, students should learn how to critically assess their own work.[166] In the LRW classroom, students should learn to use checklists, rubrics, or other devices and exercises to help them critique

---

[165] *E.g.*, Kedia, *supra* note 50, at 154 ("Perhaps the most important skill set that law students possess is the ability to learn on their own.").

[166] *E.g.*, Joi Montiel, *Empower the Student, Liberate the Professor: Self-Assessment by Comparative Analysis*, 39 S. ILL. U. L.J. 249 (2015).

their own research and writing.[167] The classroom can be designed to mirror the law firm setting, encouraging students to work collaboratively on certain tasks and to learn from each other as they work through assignments framed and sequenced by the LRW professor. This collaborative approach should be balanced with a sufficient number of independent assignments to teach students to work confidently on their own.

4. Curricular Sequence

The nature and number of LRW assignments vary widely depending on the number of credits allocated to the course, the number of semesters, and the student-teacher ratio. Ideally, students should have more than one opportunity to practice the core skills of analysis, research, and writing.[168]

Although a number of schools have three-semester programs, a two-semester program typically includes the following types of assignments:[169]

a. First Semester

The first semester generally includes *short writing and analysis assignments* that introduce discrete skills such as analyzing individual cases, synthesizing key ideas in a group of cases, and reasoning

---

[167] *See, e.g.*, Beazley, *Self-Graded Draft*, *supra* note 72; Anthony Niedwiecki, *Teaching for Lifelong Learning: Improving the Metacognitive Skills of Law Students through More Effective Formative Assessment Techniques*, 40 CAP. U. L. REV. 149, 181-93 (2012) (explaining the value of self-assessment and describing various self-assessment tools).

[168] *See generally* Sherri Lee Keene, *Are We There Yet? Aligning the Expectations and Realities of Gaining Competency in Legal Writing*, 53 DUQ. L. REV. 99, 117 (2015) (describing professional skills students should learn in a two-semester LRW course).

[169] For more details on the variety of LRW program structures and course sequences, see *2017-18 ALWD/LWI Institutional Survey*, *supra* note 99, at 19-36.

by analogy. These short assignments introduce skills on a manageable scale and keep the risk of student failure low. To encourage students to adopt a developmental mindset, LRW professors often assign little weight to these early assignments in determining the final grade for the course.

Next, the first semester course includes *objective office memoranda* of increasing complexity that gradually introduce more complex legal analysis together with legal research skills. The number of memoranda assigned depends on such variables as length and complexity of each assignment, teaching loads, and the amount of individualized feedback provided on both interim and final drafts.

For so-called "closed universe" memoranda, the professor identifies or actually provides the legal authorities, thereby "closing the universe" of research sources to be used so students can focus on legal analysis, organization, and writing. Later, the first-semester course commonly assigns one or more "open universe" memoranda. By requiring students to identify and select the authorities they need to prepare their memoranda, open-universe objective writing assignments help students learn that legal research is an essential part of the analytical process.

Research exercises range from guided research exercises seeking specific answers, to comprehensive research plans and narrative research journals. Some LRW professors elect not to require separate written research exercises but rather evaluate students' research skills as reflected in the final memoranda. Others administer a final research exam to assess these skills.

Citation exercises are widely available in books or online. Professors may choose not to require separate written citation exercises but rather evaluate legal citations as they appear in the assigned memoranda. Some LRW professors require students to demonstrate mastery of basic citation skills by giving an open-book *citation examination* near the end of the course, perhaps before students submit the final written assignment. This approach encourages students to review and practice citation skills to improve their final memorandum assignments for the course.

b. Second Semester

In the second-semester course, students write one or more *persuasive briefs*. As noted earlier, the appellate brief is the most commonly assigned persuasive document. But courses that require more than one brief often assign both a motion or trial brief and an appellate brief, sometimes based on the same fact pattern or based on the same legal issue set in a different jurisdiction. Some courses focus only on pretrial motion memoranda and trial briefs.

Oral arguments often follow the persuasive brief assignment, although some LRW programs use one of several moot court approaches.[170] Schools that assign more than one brief may correspondingly require more than one oral argument.

Some schools require second-semester students to conclude their research instruction by taking a *research examination* testing the key sources, techniques, and research strategies covered throughout the course. This exam could include some short answers to test discrete skills but might also require students to describe an efficient research process to locate relevant legal authority.

LRW courses that follow a lawyering skills approach may also require *client interviewing and counseling exercises*,[171] *negotiation and mediation simulations*,[172] and *drafting assignments*.[173] These courses may extend over three or more semesters.

---

[170] *See, e.g.*, O'Neill, *supra* note 21, at 714 (describing the first-year moot court experience as a screening device for election to the school's moot-court program).

[171] *See* Shafer, *supra* note 47.

[172] *See* O'Neill, *supra* note 21.

[173] *See, e.g.*, Entrikin & Neumann Jr., *supra* note 35.

5. *Tradeoffs and Institutional Implications*

This Part of the *Sourcebook* has discussed a wide variety of curricular options for foundational LRW programs, whether spanning several semesters or confined to the first year of the law school curriculum. Designing a basic LRW course requires considerable sensitivity to the time available to both students and professors in terms of academic credit hours, clock hours, and teaching loads. In addition, the law school must consider the practical tradeoffs between breadth and depth of coverage.

Reasonable teaching loads are essential to allow for optimal individualized critique, both in writing and in student conferences.[174] Each additional student in an LRW section results in many additional hours of work for the LRW professor to provide suitable formative assessment, including written and oral critique on a variety of student assignments.

As more professional skills are added to the basic LRW course, law schools must consider increasing the number of credit hours allocated to the required curriculum, reducing class sizes, or both. Otherwise the ever-increasing expectations imposed on LRW professors and students alike pose significant risks to the quality of the instruction in foundational analysis, research, and writing skills, compromising the law school's ability to achieve the student learning outcomes the ABA Standards expect them to embrace.

Subsequent chapters of this *Sourcebook* discuss structural aspects of program design, including management and staffing models and other personnel issues. Each alternative program design has curricular and pedagogical implications. Decisions about the scope and content of the LRW course must be made in conjunction with institutional decisions on the appropriate program structure, as well as the staffing and financial resources available to support the LRW program.

---

[174] *See infra* Chapter V for recommended teaching loads for LRW professors.

B. Remedial Foundation Courses

Experts in the legal writing academy have long debated how to incorporate remedial instruction in LRW programs for students who need it.[175] Even in the most highly selective law schools, some first-year law students come to law school with weak basic writing skills.[176] The proportion of first-year students who are ill-prepared has increased over the years for many reasons attributable to changing priorities and resource constraints in elementary, secondary, and undergraduate education.[177]

---

[175] *E.g.*, Silecchia, *Legal Skills Training*, *supra* note 33, at 267; Joseph Kimble, *Notes Toward Better Legal Writing*, 75 MICH. B.J. 1072, 1073 (Oct. 1996); *see also* Kedia, *supra* note 50, at 154 (recognizing that while some first-year law students need remedial writing instruction, "it is not the responsibility of the first-year legal writing professor to attend to remedial issues"); Lisa Eichhorn, *Writing in the Legal Academy: A Dangerous Supplement?*, 40 ARIZ. L. REV. 105, 112 (1998) (observing that the earliest legal bibliography courses included some basic writing instruction, but by the early 1970s remedial instruction was no longer a primary goal) (citing Marjorie Dick Rombauer, *First-Year Legal Research and Writing: Then and Now*, 25 J. LEGAL EDUC. 538, 539 (1973)).

[176] *See* Nancy B. Rapoport, *Changing the Modal Law School: Rethinking U.S. Legal Education in (Most) Schools*, 116 PENN ST. L. REV. 1119, 1144 (2012).

> Instead of . . . teaching high-level rhetoric and analysis, [LRW professors] have to do a fair amount of remedial training in basic writing skills. That leaves less time for training in the type of analysis and writing that good lawyers must learn. If students can't write well, they can›t think well. If they can't think well, they can't reason well. If they can't reason well, they can't solve problems well. And that means that they can't become good lawyers.

Id. (internal footnotes omitted); *see also* Lorne Sossin, *Discourse Politics: Legal Research and Writing's Search for a Pedagogy of Its Own*, 29 NEW ENG. L. REV. 883, 913 (1995) ("Students ought to be expected to come to law school able to write. Many, however, do not, even at the most elite universities. Remedial writing courses should therefore be made available to such students outside of their regular [law school] curriculum . . . .").

[177] *See* W. Warren H. Binford, *Envisioning A Twenty-First Century Legal Education*, 43 WASH. U. J.L. & POL'Y 157, 176–77 (2013); Rebecca Flanagan, *The*

Law schools vary widely with respect to identifying students who need remedial instruction and providing suitable academic support.[178] Most institutions provide comprehensive academic support programs,[179] some of which include remedial instruction in basic

Kids Aren't Alright: Rethinking the Law Student Skills Deficit, 2015 B.Y.U. EDUC. & L.J. 135, 136 (reviewing empirical research on how undergraduate education has changed over the decades and the associated challenges for law schools that admit "underprepared" students"); Nancy E. Millar, *The Science of Successful Teaching: Incorporating Mind, Brain, and Education Research into the Legal Writing Course*, 63 ST. LOUIS U. L.J. 373, 379–80 (2019); Cathaleen A. Roach, *Is the Sky Falling? Ruminations on Incoming Law Student Preparedness (and Implications for the Profession) in the Wake of Recent National and Other Reports*, 11 LEGAL WRITING 295 (2005); James Etienne Viator, *Legal Education's Perfect Storm: Law Students' Poor Writing and Legal Analysis Skills Collide with Dismal Employment Prospects, Creating the Urgent Need to Reconfigure the First-Year Curriculum*, 61 CATH. U. L. REV. 735, 752–53 (2012); *see also* Silecchia, *supra* note 116, at 248 n.57 (noting that "[t]he question of remedial writing will likely become more urgent as the declining verbal skills of high school and college graduates become a matter of greater concern"); Deborah Zalesne & David Nadvorney, *Why Don't They Get It: Academic Intelligence and the Under-Prepared Student as Other*, 61 J. LEGAL EDUC. 264 (2011) (positing that academically underprepared students can succeed if identified and offered suitable support integrated within the regular curriculum). *See generally* NAT'L COMM'N ON WRITING IN AMERICA'S SCHOOLS & COLLEGES, THE NEGLECTED "R": THE NEED FOR A WRITING REVOLUTION 7 (2003), https://www.nwp.org/cs/public/download/nwp_file/21478/the-neglected-r-college-board-nwp-report.pdf?x-r=pcfile_d (noting "the growing concern within the education, business, and policy-making communities that the level of writing in the United States is not what it should be"); Aïda M. Alaka, *The Grammar Wars Come to Law School*, 59 J. LEGAL EDUC. 343, 348 (2010).

[178] *E.g.*, Olympia Duhart & Ruben J. Garcia, *With Every Curse There Comes a Wish: Legal Education in a Time of Change*, 16 NEV. L.J. 143, 145 (2015); John F. Murphy, *Teaching Remedial Problem Solving Skills to a Law School's Underperforming Students*, 16 NEV. L.J. 173 (2015); Inglehart, Narko & Zimmerman, *supra* note 162, at 226.

[179] *See* Cynthia Schmidt & Ann L. Iijima, *A Compass for Success: A New Direction for Academic Support Programs*, 4 CARDOZO PUB. L. POL'Y & ETHICS J. 651, 651 (2006) ("The use of academic support programs (ASPs) has spread rapidly through law schools; today, virtually all law schools have such programs.

writing skills.[180] In some law schools, the LRW program plays a significant role in identifying and providing extra help for students who are insufficiently prepared for the rigors of legal writing as a specialized professional discourse.[181] Still other law schools offer

---

Although law schools have experimented with these programs for nearly twenty-five years, there is little consensus regarding what type of program is the most effective.") (internal footnotes and citations omitted); ABA Standard 309(b) ("A law school shall provide academic support designed to afford students a reasonable opportunity to complete the program of legal education, graduate, and become members of the legal profession."); *see also* Kathy L. Cerminara, *Remembering Arthur: Some Suggestions for Law School Academic Support Programs*, 21 T. MARSHALL L. REV. 249, 251 (1996) (discussing the value of academic support programs); Paul T. Wangerin, *Law School Academic Support Programs*, 40 HASTINGS L.J. 771, 774 (1989) ("Recognizing that they have admitted numerous students who may experience academic difficulty, many law schools recently have established academic support programs."). The earliest academic support programs were established to help minority students overcome the inherent barriers in legal education, but the programs have drifted away from that focus. Russell A. McClain, *Bottled at the Source: Recapturing the Essence of Academic Support as a Primary Tool of Education Equity for Minority Law Students,* 18 U. MD. L.J. RACE, RELIGION, GENDER & CLASS 139, 188 (2018).

[180] *See* Elizabeth Ruiz Frost, *Failure Begets Failure: An Examination of the Psychology of Failure and How Law Schools Ought to Respond*, 48 STETSON L. REV. 33 (2018) (reporting survey results from 113 law schools relating how they respond when a student fails the first-year required LRW course); Schmidt & Iijima, *supra* note 179, at 653. *See generally* Kristine S. Knaplund & Richard H. Sander, *The Art and Science of Academic Support*, 45 J. LEGAL EDUC. 157, 234 (1995); Patricia Grande Montana, *Peer Review Across the Curriculum*, 91 OR. L. REV. 783, 812 (2013); Louis N. Schulze, Jr., *Alternative Justifications for Academic Support II: How Academic Support Across the Curriculum Helps Meet the Goals of the Carnegie Report and Best Practices*, 40 CAP. U. L. REV. 1, 70 (2012); Adam G. Todd, *Academic Support Programs: Effective Support Through a Systemic Approach*, 38 GONZ. L. REV. 187, 188 (2002) (urging integration of academic support in the legal academy).

[181] *See* Alaka, *supra* note 177, at 352 ("In addition to teaching legal research, analysis, and critical reading skills, legal writing courses will remain the principal setting to address skills that students should have learned before they entered law school.").

focused support by legal writing specialists, writing centers, or both.[182]

This section discusses alternative ways for LRW programs to provide remedial instruction in law schools that lack sufficient resources to employ a full-time legal writing specialist or to develop a writing center. In any law school, because LRW faculty closely assess student progress, they are uniquely well-situated to identify students needing extra help to master fundamental lawyering skills.[183] An overriding concern is how to develop remedial courses in a way that avoids (or at least minimizes) stigmatizing students who need extra help.

1. Retaking the Course

The most common way law schools offer remedial instruction is to require students who receive a failing grade in first-semester

---

[182]Chapter IX comprehensively discusses the essential role of legal writing specialists and the function of legal writing centers in law schools fortunate enough to have them. *See also* Kowalski, *supra* note 72, at 347 ("[Law] schools are slowly recognizing that they need to employ specialists trained in English grammar instruction[] to teach some students remedial mechanics."). *See generally* Jeremy Francis, *The Role of a Writing Specialist in Enhancing Your Legal Writing Program*, 93 DENV. L. REV. ONLINE 69 (2016); Jeremy Francis, Daphne O'Regan & Ryan C. Black, *Designing Success: Motivating and Measuring Successful 1L Student Engagement in an Optional, Proficiency-Based Program Teaching Grammar and Punctuation*, 21 LEGAL WRITING 129, 131 (2016); Kristen E. Murray, *Peer Tutoring and the Law School Writing Center: Theory and Practice*, 17 LEGAL WRITING 161 (2011).

[183]Grace Wigal, *Repeaters in LRW Programs*, 9 PERSPS. 61, 68 (2001); Herbert N. Ramy, *Two Programs Are Better Than One: Coordinating Efforts Between Academic Support and Legal Writing Departments*, 9 PERSPS. 148, 148 (2001) ("In most law schools, legal writing instructors are uniquely positioned to assess which students will need assistance from an Academic Support Program (ASP).").

LRW to retake the course.[184] Even so, law schools that require a student to retake the course do not all follow the same approach.

Some law schools require failing students to re-enroll in the same course the next time the course is offered, which means they retake the course with a different cohort of first-year students. This approach has the advantage of minimizing classmate stigma for the repeating student. Other law schools require students who fail the first-semester course to immediately re-enroll in the same or similar course the next semester with other students, generally from other sections, who also failed the foundational LRW course. Those schools generally do not allow a student to enroll in the second-semester required LRW course until the student successfully completes the first-semester course.[185] Still others require failing students to enroll in a special remedial LRW course scheduled during the next succeeding fall semester, along with other students who failed to pass the first-year course.[186]

In some law schools, the retake course is required not only for students who received a failing grade in the first-year course but also for those who received a grade below the minimum required to enroll in the next LRW course in the progression.[187] Still others offer a course providing extra practice in legal writing and analysis that is required for students who fail the LRW course and optional for other law students.

---

[184] Frost, *supra* note 180, at 45.

[185] *See* Wigal, *supra* note 183, at 67.

[186] *Id.*

[187] *E.g.*, *id.* at 62 (describing West Virginia's LRW program requiring a student to receive a C before "passing" the course, without allowing rewrites for the last two writing assignments of the year-long course); *id.* at 63 & n.9 (identifying University of Missouri-Kansas City Law School as another that requires students to earn a C before passing the course).

A policy that requires struggling students to retake the foundational LRW course poses some challenges for both students and faculty.[188] Some students resent having to retake the course for various reasons, including embarrassment, failure to acknowledge their own writing weaknesses, and the inevitable scheduling difficulties with other courses.[189] For the LRW program, requiring students to retake the course can create staffing issues, especially for relatively small law schools with fewer LRW faculty to share the extra teaching load.[190]

2. *Specialized Remedial LRW Courses*

In the mid-1990s, Professor Sam Jacobsen of Willamette University College of Law developed a four-week intensive LRW course that was offered during the summer exclusively for first-year students who had failed to pass the foundational course.[191] Initially offered on a trial basis, the course was so successful that it became a regular summer course.[192] Other law schools have experimented with offering a remedial LRW course during the summer[193] or at

---

[188] *Id.* at 65.

[189] *Id.* at 65-66.

[190] *Id.* at 66.

[191] *Id.* (citing M.H. Sam Jacobson, *Providing Academic Support Without an Academic Support Program*, 3 LEGAL WRITING 241 (1997)); *see also* M.H. Sam Jacobson, A *Primer on Learning Styles: Reaching Every Student*, 25 SEATTLE U. L. REV. 139, 152 n.52 (2001) (noting a disproportionately high number of visual learners in the summer remedial LRW course).

[192] Wigal, *supra* note 183, at 66.

[193] *See, e.g.*, Peter Nemerovski, *Practice Makes Proficient: Writing Classes for Struggling Students*, 24 PERSPS. 55 (2016) (describing "Writing and Editing for Lawyers, a two-credit summer course for rising 2Ls (and some 3Ls) who performed poorly in their first-year courses").

other times so that academically struggling students have the opportunity to learn (or re-learn) foundational skills before progressing to more demanding required and elective courses.[194]

3. General Academic Support – Required or Voluntary

In some law schools, students whose grade-point averages do not meet a minimum threshold at the end of the first semester are either required or encouraged to participate in a formal academic support program. The services may require weekly meetings with academic support staff, help with outlining techniques, special help with exam-taking skills, or some combination. These programs are designed to provide supplemental support and structured study exercises to help students manage their time and the unusual intellectual demands of law school.[195] Some, but not all, include attention to basic writing and analytical skills.

---

[194] *See, e.g.*, Nancy Millich, *Building Blocks of Analysis: Using Simple "Sesame Street Skills" and Sophisticated Educational Learning Theories in Teaching a Seminar in Legal Analysis and Writing*, 34 SANTA CLARA L. REV. 1127, 1155–56 (1994) (proposing use of "[a] combination of 'Sesame Street Skills,' Metacognition, and The Autonomous Learning Model . . . in a remedial seminar to benefit students who have experienced difficulty with legal analysis and exam-taking").

[195] Frost, *supra* note 180, at 47-48 (describing results of a survey of over 100 law schools reporting their academic support practices for students who fail the first-year LRW course).

4. *Team-Based and Collaborative Learning Approaches*

Some experienced LRW professors have reported that team-based[196] and collaborative learning[197] courses have successfully provided special support for academically struggling students.[198] Peer editing, peer review, and special writing groups are examples of specialized collaborative learning approaches that many LRW programs have used with positive results.[199]

5. *Digital Assessment and Learning Tools*

Technological innovation has enabled law schools to rely on numerous digital tools to help students who need special academic

---

[196] *See* Anne E. Mullins, *Team-Based Learning: Innovative Pedagogy in Legal Writing*, 49 U. S.F. L. REV. F. 53 (2015); Sparrow & McCabe, *supra* note 82; Melissa H. Weresh, *Uncommon Results: The Power of Team-Based Learning in the Legal Writing Classroom*, 19 LEGAL WRITING 49 (2014).

[197] *See* Sheila Rodriguez, *Letting Students Teach Each Other: Using Peer Conferences in Upper-Level Legal Writing*, 13 FLA. COASTAL L. REV. 181, 188 (2012) ("Although experts disagree on how to define collaborative learning, 'the core assumptions' are that learners are actively engaged in learning and are taking responsibility for managing their learning.").

[198] *E.g.*, Lindsey P. Gustafson, *Remediating in Teams*, 22 LEGAL WRITING 56, 59 (2018); Inglehart, Narko & Zimmerman, *supra* note 162, at 226.

[199] *E.g.*, Davis, *supra* note 164; Michelle Falkoff, *Using Fiction Workshop Techniques in First-Year Legal Writing Classes*, 62 J. LEGAL EDUC. 323 (2012); Hill, *supra* note 72; Roberta K. Thyfault & Kathryn Fehrman, *Interactive Group Learning in the Legal Writing Classroom: An International Primer on Student Collaboration and Cooperation in Large Classrooms*, 3 J. MARSHALL L.J. 135 (2009); Walter, *supra* note 164.

support.[200] For example, *Core Grammar for Lawyers*[201] includes a diagnostic assessment of students' basic writing skills and provides tutorials for mastering each of several areas such as grammar, punctuation, and sentence structure.[202] Anne Enquist and Laurel Currie Oates co-authored the *Diagnostic Test for Grammar, Punctuation, and Usage*[203] to help identify students who have gaps in basic writing skills. Several free online assessment tools and tutorials are available for students who need focused help with basic writing skills.[204]

---

[200] Allard & Brown, *supra* note 86, at 12 (summarizing several recent technological innovations that help LRW students identify areas of needed improvement); Binford, *supra* note 177, at 175 (discussing *Core Grammar for Lawyers*); Michele Pistone, *Law Schools and Technology: Where We Are and Where We Are Heading*, 64 J. LEGAL EDUC. 586, 598-99 (2015) (discussing several innovative technological tools useful for online tutorials, online collaboration, and adaptive learning); Abigail Salisbury, *Skills Without Stigma: Using the JURIST Method to Teach Legal Research and Writing*, 59 J. LEGAL EDUC. 173, 180 (2009) (explaining how to use the legal news website *Jurist* to support LRW instruction).

[201] RUTH ANN MCKINNEY & KATIE ROSE GUEST PRYAL, CORE GRAMMAR FOR LAWYERS (4th ed.), https://www.coregrammarforlawyers.com/ (last visited Dec. 14, 2019).

[202] RUTH A. MCKINNEY & KATIE ROSE GUEST PRYAL, CORE GRAMMAR FOR LAWYERS: TEACHER'S MANUAL 4 (2014), https://papers.ssrn.com/sol3/papers.cfm?abstract_id=2322530&rec=1&srcabs=2469253&alg=1&pos=9 ("We wrote CORE GRAMMAR FOR LAWYERS to provide faculty with a tool that can be used by students directly, with or without individual or classroom help, to master the principles of grammar that are the cornerstones of great legal writing.").

[203] Anne Enquist & Laurel Currie Oates, *Diagnostic Test for Grammar, Punctuation, and Usage* (2009).

[204] *See, e.g.*, DEBORAH BOUCHOUX, ASPEN HANDBOOK FOR LEGAL WRITERS (4th ed. 2017) (including numerous links to online tools for specific writing issues).

C. Beyond Required LRW Courses: Upper-Level Writing Programs

ABA Standards require each student to "satisfactorily complete" at least "one additional writing experience after the first year," which must be "faculty supervised."[205] Virtually all law schools comply by requiring students to complete some component of the required LRW curriculum after the first year.[206] But most law schools also offer a panoply of elective courses that provide additional opportunities for students to learn lawyering skills in a writing context.[207]

In 2017-18, among a total of 182 law school respondents, only a few required law students to complete one or more specifically identified upper-level writing courses beyond the first year.[208] But 147 reported offering elective upper-level courses in legal writing.[209] Commonly required upper-level writing courses include seminars in which students write scholarly papers, various legal drafting courses, advanced appellate advocacy courses, and general advanced legal writing courses.

---

[205] ABA Standard 303(a)(2).

[206] *2017-18 ALWD/LWI Institutional Survey*, *supra* note 99, at 27, Question 6.7 # 3.

[207] *See generally* Michael R. Smith, *Alternative Substantive Approaches to Advanced Legal Writing Courses*, 54 J. LEGAL EDUC. 119 (2004).

[208] *2017-18 ALWD/LWI Institutional Survey*, *supra* note 99, at 25-27. For example, 24 law schools reported requiring a course after the first year focusing "principally" on persuasive legal writing, either basic (4 schools) or advanced (20 schools). *Id.* at 25, Question 6.7 # 1.

[209] *Id.* at 37, Question 7.2.

This section discusses the many different ways law schools provide upper-level students opportunities to learn how to write more effectively.[210]

1. Programmatic Issues

When deciding how best to incorporate upper-level writing instruction into the curriculum, LRW faculty face several issues.[211] They include deciding what kinds of upper-level courses to offer, how they should be staffed, how many credits should be allocated, and how the upper-level courses will fit into the general upper-level curriculum.

This subpart discusses the purposes, staffing options, and course designs for the variety of elective courses that can be used to fulfill upper-level writing requirements or that serve as elective upper-level writing courses. It also addresses the various ways students can learn advanced writing skills by participating in extracurricular activities.

a. The Benefits to Students of Upper-Level LRW Electives

First-year LRW programs are better staffed, better structured, and better taught now than ever before. Even the best first-year program, however, is constrained by limited time, resources, and focus;

---

[210] *See* Mary Barnard Ray, *Writing on the Envelope: An Exploration of the Potentials and Limits of Writing in Law*, 49 DUQ. L. REV. 573 (2011) (discussing various alternatives for improving advanced legal writing instruction).

[211] *See generally* Lissa Griffin, *Teaching Upperclass Writing: Everything You Always Wanted to Know But Were Afraid to Ask*, 34 GONZ. L. REV. 45 (1998-99); Silecchia, *supra* note 116; Louis J. Sirico, Jr., *Advanced Legal Writing Courses: Comparing Approaches*, 5 PERSPS. 63 (1997).

upper-level writing courses are therefore necessary to hone the skills students learn in the foundational LRW curriculum.[212]

Most mandatory LRW programs give students guided practice in writing office memoranda and appellate briefs. Many also include opportunities for writing client letters and motion memoranda or other trial briefs. But constraints on time, credit hours, and class sizes prevent most programs from introducing students to other legal writing formats, or even providing them sufficient opportunities to master the basic formats. Thus, mandatory LRW programs rarely offer more than the most rudimentary instruction in drafting contracts, statutes, and other rule-based legal documents or preparing motions, pleadings, and jury instructions—let alone researching and authoring law review articles.[213] In addition, most mandatory LRW programs end after the second or third semester. At that point, few students have yet engaged in the kind of legal work experiences that reinforce the value of the legal writing and other lawyering skills they learn in LRW. Moreover, upper-level writing courses can engage more experienced law students in ways a required first-year LRW course cannot.

Because first-year programs have so many different learning outcomes—teaching students how to identify and approach legal problems; how to research, analyze, and use authorities effectively; and how to write objectively and persuasively—it is difficult for these foundational programs to offer students enough writing opportunities to demonstrate the important nuances characteristic of truly professional written work. In some cases, student-faculty ratios may be a limiting factor as well.

---

[212]*See* Barbara J. Cox & Mary Barnard Ray, *Getting Dorothy Out of Kansas: The Importance of an Advanced Component to Legal Writing Programs*, 40 J. Legal Educ. 351 (1990).

[213]*See 2017-18 ALWD/LWI Institutional Survey*, *supra* note 99, at 38, Question 7.3.

Furthermore, time limitations in one-year programs, even those allocated a relatively high number of credits, mean that students cannot be trained to competently use each of the important legal research tools. For example, while many programs attempt to introduce first-year students to researching legislative history, administrative law materials, looseleaf services, or empirical data, beginning students cannot realistically master these resources in a two- or three-semester required program. Nor can LRW programs productively cover highly specialized materials in narrow areas of law such as bankruptcy and taxation.

Another reason for offering upper-level writing electives is to give students opportunities to learn legal writing from different professors. While professors may have some minor differences in formatting preferences or analytical vocabulary, students will nevertheless come to understand the essentials of legal writing doctrine: that context is important to all readers, that articulating the rule early in the analysis of a legal issue is a "must" for analytical writing, and that enduring principles underlie the critique that they received as first-year LRW students. The necessary adjustments upper-level students must make to adapt to new professors simply reflect those they must learn to make in practice to suit the preferences of different employers and supervising attorneys.

Offering a variety of upper-level research and writing courses also enables students to choose courses reflecting their unique areas of interest. The skills learned by practicing the analytical writing required in most first-year courses are transferable to any type of law practice that requires analytical thinking. Most students, however, also benefit from taking courses that allow them to practice writing the specific kinds of documents they will likely encounter in practice. Thus, law schools might offer drafting courses that focus on transactional documents or legislative materials, as well as advanced LRW and lawyering skills courses that allow students to write complaints, answers, various pretrial and posttrial motions, and even jury instructions.

Perhaps the most serious consequence of limiting a legal writing program to the first year is that students' legal writing skills atrophy over time if not practiced repeatedly. Even if students attain a high level of competence in the required LRW courses, their skills will deteriorate if they are not required to practice them again and again over the next two years of law school. Law students need to hone and refine the legal analysis, research, and writing skills they acquire in the first two or three semesters as they progress through the law school curriculum.

b. Special Status Issues Affecting Upper-Level Courses

Tenured and tenure-track LRW faculty, with the academic power to advocate for improved course design and an increased allocation of credits, are best positioned to ensure that LRW programs are developed to their full potential. Contract faculty are just as competent to teach LRW courses as their tenured counterparts, and adjuncts may be superior teachers in specialized subjects. But neither contract faculty nor adjuncts generally have the faculty status or faculty committee responsibilities to significantly influence curriculum decisions.

At many law schools, contract LRW faculty do not have the opportunity to vote in faculty meetings.[214] The limited number of credit hours commonly allocated to foundational LRW courses is an

---

[214]A total of 108 law schools reportedly employ at least some full-time LRW faculty on short-term or long-term contract status (other than Standard 405(c) contract status). Of that number, 45 percent reported that those full-time contract faculty have no voting rights whatsoever. *See 2017-18 ALWD/LWI Institutional Survey*, *supra* note 99, at 79, Question 10.2. Another 30 percent of responding schools reported that those faculty could not vote on hiring, promotion, or tenure matters relating to tenured and tenure-track faculty. *See generally id.* at 79-81, Questions 10.2-10.7; Sue Liemer, *The Hierarchy of Law School Faculty Meetings: Who Votes?*, 73 UMKC L. Rev. 351 (2004).

artifact of insufficient faculty status and security of position for LRW faculty. LRW faculty who cannot vote, or who lack equal status with other full-time law school faculty, are necessarily handicapped in faculty discussions about improving the law school curriculum. The quality of the upper-level writing curriculum, as well as the rigor of the foundational LRW program, often suffer as a result.

c. *Staffing Options*

As with any law school course, the preferred way to staff upper-level courses is with tenured, tenure-track, or long-term contract faculty who specialize in the relevant area. However, other viable staffing options exist. While upper-division student teaching assistants are usually inappropriate for upper-level writing courses, any other method of staffing that can be used successfully in a foundational LRW course can be used for upper-level courses. Chapter V provides comprehensive information on staffing models for LRW courses.

Adjuncts who specialize in the area of legal writing under study—transactional drafting, for example—may be particularly appropriate teachers for upper-level LRW courses. Similarly, graduate law students who have returned to school from a specialized area of practice could be retained as teachers. Some non-academics who teach tend to structure their courses around "the way we do things at my firm" rather than more generally applicable concepts and doctrine. However, this tendency can be counteracted with appropriate supervision by full-time LRW faculty.

d. *Credit Hours and Student-Faculty Ratios*

In considering the number of credit hours to allocate to an upper-level writing elective, the law school's curriculum committee must consider the realities of student and professor workload for the course. The length of a drafted document, for example, is not a suitable indicator for either the academic rigor of the student's experience or the assessment demands on the professor. In a drafting course, for example, students generally produce multiple drafts of numerous shorter documents that each require progressively more complex, sophisticated legal analysis. Allocating additional credits for the course allows for more small-group work, peer review, and other kinds of classroom exercises.[215]

The student-faculty ratio in an advanced writing course should be reasonable to allow for highly individualized feedback and assessment on multiple drafts of assigned documents. Ideally, a single section should not exceed 12 to 14 students. Moreover, the law school administration must consider the LRW professor's total teaching load. Teaching an advanced writing elective is just as demanding (if not more so) than teaching a small section of the required foundational LRW course. As noted *infra* in Chapter V, Part A.2, the total number of legal writing students for each full-time professor in any single semester should not exceed 30 to 35.

e. *Program Structures*

As law schools continue to expand upper-level LRW electives in number and scope, the variety of program structures increases.[216] A law school should design a program that meets the law school's culture and mission as well as the needs of its students, and that can be supported by available faculty resources.

A first step in designing an upper-level LRW program is to determine its chief characteristics. Fundamental program design questions include the following:

---

[215] *See* Gerald Lebovits, *Legal Writing in the Practice-Ready Law School*, 85 N.Y. St. B.J. 72, 67 (Sept. 2013) ("Law schools should offer writing courses that allot a fair number of credits and sufficient class hours for the work their writing students must do.").

[216] A Teaching Bank, including numerous syllabi for upper-level legal writing courses, is accessible to members of the Legal Writing Institute at https://www.lwionline.org/resources (last visited Dec. 14, 2019).

- Should any upper-level courses be required rather than optional?
- Does the program include a specific sequence of courses or a smorgasbord of elective courses?
- Do upper-level courses focus on research and writing skills, or is upper-level writing integrated with a specific area of legal doctrine?
- Is writing integrated into every aspect of legal education, as in a "Writing Across the Curriculum" approach?
- Does the law school offer a certificate program to encourage students to develop special expertise in LRW skills?

Answers to each of these questions help to sketch the outline of an advanced writing program tailored to a school's specific needs.

i. Required or Optional

In offering upper-level writing instruction, perhaps the most important design decision is whether a particular course should be required or optional. As noted earlier, the ABA Standards have long required at least one faculty-supervised upper-level writing experience beyond the first year.[217] Many law schools offer seminar and independent study courses that may satisfy the upper-level writing requirement. While those courses offer writing *experiences,* they typically provide little in the way of writing *instruction.*[218] Requiring

---

[217] ABA Standard 303(a)(2).

[218] *See, e.g.,* Jessica Wherry Clark & Kristen E. Murray, *The Theoretical and Practical Underpinnings of Teaching Scholarly Legal Writing*, 1 TEX. A&M L. REV. 523, 525 (2014) ("Over half of all law schools require their J.D. students to write a scholarly paper to satisfy an upper-level writing requirement, yet most of these students will take on these tasks without specific instruction on the process of writing a scholarly paper, and with minimal guidance and feedback throughout the scholarly writing process."); Lebovits, *supra* note 215, at 67 ("Students must satisfy a writing requirement in their second or third year, but their papers typically are academic, not practice-based, and are rarely line edited, as are the writing course's papers.").

an upper-level LRW course sends the message to law students that writing is an essential lawyering skill.[219]

Only a small percentage of the students will likely enroll in optional advanced LRW courses, and elective courses are less likely to remain a permanent part of the curriculum. Whether required or optional, the number of credits allocated for an upper-level LRW course communicates not only the value of the course but also the workload and discipline expected of students who enroll in the course.

ii. Sequence or Smorgasbord

Upper-level writing instruction can consist of a limited number of courses from which students must select, or a "smorgasbord" menu of courses. Some law schools that adopt the former approach require students to enroll in a third semester of the foundational course that satisfies the upper-level writing requirement.[220] The required third semester could be offered as part of the law school's second-year curriculum, or a student could enroll in the course in a later semester.

Alternatively, a law school might offer several courses with a substantial drafting component, such as transactional, legislative, or litigation-related drafting. Students might have the option to take the full sequence or enroll selectively in courses to suit their individual preferences and schedules. The latter option puts less strain on faculty resources. Offering a smorgasbord of electives also allows students to enroll in advanced writing courses when motivated to

---

[219] *See, e.g.,* Schrup & Provenzano, *supra* note 51, at 99 (encouraging law schools to require two to four credits of advanced legal writing coursework to satisfy the upper-level writing requirement rather than a traditional seminar course).

[220] *See* William Y. Chin, *The "Relay" Team-Teaching Approach: Combining Collaboration and the Division of Labor to Teach a Third Semester of Legal Writing*, 13 Persps. 94 (2005); Dennis, *supra* note 18 (explaining the value of a three-semester required program and offering recommendations).

develop or refresh particular skills, or perhaps to prepare for specific job opportunities.

iii. Focused or Integrated Writing Instruction

An advanced course may focus specifically on teaching writing skills or may integrate the writing instruction with one or more doctrinal courses.[221] The integrated approach demands a professor with the willingness and ability to teach both doctrine and writing skills effectively, and to devote substantial time to review and respond individually to writing assignments. As a practical matter, an integrated course also requires a conscious reduction in coverage of doctrinal material.

The most progressive and intensive approach to integrating skills with doctrine is to design a curriculum in which all courses further the goal of teaching writing, following a "Writing Across the Curriculum" model.[222] Alternatively, a law school may choose to combine the integrated approach with an optional or required program that specifies advanced writing skills covered by particular courses. For example, all public law courses might include a legislative drafting exercise, and all family law or small business courses might include client letter assignments.[223]

---

[221] *See generally* Alice Noble-Allgire, *Desegregating the Law School Curriculum: How to Integrate More of the Skills and Values Identified by the MacCrate Report into a Doctrinal Course*, 3 NEV. L. J. 32 (2002); John B. Mitchell, Betsy R. Hollingsworth, Patricia Hall Clark & Raven Lidman, *And Then Suddenly Seattle University Was on Its Way to a Parallel, Integrative Curriculum*, 2 CLINICAL L. REV. 1 (1995).

[222] *See supra* Chapter I, Part D.

[223] *See, e.g.*, Lisa A. Rich, *Teaching Public Policy Drafting in Law School: One Professor's Approach*, 55 DUQ. L. REV. 151 (2017); Bobette Wolski, *Why, How, and What to Practice: Integrating Skills Teaching and Learning in the Undergraduate Law Curriculum*, 52 J. LEGAL EDUC. 287, 296 (2002) (showing how Australian law schools require various skills to be covered as part of doctrinal courses).

iv. Certificate Programs

A unique option encouraging excellence in legal writing is the writing certificate program. Just as some law schools design specialty areas or areas of concentration for doctrinal areas such as tax or international law, the option might be similarly available for legal writing.[224] A certificate program in advanced legal writing, research, and drafting can be structured to allow students to take advanced writing courses and doctrinal courses with substantial writing components to build a comprehensive legal writing portfolio.[225]

2. *Types of Upper-Level Courses*

This subpart addresses four general categories of upper-level courses. First, "horizontal" courses focus on broadening students' knowledge of legal writing by exposing them to various types of legal documents. Second, "vertical" courses deepen students' understanding of legal writing by providing more advanced instruction and practice in specific legal writing methods. Third, "survey" or "hybrid" advanced writing courses both broaden and deepen students' knowledge and understanding of legal writing. Finally, "integrated" courses use a variety of methods, including writing, to teach course material.

---

[224] *See* Linda H. Edwards, *Certificate Program in Advanced Legal Writing: Mercer's Advanced Writing Curriculum*, 9 PERSPS. 116 (2001).

[225] *See, e.g.*, SULLIVAN ET AL., *supra* note 7, at 174 (encouraging the use of student portfolios to assess complex practice skills); Johansen, *supra* note 76; Deborah Jones Merritt, *Pedagogy, Progress, and Portfolios*, 25 OHIO ST. J. ON DISP. RESOL. 7, 14 (2010); Carol McCrehan Parker, *The Signature Pedagogy of Legal Writing*, 16 LEGAL WRITING 463, 472 (2010) ("Learning portfolios provide a means of linking clearly articulated goals to assessment measures, consistent with the learning expectations of just-in-time learners."); Vicki Waye & Margaret Faulkner, *Embedding E-Portfolios in a Law Program: Lessons from an Australian Law School*, 61 J. LEGAL EDUC. 560 (2012).

a. Horizontal Courses

As the name implies, a "horizontal" course seeks to broaden students' knowledge of the various types of legal documents lawyers prepare in both practice and scholarship. The typical first-year LRW course concentrates on litigation-oriented office memoranda and persuasive briefs. These documents give students practice in developing an analytical method, using legal writing doctrine to communicate information, and researching particular areas of the law. But each type of legal document has unique analytical, content, and format requirements, and exposing students to a wider range of legal documents increases their knowledge in all of these areas.

Common examples of horizontal courses include drafting courses, seminar courses, and judicial opinion-writing courses.

i. Legal Drafting Courses

Law schools traditionally ignored the important lawyering skill of legal drafting as distinct from legal writing generally.[226] Although virtually every practitioner must draft documents in practice, only 27 of 182 responding law schools required law students to complete some kind of legal drafting course in 2017-18.[227]

Over the last few years, many law schools have increased the number of elective courses in legal drafting.[228] They follow several different models: general or survey legal drafting courses; transactional, legislation, and litigation drafting courses; subject-specific drafting courses; drafting instruction integrated in doctrinal courses; and clinical courses incorporating drafting instruction.

---

[226] Entrikin & Neumann Jr., *supra* note 35, at 14-17.

[227] *2017-18 ALWD/LWI Institutional Survey*, *supra* note 99, at 21-23, Question 6.4.

[228] *See* Carpenter, *supra* note 36 and accompanying text; *see also* Joseph Kimble, *Teaching Legal Drafting*, 3 Scribes J. Legal Writing 148 (1992).

General or Survey Legal Drafting Courses. In a survey legal drafting course, students are taught the fundamentals of good legal drafting. They draft several different types of documents that deal with diverse areas of law. For example, students may draft a contract, a will or trust, a statute, and a set of jury instructions, providing a broad range of experience with transactional, legislative, and litigation drafting. Alternatively, a general course might focus on just one type of document in a transactional drafting or legislative drafting course. Regardless of the specific subject matter, these courses have a shared emphasis on the fundamentals of good legal drafting that all kinds of transactions and documents have in common.[229]

Thus, the survey course may emphasize the drafting process from investigation, to conceptualization and planning, to writing and revising; the need to write for a specific audience or for multiple audiences; the need to integrate structure and content; the significance of special words such as "shall," "will," and "may"; the need to define key terms; the use of checklists and forms; and the use of plain-language drafting techniques. To cover legal drafting skills so generally, however, these courses must inherently sacrifice depth. Like introductory courses in objective or persuasive writing, survey drafting courses must focus primarily on the skill itself rather than the substantive law underlying each drafting assignment.

Transactional, Litigation, and Legislative Drafting Courses. Law schools that offer these courses generally depend on the availability of faculty with specific interests in each area. Some focus on drafting in an advanced litigation context such as Advanced Litigation Drafting, Complex Litigation, Criminal Procedure, Advanced Constitutional Law and Litigation, and International Litigation.

---

[229] *See, e.g.*, GEORGE W. KUNEY & DONNA C. LOOPER, LEGAL DRAFTING, PROCESS, TECHNIQUES, AND EXERCISES (3d ed. 2017); RICHARD K. NEUMANN & J. LYN ENTRIKIN, LEGAL DRAFTING BY DESIGN: A UNIFIED APPROACH xxxvii, 5-6, 499-500 (2018).

However, some of these litigation-oriented courses devote far more attention to oral advocacy than legal writing.

Other specialized courses focus on a specific practice area, such as transactional drafting within a business context[230] or statutory drafting in the context of the legislative process. More specialized drafting courses are sometimes taught by doctrinal faculty members or adjuncts who have experience and interest in a particular area of law.

Subject-Specific Drafting Courses. This model focuses on drafting in one area of law such as real estate, commercial law, estate planning, or bankruptcy.[231] In a real estate drafting course, for example, assignments may include a real estate conveyance or deed, a contract to convert premises to a condominium, a commercial lease with a specific clause providing contingencies for the relocation of a major highway, or other typical real estate instruments. Students are expected to research the background law and the transactional facts, and to explore forms and checklists for sample clauses.

The benefit of this model is that the students learn the relationship between doctrine, analysis, and writing as they acquire detailed knowledge of a substantive field and master the fundamentals of legal drafting.[232] The writing assignments reinforce and deepen students' understanding of legal doctrine. A shortcoming of this approach is that individual students' lack of interest in the particular subject area may cause them to pass up learning drafting skills.

Drafting Assignments in Doctrinal Courses. Some schools may not have the resources to provide legal drafting courses. As noted

---

[230] *See, e.g.,* SCOTT J. BURNHAM, DRAFTING AND ANALYZING CONTRACTS: A GUIDE TO THE PRACTICAL APPLICATION OF THE PRINCIPLES OF CONTRACT LAW (4th ed. 2016); TINA STARK, DRAFTING CONTRACTS: HOW & WHY LAWYERS DO WHAT THEY DO (2d ed. 2013).

[231] *See, e.g.,* Karen J. Sneddon, *Trusts and Estates Drafting: Avoiding Rigor Mortis in the Law School Curriculum*, 63 MERCER L. REV. 1071 (2012) (describing the development of a subject-specific drafting course).

[232] *See* Noble-Allgire, *supra* note 221.

above, effective drafting classes should have small student-faculty ratios because students draft multiple documents requiring detailed individualized feedback. However, a law school lacking sufficient faculty resources can still provide some instruction in legal drafting by structuring upper-level doctrinal electives to include drafting instruction and assignments related to the subject matter of the course.[233]

For example, in a Corporations class, the professor may set aside class time to offer instruction in drafting, and then assign the class to draft articles of incorporation, by-laws, or a corporate buy-out plan.[234] Every course offers ample opportunities for incorporating drafting exercises—from marital settlement agreements to intellectual property filings. While not as effective as a separate semester-long course in legal drafting, a drafting assignment in a doctrinal course can introduce students to the fundamentals of drafting: collecting facts, researching the law and transactional background, using checklists and forms, and writing for a specific audience. Students also learn that drafting is an essential skill for any practicing lawyer regardless of subject-matter specialty.

Some professors include a drafting assignment as a part of the final course grade. If many different courses offer one or two drafting assignments, the burden of critiquing and providing feedback is more equitably spread across the faculty, and students benefit from the variety of drafting contexts and approaches. As in subject-specific drafting courses, the interactions between writing and

---

[233] *See, e.g.*, Monica Todd, *Matchmaking in Law School: Practical Skills and Doctrine in Family Law Course Design*, 46 W. St. L. Rev. 127 (2019) (describing the transformation of a family law course into an advanced professional skills course).

[234] *See, e.g.*, Joan M. Heminway, *Fresh Approaches to Teaching Transactional Drafting: Drafting Corporate Bylaws: From Alpha to Omega,* 18 Transactions 399, 399-420 (2016); Laura R. Winter, *Computer-Enhanced Collaborative Drafting in Legal Education*, 52 J. Legal Educ. 278 (2002) (describing how to draft basic legal documents for a corporation).

doctrine reinforce each other, providing a practical context for the theoretical material offered in the course.

For more information about incorporating legal writing into doctrinal courses, see *infra* Part D of this chapter.

Clinical Courses with Drafting Instruction. Many law schools provide drafting instruction as part of in-house legal clinics.[235] Typically, the training is done by clinical professors when a student is called upon to draft a document, such as a will or a legal pleading, to carry out a client's goals. The clinical professor may offer guidance, refer the student to form books or existing clinic forms and samples, and review and edit the students' document drafts. Many clinics offer a classroom component that may include formal instruction in drafting techniques.

When evaluating a law school's course offerings in legal drafting, the following factors warrant consideration:

Whether the course is required or elective: Although few law schools require training in legal drafting, surveys of the legal profession make clear that drafting can be effectively taught in law school, that drafting is not well-taught in practice (especially in smaller firms or solo practices), and that most lawyers' drafting skills are woefully inadequate.[236] Thus, schools that require

---

[235] *See* Bowman & Brodoff, *supra* note 20; Angela J. Campbell, *Teaching Advanced Legal Writing in a Law School Clinic*, 24 Seton Hall L. Rev. 653 (1993); Kowalski, *supra* note 72, at 286; Robert R. Statchen, *Clinicians, Practitioners, and Scribes: Drafting Client Work Product in a Small Business Clinic*, 56 N.Y. L. Sch. L. Rev. 233 (2012).

[236] *See, e.g.*, Jamison Wilcox, *Teaching Legal Drafting Effectively and Efficiently—By Dispensing with the Myths*, 57 J. Legal Educ. 448, 448 (2007). "'[L]awyers are called on to prepare definitive legal instruments almost daily. No legal discipline is more pervasive.' Yet few lawyers possess these skills at a proficient level." *Id.* (quoting Reed Dickerson, The Fundamentals of Legal Drafting 1 (1986)); *see also* Joseph Kimble, *You Think Lawyers Are Good Drafters?*, 94 Mich. B.J. 54, 54 (May 2015) ("[M]ost lawyers are not skilled drafters.");

graduates to develop good drafting skills give their students a competitive edge in the job market.

Student-faculty ratio: Learning legal drafting requires more than listening to lectures or reading examples. The best way to learn this important skill is by drafting documents on which the professor provides timely, detailed individualized feedback. As with any other skills course, the student-faculty ratio in a drafting course must be small enough to enable the professor to offer sufficient assignments and provide quality critiques of student work.

Number of drafting assignments: One law school drafting experience is better than none at all. However, legal drafting, like any other professional skill, is truly learned only when the student has the opportunity to continuously practice the new skill. A student cannot become a polished and professional drafter after preparing just one contract or lease. The fundamentals of good drafting can be inculcated only by continued practice. Thus, an effective drafting course must provide at least three and as many as six or seven graded and critiqued drafts and assignments.

Nature of drafting assignments: Care, attention, and experience are needed to design effective drafting assignments. A drafting assignment need not be long to be challenging for students. Drafting a lengthy document that includes a substantial amount of boilerplate is not as valuable a learning exercise as drafting a unique one-paragraph provision to address a specific problem or to prevent a particular legal issue or contract dispute.

Assignments that merely require students to obtain and fill in forms provide only limited educational or practical value. Students should be taught the fundamentals of legal drafting to enable

---

Peter Siviglia, *Teaching the Drafting of Contracts*, 70 N.Y. St. B.J. 46, 46 (May/June 1998) (documenting the need to train law students in legal drafting). *See generally* Preston M. Torbert, *Contract Drafting: A Socratic Manifesto*, 14 Scribes J. Legal Writing 93 (2011-2012).

them to create documents with few or no existing forms to follow. Although formbooks offer helpful checklists and samples, students should be taught how to use these forms intelligently. Students should be encouraged to prepare a document to suit a specific set of circumstances, rather than blindly following a form just because it has been used for years or because it appears in a standard work.[237]

Pedagogy: In addition to lecture and demonstration, a quality legal drafting program uses a variety of exercises (including interactive exercises such as negotiation), collaborative learning techniques, mock interviews, extensive feedback, and individual conferences. Moreover, legal drafting professors should stress special ethical considerations in legal drafting such as mining metadata, responding to drafting errors made by opposing counsel, and drafting unenforceable provisions.[238]

---

[237] *See, e.g.*, Kirsten K. Davis, *Legal Forms as Rhetorical Transaction: Competency in the Context of Information and Efficiency*, 79 UMKC L. REV. 667, 675 (2011) (noting that "a form that is not sufficiently interrogated for the actual expertise it brings to a particular client's problem can result in incompetent performance"); William E. Foster & Andrew L. Lawson, *When to Praise the Machine: The Promise and Perils of Automated Transactional Drafting*, 69 S.C. L. REV. 597, 617 (2018) (noting that "expanded availability [of forms] has carried with it a potentially deleterious effect on the quality of transactional representation").

[238] *See* Scott J. Burnham et al., *Transactional Skills Training: Contract Drafting—Beyond the Basics*, 2009 TRANSACTIONS 253 (2009) (addressing the ethics of ambiguity, drafting with precedents, using information technology in drafting, outsourcing, and metadata); Gregory M. Duhl, *The Ethics of Contract Drafting*, 14 LEWIS & CLARK L. REV. 989 (2010); Lori D. Johnson, *The Ethics of Non-Traditional Contract Drafting*, 84 U. CIN. L. REV. 595 (2016); Christina L. Kunz, *The Ethics of Invalid and "Iffy" Contract Clauses*, 40 LOY. L.A. L. REV. 487 (2006).

ii. Seminar Courses or Independent Study

To satisfy the ABA's upper-level writing requirement,[239] a large number of law schools require each student to write a scholarly paper under faculty supervision, either in the context of an upper-level doctrinal seminar course or as an independent study project. For many students, this upper-level writing experience is their only exposure to scholarly legal writing. The underlying theory is that the student will work with complex materials, receive advanced experience in legal research, and engage in a type of critical legal thinking unlike the analysis required for practice-oriented legal writing and drafting. A scholarly writing experience provides an additional opportunity for students to benefit from detailed feedback on their writing skills. Some students even publish their scholarly work.[240]

Unfortunately, a seminar or independent study does not always provide a good research or writing experience. The faculty supervisor may not provide sufficient individualized feedback to the student. Even if feedback is given, the professor often focuses only on substance and offers little or no instruction or feedback on research and writing. In this situation, the student completes only one paper and does not learn the underlying principles of legal writing that can be generalized to future projects.

But with proper faculty supervision,[241] the upper-level scholarly paper may provide an important research and writing experience for students. In the final year in law school, the student is more likely to have developed sufficient doctrinal knowledge and analytical skills to undertake a highly sophisticated scholarly project. Because the

---

[239] ABA Standard 303(a)(2).

[240] Several law reviews accept student-authored articles from other law schools. *See* Nancy Levit et al., *Submission of Law Student Articles for Publication* (Sept. 2, 2016), SSRN: https://ssrn.com/abstract=1656395 or http://dx.doi.org/10.2139/ssrn.1656395.

[241] *See* Elizabeth Fajans & Mary R. Falk, *Comments Worth Making: Supervising Scholarly Writing in Law School*, 46 J. Legal Educ. 342 (1996).

student generally selects the specific topic, the student often has a strong incentive to prepare a quality paper with the guidance of a dedicated faculty mentor.

Seminar or independent study professors may wish to assign a text that addresses methods of scholarly writing.[242] Producing a scholarly paper is as much about the writing experience as the doctrinal substance. To ensure a more rewarding student experience, the professor should resist the tendency to focus primarily on doctrine and should structure the course so students begin the writing process early enough to allow time for several drafts. For example, the professor might review an annotated outline near the beginning of the semester, a first draft at mid-semester, and the final draft at the end of the semester.

If the professor offers guidance on writing as well as the doctrinal substance of the paper, conscientiously critiques the student's work, and requires several drafts and rewriting, the scholarly writing course can be an excellent educational experience.

iii. Judicial Opinion Writing

Judicial opinion writing, a more recent addition to the menu of advanced legal writing courses, offers a unique perspective on the legal process. Although law students read opinions in every course, they spend little time examining opinions as a unique writing format or analyzing how opinions are written and organized. Understanding the process of writing a judicial opinion helps students critically read and interpret opinions. The course may be especially valuable to students who aspire to become judicial clerks.

---

[242] *E.g.*, Jessica L. Clark & Kristen E. Murray, Scholarly Writing: Ideas, Examples, and Execution (2d ed. 2012); Elizabeth Fajans & Mary R. Falk, Scholarly Writing for Law Students: Seminar Papers, Law Review Notes & Law Review Competition Papers (5th ed. 2017); Eugene Volokh, Academic Legal Writing: Law Review Articles, Student Notes, Seminar Papers, and Getting on Law Review (5th ed. 2016).

The course provides an overview of the nature, types, purposes, philosophies, styles, and technical aspects of opinion writing by judges at all levels (state and federal, trial and appellate).[243] The course may explore such topics as the role and function of the judge in resolving conflicts and developing law, acceptable modes of judicial reasoning, the nature and scope of judicial discretion, methods of proof, distinguishing between law and fact, and the impact of judicial decisions on public policy. The course may include exercises in resolving hypothetical or pending cases and writing opinions or orders.

In 2017-18, 38 law schools reported offering an upper-level course devoted to judicial opinion writing for at least three consecutive academic years.[244]

b. Vertical Courses

In contrast to "horizontal" courses that allow LRW professors to introduce upper-level students to new and different types of legal documents, "vertical" writing courses are designed to delve more deeply into previously covered skills. Vertical courses allow students

---

[243] *See, e.g.,* RUGGERO J. ALDISERT, OPINION WRITING (3d ed. 2012); JILL BARTON, SO ORDERED: THE WRITER'S GUIDE FOR ASPIRING JUDGES, JUDICIAL CLERKS, AND INTERNS (2017); FEDERAL JUDICIAL CENTER, JUDICIAL WRITING MANUAL: A POCKET GUIDE FOR JUDGES (2d ed. 2013), https://www.law.upenn.edu/live/files/5466-writing-judicial-opinions; JOYCE J. GEORGE, JUDICIAL OPINION WRITING HANDBOOK (5th ed. 2007); PAUL W. KAHN, MAKING THE CASE: THE ART OF THE JUDICIAL OPINION (2016); Robert A. Leflar, *Quality in Judicial Opinions*, 3 PACE L. REV. 579 (1983); Richard A. Posner, *Judicial Opinions and Appellate Advocacy in Federal Courts—One Judge's Views*, 51 DUQ. L. REV. 3, 22-35 (2013); S. I. Strong, *Writing Reasoned Decisions and Opinions: A Guide for Novice, Experienced, and Foreign Judges*, 2015 J. DISP. RESOL. 93; James Boyd White, *Judicial Opinion Writing: What's an Opinion For?*, 62 U. CHI. L. REV. 1363 (1995).

[244] *2017-18 ALWD/LWI Institutional Survey*, *supra* note 99, at 38, Question 7.3.

to practice more complex aspects of a specific genre of legal writing to which they have already been introduced.

As discussed earlier in this chapter, the two most common legal documents covered in first-year LRW courses are the objective memorandum and the persuasive brief. Most vertical upper-level courses build on first-year instruction by covering more sophisticated aspects of objective and persuasive legal writing. Vertical courses include at least four subcategories: Advanced Appellate Advocacy, Advanced Persuasive Writing, Advanced Objective Writing, and Advanced Legal Research.

i. Advanced Appellate Advocacy

The most common vertical course is Advanced Appellate Advocacy.[245] This course builds directly on the first-year brief-writing experience by exploring more sophisticated aspects of appellate practice. In an Advanced Appellate Advocacy course, each student writes and rewrites one or more appellate briefs involving complex or novel legal issues. Generally the course covers the rules of appellate procedure, scope and standards of review, preservation of error, and the harmless error doctrine. Students are also instructed in the more advanced dimensions of appellate argument.

Many programs attempt to use complete records from actual cases, which may be obtained from appellate court files or other public agencies.[246] Some professors schedule visits to observe actual court arguments or arrange for appellate courts to hold arguments at

---

[245] *See* Smith, *supra* note 207.

[246] Appellate records suitable for persuasive writing assignments are published annually in *The Moot Court Casebook* by the New York University School of Law's Moot Court Board, https://www.nyumootcourt.org/casebook/ (last visited Jan. 11, 2020). Federal court records are available online from Public Access to Court Electronic Records (PACER), https://www.pacer.gov/ (last visited Jan. 11, 2020). Some court documents are also available from various online legal research services.

the law school. Sometimes the course is limited to moot court members or otherwise linked to student moot court competitions.

Advanced Appellate Advocacy courses allow students to confront more challenging issues than they were able to handle as first-year students. The opportunity to use full appellate records rather than the more limited records used in most first-year courses provides students valuable experience in identifying relevant facts and organizing briefs to address more complex legal issues.

ii. Advanced Persuasive Writing

The second type of vertical course is Advanced Persuasive Writing. Like Advanced Appellate Advocacy, these courses cover more advanced aspects of persuasive legal writing. However, the art of persuasive writing is explored more generally, beyond a specific type of document or legal practice.[247]

Rather than focusing on the components and format requirements of any specific legal instrument, Advanced Persuasive Writing courses address specific techniques and strategies of persuasion relevant to many types of persuasive writing. These courses also explore the theory behind effective persuasive writing, often borrowing from other disciplines such as classical rhetoric, psychology, and literary theory.[248]

---

[247] *See, e.g.*, MICHAEL R. SMITH, ADVANCED LEGAL WRITING: THEORIES AND STRATEGIES IN PERSUASIVE WRITING 5 (3d ed. 2013). *See generally* LOUIS J. SIRICO, JR. & NANCY L. SCHULTZ, PERSUASIVE LEGAL WRITING (4th ed. 2015). Professors Sirico and Schultz make this point most clearly in Chapters 13 and 14, which provide instruction in writing persuasively for a number of different audiences. *Id.* at 133-64.

[248] *See* SMITH, *supra* note 247, at 4-5; *see also* SIRICO, JR. & SCHULTZ, *supra* note 247, at 1-18 (discussing history of classical rhetoric and "The Psychology of Persuasion"). *See generally* JAMES BOYD WHITE, THE LEGAL IMAGINATION: STUDIES IN THE NATURE OF LEGAL THOUGHT AND EXPRESSION (1973) (exploring the "legal imagination" in reading and writing based on an eclectic mix of materials from various disciplines).

The assignments in these courses follow two basic models. The first is similar to that used in first-year courses and Advanced Appellate Advocacy courses: students draft one or two longer documents that apply all skills covered in the course. The second calls for numerous shorter exercises, each focusing on one specific persuasive writing skill or technique.[249]

iii. Advanced Objective Writing

Advanced Objective Writing is the third type of vertical upper-level legal writing course. Courses of this type build on first-year instruction on writing predictive law office memoranda. These courses allow the professor and students to explore more advanced dimensions of effective memo writing, often in the context of an assignment that calls for more sophisticated research and legal analysis.

Professors following this approach sometimes use an introductory legal writing text that provides more in-depth coverage and more complex assignments. Other professors use selected portions of more general advanced legal writing texts.

iv. Advanced Legal Research

A few law schools require an upper-level course addressing advanced techniques of legal research[250] or offer research training in specialized fields.[251] An increasing number offer advanced research

---

[249] *See* MICHAEL R. SMITH, TEACHER'S MANUAL: ADVANCED LEGAL WRITING: THEORIES AND STRATEGIES IN PERSUASIVE WRITING (3d ed. 2013).

[250] *See* Peter C. Schanck, *Mandatory Advanced Legal Research: A Viable Program for Law Schools?*, 92 LAW LIBR. J. 295 (2000).

[251] *See* Ann Hemmens, *Advanced Legal Research Courses: A Survey of ABA-Accredited Law Schools*, 94 LAW LIBR. J. 209 (2002); Matthew C. Cordon, *Beyond Mere Competency: Advanced Legal Research in a Practice-Oriented Curriculum*, 55 BAYLOR L. REV. 1 (2003); S. Blair Kaufman, *Advanced Legal*

courses as electives.[252] If these courses require students to prepare written documents, they provide important opportunities for students to hone writing skills as well.

One model allows students to choose a section devoted to a particular doctrinal specialty such as business law, family law, taxation, labor law, or intellectual property law. Students are taught how to use specialized treatises, administrative materials, looseleaf services, legislative histories, computerized data bases, and empirical data related to the specific field. Each student uses specialized research tools for the subject matter of the course to prepare one or more legal documents.

Another model focuses on research generally. Students explore research tools in depth and prepare "road maps" or "pathfinders" that explain how to find answers to legal questions within a specific subject matter using specialized research tools and sources.

Advanced Legal Research courses provide ideal opportunities to use qualified law librarians as instructors or as part of a team teaching the course. Law schools whose librarians are also lawyers have a uniquely valuable resource for offering specialized research instruction beyond the foundational skills students learn in required LRW courses.[253]

Research Courses: A New Trend in American Legal Education, 6 LEG. REF. SERV. Q. 123 (1986).

[252]Between 2002 and 2010, 33 law schools added an Advanced Legal Research course to the curriculum. Genevieve Tung, *Academic Law Libraries and the Crisis in Legal Education*, 105 LAW LIBR. J. 275, 288-89 (2013) (citing CARPENTER, *supra* note 36, at 74 fig. 60)).

[253]*See generally* Genevieve Tung, *Collaboration Between Legal Writing Faculty and Law Librarians: Two Surveys*, 23 LEGAL WRITING 215 (2019).

c. *Survey or Hybrid Courses*

The third general approach to teaching advanced legal writing combines the first two approaches. Survey or hybrid courses supplement foundational instruction in objective and persuasive writing by exploring advanced aspects of those skills (the vertical approach) and by introducing students to various new types of legal documents such as correspondence, contracts, litigation documents, scholarly articles, and judicial opinions (the horizontal approach). Some courses also include remedial instruction in basic legal writing skills.[254]

A survey course allows students to explore a wide array of advanced legal writing topics; on the other hand, breadth of coverage necessarily means less depth. For law schools lacking the faculty resources to offer multiple advanced writing courses, a survey course provides valuable experience for upper-level students, building on the foundational skills covered in required LRW courses.

d. *Integrated Courses*

Integrated courses represent the fourth general approach to teaching advanced legal writing. These courses can build on the required LRW program by integrating advanced writing instruction with another professional lawyering skill or with a doctrinal subject.[255]

---

[254] *See, e.g.*, ELIZABETH FAJANS, MARY R. FALK & HELENE S. SHAPO, WRITING FOR LAW PRACTICE: ADVANCED LEGAL WRITING (3d ed. 2015); MARY BARNARD RAY & BARBARA J. COX, BEYOND THE BASICS: A TEXT FOR ADVANCED LEGAL WRITING (3d ed. 2012).

[255] *See generally, e.g.*, Cynthia Batt, *A Practice Continuum: Integrating Experiential Education into the Curriculum*, 7 ELON L. REV. 119 (2015); Peter A. Joy, *The MacCrate Report: Moving Toward Integrated Learning Experiences*, 1 CLINICAL L. REV. 401 (1994).

i. Experiential Learning and Simulations

Experiential and simulation courses are two primary examples of integrated courses that sometimes include substantial advanced instruction and experience in professional legal writing along with other professional lawyering skills.

Current ABA accreditation standards require law students to complete a minimum of six credit hours in experiential courses,[256] which must, among other things, "integrate doctrine, theory, skills, and legal ethics, and engage students in performance of one or more . . . professional skills [needed for competent and ethical participation as a member of the legal profession]."[257] Experiential courses take three primary forms: simulations, live-client law clinics, and field placements.[258]

An important caveat to the ABA Standards cautions that an experiential course cannot satisfy more than one curriculum requirement.[259] For that reason, even if an upper-level experiential course

---

[256] ABA Standard 303(a)(3); *see* ABA Standard 304 (enumerating and defining experiential courses that satisfy Standard 303(a)(3)).

[257] ABA Standard 304(a)(1); *see* ABA Standard 302(d); ABA Interpretation 302-1 (enumerating "professional skills" inclusively "such as, interviewing, counseling, negotiation, fact development and analysis, trial practice, document drafting, conflict resolution, organization and management of legal work, collaboration, cultural competency, and self-evaluation"); *see also* Margaret Moore Jackson, *From Seminar to Simulation: Wading Out to the Third Wave*, 19 J. GENDER RACE & JUST. 127, 131 (2016) ("The revised [ABA] Standards also redefined the components of courses that satisfy what was formerly known as 'the skills requirement,' and which now should be called the 'experiential education' requirement." (citing ABA Standards 303, 304, 305 (2014-2015)).

[258] ABA Standard 304(a)-(d).

[259] ABA Standard 303, Interpretation 303-1.

> A law school may not permit a student to use a course to satisfy more than one requirement under this Standard. For example, a course that includes a writing experience used to satisfy the upper-class writing

includes a substantial, faculty-supervised legal writing experience, it cannot satisfy both the experiential course requirement and the upper-level writing requirement.[260]

Experiential or skills-based integrated courses combine upper-level instruction in legal writing with other professional skills such as client interviewing, client counseling, legal drafting, pretrial practice, trial practice, negotiation and other transactional skills, alternative dispute resolution, or appellate practice.[261] This kind of integrated legal writing instruction can take the form of a simulation course[262] or a legal clinic.[263]

> requirement [Standard 303(a)(2)] cannot be counted as one of the experiential courses required in Standard 303(a)(3). This does not preclude a law school from offering a course that may count either as an upper-class writing requirement or as a simulation course [Standards 304(a) and 304(b)] provided the course meets all of the requirements of both types of courses and the law school permits a student to use the course to satisfy only one requirement under this Standard.

Id. (brackets in original).

[260] *See* ABA Standard 303(a)(2) (requiring "one writing experience in the first year and *at least one additional writing experience after the first year*, both of which are faculty supervised" (emphasis added)).

[261] *See, e.g.*, Carol Goforth, *Transactional Skills Training Across the Curriculum*, 66 J. LEGAL EDUC. 904 (2017); Harris & Susman, *supra* note 46; Elizabeth M. Schneider, *Integration of Professional Skills into the Law School Curriculum: Where We've Been and Where We're Going*, 19 N.M. L. REV. 111 (1989); *cf.* Schultz, *supra* note 22.

[262] *See* ABA Standard 304(b). A simulation course "provides substantial experience not involving an actual client, that is reasonably similar to the experience of a lawyer advising or representing a client or engaging in other lawyering tasks in a set of facts and circumstances devised or adopted by a faculty member." *Id.*

[263] *See* ABA Standard 304(c). A clinical course "provides substantial lawyering experience that involves advising or representing one or more actual clients or serving as a third-party neutral." *Id.*; *see, e.g.*, Maureen E. Laflin, *Toward the Making of Good Lawyers: How an Appellate Clinic Satisfies the Professional Objectives of the MacCrate Report*, 33 GONZ. L. REV. 1 (1998); *supra* note 235 and

Experiential courses that integrate legal writing and legal drafting skills often require students to draft various types of legal documents related to the representation of a real or hypothetical client through the many stages of the legal process. These documents may include transactional documents, correspondence, memos, motions, pleadings, interrogatories, negotiation settlement agreements, jury instructions, trial briefs, and appellate briefs.

One strong advantage of integrating legal writing into an experiential course is that it teaches legal writing in a realistic professional context. Although law schools are increasingly adding professional context to first-year courses, many continue to teach foundational LRW in a "silo" by isolating it as an independent skill. As a consequence of integrating legal writing in the context of lawyering and legal problem-solving skills generally, upper-level students learn how legal analysis, research, and the writing process itself inform all other aspects of client representation.[264]

ii. Doctrine-Based Courses

The second approach integrates advanced legal writing instruction with a specific upper-level doctrinal subject such as real estate transactions or business associations.[265] Integrated courses of this kind focus on practical legal writing skills associated with a specific

accompanying text (citing other sources on integrating legal writing in law clinic courses).

[264] *See* Adam Lamparello & Charles E. MacLean, *Experiential Legal Writing: The New Approach to Practicing Like a Lawyer*, 39 J. LEGAL PROF. 135 (2015).

[265] *See, e.g.*, Barbara J. Busharis & Suzanne E. Rowe, *The Gordian Knot: Uniting Skills and Substance in Employment Discrimination and Federal Taxation Courses*, 33 J. MARSHALL L. REV. 303 (2000); Susan L. DeJarnatt, *In re MacCrate: Using Consumer Bankruptcy as a Context for Learning in Advanced Legal Writing*, 50 J. LEGAL EDUC. 50 (2000); Robert M. Jarvis, *Using Entertainment Law to Teach Legal Writing*, 3 ENT. & SPORTS L.J. 243 (1986); Susan E. Thrower, *Teaching Legal Writing through Subject-Matter Specialties: A Reconception of Writing across the Curriculum*, 13 LEGAL WRITING 3 (2007).

doctrine, as distinguished from traditional seminar courses that teach scholarly legal writing.[266] Integrating practice-oriented legal writing and analysis with doctrine allows students to appreciate how practical lawyering skills are necessarily interrelated with mastering the substance of a particular area of legal doctrine.[267]

Like experiential courses that integrate legal writing with other professional skills, courses that integrate legal writing with a particular doctrinal subject often require students to produce various types of legal documents relevant to the specific subject matter of the course.[268]

3. *Cocurricular and Extracurricular Advanced Instruction*

In addition to formal upper-level courses, numerous co-curricular and extra-curricular activities provide opportunities for advanced legal writing instruction. They include scholarly writing opportunities, moot court teams, bar exam preparation, and career placement services.

---

[266] *See supra* notes 239-42 and accompanying text (discussing traditional seminar courses).

[267] *See generally* Busharis & Rowe, *supra* note 265; Leigh Hunt Greenshaw, *"To Say What the Law Is": Learning the Practice of Legal Rhetoric*, 29 VAL. U. L. REV. 861 (1995). As one scholar explained, "[t]he effect is synergistic: students learn doctrine by using it practically and learn practical skills through an increasingly familiar branch of doctrine." DeJarnatt, *supra* note 265, at 56; *see also* Busharis & Rowe, *supra*, at 303-19 (discussing the "false dichotomy between 'skills' and 'substance'"); Greenshaw, *supra*, at 867 ("Legal composition and legal subject matter interact in ongoing rhetorical activity and are therefore best understood and best studied together.").

[268] *See, e.g.*, Busharis & Rowe, *supra* note 265, at 319-39 (discussing the various types of assignments in two integrated legal writing courses); DeJarnatt, *supra* note 265, at 62-68 (discussing the various types of assignments in an integrated legal writing and bankruptcy course).

a. Scholarly Writing

Nearly every law school provides students valuable opportunities to participate in law review. Most law reviews are competitive enterprises, but some law schools offer elective opportunities for students to participate in publishing online journals on special topics. In addition, many law-related organizations encourage students to engage in extracurricular writing opportunities by sponsoring scholarly writing competitions.[269]

i. Law Review

Members of a law school's law review generally undertake two kinds of responsibilities that provide advanced instruction in legal writing. The first involves their roles as authors of scholarly articles. The second involves their role as student editors of scholarly articles written by scholars or other students.

Authoring Scholarly Articles. Most law reviews require each member to write at least one scholarly paper of publishable quality. The paper may be written in the context of a write-on competition for law review membership or as a requirement for all law review members. Either way, these writing projects provide students with the opportunity to practice scholarly legal research and writing.

Law professors are frequently called upon to supervise or advise these projects. If a law school allows a student to satisfy the ABA's upper-level writing requirement by participating in law review, faculty supervision is required.[270] Of course, the nature and scope of faculty supervision must comply with the law review's rules and procedures.

---

[269] *See* Clark & Murray, *supra* note 218, at 531.

[270] *See* ABA Standard 303(a)(2) (providing that the required upper-level writing experience must be "faculty supervised").

Soliciting and Editing Scholarly Articles. The primary functions of a student law review are to solicit, edit, and publish scholarly articles. Consequently, law review members review, edit, and cite-check the scholarly work of others. Yet few law review members have experience or training in editing.

Whether acting formally as a law review faculty advisor or overseeing a more informal training session, an LRW faculty member can offer valuable instruction to law review members on a range of topics that will support their editorial roles. These topics include the nature of scholarly legal writing and how it differs from other forms of legal writing; the structure and components of effective scholarly writing including grammar, writing style, and citation; and the editorial process. Thus, law review responsibilities offer a variety of additional writing instruction in scholarly editing.

ii. Scholarly Writing Competitions

Each year, numerous legal organizations sponsor national writing competitions soliciting scholarly articles on a specified subject.[271] Most law schools maintain a current list of legal writing competitions on their websites.[272] Many of these competitions award money, prizes, and publication opportunities to law students. Law professors are frequently asked to supervise a student's submission.

A supervising professor should first become familiar with the rules of the competition. Most competitions set out detailed rules on such matters as the topic of the paper, eligibility requirements, the submission process, and format requirements. The professor should

---

[271] *See, e.g., Writing Competitions and Contests*, ABA FOR LAW STUDENTS, https://abaforlawstudents.com/events/law-student-competitions/writing-competitions/ (last visited Jan. 11, 2020). *See generally* LARRY L. TEPLY, LAW SCHOOL COMPETITIONS IN A NUTSHELL 9-10 (2003).

[272] *See, e.g., Law Student Writing Competitions & Associated Scholarships*, LEWIS & CLARK LAW SCHOOL, https://law.lclark.edu/academics/student_writing_competitions/ (last visited Dec. 14, 2019).

particularly note any rules that limit the scope of faculty guidance or supervision.

If competition rules permit, a professor can offer assistance in creating a schedule for accomplishing specific tasks; choosing a topic (to the extent competition rules allow flexibility); developing a thesis; developing research strategies; understanding the nature and conventions of scholarly writing and how it differs from other forms of legal writing; and critically analyzing the topic. A professor can also assist by reviewing drafts and providing feedback on substance and writing.

b. Moot Court Competitions

Interscholastic moot court competitions provide rich opportunities for learning more about persuasive legal writing.[273] Because many competitions limit the ways faculty can supervise brief-writing, the moot court writing experience is largely self-taught. Moreover, most competition rules provide that moot court briefs are written collaboratively by two or more moot court team members. Both features of moot court competition generally limit a student from using the moot court brief to satisfy the ABA's upper-level writing requirement.

Some schools teach an Advanced Appellate Advocacy course, which may be required for members of moot court competition teams. The course allows advanced coverage of such topics as standards of review, effective writing methods, oral argument techniques, and collaborative writing.[274]

---

[273] *See, e.g.*, LEGAL WRITING INSTITUTE ET AL., THE MOOT COURT ADVISOR'S HANDBOOK: A GUIDE FOR LAW STUDENTS, FACULTY, AND PRACTITIONERS (2015); SUE PAINTER-THORNE & KAREN J. SNEDDON, MOOT COURT WORKBOOK: FINDING EDUCATIONAL SUCCESS AND COMPETITION GLORY (2017); LARRY A. TEPLY, SUCCESSFULLY COMPETING IN U.S. MOOT COURT COMPETITIONS (2014); Dickerson, *supra* note 118; Hernandez, *supra* note 118.

[274] *See supra* notes 245-46 and accompanying text.

c. Bar Exam Preparation

Before 2008, ABA Standards either barred law schools from awarding any credit for bar examination preparation courses, or they precluded law schools from counting such credits toward the minimum number required to earn the law degree.[275] Two years after those limitations were dropped, close to half the law schools participating in an ABA curriculum survey were awarding academic credit for bar preparation courses.[276]

LRW faculty are sometimes consulted about the design of a bar preparation course. In some instances, they may be asked to teach it because of their specialized knowledge related to the legal analysis and writing skills assessed on the bar exam, particularly the Multistate Performance Test.[277] More significantly, a student's bar passage challenges are often a result of difficulties in expressing legal

---

[275] *See* Catherine L. Carpenter, *Recent Trends in Law School Curricula: Findings from the 2010 ABA Curriculum Survey*, 81 Bar Examiner 6, 9, 11 & n.12 (June 2012); Aleatra P. Williams, *The Role of Bar Preparation Programs in the Current Legal Education Crisis*, 59 Wayne L. Rev. 383, 401 (2013). Since 2008, law schools may "offer bar preparation courses for credit without any restrictions on the use of the credit earned." Carpenter, *supra*, at 11 & n.12.

[276] Carpenter, *supra* note 275, at 9; *see* Schulze, Jr., *supra* note 180, at 24–25 & n.161 (noting that since the ABA amended the Standards in 2008 to allow academic credit for bar preparation courses, "schools are intentionally using these classes to prepare students for success on state bar exams").

[277] *See* Sabrina DeFabritiis, *1L Is the New Bar Prep*, 51 Creighton L. Rev. 37, 38 (2017) ("[T]he skills we teach our students in their first-year legal-writing course . . . lay the foundation for success on the bar exam."); Maureen Straub Kordesh, *Reinterpreting ABA Standard 302(f) in Light of the Multistate Performance Test*, 30 U. Mem. L. Rev. 299 (2000). *See generally Multistate Performance Test,* Nat'l Conference of Bar Examiners, http://www.ncbex.org/exams/mpt/ (last visited Dec. 14, 2019).

> The MPT is designed to test an examinee's ability to use fundamental lawyering skills in a realistic situation and complete a task that a beginning lawyer should be able to accomplish. The MPT is not a test of substantive knowledge. Rather, it is designed to evaluate certain fundamental

analysis in writing, so a bar preparation course can encourage students at risk of failing the bar exam to consult with a legal writing professional.

Because bar preparation courses require intense one-on-one interaction, and because they are often best tailored to the particular needs of each student, the student-faculty ratio should be realistically low. Teaching loads for LRW faculty who are asked to add a bar exam preparation course should be adjusted accordingly.

d. Career Placement Workshops

The Placement or Career Services Office is generally just as concerned with the quality of students' legal research and writing skills as are LRW faculty. Based on their personal experience with practicing lawyers and hiring partners, those charged with helping law students find jobs know how important these skills are to employers. Placement office workshops that focus on how to write cover letters, prepare resumes, and select writing samples can provide good opportunities for cooperation between LRW faculty and placement officers.

The level of involvement varies widely depending on the resources and culture of each law school. Some LRW courses assign students to write cover letters and resumes as exercises in persuasion and as part of the regular coursework. Writing faculty may offer to present workshops, consult with career services staff on designing workshops, or merely serve as a resource, either to meet faculty service obligations or for additional compensation.

---

skills lawyers are expected to demonstrate regardless of the area of law in which the skills are applied.

Id.

D. Incorporating Writing in Other Courses

Although writing is most commonly understood to be a form of communication, writing is also "a form of thinking."[278] As noted earlier in this *Sourcebook*, "writing to learn" is an approach that can be used in any class to help students think and "to enhance students' learning of the underlying subject matter" of the course.[279] Enhanced learning is unquestionably a desirable outcome for student learners, but professors also benefit when they embrace writing as a teaching tool:

> Professors who successfully integrate writing and other critical thinking activities into their courses often report a satisfying increase in their teaching pleasure: students are better prepared for class, discussions are richer, and student performance improves.[280]

What teacher would not want to see such results? The challenge for most, however, is how to do it.

1. How Writing Promotes Deep Learning

Writing helps students learn in several ways. First, writing enhances the classroom experience. "Good assignments . . . give students opportunities to receive early feedback on their work, encourage meaning-making, and clearly explain the instructor's expectations & purpose."[281]

---

[278] WILLIAM ZINSSER, WRITING TO LEARN vii (1988).

[279] *See supra* Chapter I, Part D.

[280] JOHN C. BEAN, ENGAGING IDEAS: THE PROFESSOR'S GUIDE TO INTEGRATING WRITING, CRITICAL THINKING, AND ACTIVE LEARNING IN THE CLASSROOM 2 (2011).

[281] *Id.* at 1 (citing P. Anderson et al., *Using Results from the Consortium for the Study of Writing in College*, NAT'L SURVEY OF STUDENT ENGAGEMENT (2009) (webinar handout)). The webinar handout is available at http://nsse.indiana.edu/html

Writing also promotes engagement with the subject matter. As a matter of fact, "[t]he relationship between the amount of writing for a course and students' level of engagement—is stronger than the relationship between students' engagement and any other course characteristic."[282] This relationship holds true "whether engagement is measured by time spent on the course, or the intellectual challenge it presents, or students' level of interest in it."[283]

Finally, and perhaps most importantly for law students, writing improves critical thinking:

> [T]he most intensive and demanding tool for eliciting sustained critical thought is a well-designed writing assignment on a subject matter problem. [W]riting is closely linked with thinking and . . . in presenting students with significant problems to write about . . . we can promote their general cognitive and intellectual growth. When we make students struggle with their writing, we are making them struggle with thought itself. Emphasizing writing and critical thinking, therefore, generally increases the academic rigor of a course. Often the struggle of writing . . . awakens students to the real nature of learning.[284]

2. *Misapprehensions About Using Writing in the Classroom*

If writing enhances student learning, student engagement, and teacher satisfaction, why don't all law professors incorporate

---

/NSSEPubSearch.cfm?SearchPubFormFlag=yes&search_keywords=Writing#webinars (last visited Nov. 6, 2019).

[282] BEAN, *supra* note 280, at 1 (citing RICHARD J. LIGHT, MAKING THE MOST OF COLLEGE: STUDENTS SPEAK THEIR MINDS 55 (2001)).

[283] *Id.*

[284] *Id.* at xvi.

writing projects into their teaching? Several common misapprehensions prevent teachers of traditional law school courses from adding writing projects to their teaching tool kit. Most of these misapprehensions are rooted in a tendency to think of "writing" only as a subject—i.e., Freshman Composition—rather than as a teaching and learning tool.

Perhaps the most common misapprehension is the belief that one can add writing to the course only by subtracting something more valuable: subject matter content and coverage. A teacher can use writing, however, without having to teach writing. Indeed, although many—if not most—law professors use the traditional essay as a summative assessment of student knowledge at the end of a course, most of them do not devote class time to teaching essay-writing. An easy way to harness the power of writing as a teaching and learning tool is to use it for formative assessment throughout a course.

Numerous resources provide short, "low-stakes" writing assignments that are easy to incorporate into any class without diverting significant time or attention from subject matter coverage. Reading logs, guided note-taking, class summaries, and countless other short assignments can help students learn to focus their study time and sharpen the in-class experience. Writing practice exam questions can help students identify the key concepts and skills that the professor is trying to teach in a particular class.[285]

Other more complex assignments can help students synthesize material and improve long-term retention. One of the contributors to this *Sourcebook*, for example, requires her Family Law students

---

[285] *See generally, e.g.*, *WAC Clearinghouse,* Colo. State Univ., https://wac.colostate.edu/resources/wac/intro/wtl/wtlactivities/ (last visited Dec. 14, 2019); *Low-Stakes Assignments,* DePaul Teaching Commons, https://resources.depaul.edu/teaching-commons/teaching-guides/feedback-grading/Pages/low-stakes-assignments.aspx (last visited Dec. 14, 2019).

to create one-page conceptual or analytical depictions of discrete subjects such as the legal requirements for a valid marriage. Working in pairs or trios outside class, students must synthesize the material they have studied, understand how the various topics are connected, and create a "picture" of the subject—e.g., a flow chart, concept map, or similar visual depiction—rather than a traditional outline of information. The activity promotes deeper learning and broader understanding by requiring students to wrestle with the subject in a meaningful way. A short in-class discussion of the students' work requires no more time than an end-of-semester exam review, but the timeliness of the review promotes long-term retention.

Professors may also avoid incorporating writing into their classes based on the erroneous belief that the associated grading load will divert time from other job responsibilities such as scholarship, class preparation, and service. In fact, however, a professor has several alternatives to ensure that students receive adequate and meaningful feedback on their work without the need to review and respond to each assignment individually.

Checklists and rubrics can be used very effectively, and while they require some preparation time up front, once created they can be reused and adapted from year to year. Teachers can use these tools to review student work themselves, but they can also be used as tools for student self-assessment or peer review.

Another effective assessment tool for small, focused writing assignments is "calibrated peer review" (CPR), developed at the University of California-Los Angeles.[286] Although first used in chemistry courses, the approach has been used in a variety of

---

[286] *See* Arlene A. Russell, *Calibrated Peer Review—A Writing and Critical-Thinking Instructional Tool*, *in* TEACHING TIPS: INNOVATIONS IN UNDERGRADUATE SCIENCE INSTRUCTION 54 (Marvin Druger et al. eds., 2004).

disciplines, including law.[287] A CPR assignment requires students to complete a short writing assignment—often just a paragraph—and submit it online. "Calibration" examples are provided to train students how to be effective reviewers of the assignment. The students first review the work of three peers and then review their own work. Professors must prepare the assignment and the "calibration" examples, but the rest of the work is done online by the students. As with checklists and rubrics, many self- and peer-review assignments, like CPR, can be reused with little if any revision. To reap the benefits of writing-to-learn, professors may need to devote some time to planning, but thereafter they need not devote time to grading and assessing reams of student work.

Some professors labor under a related misapprehension that feedback on writing means correcting grammar, punctuation, and citation—things the professors may not want to do or fear they lack the training to do. Not all writing, however, needs to be assessed for these technical skills. An effective writing-to-learn assignment begins with a specific pedagogical purpose; student work should be evaluated to determine if the purpose of the assignment was achieved. Unless a professor intends to teach writing mechanics, there is no need to assess students' mechanical proficiency.

This is not to say that professors will not become aware of deficiencies in some students' basic writing skills. They will. But this awareness will provide professors with valuable insight into their students' level of general preparedness for legal study. The practice also helps professors determine whether a student doesn't understand a substantive concept, or does understand it but can't

---

[287] For example, Professors Iva Ferrell and Susan King of Widener University Delaware Law School delivered a presentation at the 2014 Legal Writing Institute Biennial Conference on using CPR in a law school class. *See* Iva J. Ferrell & Susan A. King, *Calibrated Peer Review: Report from a Two-Year Study*, https://www.lwionline.org/conferences/2014-biennial-conference (link to conference resources) (last visited Dec. 14, 2019).

convey that understanding effectively in writing. Professors who rely solely on Socratic dialogue and in-class discussion may not have the opportunity to discover that many students face these kinds of learning challenges. When a writing assignment reveals writing and thinking problems, that information can inform and improve one's teaching. The feedback from students also enables professors to refer a student for additional support while the student still has time to take meaningful steps to improve.

The final major misapprehension about using writing as a teaching tool is the belief that writing projects "work" in courses like Appellate Advocacy, Judicial Writing, Legislative Drafting, or Contract Drafting, but not in doctrine-specific courses such as Family Law, Secured Transactions, or Conflicts. This belief confuses genre and document design with content. Appellate briefs, judicial opinions, statutes, and transactional documents are specific genres or legal documents; they are subject to certain content requirements and structural conventions that skilled lawyers must master to qualify as "legal writers." Writing-to-learn assignments, on the other hand, can be designed to serve any pedagogical goal, from remembering the elements of a rule in Torts to engaging in self-reflection in a field placement. The content and structure are not pre-ordained but rather chosen by the professor to enhance learning and achieve specific objectives. If a professor has a lesson to teach, a writing assignment can be the perfect way to teach it.

3. *How to Make It Work*

When a faculty member decides to incorporate writing into a course, the bulk of the work must be done before the course begins. Advance planning is essential to assure that a project is well-designed and well-implemented. To realize the greatest benefit from writing as a teaching and learning tool, a teacher must do the planning with three things in mind: (1) what students should learn, (2) the kind of writing assignment or project that will best advance that learning objective, and (3) the amount of time students and faculty can reasonably allocate to the project.

When using writing as a teaching tool, less is more: "[F]or promoting engagement and deep learning the number of writing assignments in a course may not be as important as the design of the writing assignments themselves."[288] Accordingly, it is wise to begin with one or two simple assignments. For example, a professor might hand out index cards and ask students to spend the last three to five minutes of class jotting down the key "take-aways" from the day's class or explaining why the student would like further instruction on a particular concept or topic. Similar easy-to-execute ideas can be found online, and many universities have teaching and learning centers and writing specialists who are well-equipped to help professors design effective low-stakes writing projects.

Having experienced success with a simple project, professors can consider other opportunities to incorporate writing into their classes as they teach the course. They will then have ample time to design other projects before teaching the class again. When a professor embraces writing as a tool to improve teaching and enhance student learning and engagement, all members of the learning community benefit.

---

[288] BEAN, *supra* note 280, at 1 (citing P. Anderson et al., *supra* note 281).

III. PEDAGOGICAL METHODS IN FIRST-YEAR COURSES

A. Teaching Classes

Effective, well-planned teaching is critical to student success and satisfaction. This is especially true in a first-year LRW course. Though some form of Socratic method is used in most law school courses, there is no single, consensus approach for teaching LRW. Given the hands-on approach to skills instruction and the growing understanding of the value of experiential learning, LRW classes rarely rely on the Socratic method. In addition, LRW is typically the only skills course in the first-year curriculum; therefore, there are often stark differences between how LRW is taught and how most other first-year courses are taught.

Because analysis, writing, and research skills are seldom taught effectively by lecture or Socratic dialogue alone, creativity and variety in planning each class session are essential in the LRW classroom. Teaching a "how-to" process is a more complicated activity than a deliver-and-absorb process of teaching information. LRW professors typically teach research and writing skills in the context of applying legal doctrine to solve problems, so LRW professors must be prepared to teach both substance and skills in their classrooms. While some of these skills can be learned by reading and unguided practice, most can be developed only with guided practice and feedback.

1. Teaching Techniques

To teach skills, LRW courses rely fundamentally on students drafting and redrafting memoranda and other written assignments, and professors providing feedback on that work. But LRW professors also choose from a variety of other teaching techniques to complement the core assignments. The following techniques can work separately or together:

Short lecture. Lecture can be an effective means of introducing new information or providing skills instruction. The LRW professor should ensure that lecture material neither merely repeats assigned readings nor disregards assigned readings entirely. Students will soon stop reading their texts if they learn that the class period will be devoted to the professor reciting assignments verbatim or that the readings have no bearing on the course content or instruction. Professors should use assigned reading as a foundation to build on in class and at a minimum add new information and examples. Many professors also give short reading quizzes to keep students accountable for the assigned reading. Increasingly, faculty are providing short lectures in recorded format for students to review before or after a given class session.

Interactive discussion. A professor may choose to combine lecture with Socratic dialogue.[1] This approach engages the students more than passive listening and also allows the professor to better gauge whether the students understand the material. For instance, Socratic dialogue can be effective when students are analyzing the cases they will use in drafting a written assignment, particularly for synthesizing ideas from several cases. It can also be useful in group work as the professor moves from group to group, engaging in a short Socratic dialogue with each. In this type of discussion, students can be asked to provide written responses, such as writing on a blackboard, whiteboard, or editable electronic document.

Collaborative learning. Collaborative learning can be empowering for students and helpful in developing teamwork and community. It can be the basis for small projects or an entire course.[2]

---

[1] *See* Mary Kate Kearney & Mary Beth Beazley, *Teaching Students How to "Think Like Lawyers": Integrating Socratic Method With the Writing Process*, 64 TEMP. L. REV. 885 (1991).

[2] *See* Elizabeth L. Inglehart, Kathleen Dillon Narko & Clifford S. Zimmerman, *From Cooperative Learning to Collaborative Writing in the Legal Writing Classroom*, 9 LEGAL WRITING 185 (2003).

Collaborative learning requires students to learn from each other and to experience alternative ways of approaching a task.[3] For instance, students who work collaboratively on a research project can help each other learn how to use the resources, overcome obstacles that one person might not be able to navigate alone, and offer alternative viewpoints that one student alone could not generate. Professors can also promote the value of collaboration as a lawyering skill and use that idea as a starting point for further collaborative work. Students can discuss the pros and cons of collaboration in the workplace, conduct a self-assessment of their own strengths and weaknesses in a collaborative setting, and evaluate each other at the end of collaborative projects.

In-class and out-of-class exercises. A professor may use exercises designed to help students prepare for class or to practice a specific skill. For example, a professor might have students work individually or in groups to make a sample brief more persuasive. Professors can also ask students to tackle research assignments together or to prepare a settlement agreement working in teams.

Short writings. Short writings at the beginning or end of class and short reaction papers give students an opportunity to reflect on what they are learning and to gather their thoughts before or after a class session. These short writings also provide valuable feedback to the professor on what students are learning.

Small-group work. Dividing a class into small groups and assigning tasks to those groups can foster collaborative learning and teach the skills necessary to work in groups or teams on LRW tasks. Because group work may present unique challenges, a professor should strive to design group work carefully, to articulate the performance requirements clearly, to have a well-articulated system for student assessment, and to budget time for both group work

---

[3] *See* Clifford S. Zimmerman, *"Thinking Beyond My Own Interpretation:" Reflections on Collaborative and Cooperative Learning Theory in the Law School Curriculum*, 31 ARIZ. ST. L.J. 957 (1999).

and sharing information after group work. While allowing students to form their own groups can be a comfortable way to start group work, professors should also assign students to groups so each student engages with more classmates and learns to work with different personality types.

Role-playing. Role-playing is an effective and exciting teaching method for skills that involve interaction with another person. Students can interview a client, mediate a dispute, or engage in oral argument. Students can learn from playing the role of a lawyer, a client, or a judge. The most effective use of role-playing provides students the opportunity to reflect on the experience with an oral or written "debriefing."

A level of realism can be brought to the role-play by having non-class members play some or all of the parts. Professors have also engaged non-LRW professors and school administrators in role-playing, which accomplishes two purposes. It gives students the opportunity to work with an unfamiliar person, and it allows non-LRW colleagues to see up close the important work done in the LRW classroom.

Modeling. The LRW professor may model a skill for the students. For example, a professor may model the process of editing a draft document or introducing an oral argument. Demonstrating the process often makes students aware of the thought processes as well as the actions involved in the task. In addition, the professor may present a model document, showing students a particular type of document and labeling its various analytical parts.

Peer critique. Students can be taught how to critique each other's drafts.[4] Effective peer critique initially requires teaching the students how to offer feedback, and then guiding or structuring their peer-review work, perhaps by offering checklists or a list of

---

[4]*See* Jo Anne Durako, *Peer Editing: It's Worth the Effort*, 7 PERSPS. 73 (1999); Kirsten K. Davis, *Designing and Using Peer Review in a First-Year Legal Research and Writing Course*, 9 LEGAL WRITING 1 (2003).

prompts. Supervision of the peer critique process will be necessary at first to ensure that students are participating fully and giving balanced and helpful comments.

Group critique. An LRW professor may choose to offer group critiques on some assignments. Rather than commenting individually on papers, or in addition to giving abbreviated comments on each paper, the professor may make copies of representative drafts and use them to discuss common problems and areas to correct. While this approach is faster than commenting fully on each student's individual draft, the professor must go through all the drafts to know what problems to highlight and must take care that students do not feel singled out. Group critique can also be used as an in-class exercise: small groups can critique the samples together before engaging in a large-group discussion.

Quizzes. As mentioned earlier, a short quiz at the beginning or end of class—or delivered online between class meetings—can highlight material students are expected to know and give the professor feedback on whether the students are learning the assigned material. Such quizzes can provide useful checks on student reading or promote review of class instruction. Even a short quiz on reading comprehension can be enough to incentivize student engagement with the material.

Pre-recorded demonstrations. Many organizations and commercial publishers offer recorded scenarios for skills training.[5] Using a pre-recorded scenario offers variety and focused instruction, especially when students are asked to engage in discussion afterwards or to respond in writing to questions raised by the experience.

Guest lectures. A guest lecturer can effectively provide context for a skill that students are learning or impress upon them the importance of the skill. Possible guests range from upper-level

---

[5] *See generally, e.g.*, National Institute for Trial Advocacy (NITA), http://www.nita.org (last visited Dec. 14, 2019).

students reporting on their experiences in clerkships and internships to judges discussing effective written and oral advocacy.

Field trips. Students can take field trips to local courts to hear oral arguments, to watch hearings or trials, and to meet with judges or judicial clerks. These trips can be made as a whole class, in small groups, or as individuals. They should be done with purpose and include a post-trip reflection or debriefing.

It is critical for the professor to be selective and thoughtful about both field trips and classroom visitors. In addition to "success" as a lawyer or in other legal work, consider professionalism, diversity, and a commitment to ethical lawyering when selecting speakers or hosts for field trips.

Workshops and tutorials. Optional workshops and tutorials can be used to augment classroom coverage of certain topics. Optional workshops can provide instruction focused on a single skill or issue and can offer instruction that is more basic or advanced than general class instruction. These workshops can be offered by the professor, teaching assistants, writing specialists, academic support staff, or others. As supplements to the normal course content, they can be offered to all students who self-select additional instruction, or to students referred for additional instruction based on an observed need.

Alternative learning opportunities. In addition to the more traditional learning opportunities detailed above, professors should think expansively about how to create a community of learners. Some professors have experimented with classroom instruction in different venues: the idea is to offer a more accessible location to build trust and community. In these alternative sites, professors review papers, offer feedback, or conduct conferences. Professors have met with their class in coffee shops, in the law school library, in the atrium, or in other meeting spaces on campus. One professor hosts a "Lounge" or Writing Lab at night to encourage students to join one another to edit and review their papers.

2. *Teaching and Learning Theories*

In addition to implementing a range of teaching techniques, the LRW community is increasingly turning to teaching and learning theory to shape classroom instruction.[6] These learning theories include sensory-based theory, cognitive theory, personality-based theory, and adult learning theory. While a full discussion of each theory is beyond the scope of this *Sourcebook*, detailed readings can be found in the footnotes. The following paragraphs set out a brief description of each learning theory.

Sensory-based theories analyze learning based on whether information is taken in visually, aurally, or kinesthetically.[7] Typical law school instruction is primarily visual and secondarily aural; students read to absorb information visually and then engage in Socratic dialogues or listen to lectures that require auditory input. The LRW course is often the only first-year course with a kinesthetic or "learning by doing" component, such as walking through the library to conduct legal research or standing before a judge to deliver an oral argument.

Cognitive theories analyze the way the brain works in taking in and processing new information. Cognitive theories may be based on age-related developmental stages, on student preferences for reflective or active interaction with the information, or on sophistication in the ability to manipulate information.[8] In considering a theory

---

[6] *See, e.g.*, Robin A. Boyle, *Employing Active-learning Techniques and Metacognition in Law School: Shifting Energy from Professor to Student*, 81 U. DET. MERCY L. REV. 1 (2003); *see also* Michael Hunter Schwartz, *Teaching Law by Design: How Learning Theory and Instructional Design Can Inform and Reform Law Teaching*, 38 SAN DIEGO L. REV. 347 (2001) (criticizing traditional law school teaching and proposing a pedagogy consistent with insights from learning theory).

[7] *See* M.H. Sam Jacobson, *A Primer on Learning Styles: Reaching Every Student*, 25 SEATTLE U. L. REV. 139 (2001).

[8] *See id.*

that sets out sequenced stages of information processing, professors might similarly sequence their courses to start with simple levels of information processing such as memorization, and progress to more sophisticated levels such as synthesis.

Personality-based theories include the popular Myers-Briggs Type Indicator (MBTI). They analyze learning preferences by relating them to personality categories.[9] Some schools use these theories extensively, testing not only incoming students but also faculty members to enable them to understand their students' learning preferences as well as their own teaching preferences.

Adult learning theories analyze the ways that adults prefer to learn. Adult learning theories emphasize respect for the life experiences that adult learners bring with them and the importance of offering choice and control over the learning environment.[10] They also emphasize that adult learners are practical and goal oriented. Professors who shape their teaching to the needs of adult learners may share, rather than impose, some teaching decisions to allow adult learners to contribute to the construction of their learning environment.

Metacognitive practices, which explicitly build in time for self-reflection and steps to better guide students' thought processes, have also been increasingly added to the LRW curriculum. As lifelong learners, lawyers must develop a strong skill for self-regulated

---

[9] *See* Vernellia R. Randall, *The Myers-Briggs Type Indicator, First Year Law Students and Performance*, 26 CUMB. L. REV. 63 (1995). *But see* M.H. Sam Jacobson, *Using the Myers-Briggs Type Indicator to Assess Learning Style: Type or Stereotype?*, 33 WILLAMETTE L. REV. 261 (1997).

[10] Adult learning theory is widely discussed in clinical education. *See, e.g.*, Betty J. Luke, *The Ethos and Pathos of Ethics and Law Students: A Clinician's Perspective*, 45 S. TEX. L. REV. 843 (2004).

learning.[11] Self-reflective practices that reinforce metacognition are one step toward this goal. For example, some professors include a "cognitive protocol"[12] with assignments. These short exercises help students think explicitly about their writing process. The goal is to help them duplicate steps that made them successful and avoid steps that were not helpful. Cognitive protocols can be completed before and after assignment submission, and then reviewed just before graded assignments are returned. Some LRW textbooks are now explicitly incorporating prompts to spark metacognitive practices around legal writing.[13]

B. Commenting on Papers

One of the most important teaching methods used in LRW instruction is direct commenting on students' written work. This type of direct feedback, typically offered throughout an LRW course, stands in stark contrast to the typical "final exam" or "mid-term and final exam" model of assessment used in most law school courses. Direct feedback on student work can take multiple forms including critiquing papers (either in writing with electronically embedded comments or orally with audiotaped comments), offering in-class review, holding individual student-teacher conferences, and grading. The critique of student work is a critical anchor in the feedback loop between professor and student. It is also a staple of

---

[11] Anthony Niedwiecki, *Lawyers and Learning: A Metacognitive Approach to Legal Education*, 13 Widener L. Rev. 33 (2006).

[12] Professor Sophie Sparrow has been recognized for developing the use of cognitive protocols in LRW assignments. For a list of selected publications, see her faculty biography at https://law.unh.edu/person/sophie-sparrow (last visited Dec. 14, 2019).

[13] *See* Camille Lamar Campbell & Olympia Duhart, Persuasive Legal Writing: A Storytelling Approach (2017).

formative assessment,[14] an area that has gained traction in doctrinal classes because of substantially revised ABA Standards.[15] In LRW circles, however, formative assessment has long been the cornerstone of effective instruction.

1. Critiquing Written Work

Critiquing individual memos with written or oral comments is the most common way LRW professors give students feedback on written work. Several extensive articles and every legal writing conference offer detailed instruction on how to comment effectively on papers.[16] Characteristics of effective critique include the following:

- *Effective use of margin and end comments.* Effective critique offers comments both within and at the end of the text. Comments within the text focus on specific features: the use of a case, the precision and accuracy of an idea, the wordiness of a passage, or the format of a citation. Comments at the end of the text—end or global comments—often focus on general strengths and weaknesses of the paper and identify what the student should work on in the next draft or assignment (e.g.,

---

[14] Olympia Duhart, *The 'F' Word: The Top Five Complaints (and Solutions) About Formative Assessment*, 67 J. LEGAL EDUC. 531 (2018).

[15] Section of Legal Educ. & Admissions to the Bar, *ABA Standards and Rules of Procedure for Approval of Law Schools (2019-2020)*, ABA: AM. BAR. ASS'N, Standard 314 (Assessment of Student Learning), https://www.americanbar.org/content/dam/aba/administrative/legal_education_and_admissions_to_the_bar/standards/2019-2020/2019-2020-aba-standards-chapter3.pdf. *See supra* Chapter I, Part B.

[16] *See, e.g.*, Linda L. Berger, *A Reflective Rhetorical Model: The Legal Writing Teacher as Reader and Writer*, 6 LEGAL WRITING 57 (2000); Anne Enquist, *Critiquing and Evaluating Law Students' Writing: Advice from Thirty-Five Experts*, 22 SEATTLE U. L. REV. 1119 (1999); Jane Kent Gionfriddo, *'The Reasonable Zone of Right Answers': Analytical Feedback on Student Writing*, 40 GONZ. L. REV. 427 (2005); Kearney & Beazley, *supra* note 1.

"Three strengths of your paper are . . . . Three areas that you need to work on are . . . .")[17]

- *Distinguishing between formative and summative comments.*[18] The terms *formative* and *summative* distinguish between comments that help improve the paper and those that assess the demonstrated level of merit or proficiency. When commenting on drafts, LRW professors offer formative comments. These comments may ask a question, refer the student to the text or a class session, make a suggestion, or offer a possible change. Summative comments that a draft (or part of it) is "good" or "on the right track," without more, do not explain how the student might improve the work. They merely assess the quality of the writing at the time the professor wrote the comment.

- *Drafting comments that help the student improve the draft while retaining student ownership of it.* Comments should be sufficient for the student to understand and act upon, but not overwhelming. Comments should be in the form of instruction rather than editing. Students will often view a professor's editing as "the things that need to be fixed" and limit revisions to those specific issues or instances. Experienced LRW faculty avoid editing or rewriting the student paper themselves. A critique—in which the teacher points out problems, identifies strengths, and suggests avenues for research or revision—is significantly different from an edit, in which a reviewer crosses out words and inserts new ones and adds

---

[17] *See* Richard K. Neumann Jr., *A Preliminary Inquiry into the Art of Critique*, 40 Hastings L.J. 725 (1989).

[18] *See* Brooke K. Horvath, *The Components of Written Response: A Practical Synthesis of Current Views*, *in* The Writing Teacher's Sourcebook 207-08 (Gary Tate & Edward P.J. Corbett eds., 2d ed. 1988) (article originally published in 2 Rhetoric Rev. 136 (1984)).

or deletes citations to specific authorities.[19] A student whose paper is edited merely manufactures the editor's suggested product. A student whose paper is properly critiqued must still make the research, writing, and revision decisions necessary to create a new product.

One challenge in providing comments on student writing is balancing the desire to identify all student errors (thereby putting the student on notice and justifying the grade) with providing an amount of feedback that a student can process (thereby maximizing student improvement and assisting a student in evaluating the relative importance of mistakes). Experienced LRW faculty offer fewer comments and explain more explicitly which errors are significant and which are merely technical. The "less is more" approach recognizes two important truths: (1) students can get overwhelmed, lost, or both if faced with too many edits on a page, and (2) LRW faculty members are always pressed for time and therefore must be selective in giving feedback.

- *Drafting comments that the student understands.* Offering effective comments is time-consuming because they are more often narratives rather than labels. Writing "awk" or "good" in the margin is quick, but not very helpful to a student who has no idea what "awk" means, why the writing is "awk," or how to remedy the "awk-ness."

  Increasingly, LRW professors are using word processing software[20] to comment on student writing. Collecting, commenting on, and returning student work in digital form can

---

[19] *See generally* STEPHEN V. ARMSTRONG & TIMOTHY P. TERRELL, THINKING LIKE A WRITER: A LAWYER'S GUIDE TO EFFECTIVE WRITING AND EDITING (3d ed. 2008).

[20] One popular program, for instance, is Annotate. *Annotate PRO: Legal Writing Edition*, ANNOTATE PRO, http://www.11trees.com/live/annotate-pro/annotate-for-word-legal-writing-edition/ (last visited Dec. 14, 2019).

reduce paperwork, make one's stack of memos to be graded more portable, and provide comments that are more readable than (at least some) professors' handwriting. Technology can also facilitate the commenting process by allowing for the use of macros that address the most common writing problems and thus fairly quickly produce a personalized comment sheet or embedded comments in the student's paper. A similar approach can be used with a printed sheet of generic comments referenced by number at appropriate places on the student's paper. But the LRW professor must still be careful to individualize comments for those problems that are not generic and are critical to the author's ability to revise effectively.

- *Drafting balanced comments.* LRW professors should strive for balance in their comments, pointing out strengths as well as weaknesses in a student's writing. It is easy for a novice LRW professor to see little good in a draft (out of inexperience, the novice professor may expect that students will be able to successfully apply everything they have been taught thus far in the course) and react with a series of harsh comments intended to be constructive. A student who is too discouraged by a barrage of negative comments, however, may see little point in trying to fix the draft and disengage from the learning process altogether. Often, an invitation to the student to explain the student's thinking can provoke more progress than a condemnation of the poorly written or thought-out passage.
- *Offering comments that relate to the basis for evaluation.* Comments on a draft should relate to the criteria used in evaluating the final product. One way to relate comments to grading criteria is to create a commenting/grading rubric or checklist and to use variations of it for both commenting on the draft and evaluating the final product. If time permits, involving the class in drafting the checklist is an effective teaching tool. Professors must remain free, however, to modify the rubric

as they proceed with the evaluation process and see what students are actually doing.

Yet a rubric/checklist[21] alone is an ineffective method of critiquing a draft. Checking off items on a checklist is more summative than formative, unless the items offer narrative instructions on how the student can improve. Combining sufficient individualized margin comments with an end comment that includes a rubric/checklist is a good solution.

- *Drafting comments that prepare the student for an effective writing conference.* Legal writing faculty who offer or require conferences should keep those conferences in mind when drafting comments. For example, the final comment can set an agenda for the conference, identifying topics for discussion. The professor may even require the student to complete some sort of preparation for the conference. For example, if research is weak, the professor may suggest a research path and ask the student to bring the results to the conference. If the student seems to have misunderstood a significant case, the professor can ask the student to brief the case and bring both the case and the brief to the conference.

- *Clarifying responsibility for revision.* Students should understand all the sources from which they will get feedback on a paper and their responsibility to draw on all those sources when revising a draft. Students should understand that the lack of a written comment on a paper does not excuse them from correcting a problem not specifically marked. While the LRW professor should certainly address major problems in a draft by offering written comments or discussing them in a student conference, other problems may be addressed in group critiques, in a feedback memo to the class, or by other less-individualized approaches. Students should be aware that

[21] Sophie M. Sparrow, *Describing the Ball: Improve Teaching by Using Rubrics—Explicit Grading Criteria*, 2004 MICH. ST. L. REV. 1, 1 (2004).

simply fixing—or attempting to fix—everything marked on a paper will not guarantee a better grade.

To give quality feedback and comment effectively on student papers, LRW professors must be able to identify the strengths and weaknesses in a paper, communicate those strengths and weaknesses in a way that is understandable to the student writer, and suggest ways to improve upon the weaknesses clearly enough that the student can carry out the suggested revisions. Often, however, effective critique requires more elaboration than is feasible on the student's paper. If the critique will be followed by an individual student conference, the comments might include a prompt to discuss certain points more fully then.

2. *In-Class Review*

In-class reviews after each assignment give the LRW professor the opportunity to review with the entire class the goals of an assignment, the process followed in researching and writing the assignment, the strengths and weaknesses demonstrated in the papers submitted, and the lessons to be carried over to subsequent assignments. In-class review is most effective if given soon after the completion and grading of the assignment. Thus, courses in which major assignments are due at the end of the semester may lack many opportunities to use this commenting approach. When time permits, in-class review can be useful both to give global comments and to show examples of model (or prior years') student papers. It allows students to ask questions and share observations about an assignment and to hear other students' questions and observations as well.

Professors need to be aware, however, that first-year law students have a difficult time transferring comments from one situation (another student's paper) to their own. This difficulty in analysis and transference is often most pronounced in students who are most in need of helpful comments. For those students and others, in-class review cannot substitute for adequate individual comments.

That said, in-class review that includes examples is an especially effective technique for students who literally need to see other examples to understand how their own paper could have been drafted more effectively. For this reason, showing examples of common mistakes, coupled with more correct examples, is often a good technique. In-class review also pulls together all aspects of an assignment and paves the way for the next one.

3. *One-on-One Review Conferences*

Many students report that one-on-one conferences are the most effective way to get feedback,[22] particularly when a rewrite requirement follows the conference. Conferences allow for immediate and focused discussion between professor and student about an assignment and the comments. They are an excellent way to push students to a higher level of analysis and to rewire student thinking to produce an "Aha!" insight about the assignment.[23] One of the benefits of one-on-one conferences is the opportunity for a true dialogue in which the student's decision-making and writing process can be examined in a manner not possible simply by reading the draft.

On the other hand, depending on class sizes and teaching loads, conferences can be extremely time-consuming. As discussed below, resource allocation must be considered when fitting conferences into the course syllabus.

Effective conferences have the following characteristics:

- *They have a planned agenda.* Students must understand how a conference will be conducted and their responsibility to prepare for the conference—often by reading the comments and formulating a list of questions for discussion. This

---

[22]For a good discussion on individual student conferences, see Robin S. Wellford-Slocum, *The Law School Student-Faculty Conference: Towards a Transformative Learning Experience*, 45 S. TEX. L. REV. 255 (2004).

[23]*See generally* Neumann Jr., *supra* note 17.

requirement must be taken into account when the professor plans the semester. Critiqued papers must be returned early enough to allow students to review them before the conference. Professors often retain a copy of the critiqued draft and briefly review it in preparation for each conference.

- *They contribute to a constructive relationship between the professor and the student.* An effective conference should demonstrate the student's willingness to learn from a professor who, in turn, is able to address the individual needs of that student. The atmosphere in an effective writing conference is one of collaboration, not confrontation, and of teaching, not haggling over grades.

- *They lead to an improved written product.* An effective conference should enable the student to improve the paper by rewriting it. This improvement should not result from simply following a list of directives in a robot-like fashion, but rather fully discussing and understanding the paper's strengths and weaknesses. Students should leave the conference with the writing skills needed to make the necessary improvements. That might require the student to practice revising in the conference; for example, the professor and student might revise a passage together. A follow-up conference might be needed for students who are especially insecure about their writing, or who must devote significant work to improving their writing.

- *They are not an isolated occurrence.* A quality legal writing program includes one-on-one conferences as part of the course syllabus and schedules them at least once each semester. The conferences must be long enough to give students time to explore their concerns and to allow for meaningful learning. Deciding how many conferences to conduct, how long they should be, and when to schedule them, however, depends on many variables. Some conferences are as short as 15 minutes, and others as long as 30 minutes.

Given the time-consuming nature of conferences, LRW professors should think creatively about how to free up time to focus on the conferences. One solution may be to schedule course-related speakers or workshops that do not require individual preparation by LRW faculty. For example, during conferences on the appellate brief, students could attend a panel presentation by judges speaking on oral advocacy. Another option is to cancel classes for one or two "conference" weeks.

Above all, students should understand that individual conferences are opportunities to hone another important lawyering skill—meeting with a supervisor. Some professors have renamed student conferences "Meetings with the Partner" to highlight this goal. Students are expected to dress professionally, prepare an agenda for the conference, and essentially "run" the meeting.

4. Grades

While there are many approaches to assigning grades, LRW professors must decide whether to grade holistically[24] or to grade using a rubric or checklist of individual objective criteria. They must also decide whether to grade interim assignments in the same way final grades are reported (e.g., numerical or letter grades). It is vital to ensure that the grading process is both fair and workable. It must appear objectively reasonable to the students, and it must offer the professor some flexibility even when required to adhere to a mandatory curve distribution.

Experienced LRW professors may prefer to grade holistically because they have seen enough student papers to assess each in comparison to papers previously reviewed. Holistic grading allows flexibility to consider unexpectedly good (or bad) thinking and writing and reward (or penalize) it accordingly, without the constraint of

---

[24] *See* Willa Wolcott, *Holistic Scoring*, 13 PERSPS. 5 (2004).

a pre-existing grading rubric/checklist. For similar reasons, experienced professors may prefer "live critiquing/grading," particularly for interim or draft assignments. By eliminating the pre-reading step, a professor can read and assess the assignment with the student present, engaging in a discussion about the strengths and weakness of the document without giving extensive written comments.[25]

Novice LRW professors may have a more difficult time grading holistically because they can too easily focus on what is wrong with a paper and inadvertently discount the features that are effective. Using a rubric/checklist may therefore result in a more balanced assessment of the writing. Moreover, using a rubric/checklist assures students that identified criteria are used to evaluate all students' work, helping to ease any concerns about subjective grading. A rubric/checklist may, however, constrain the professor who finds that a paper does not quite fit within the criteria contemplated. LRW professors must retain some flexibility to revise a rubric/checklist after grading the first several papers, much as doctrinal faculty do when grading final exams.

Grading interim drafts in the same way as final memos has advantages and disadvantages. On the one hand, giving a final grade on each draft makes it difficult for a professor to curve grades if the program or school requires it. Furthermore, this system may over-reward those students who had better pre-law preparation in skills relevant to legal writing and to under-reward those who acquire the skills during the LRW course. If early drafts are a significant part of the final grade, two students may receive vastly different grades even if their final products are of the same quality. In addition, students whose first law school grades are assigned in the LRW class (as often happens) tend to react negatively to both the course and

---

[25] Barbara P. Blumenfeld, *Rhetoric, Referential Communication, and the Novice Writer*, 9 LEGAL COMM. & RHETORIC: J. ALWD 207, 222 (2012).

the professor if grades are not consistent with students' expectations (as they rarely are).[26]

For these reasons, some LRW faculty give interim drafts grades with little or no value, or they use a purely symbolic system (e.g., check, check-plus, check-minus). Care must be taken to provide other performance incentives when using such a system, such as deducting points from the final grade for students whose interim drafts did not meet a good-faith standard. Alternatively, assigning a numeric raw score and giving students information about the class range and average permit students to assess their own performance without specific grades that can distract and disillusion them.

On the other hand, good reasons support grading interim drafts. Some students are more talented at the initial analysis that forms the foundation of the draft but less adept at revising the memo into a polished final product. Grading only the final memo devalues a student's particularly effective initial cut at the analysis, which is unfair to these students. It also communicates the dangerous message that the analytical basis of a legal document is less important than the mechanics.

In a curriculum that grades drafts as well as final memos, one way to equalize student abilities is to begin with a practice memorandum on which students receive intensive critique and an opportunity to revise their work, but not a specific grade. This strategy levels the playing field by allowing all students to learn legal writing skills without the risk of a low grade on either a draft or final writing assignment.

LRW professors who teach in a law school that applies grade normalization or grading curves in first-year classes should also consider those constraints when grading memos. To the extent possible,

---

[26] *See* Melissa Marlow-Shafer, *Student Evaluation of Teacher Performance and the "Legal Writing Pathology": Diagnosis Confirmed*, 5 N.Y. City L. Rev. 115 (2002); Judith D. Fischer, *How to Improve Student Ratings in Legal Writing Courses: Views from the Trenches*, 34 U. Balt. L. Rev. 199 (2004).

it is best to consider the grading range even on interim assignments. Such adjustments can help students avoid the "sticker shock" of receiving higher grades on early assignments and then getting a final grade suppressed by the grading curve. It is also helpful to talk to students about the grade normalization scheme throughout the semester so they can manage expectations about final grades.

5. *Portfolios and Self-Assessment*

In effort to help students better track their writing progress and build a full body of work, some professors require portfolios in their LRW classes. Writing portfolios can be compiled electronically or in binders. They provide several pedagogical advantages.

Quite simply, a portfolio is a collection of one student's writing samples.[27] The highest value of the portfolio is that it allows students to reflect on their own work and to make choices about their strongest work.[28] Both practices promote self-regulated learning and self-assessment, two skills that are essential in both LRW and law practice.

Two common portfolio types are Work in Progress and Best Work.[29] Some professors rely on the Work in Progress portfolio to track the development of a single assignment over time. This type of portfolio follows a document from draft to final form. Other professors use the Best Work portfolio to highlight strong writing products. It features examples of various writing products in their best and final stages. Some professors use a combination of the two kinds of portfolios in a single course.

---

[27] *See, e.g.*, *Using Portfolios in Writing-Enhanced or Writing Rich Courses*, STETSON UNIV., http://www.stetson.edu/other/writing-program/resources/writing-intensive-courses/using-portfolios.php (last visited Dec. 14, 2019).

[28] Steven J. Johansen, "*What Were You Thinking?": Using Annotated Portfolios to Improve Student Assessment*, 4 LEGAL WRITING 123, 135 (1998).

[29] *Id.*

Portfolios can also make good use of annotations or comments to support student reflection. This process usually includes an opportunity for students to make comments or annotations defending the decisions they made in the writing process.[30] Questions can range from the specific ("Why did you choose the cases that you used in your Rule Explanation?") to more general ("How has your writing improved over the past four weeks?"). These questions help students unpack the writing process—which is marked by several decisions over the course of drafting a document. A student's answers to these questions also allow the professor to better assess the student's legal reasoning. Such insight can reveal flaws and prompt course corrections.

Finally, portfolios can be very useful to potential employers. The annotated portfolios are much more robust than a short writing sample. Specifically, they allow employers to look at a single document to better understand a student's writing strengths and reasoning abilities. Writing portfolio proponents have also noted that the discipline of maintaining a student writing portfolio sends a strong signal to employers about the industry of the student under consideration. "Imagine the signal such a portfolio would send to an employer: This is a student who is serious about his [or her] writing, has had a variety of writing experiences, and is able to recognize his [or her] writing strengths."[31]

C. Issues Specific to Effective Teaching of Research

Much of the discussion in Part A of this chapter applies as well to teaching research skills. Research instruction also raises issues regarding the appropriateness of specific teaching techniques and the use of computer-assisted legal research (CALR).

---

[30] *Id.*

[31] *Id.*

Legal research was historically taught as a separate course that focused on characteristics of individual sources and tools rather than the relationships among them and the selection of one over another. Today, most LRW programs have moved away from the "bibliographic" approach to an integrated approach.[32] Research is increasingly taught as an integral part of an LRW course rather than separately.[33] The variety of approaches range from fully integrated legal research and writing courses, to separate courses with some collaboration, to entirely separate legal research and legal writing courses. The decision to adopt a particular approach largely determines who teaches legal research, whether research and writing assignments are integrated, and how students' research skills are evaluated.

1. Pedagogical Approaches

The initial structural decision may be a matter of practicality (e.g., staffing or credit allocation) or a matter of pedagogical choice. The main considerations are as follows:

a. Integrated Versus Isolated

An "integrated" approach to teaching legal research has two meanings: structural, in that research is taught as part of the LRW course; and pedagogical, in that research is taught as part of a problem-solving process that begins with a legal question and

---

[32] David S. Romantz, *The Truth About Cats and Dogs: Legal Writing Courses and the Law School Curriculum*, 52 U. Kan. L. Rev. 105, 128-36 (2003) (discussing the historical changes in legal research and writing courses from a bibliographic approach to a more integrated approach).

[33] In 2004, 141 schools taught an integrated course; 60 taught research and writing separately. Ass'n of Legal Writing Dirs. & Legal Writing Inst., *Report of the 2004 Survey* 8, Question 18 (2005), https://staging-mp6ykpkm7cbbg.us.platform.sh/sites/default/files/2004-survey-results.pdf; *see also* Helene S. Shapo & Christina L. Kunz, *Teaching Research as Part of an Integrated LR & W Course*, 4 Persps. 78 (1996); *supra* Chapter II, Part A.3.c (discussing the trend in favor of integrating legal research instruction with legal analysis and writing).

results in the development of an answer. Legal research can be integrated in one or both ways in a given setting.

Both stand-alone courses taught by highly skilled law librarians and integrated courses can provide effective research instruction. The critical component is the pedagogy. Research instruction should go beyond mere identification and cursory examination of the sources and involve students in meaningful use of the sources. Students should engage in hands-on, experiential research work that provides opportunities to identify a legal issue, to develop a research plan, to select proper sources, to glean legal knowledge from the sources, to report on research findings, to receive feedback, and to engage in self-reflection.

In practice, of course, legal research is rarely performed in a vacuum. Rather, research is performed with a purpose: to answer a legal question and to communicate that answer to a client, another attorney, or a court. This task can be taught effectively by expert law librarians or legal writing faculty if the course is well-designed and delivered.

b. Process Versus Product

As with writing instruction generally, recent decades have witnessed a shift in legal research instruction from valuing product to valuing process. An emphasis on process typically includes teaching students how to develop a research plan, how to choose among sources, how to recognize and fill in gaps in their research, and how to know when they have sufficiently researched the legal question before them.

Students learn that research, analysis, and writing are not independent steps. Rather, students are taught to begin writing and analyzing as they go through the research process. As students find and read new sources, for instance, they realize they must revise their initial ideas; these new ideas in turn may affect the student's early thoughts on how to draft the document. They are encouraged to then revise their writing by adding the new ideas or expanding the discussion.

Generally, process-oriented instruction focuses on mastering skills students can apply to future problem-solving assignments.

An emphasis on product can be useful for teaching and evaluating discrete skills. It can do so either by simply requiring direct evidence of success (did the students find the correct answer?) or through a more inferential evaluation (did the written document or research product demonstrate use of appropriate authority?). In the latter approach to assessment, an adequate research process is inferred from the substantive quality of the end product.

2. *Decisions About Staffing*

Staffing for research instruction can take several forms. At one end of the spectrum is integrated research instruction taught solely by the professor who teaches the entire LRW course; at the other end is the librarian-taught, stand-alone research course. Between those two extremes lie collaborative and cooperative teaching models. A second dimension in considering staffing options focuses on the qualifications and status of both LRW professors and law librarians.

a. LRW Professor Model

Integrated research instruction taught solely by the professor who teaches the entire LRW course requires a high level of preparation and training. There are many advantages to this model; the full integration of the research and writing processes most closely approximates the practice of those skills in a real-world setting, and the LRW professor can weave the two skills together in a fluid and flexible manner whenever appropriate.

A potential disadvantage is the relative lack of teaching experience among newly hired LRW professors. Recent law school graduates may not have received in-depth training in legal research. LRW professors who come from practice are most familiar with and often favor the resources that were available to them in practice. Professors who self-identify as primarily writing and analysis experts may allocate the course hours in a way that minimizes legal research instruction, or they may signal to students that legal research instruction is a less important component of the integrated course.

Schools using this staffing model should strive to ensure that new LRW professors recognize the need for students to master the research portion of the course. The law librarians' assistance can be invaluable in training new LRW professors. Schools using this staffing model should also evaluate the balance of writing, analysis, and legal research instruction to ensure proper development of students' legal research skills.

b. Collaborative Model

Alternatively, the LRW professor may teach research collaboratively with law librarians and perhaps online research vendor representatives. This approach gives students the benefit of a group of teachers with different points of view and expertise. The extent to which legal research is integrated into the rest of the curriculum, however, depends upon the nature and degree of collaboration between the LRW professor and the librarian (and to a lesser extent the online research vendor representatives). It also depends how the course or courses are structured. Who is designated as the primary professor, who does the grading, and who most frequently and consistently instructs students all signal to students the relative importance of the instructors' respective messages.

In one version of this model, the LRW teacher simply turns over some portions of basic research instruction to librarians or vendor representatives. Usually in this model, basic research is taught separately from the students' memo assignments. While this model uses resources economically, it has the serious drawback of communicating to students that legal research is separate from analysis and the writing process. For that reason, the approach undermines students' development of sophisticated research strategy approaches and overall problem-solving skills. This model also tends to reduce librarians to "guest lecturers" and thus discourages them from contributing the full scope of their considerable expertise to teaching students or developing the research aspect of the LRW curriculum.

In another version of the collaborative model, the LRW teacher and librarian work closely together to plan the research curriculum. For instance, the "team" might determine together how best to integrate research instruction in proper sequence leading up to written memorandum assignments; to plan individual classes for which co-teaching would best illustrate the close relationship of analysis and research; to develop individual research exercises based on the legal writing problem; or to discuss how best to evaluate students' research skills. This model provides students with a rich experience in learning basic research skills in the context of solving a particular legal problem. In addition, students are exposed to the different perspectives and expertise of professional librarians and LRW professors, enriching the students' experience beyond the instruction either group could deliver separately. Under this model, an LRW teacher might gain time by not having to teach all aspects of research. But an equivalent amount of time will probably be spent collaborating with a librarian (and perhaps research vendors) to plan and integrate legal research instruction into the rest of the LRW curriculum.

Integrating vendor representatives also provides an opportunity for an LRW professor to offer expert research instruction to the students. However, this approach must be considered carefully. Vendor representatives are invariably well-versed in the features of the products they support and can be highly informative for students on the use of their particular products. But the vendor representative's perspective is not usually about the research task as a whole. Vendors inevitably slant presentations to emphasize their products' purported superiority over those of competitors.

Vendor representatives are also unlikely to be intimately familiar with each school's LRW course structure or the legal problem the students are researching. They may not objectively assess the value of one research medium over another, let alone the merits of their competitors' products in accomplishing the necessary research. LRW faculty and librarians can provide an objective perspective to counter what some students may perceive as a "sales pitch" by vendor representatives. Providing the vendor representatives with specific lesson goals and discussing their lesson plans ahead of time can be very helpful.

c. Librarian Model

Finally, law librarians can teach legal research as a stand-alone research course. Law librarians bring additional expertise to the legal research instruction process. If hired based on teaching ability, they can provide excellent, pedagogically sound instruction. Similarly, if teaching is a significant part of their job responsibilities, they can allocate appropriate time to preparation, teaching, and grading. As for all legal writing courses, this kind of preparation and feedback is time intensive.

While it is possible to relate research exercises in a stand-alone course to the writing assignments in a separate writing course, it is unlikely that the exercises can be effectively coordinated. Presumably, the purpose of a stand-alone research course is, at least in part, to permit those teaching it to select exercises and materials independent of the legal writing course material. Consequently, students may be less likely to learn how the research process inherently affects the analysis and writing process. When using this model, special care should be taken to teach legal research in way that goes beyond merely bibliographic knowledge and instructs students on the skill of legal research in the context of the writing and analysis process.

Like LRW courses generally, separate legal research courses should be taught in smaller sections with significant opportunities for exercises and feedback. Similar attention should be paid to class size and the overall workload of the law library faculty.

Some of the concerns inherent in this model can be ameliorated by having students learn legal research separately, and then take those skills to a legal writing class in which the teacher works to help them integrate research and writing skills. However, this approach has the disadvantage of delaying essential legal writing instruction.

3. *Evaluation of Students' Research Skills*

Students' research skills can be evaluated by self-reporting, by commercial or teacher-created research exercises, by inferences drawn from written work based on their research, by oral or written examination, or by any combination of these methods.

Self-reporting by students can take a variety of forms, including simple or annotated research lists and logs that record the student's process and results. The effectiveness of research lists and logs in evaluating students' mastery of research skills depends on where the students are in their learning process, whether students understand the importance of such lists or logs, and how much time the LRW professor has to review the students' work.

For example, a list of research results can be an effective tool for ensuring that students have found the correct authorities before they begin to write, but the list may reveal nothing about the process they followed to find those authorities. On the other hand, such a list is easy to evaluate.

A particularly process-focused self-report might ask the students to report not just what they found but the entire process by which they found it. A research log that includes a student's description of the research process can be tedious to review if assigned early in the first semester when students are likely to lack effective research planning skills and therefore report false starts and the location of irrelevant material. Later in the year, however, a research log can offer a good way to check on a student's development as an independent researcher. At any time during the year, students may view any such assignment as "busy work"; to counter that perception, professors need to help students understand the value of articulating their research process and then receiving teacher feedback on their successes and mistakes.

Research exercises can be selected from commercial sources or teacher-created. Many legal research texts include exercises developed by the author to complement the research approach set out in the text. These exercises are unlikely to tie in with a particular writing assignment, however, and thus may not be compatible with a fully integrated approach. Before using any commercial exercise, the LRW professor (or a teaching or research assistant) must perform a dry run to be sure that the exercise can be completed with the resources available at that school and that the exercise has not been pre-empted by updates in the materials.

Professor-created research exercises can be tailored to a fully integrated research and writing sequence and to the holdings of that school's law library, but drafting them is extraordinarily time-consuming. In addition, developing a fact pattern that works for both a writing assignment and a specific research task involving specific sources requires significant planning.

Drawing inferences as to students' research ability from their written work is a product-oriented approach to evaluating research skills. While it has a certain bottom-line appeal, its drawback is that the LRW professor cannot assess the student's research process.

Class discussions can also be very effective if they occur during or soon after students have completed a research assignment. Such discussions can illuminate the range of possible methodologies and strategies to attack a particular research problem, the intimate relationship between analysis and research, and effective and ineffective techniques for using specific research tools.

Examinations, oral or written, can help the LRW professor evaluate students' mastery of factual information about research sources and the research process. An oral examination gives the examiner an opportunity to pursue individual lines of inquiry, but it is extremely time-consuming to administer. In one approach, students schedule meetings with "the senior partner" to report on their research process and results in preparation for drafting a memorandum or brief.

A written examination is easier to administer but cannot be individualized for each student. A written examination can be drafted by the individual LRW professor, by the program director, or as a collaborative effort among a program's faculty. While writing an examination that works for all LRW professors is a time-consuming and painstaking process, using a common exam allows a program to assess how students in all sections are performing.

Care must be taken, however, to draft an exam that tests beyond simple bibliographic information. One effective exam structure requires students to actually perform research with a packet of photocopied authorities to answer exam questions. Another effective option requires each student to complete a "take-home" exam in the library using print and online sources, and then to write up both the "answer" and the process the student used to reach that conclusion.

4. Computer-Assisted Legal Research (CALR)

An additional consideration in teaching research effectively is when and how to introduce CALR. Today's law student is increasingly wedded to the computer, not only for legal research but also for answering questions that arise in everyday life. It is no exaggeration to say that once students are able to access online resources, they are loath to spend much time in the law library stacks with print materials.

Many LRW programs begin teaching research skills in print and do not permit students to have complete access to CALR until the end of the fall or the beginning of the spring semester. But increasingly, programs teach CALR earlier in the first year or even simultaneously with print research.

Several rationales support teaching print research first. Computer sources are based on print sources (and indeed are constantly redesigned to replicate the print sources more closely). Print sources help students build the vocabulary they need to use computers effectively. Researching in books gives students a sense of the structure of the law that they cannot get from Boolean or natural language searching. Students will never learn how to research using print sources unless they are initially denied computer access. Finally, many law offices and government agencies expect students to know how to research in print as well as online.

The dominant trend, however, is to teach legal research in all media from the beginning of the course and to teach students to evaluate the merits and drawbacks of various media as they learn. This approach has the advantage of avoiding the "forbidden fruit" appeal of CALR, and it allows the research teacher the opportunity to guide the students in meaningful evaluation of the various research tools in both written exercises and class discussion.

Whichever approach a program uses, the end goals of research instruction should be to train students to use both print and computer-based resources competently and to make well-founded choices about when to use each separately and when to use them in combination. Students should also be aware of the costs inherent in all media and how to use them cost-effectively.

D. Technology and LRW

Even for the self-proclaimed Luddite, technology in the modern LRW classroom is unavoidable. That is a good thing. Technology allows professors to make their classroom instruction more efficient and exciting. Technology also supports hybrid classes and "flipped" instruction models that create more space for interaction during class. Students can review more accessible materials themselves online, freeing up time to tackle more complex subjects in class. Furthermore, technology offers more variety to professors in the feedback loop; specifically, programs are now available to help professors offer more concrete feedback and critiques of student work.

Presentation technology: PowerPoint has long been a popular way to deliver information with visual aids. Programs make it easier than ever to design effective PowerPoint slides that can be used in class to share information with students. PowerPoints can also be posted on online classroom platforms to share information with students. Beyond PowerPoints, some professors integrate more dynamic programs such as Prezi to make material visually exciting.

Formative assessment: Technology can be used in several ways to support formative assessment and feedback. Clickers are one way to conduct electronic polling in the classroom to test out case theories, check on citations, or engage students on assigned readings. An even easier and more affordable solution is using free polling programs available as cellphone applications. Game-based learning platforms such as Kahoot! and Poll Everywhere offer free, simple polling options for professors to use in class. Answers can be displayed on the screen, and students can participate as long as they have a cellphone and the classroom has internet access.

Teaching aid technology: Technology can also be used to supplement classroom instruction. Online platforms are required in many LRW programs and have numerous benefits. They allow professors to easily communicate updates and scheduling changes to students; they are portals for course materials, handouts, and assignments; they can be used for scheduling conferences and meetings; they can be used for quizzes and assignments; and they can also host discussion boards. Westlaw and LexisNexis both offer online classroom platforms. Others include Top Hat and Canvas.

Technology can also facilitate critique of student papers. Many professors have moved from handwritten comments to typed feedback. Electronic feedback allows professors to track changes, insert comments, or link to additional resources in a Word document. Students also appreciate that comments are easier to read and understand. If professors are committed to grading electronically, they might consider using a program to enhance the feedback. Annotate Pro[34] is one popular program that allows professors to give students individualized feedback on writing assignments. The advantage of

---

[34] *See supra* note 20.

such programs is that they offer a digital library of comments that can still be personalized. However, some professors are reluctant to grade online because the technique requires a computer.

Learning Technology: Technology can also be invaluable in helping students complete independent lessons. Some professors assign learning modules prepared by commercial vendors to assist in teaching research or citation. Other professors have encouraged or required students to address writing deficiencies through the completion of online grammar support programs such as *Core Grammar for Lawyers*.[35]

Multimedia: As nearly all classrooms are now equipped with smartboard and internet access, LRW professors today have even more flexibility about how to best integrate technology in their classrooms. The possibilities are truly endless and should be guided by the professor's comfort levels and students' interest levels. Many professors use student recordings and playbacks to prepare for oral arguments. Others make podcasts to supplement or make up classes. YouTube videoclips are very popular to illustrate everything from negotiation to lawyering examples (and nonexamples), and some professors display footage from real courtrooms. Some professors even play music regularly during collaborative work or other classroom activities. One professor, for example, engaged the class by sharing her playlist of "collaboration music" during an in-class group project on collaboration.[36]

While using technology in the LRW classroom offers numerous advantages, technology cannot substitute for live interaction between professors and students. Professors who seek to integrate more technology in the LRW classroom should be mindful not to

---

[35] *See* RUTH ANN MCKINNEY & KATIE ROSE GUEST PRYAL, CORE GRAMMAR FOR LAWYERS, https://coregrammarforlawyers.com/ (last visited Dec. 15, 2019).

[36] The songs included *It Takes Two* by Rob Base and D.J. E-Z Rock (1988) and *Come Together* by The Beatles (1969).

overuse it for fear of inadvertently creating a community of passive learners.

Best teaching practices call for a variety of technology models, keeping the integration of technology brief (e.g., do not prepare a two-hour PowerPoint presentation for class) and leveraging students' expertise and familiarity with technology. Instead of merely delivering a PowerPoint on collaboration, for example, ask students to work together in class to build their own PowerPoint presentation on the same topic. Even in 15 minutes, a group of law students can generally create an effective and engaging PowerPoint. They are often more adept than professors at integrating the "bells and whistles" that make the PowerPoint effective. The best PowerPoint for a particular lesson can also be shared with the class on a learning platform or emailed to the class for review. Students can also be invited to write a blog, Tweet on a topic, create a "playlist" for a theme of a case, or find a meme that reflects the underlying theory of a case. When given the opportunity, students can be very creative in using technology to bolster learning. The active engagement promotes deep learning and creates a positive community in the LRW classroom. And the results can be used in the future as teaching aids.

When used effectively, classroom technology can be exciting and efficient. Program directors can sponsor "Teaching Tips" to share the latest in technological advances, or professors can reach out to law school colleagues or vendors for training. Several books are available that offer guidelines on the most effective use of technology in the classroom.[37] LRW conferences increasingly offer technology demonstrations. Continuing education in using these tools is also critical.

---

[37] *See, e.g.*, MICHELLE D. MILLER, MINDS ONLINE: TEACHING EFFECTIVELY WITH TECHNOLOGY (2016).

E. The Importance of Good Judgment in Teaching

Like their colleagues in doctrinal courses, LRW professors must use good judgment in classroom teaching, in individual meetings with students, and in written or oral comments on assignments. The LRW course at many schools is the sole first-year course in which the professor knows each student as a person. LRW professors, therefore, have special power to shape students' perceptions of their entire first-year experience.

LRW courses are designed in part to introduce students to appropriate professional behavior. A professor who is respectful to students without bias or favoritism serves as a good professional role model for law students.

In addition, LRW professors must be credible to their students. Just as a teacher of first-year Contracts must be an expert in contract law and how to teach it well, LRW teachers must bring expertise to their subject. Because students must apply the skills they are taught, any deficiencies in instruction become evident sooner in LRW courses than in doctrinal courses.

Because LRW professors enjoy more significant contact with students than most doctrinal professors, students may assess them more frequently and more critically (after all, familiarity breeds, at the very least, a perceived license to comment). LRW professors must maintain a careful balance—to be friendly, but not familiar; demanding, but not unreasonable; supportive, but not smothering; understanding, but not easily manipulated.

The LRW professor may have more impact on first-year students' sense of what it means to be an attorney than any other first-year law professor. For this reason, those who teach LRW must possess good judgment and exhibit that judgment in all aspects of student contact.

IV. ASSESSMENT AND GRADING

Although LRW professors have always relied on various assessment techniques to teach their students, law schools are now required to incorporate learning outcomes and assessment across the curriculum. This is nothing new for LRW professors; LRW courses are generally taught using multiple drafts of an assignment with individualized critiques and student conferences. Assessment in LRW courses has generally been done in isolation and without reference to the broader curricular goals of a law school, but this "silo" approach is changing.

The biggest driver of the increase in assessment in law schools is the ABA Section of Legal Education and Admissions to the Bar, the main accreditor of law schools. The ABA Standards now require law schools to integrate learning outcomes and assessment into the curriculum with the goal of improving student learning.[1] Additionally, students at every law school must now complete at least six credit hours of experiential learning courses. Overall, the standards are meant to better prepare students for the practice of law while establishing assessment techniques that evaluate whether the students are indeed prepared.

The ABA Standards require law schools to develop and publish learning outcomes that clearly state what they want students to be able to do and know by the time they graduate. The ABA Standards also require an assessment plan that includes both student assessment in courses as well as institutional assessment of the program of legal education. Put simply, the ABA Standards require that law schools answer two questions:

---

[1] *See* Section of Legal Educ. & Admissions to the Bar, *ABA Standards and Rules of Procedure for Approval of Law Schools (2019-2020)*, ABA: Am. Bar Ass'n, Standards 301, 302, 314, 315 [hereinafter *ABA Standards (2019–2020)*], https://www.americanbar.org/content/dam/aba/administrative/legal_education_and_admissions_to_the_bar/standards/2019-2020/2019-2020-aba-standards-and-rules-of-procedure.pdf.

1. What does the law school want its students to know and be able to do when they graduate?
2. How will the law school know that its students have attained these competencies?

The ABA separates the standards for student assessment and the standards for institutional or programmatic assessment.[2] For student assessment, the ABA requires that every law school "utilize both formative and summative assessment methods in its curriculum to measure and improve student learning and provide meaningful feedback to students."[3] The standards explain that formative assessments are measurements that help promote student learning through effective and "meaningful feedback."[4] The standards define summative assessments as tools that measure the students' competency at the conclusion of any course or any part of a student's legal education.[5]

For institutional and programmatic assessment, the standards require schools to use the data and information taken from student assessment to evaluate the school's success and adjust its curriculum as needed.[6] The standards suggest some approaches for this type of programmatic and institutional review, including direct and indirect forms of assessment.[7] Direct forms of assessment measure the students' achievement of the learning outcomes by evaluating their actual work product. The ABA Standards include student learning portfolios and performance in capstone courses as examples of direct assessment tools. Indirect assessment gathers data by examining indicators of learning rather than looking at students' work product. Examples of indirect assessment listed in the ABA Standards include job placement rates and surveys of employers and alumni.[8]

---

[2] *See* ABA Standards 314, 315.

[3] ABA Standard 314.

[4] ABA Standard 314, Interpretation 314-1.

[5] *Id.*

[6] *See* ABA Standard 315.

[7] *See* ABA Standard 315, Interpretation 315-1.

[8] *Id.*

Educational psychologist Michael Scriven developed a distinction between two types of assessment in education—summative assessment and formative assessment.[9] Generally, summative assessment refers to the process of evaluating whether a student has satisfied the learning outcomes of a course, while formative assessment refers to the intermediate feedback given to students to help them learn and complete some educational task.

Summative assessment evaluates how much learning has occurred in the class at a particular moment in time. Its purpose is to measure the success of the students in a course, and in most law schools, the relative abilities of the students in a course. Examples of summative assessment tools are final exams in law school and the state bar exam.

Formative assessment, on the other hand, is specifically intended to provide feedback to the students during the learning process to improve the students' learning. Formative assessment generally occurs before summative assessment. Formative assessment provides information to both the students and teacher so they can adjust the learning and teaching process to promote further learning. It is an ongoing process that requires frequent testing, appropriate feedback, and additional opportunities to improve learning. Examples of formative assessment tools used in law schools include midterm exams, feedback on drafts of student papers, and short reflective papers throughout a course.

A. Goal of Good Assessment: Transfer of Learning

Transfer of learning is the application of previously acquired skills, knowledge, and professional values to new contexts.[10] A new context could be the next day's assignment or a client's case years in the future. Although effective transfer is the obvious end-goal for any educational program, it can be surprisingly elusive. The key principle is that humans store learning in schemas according to

---

[9] *See* MICHAEL SCRIVEN, THE LOGIC OF EVALUATION 13, 44-46 (1981) (distinguishing formative from summative evaluation).

[10] *See, e.g*, Tonya Kowalski, *True North: Navigating for the Transfer of Learning in Legal Education*, 34 SEATTLE U. L. REV. 51, 53-55 (2010).

the context in which the information was learned. When the context changes, the mind's "search engine" tends to skip learning that, on the surface, doesn't appear to come from a matching context.

The effect of ever-shifting contexts (new classrooms, new subjects, new professors, and new clients) can be ameliorated by a number of strategies and cultivated mindsets. For example, professors can help their students by building awareness of the context barrier to learning transfer, helping them imagine future applications for the new skills they are learning, creating multiple opportunities to apply skills across increasingly different contexts to generalize the skill set, and so on.[11]

Both formative and summative assessment play an important role in cueing opportunities for transfer, as well as for cultivating "transfer thinking." As discussed in the summative assessment section below, feedback and rubrics can be used to cue past learning, to place learning struggles into the context of long-term goals and professional growth, to envision future workplace applications, and to explain how subtle shifts in context may have caused a misapplication of previously learned skills or knowledge.

B. Summative Assessment

Summative assessment is the final evaluation of a student's coursework, whether a major assignment or the entire course. An assignment grade or course grade provides an opportunity for the instructor to determine how well a student has progressed toward meeting the original learning objectives. Because summative assessments in LRW courses typically include some form of feedback,

---

[11] *See generally* David N. Perkins & Gavriel Salomon, *Teaching for Transfer*, EDUC. LEADERSHIP 22-32 (Sept. 1988); TRANSFER OF LEARNING IN PROFESSIONAL AND VOCATIONAL EDUCATION: A HANDBOOK FOR SOCIAL WORK TRAINERS (Viviene E. Cree & Cathlin Macaulay eds., 2001).

they can also serve a formative purpose if students use that advice to improve performance in later assignments or courses.

This part discusses current and best practices for summative assessment in LRW final writing assignments and course grades.

1. Graded Courses

The great majority of law schools responding to an annual survey of LRW programs assign students grades in first-year objective LRW courses and include them in students' cumulative grade point averages. For example, the ALWD/LWI Annual Survey shows that for the objective LRW course, the most common entry-level LRW course, 94% of the reporting law schools assigned course grades. The other 6% used a pass/fail or hybrid grading system. The past five years have shown a gradual increase in graded courses from the previous five, during which the proportion tended to hold steady at around 87%.[12] Of the many law schools that include students'

---

[12]As reported in the 2016-2017 ALWD/LWI Annual Survey, 164 of 175 responding schools (94%) grade their objective LRW courses and include them in grade-point averages. Only eight schools use an enhanced pass/fail system, and only three use a simple pass/fail system. Ass'n of Legal Writing Dirs. & Legal Writing Inst., *ALWD/LWI Annual Legal Writing Survey: Report of the 2016-2017 Survey* 32-33, Question 6.12 (2017) [hereinafter *2016-2017 ALWD/LWI Survey*], https://www.lwionline.org/sites/default/files/Report-of-the-2016-2017-Survey.pdf. Allowing for some margin of error, the figures leading up to the 2016-2017 survey were as follows:

2007: 155/181=86%;

2008: 158/181=87%;

2009: 145/166=87%;

2010: 159/185=85%;

2011: 163/187=87%;

2012: 160/183=87%;

2013: 168/190=88%;

grades in the objective LRW course in the grade-point average (GPA), a large majority also require a mean GPA or grade distribution that differs from upper-division courses, which might or might not be the same as that used for other first-year courses.[13]

Arguably, law schools' preference for graded LRW courses reflects the increasing demand for quality legal skills education by both students and employers. A fully graded course also encourages new students to better respect both the material and the instructor.

2. *Anonymous Grading*

Anonymous grading conceals the student's identity during the assessment process. Trends associated with anonymous grading in LRW are difficult to track due to a lack of long-term data. In 2017, a little over two-thirds of LRW programs reported using some degree of anonymous grading in the entry-level objective LRW course, while nearly one-third did not grade anonymously at all.[14]

In terms of best teaching practices, professors should strive for robust anonymous grading policies for written assignments to reduce the effects of implicit bias. In a recent meta-analysis, researchers surveyed all available controlled studies on grading bias. They found clear evidence of implicit bias in student assessment when instructors had access to information about the student's race, gender, or other non-relevant personal information. This finding remained statistically valid across all education tiers and across

---

2014: 159/178=89%;

2015: 178/193=92%.

See responses to Question 15 (an earlier version of Question 6.12) for all surveys, https://www.lwionline.org/resources/surveys (last visited Dec. 15, 2019).

[13] *See 2016-2017 ALWD/LWI Survey*, *supra* note 12, at 32-33, Question 6.12.

[14] *Id.* at 31, Question 6.11.

several countries.[15] In a separate study, a related research team also found evidence of a positive or negative "halo" effect in grading. The halo effect is a form of implicit bias that occurs when an instructor expects a student to perform well or poorly based on previous work and perceives the quality of the student's later work to be consistent with those expectations.[16] In both situations, the researchers named anonymous grading and rubrics as two of the key factors in reducing the effects of bias.

While it can be difficult to achieve perfect anonymity in smaller courses with a great deal of individualized instruction and feedback, first-year students tend to struggle with very similar analytical and mechanical challenges. As a result, it is unusual to easily distinguish one LRW student's memo or brief from another with any certainty, save for the occasional highly idiosyncratic style.

Pervasive anonymous grading can, however, make it more difficult for instructors to track long-term student performance for purposes of intervention. Course software and the use of identification numbers largely alleviate these concerns about anonymous grading. They allow for relative ease in grading anonymously and provide a method for monitoring individual students' development. Anonymous grading policies are also likely to enhance a professor's reputation among students for fairness.[17]

---

[15] John M. Malouff & Einar B. Thorsteinsson, *Bias in Grading: A Meta-Analysis of Experimental Research Findings*, 60 Australian J. Educ. 245-46 (2016).

[16] John M. Malouff et al., *Preventing Halo Bias in Grading the Work of University Students*, 1 Cogent Psychology 1 (2014), https://www.cogentoa.com/article/10.1080/23311908.2014.988937.pdf.

[17] Vikram David Amar, *Why "Blind" Grading Makes Good Sense, and Should Be Used More Extensively Outside of the Context of Law School Exams*, Justia: Verdict (Jan. 17, 2014), https://verdict.justia.com/2014/01/17/blind-grading-makes-good-sense-used-extensively-outside-context-law-school-exams.

3. *Summative Feedback*

In LRW courses, professors customarily provide feedback not just for student use in revising drafts, but also for purposes of reflection after students submit final papers. LRW professors use a variety of methods to provide feedback that has the potential to reinforce course goals, facilitate transfer of learning, and even reduce stereotype threat.[18]

In 2015, the ALWD/LWI Annual Survey retrospectively compared feedback methods on major LRW assignments. In about two-thirds of LRW programs, major writing assignments are usually graded with a more complex method than a simple pass/fail or checkmark system.[19] LRW faculty continue to use a variety of approaches to provide summative feedback on major writing assignments. Of the 193 law schools responding in 2015, all but one used individualized margin comments as at least one form of feedback, strongly suggesting an LRW industry standard in favor of that practice. In addition, most LRW programs provide feedback in additional formats, including end comments, general comments addressed to all students, rubrics, in-person conferences, audio recordings, or a combination.[20] The data is not yet clear as to whether feedback methods become less robust after major work has been revised and submitted for final credit.

---

[18]Stereotype threat is the "cognitive barrier" that members of a social group face when their group tends to be undervalued or denigrated. A student who belongs to that group may fear underperforming because it will affirm outsiders' stereotypes of the entire social group. Perhaps ironically, that fear can then negatively impact performance. *See* Paula J. Manning, *Word to the Wise: Feedback Intervention to Moderate the Effects of Stereotype Threat and Attributional Ambiguity on Law Students*, 18 U. Md. L.J. Race, Religion, Gender & Class 99, 99–100 (2018).

[19]Ass'n of Legal Writing Dirs. & Legal Writing Inst., *Report of the 2015 Annual Legal Writing Survey* 17, Question 25 (2016) [hereinafter *2015 ALWD/LWI Survey*], https://www.alwd.org/images/resources/2015%20Survey%20Report%20(AY%202014-2015).pdf.

[20]*Id.* Question 24. These programs formally grade at least 76% of all major assignments.

While best practices for providing feedback are described elsewhere in the *Sourcebook*, it is worth stressing here the role that summative feedback plays in an LRW student's long-term development. Particularly with summative assessments, the instructor and student have an opportunity to reflect upon how far a student has come, even if the student continues to struggle. The professor will also identify long-range goals for the student to work toward in future projects to reach or exceed core proficiency. By treating performance as a point along a continuum rather than a fixed state, bigger-picture summative feedback should encourage a growth-based mindset toward intelligence and learning—a mindset that is important for teachers to habitually cultivate as well.[21]

In a very similar way, meaningful final feedback can also play an important role in helping students transfer new skills to future assignments, whether in school or in the workplace. This practice can go well beyond telling a student how to fix a present deficiency in structure or proof. For example, as with growth mindset, one basic transfer strategy involves helping the student to see the assignment's place in the larger scheme of legal education. This strategy can be called forward- and backward-reaching transfer.[22] For example, the LRW professor may remind students that past classroom exercises helped prepare them to carry out a given task in a writing assignment, and that the same skill will be important not only in the next assignment, but also in the workplace.

Finally, summative feedback plays a role in one of our most important jobs as educators: making our LRW classrooms more inclusive by reducing stereotype threat. Students may feel marginalized, disaffected, underprepared, or otherwise threatened by fear of

---

[21] Carol Dweck, *Carol Dweck Revisits the "Growth Mindset,"* EDUCATION WEEK (Sept. 22, 2015), https://www.edweek.org/ew/articles/2015/09/23/carol-dweck-revisits-the-growth-mindset.html. *See generally* CAROL DWECK, MINDSET: THE NEW PSYCHOLOGY OF SUCCESS (2006).

[22] Shaun Archer et al., *Reaching Backward and Stretching Forward: Teaching for Transfer in Law School Clinics*, 64 J. LEGAL EDUC. 258 (2014).

their instructor's (or their own) deeply held beliefs based on stereotypes. Those stereotypes can be about race or gender, but may also concern less-studied attributes or statuses such as gender identity, body shape, immigration, age, and military service, among others. As with feedback on other key assignments, LRW instructors may use summative feedback to employ the "Wise" strategy to build trust with students and encourage a growth mindset.

The Wise feedback method has been proven to ameliorate lost trust between racially marginalized adolescent students and their teachers by inviting students to see the instructor's motivations for offering critical feedback, using a set of simple interventions. The interventions were designed to persuade students that the instructor's critique was motivated both by high standards and a sincere belief in the students' ability to meet those standards.[23] One of the key indicators of these interventions' effectiveness was substantially improved performance from first draft to second by a majority of students. Another was a gain of one-third of a grade point on a 4.0 scale, and a third was persistent improvement in the level of student trust in the teachers.

Both motivations—high standards and sincere belief in student ability—must be conveyed credibly for the interventions to succeed. The key strategy for providing Wise summative feedback is to convey—simply, clearly, and sincerely—both motivations to the student. These interventions are simple and low-cost for the LRW professor.

4. *Summative Rubrics*

A rubric is a set of criteria used to assess student performance on a given assignment. As of 2015, just over two-thirds of LRW

---

[23]David Scott Yeager et al., *Breaking the Cycle of Mistrust: Wise Interventions to Provide Critical Feedback Across the Racial Divide*, 143 J. Experimental Psychology: Gen'l 804 (2014); Manning, *supra* note 18.

programs reported using some form of grading grid or score sheet not only to assess major writing assignments, but also to provide another vehicle for feedback.[24]

Rubrics serve several important purposes including reinforcing learning objectives, increasing objectivity, and enhancing transfer. The likelihood of achieving all three purposes is enhanced when students have access to the rubric before and after completing their work on the assignment.

Learning objectives. Particularly for summative rubrics, the major grading criteria should be tied directly to the course objectives outlined in the syllabus. Ideally, grading criteria should be tied to LRW or J.D. program learning outcomes as well. This approach enhances a mindful, integrated approach toward assessment that flows from early course design to final letter grades and later reflection. One simple way to integrate criteria is to number the course objectives and then use the same numbers for corresponding skill sets identified on the rubric.

Arguably, the most effective rubric style for a skills course is one that describes for students the typical characteristics of low-, average-, and high-performing work products. Professor Sophie Sparrow pioneered the application of this rubric style to the law school environment. Her research and sample rubrics are currently available from the Institute for Law Teaching and Learning.[25]

For example, one of the key learning objectives in a first-year LRW course is using analogical reasoning to prove a rule

---

[24] *2015 ALWD/LWI Survey*, *supra* note 19, at 17, Question 24.

[25] *See Resources*, INST. FOR LAW TEACHING & LEARNING, http://lawteaching.org/resources/ (last visited Dec. 15, 2019); *see also* Sophie Sparrow, *Describing the Ball: Improve Teaching by Using Rubrics – Explicit Grading Criteria*, 2004 MICH. ST. L. REV. 1; Sandra L. Simpson, *Riding the Carousel: Making Assessment a Learning Loop Through Continuous Use of Grading Rubrics*, 6 CANADIAN LEGAL EDUC. ANNUAL REV. 35 (2011).

application. A performance-driven rubric provides the LRW instructor with an opportunity to reflect on what makes a strong analogical proof, and what average skill level is achievable in that semester. The professor might decide that at minimum, the student needs to get past the hurdle of merely applying a black-letter rule directly to the facts. There must be some effort to build an analogy between key aspects of the client's fact pattern and corresponding facts from one or more judicial opinions. At the same time, the professor hopes that at least some students will grasp the material quickly enough that instead of making rudimentary comparisons, they are able to cut through to the deepest layers of judicial reasoning, which are sometimes only implicitly expressed. The description for those students not yet past the hurdle could be placed in the rubric column for below-average performance, which might also be called *under-developed* or *developing*. The description for those students with the deepest analysis might be *high performing* or *exceeds expectations*, and the *average* or *proficient* column could refer to analogies that use at least the main determinative facts.

Objectivity. Like anonymous grading, rubrics have the potential to increase actual and perceived fairness for both professors and students. First, a clear set of criteria ensures that scores are based on the same factors for all students. Second, using the rubric to draw the line between different performance levels also helps to reduce inconsistency when marking student papers. This extra assurance of consistency is especially important when anonymity is not realistic, such as when scoring oral arguments.

Transfer. Finally, rubrics tied to course objectives and performance criteria tend to remind students of their long-term goals, with the potential to increase intrinsic motivation and other positive orientations toward learning such as growth mindset and "transfer thinking." The more LRW professors reinforce this system of goals, growth, and outcomes in their teaching materials and discussions, the more likely students will internalize motivation for learning.

C. Formative Assessment

The goal of formative assessment, whether used in an LRW course or other law school course, is to use feedback to improve the student's work and to inform the professor's decisions about next steps for instruction. In other words, it is designed to help students and professors alike better understand the learning process and ultimately increase student learning. Indeed, one main goal of formative assessment is to empower students to become self-regulated learners who actively monitor their learning efficacy.

Good formative feedback adheres to the following seven principles: [26]

1. *It helps clarify what good performance is (goals, criteria, expected standards).* In addition to explicitly clarifying the goals and standards for a particular task, professors can make the formative assessment process more effective by providing exemplars of excellent work for students to review. Demonstrating what a "good" work product is during the course of formative assessment by providing a sample "answer" for the task can increase students' self-regulation as learners. Professors can also explain the various assignment criteria and performance levels on a rubric, or even have the students assist in creating the rubric.

2. *It facilitates the development of self-assessment (reflection) in learning.* Formative feedback allows students to identify criteria for good work and to apply those standards to their own work. Additionally, reviewing peers' work products can help students learn to make objective judgments about the relevant standards.

---

[26] David J. Nicol & Debra Macfarlane-Dick, *Formative Assessment and Self-Regulated Learning: A Model and Seven Principles of Good Feedback Practice*, 31 STUD. IN HIGHER EDUC. 199, 205 (2006).

3. *It delivers high-quality information to students about their learning.* Formative feedback should be related to the goals, standards, and criteria that professors have set out. Feedback that is given often and regularly enables students to better monitor and regulate their own progress toward achieving those goals. Additionally, professors can provide feedback that is limited in quantity and prioritized to indicate main areas of needed improvement.

4. *It encourages professor and peer dialogue about learning.* Feedback that is a dialogue rather than just transmission of information is often more effective; it allows students the opportunity to engage the professor about the meaning, significance, and nuance of the feedback. This dialogue can occur in one-on-one sessions, in small groups of peers, or even through the use of technology such as email conversations or discussion boards.

5. *It encourages positive motivational beliefs and self-esteem.* The tone of the feedback can impact both the students' goals and their commitment to those goals. Feedback that praises effort and strategic behaviors (rather than innate intelligence or skill) can help focus students on the ultimate goals of the project and lead to higher achievement. Additionally, frequent low-stakes assessment opportunities (as opposed to a few high-stakes assessments) can help build students' motivation and self-esteem.

6. *It provides opportunities to close the gap between current and desired performance.* The best way to encourage learning from formative feedback is to allow students to respond in some way to it—by rewriting a document or redoing a quiz. Even allowing students to reflect in writing on what they can do differently next time can help make the connection between their current level of performance and the ultimate goal.

7. *It provides information to professors that can be used to help shape the teaching.* Frequent formative assessment can

> help professors determine whether to make changes in the classroom. These assessments may reveal that many students are struggling with one particular skill or concept that a professor may wish to repeat or review. Or professors may learn that most of the students have mastered a particular topic and that the classroom discussion can move forward to new material.

Formative assessment can include any number of in- or out-of-class tasks. Typical formative assessment tools in law school classrooms include midterm exams and feedback on papers or sample exam questions. These tools typically include detailed (and hopefully timely) feedback to the students, and if a rewrite opportunity is provided, students can better learn to use the feedback received on the initial submission.

Other types of formative assessment can be useful rather than commenting on numerous drafts of a paper or other assignment, and are often more practical for professors.

Minute papers are common formative assessment tools because they are quick, they allow students to communicate directly to the professor, and they are easy to review and categorize. The premise, as the name suggests, it to allow students one minute to answer a particular reflective question, such as "What was the most important topic we learned today?" or "What is still unclear about the topic we covered?"

Think/pair/share activities allow students a moment by themselves to answer a particular question posed by the professor, a moment to share their responses with a neighbor, and a moment to share their ideas with the class at large. This format gives each student the opportunity to formulate an answer and then get feedback in the form of discussion with a peer and eventually with the entire class.

Multiple-choice questions can be used in the classroom to quickly gauge students' comprehension of a particular topic. Professors can have students raise their hands, hold up note cards, or use technology (clickers, instant polls, etc.) to indicate an answer. The results on the question posed allow professors to get a big-picture perspective on how well students understand the subject matter.

Team-based learning is a teaching strategy based on the idea that a team achieves more than the same number of individuals working alone. In this learning environment, students are divided into teams, and as a team they discuss the reading for that day's class and are assessed as a group (often through a short quiz) on their comprehension of the material. One way to incorporate team-based learning into a classroom is to have students take a quiz individually and then retake the same quiz working in groups. This process gives students the opportunity to develop an answer on their own and then get feedback from others in the group about their understanding before learning the right answers to the quiz.

Simulations allow students to apply what they have learned in class to a real-life situation. For example, students could prepare a short oral argument about a topic, or they could engage in a client interview to demonstrate what they have learned about a particular subject.

Quizzes can provide quick feedback to both students and professors about student learning, and they can take any number of forms: an open-book, two-question quiz at the start of class to assess student understanding of the reading; an in-class quiz taken individually or in groups (or both); a short quiz at the end of class to evaluate comprehension of the discussion that day; or an on-line quiz at the end of the week to assess big-picture concepts.

Rubrics are a set of detailed written criteria that can be used to provide formative assessment in a variety of ways. Professors can give rubrics to students in advance to show how writing assignments will be evaluated. Students can be asked to evaluate work (their own, that of a peer, or even a sample created by the professor) against a rubric to better understand the criteria for success. Professors can even have students assist in creating the rubric and identifying the standards for effective work.

V. FACULTY STATUS AND GOVERNANCE

Ideally, all required LRW courses should be taught by full-time faculty who are experts in the discipline.[1] The requisite expertise is usually acquired through significant law practice or teaching experience or both. Since the last edition of the *Sourcebook* was published in 2006, the percentage of law schools employing exclusively full-time LRW faculty[2] to teach the required first-year course has increased from approximately 50 to 69 percent.[3] An additional 22 percent (32 of 144 schools) use a hybrid staffing model[4] that includes full-time faculty.[5] Thus, up to 91 percent of law schools

---

[1] These courses include the first-year course required by Standard 303(a)(2) of the ABA Accreditation Standards and any course required by a law school in the second year as part of a three-semester program. *See* Section of Legal Educ. & Admissions to the Bar, *ABA Standards and Rules of Procedure for Approval of Law Schools (2019-2020)*, ABA: Am. Bar. Ass'n [hereinafter ABA Standard(s)], https://www.americanbar.org/content/dam/aba/administrative/legal_education_and_admissions_to_the_bar/standards/2019-2020/2019-2020-aba-standards-and-rules-of-procedure.pdf.

[2] "LRW faculty" as used throughout this chapter refers to writing faculty who may also teach legal research as part of their courses. For an explanation of the terminology used in this *Sourcebook*, see Chapter I, Part A.3.

[3] *Compare* Ass'n of Legal Writing Dirs. & Legal Writing Inst., *Report of the 2017-2018 Institutional Survey* 9, Question 4.4 (2018) [hereinafter *2018 ALWD/LWI Survey*] (indicating that 123 out of 184 schools—with two schools apparently double-counted—employed full-time faculty to teach LRW), https://www.alwd.org/images/resources/ALWD-LWI-2017-18-Institutional-Survey-Report.pdf, *with* Ass'n of Legal Writing Dirs. & Legal Writing Inst., *2006 Survey Results* 6, Question 10 (2006) [hereinafter *2006 ALWD/LWI Survey*] (indicating that 92 out of 184 schools employed full-time tenured or non-tenured faculty specifically to teach LRW), https://www.alwd.org/images/resources/2006%20Survey%20Report%20(AY%202005-2006).pdf.

[4] A hybrid staffing model is one that usually employs a combination of full-time, part-time, and adjunct faculty, or hires faculty on short-term contracts that are convertible to long-term contracts or tenure. *See infra* Part D of this chapter.

[5] *See 2018 ALWD/LWI Survey*, *supra* note 3, at 10, Question 4.10 (indicating that 46 out of 48 schools with hybrid programs—25 percent of 182 schools—

surveyed now use all or some full-time faculty to teach the traditional first-year legal writing course.

Just as the percentage of LRW faculty who teach full time has increased, so has their status. LRW faculty are now eligible for tenure at roughly 27 percent of U.S. law schools.[6] Additionally, LRW faculty have ABA Standard 405(c) contracts at roughly 42 percent.[7] In terms of first-year LRW programs alone, it is safe to say that 69 percent of schools surveyed in 2018 offer full-time LRW faculty some form of tenure or a status reasonably similar to tenure.[8]

Thus, law schools are increasingly realizing the benefits of offering long-term employment opportunities to LRW professors.

---

employed at least some full-time legal writing faculty in their first-year or combined first-year and upper-level programs). That percentage has decreased from 29 percent in 2006, presumably because more schools are employing exclusively full-time faculty. *See 2006 ALWD/LWI Survey*, *supra* note 3, at 7, Question 11 (indicating that 53 out of 184 schools with hybrid programs—29 percent of 184 schools—employed at least some full-time legal writing faculty in the first year).

[6] *2018 ALWD/LWI Survey*, *supra* note 3, at 11, Question 4.11 (indicating that 49 schools with a first-year or combined first-year and upper-level program have legal writing faculty with some form of tenure). The Professional Status Committee of the Legal Writing Institute also maintains a list of schools offering tenure to LRW faculty as well as the program director (if any). *See The Professional Status Committee and Status-Related Advocacy*, LEGAL WRITING INST., https://www.lwionline.org/resources/status-related-advocacy (last visited Dec. 15, 2019) [hereinafter *LWI Professional Status Committee Advocacy*]. While the majority—76 percent—of these schools offer their LRW faculty traditional tenure (37 out of 49 schools), some offer programmatic tenure (12 out of 49 schools). *2018 ALWD/LWI Survey*, *supra* note 3, at 11, Question 4.11. While traditional tenure is achieved using the same standards for all faculty, programmatic tenure is "achieved through a separate track/using different standards than traditional tenure awarded to doctrinal faculty." *Id.* at viii. For more information on the different forms of tenure, see *infra* Part B.1 of this chapter.

[7] *See 2018 ALWD/LWI Survey*, *supra* note 3, at 11, Question 4.11 (69 out of 182 schools); *see also* ABA Standard 405(c).

[8] *See 2018 ALWD/LWI Survey*, *supra* note 3, at 11, Question 4.11.

Writing professors, like all professors, need time to develop their expertise. Students benefit most by learning from experienced professors who are invested in the school and the writing program and who are committed to excellence in teaching LRW. In addition, LRW professors who are long-term members of the faculty can make further contributions to the school through teaching other courses, writing law review articles and textbooks, and engaging in public service that enhances the school's reputation. Not surprisingly, the vast majority of LRW faculty with tenure or ABA Standard 405(c) status are required, expected, or encouraged to produce scholarship as a condition of their promotion.[9]

Consistent with the increase in LRW faculty status, law schools are also moving away from directed programs. Full-time professors with tenure or ABA Standard 405(c) status with voting rights have the requisite expertise to provide students with the highest level of instruction, a demonstrated commitment to the discipline, and the time and energy to mentor new legal writing colleagues. In 2018, roughly 31 percent of law schools surveyed had "autonomous programs," meaning without a director.[10] When programs move to an autonomous model, the perception of hierarchy is removed, allowing all LRW faculty to integrate fully with the law faculty as a whole.

A. Preliminary Considerations on Qualifications, Status, and Workload

Choosing the right faculty status for those teaching LRW courses, both required and elective, is critical to a program's success. While financial concerns cannot be ignored, the least expensive models are rarely the most effective. Inexperienced, part-time,

---

[9] *See id.* at 118, Question 11.34.

[10] *See id.* at 8, Question 4.3 (57 out of 184 schools, with two schools apparently double-counted). Some of these programs appoint a coordinator (akin to a department chair) to handle a program's administrative needs.

or adjunct faculty who cannot invest in a program's long-term goals or develop their teaching skills over time rarely provide the best learning experience for students. Accordingly, the ABA Standards require that "substantially all of the first one-third of each student's coursework" must be taught by full-time faculty.[11]

ABA Standard 405(d) currently requires that law schools "afford legal writing teachers such security of position and other rights and privileges of faculty membership as may be necessary to (1) attract and retain a faculty that is well qualified to provide legal writing instruction . . . , and (2) safeguard academic freedom."[12] Despite this modest requirement, law schools have increasingly recognized the significant value LRW faculty bring to legal education in terms of teaching, scholarship, and service, and the concomitant need to improve their overall standing in the legal academy. As a result, and as noted above, 69 percent of schools provide full-time LRW faculty with status superior to that required by ABA Standard 405(d).

Regardless of the program model, full-time LRW faculty should be considered the norm and should have the following qualifications and characteristics:[13]

- sufficient experience as a practicing attorney, with a well-rounded view of the legal profession and the settings in which legal writing occurs;

---

[11] ABA Standard 403(a).

[12] ABA Standard 405(d).

[13] Statistics demonstrate that LRW faculty increasingly possess these characteristics and credentials. *See, e.g.*, Susan Liemer & Hollee Temple, *Did Your Legal Writing Professor Go to Harvard?: The Credentials of Legal Writing Faculty at Hiring Time*, 46 U. LOUISVILLE L. REV. 383 (2008); Melissa H. Weresh, *Stars Upon Thars: Evaluating the Discriminatory Impact of ABA Standard 405(c) "Tenure-Like" Security of Position*, 34 LAW & INEQ. 137, 143 (2016) ("Many, if not most, legal writing faculty members produce scholarship and perform service. Further, legal writing faculty members often have academic credentials equal to their tenure-line peers.")

- demonstrated excellence in legal analysis, research, and writing, as well as other skills that might be required by the curriculum such as interviewing, counseling, negotiation, and advocacy;
- an interest in pedagogy and scholarship related to the LRW discipline; and
- the ability to communicate effectively, both in the classroom and in one-on-one conferences with students.

Over the past decade, some LRW program models have virtually disappeared. For example, the percentage of schools using solely adjuncts in the first year has dropped from 12.5 to 4 percent,[14] and the percentage of schools using upper-level students to teach or provide substantial written feedback in the first year has dropped from 6 to 2 percent.[15] Only two schools exclusively use teaching fellows.[16] The program models primarily in use today for LRW programs, which may be autonomous, can be summarized as follows: [17]

- Full-time professors, tenured or eligible for tenure;
- Full-time professors with long-term, presumptively renewable contracts under ABA Standard 405(c);

---

[14] *Compare 2006 ALWD/LWI Survey*, *supra* note 3, at 6, Question 10 (indicating that 23 out of 184 schools used solely adjuncts) *with 2018 ALWD/LWI Survey*, *supra* note 3, at 9, Question 4.4 (indicating that 7 out of 184 schools—with two schools apparently double-counted—used solely adjuncts for their first-year or combined first-year and upper-level programs).

[15] *Compare 2006 ALWD/LWI Survey*, *supra* note 3, at 6-7, Questions 10 & 11 (indicating that 13 out of 184 schools used upper-level students as described above) *with 2018 ALWD/LWI Survey*, *supra* note 3, at 9-10, Questions 4.4 & 4.10 (indicating that 4 out of 182 schools used upper-level students this way).

[16] *See 2018 ALWD/LWI Survey*, *supra* note 3, at 9-10, Questions 4.4 & 4.10 (indicating that up to 8 schools use teaching fellows as part of a hybrid first-year or combined first-year and upper-level program).

[17] Historically, the more "elite" the law school, the lower the status of the LRW faculty and curriculum. *See generally* Mitchell Nathanson, *Dismantling the Other: Understanding the Nature and Malleability of Groups in the Legal Writing Professor's Quest for Equality*, 13 Legal Writing 79 (2007).

- Full-time professors with varying contract status and voting rights;
- Full-time professors with short-term contracts that provide little or no job security or voting rights;
- Teaching fellows or visiting assistant professors;
- Part-time or adjunct faculty;[18] and
- A hybrid of the above options.

A school's ultimate choice of program model necessarily depends not only on the merit of the model itself, but also on local factors such as the needs of the curriculum; faculty, law school, and university policies; law school tradition; and other concerns and priorities. Each model has inherent advantages and disadvantages, although ABA Standards 303, 314, 315, and 403,[19] along with the

---

[18]Part-time and adjunct faculty members are distinguished on the basis of their time commitment to the school. A part-time faculty member is defined as follows:

> A faculty member, regardless of other status, who is hired to perform duties less than what is considered a normal full teaching or administrative load at the school. As distinguished from Adjunct faculty, a Part-[t]ime faculty member is typically obligated to work a set number of hours in a given time period (e.g., per week or per semester). This term does *not* include other types of faculty who have reduced loads on a temporary basis for whatever reason.

2018 ALWD/LWI Survey, *supra* note 3, at viii. An adjunct is defined as

> [a] faculty member hired to teach one or more courses, who may or may not have substantial outside employment. As distinguished from Part-[t]ime faculty, an Adjunct faculty member is typically obligated to teach one or more specific courses but does not typically have an obligation to work a set number of hours in a given time period (e.g., per week or per semester).

Id. at vi.

[19]ABA Standard 303(a)(2) requires each student to take "one writing experience in the first year and at least one additional writing experience after the first year, both of which [must be] faculty supervised;" ABA Standard 303(a)(3)

persistent and sometimes urgent call for better skills training in legal education,[20] suggest that the best practice is to adopt either a tenure-track model or an ABA Standard 405(c) model.[21] The more equitable the status of LRW faculty, the more likely those faculty will receive adequate support for both teaching and scholarship. Scholarship support is important because it enhances teaching, benefits students, and helps build the LRW discipline.[22]

To that end and to the extent possible, LRW faculty should have the same rights and privileges afforded other faculty, particularly those of the same rank or title, including:

---

requires each student to complete "one or more experiential course(s) totaling at least six credit hours." ABA Standards 314 and 315 require law schools to use formative and summative assessment methods to improve student learning and to routinely evaluate their students' degree of competency by measuring their progress on learning outcomes. Together, these standards seek to ensure that students learn both the theory and practice of law.

[20] *See, e.g.*, ABA SECTION OF LEGAL EDUC. & ADMISSIONS TO THE BAR, LEGAL EDUCATION AND PROFESSIONAL DEVELOPMENT – AN EDUCATIONAL CONTINUUM: REPORT OF THE TASK FORCE ON LAW SCHOOLS AND THE PROFESSION: NARROWING THE GAP (1992) [*hereinafter* MACCRATE REPORT]; ABA Task Force on the Future of Legal Educ., *Final Report and Recommendations* (2014), https://www.americanbar.org/groups/professional_responsibility/taskforceonthefuture legaleducation/; WILLIAM M. SULLIVAN ET AL., EDUCATING LAWYERS: PREPARATION FOR THE PRACTICE OF LAW (Carnegie Found. for Advancement of Teaching 2007); Ruth Anne Robbins, Amy Sloan & Kristen K. Tiscione, *Analysis, Research, and Communication in Skills-Focused Courses, in* BUILDING ON BEST PRACTICES: LEGAL EDUCATION IN A CHANGING WORLD 111 (Deborah Maranville et al. eds., 2015); David Segal, *What They Don't Teach Students: Lawyering*, N.Y. TIMES, Nov. 19, 2011, https://perma.cc/FR64-AJWE.

[21] On implementing ABA Standard 405(c), see Melissa H. Weresh, *Best Practices for Protecting Security of Position for 405(c) Faculty*, 66 J. LEGAL EDUC. 538 (2017).

[22] *See, e.g.*, Linda L. Berger, Linda H. Edwards & Terrill Pollman, *The Past, Presence, and Future of Legal Writing Scholarship: Rhetoric, Voice, and Community*, 16 LEGAL WRITING 537, 564-66 (2010).

- comparable teaching and service loads;
- small enough classes to allow professors to teach well and still have time to engage in scholarship and service;[23]
- teaching assistants when the nature of the course or course load so requires;
- support for scholarship, including research assistants, paid sabbaticals, and research leave; [24]
- support for continuing professional development, including attendance at and participation in regional and national conferences and organizations;
- voting rights;[25]
- the full measure of academic freedom;[26] and

---

[23] *See generally* Jan M. Levine, *From the Podium*, SCRIVENER, Summer 2001, at 2; 2 Legal Writing Inst., *The New Teacher's Deskbook,* THE MONOGRAPH SERIES (a selection of articles addressed to new LRW faculty); 3 Legal Writing Inst., *Teaching Legal Writing: Theory*, THE MONOGRAPH SERIES (a selection of foundational articles on theoretical approaches to teaching legal analysis and writing). For the full Monograph Series, see https://www.lwionline.org/publications/mono graph-series (last visited Dec. 15, 2019) [hereinafter *LWI Monograph Series*].

[24] *See* Deborah Maranville, Ruth Anne Robbins & Kristen K. Tiscione, *Faculty Status and Institutional Effectiveness, in* BUILDING ON BEST PRACTICES: LEGAL EDUCATION IN A CHANGING WORLD 432, 437-38 (Deborah Maranville et al. eds., 2015); Lisa Eichhorn, *Writing in the Legal Academy: A Dangerous Supplement?*, 40 ARIZ. L. REV. 105 (1998); Steven D. Jamar, *Doing It All—Over Time*, 16 SECOND DRAFT, Dec. 2001, at 15; Susan P. Liemer, *The Quest for Scholarship: The Legal Writing Professor's Paradox*, 80 OR. L. REV. 1007 (2002) [hereinafter Liemer, *Paradox*].

[25] At a number of law schools, particularly those offering only short-term contracts, LRW faculty still cannot vote. *See 2018 ALWD/LWI Survey*, *supra* note 3, at 79, Question 10.2 (indicating no voting rights for full-time LRW faculty on long-term, presumptively renewable; long-term, non-presumptively renewable; and short-term contracts at 2, 15, and 34 schools respectively). *See generally* Maranville, Robbins & Tiscione, *supra* note 24, at 436-37; Susan P. Liemer, *The Hierarchy of Law School Faculty Meetings: Who Votes?,* 73 UMKC L. REV. 351 (2004) (addressing law faculty voting rights).

[26] *See* Am. Assoc. of Univ. Professors (AAUP), *1940 Statement of Principles on Academic Freedom and Tenure*, https://www.aaup.org/report/1940-statement

- any other standard faculty perquisites, such as health insurance coverage and retirement benefits.

The remainder of this Part discusses general considerations when adopting or transitioning to a particular LRW program model, as well as the hiring process and status of the faculty teaching in the program.

1. Equal and Fair Treatment, Governance Rights, and Academic Freedom

The rights and privileges suggested above are essential to full citizenship for LRW faculty, a status that benefits the school, faculty at large, and student body. Full citizenship includes equal and fair treatment and the ability to participate in faculty governance.[27] In 2015, the Legal Writing Institute, the Association of Legal Writing Directors, and the Society of American Law Teachers adopted a statement in support of full citizenship rights for all faculty, regardless of the subject matter they teach.[28] When LRW faculty are recognized for their contributions to the school's mission, they are inspired both to grow as scholars and teachers and to build the LRW discipline. In contrast, a school that devalues its LRW faculty sends

---

-principles-academic-freedom-and-tenure; Maranville, Robbins & Tiscione, *supra* note 24, at 435-36; Liemer, *supra* note 25, at 373-75.

[27] *See* Maranville, Robbins & Tiscione, *supra* note 24, at 437.

[28] The statement reads,

> No justification exists for subordinating one group of law faculty to another based on the nature of the course, the subject matter, or the teaching method. All full-time law faculty should have the opportunity to achieve full citizenship at their institutions, including academic freedom, security of position, and governance rights. Those rights are necessary to ensure that law students and the legal profession benefit from the myriad perspectives and expertise that all faculty bring to the mission of legal education.

The three sponsoring organizations also collected over 570 individual signatures in support of the statement. *See LWI Professional Status Committee Advocacy*, *supra* note 6 (signatures on file with the Legal Writing Institute).

a message to both faculty and students that the law school does not value skills-focused courses as much as other courses. That message can cause students to spend less time and effort on LRW courses and discourage them from seeking recommendations from faculty who often know them and their written work best.[29]

Full citizenship also includes the right to vote at faculty meetings;[30] to participate in, vote in, and chair faculty committees;[31] to enjoy the same eligibility for resources that support the production of scholarship, such as sabbaticals and research leave, research stipends, research assistants, and professional development funding;[32] and to be considered for faculty leadership positions.[33] Full-time LRW faculty who teach and serve on committees, whether or not they are required to produce scholarship, should have a voice in faculty meetings, particularly when the school hires legal writing faculty or changes the LRW curriculum.

Finally, all faculty should enjoy the full measure of academic freedom, which includes the ability to choose course textbooks, design a syllabus, and create assignments.[34] Academic freedom for all

---

[29] *See* Kristen K. Tiscione & Amy Vorenberg, *Podia and Pens: Dismantling the Two-Track System for Legal Research and Writing Faculty*, 31 COLUM. J. GENDER & L. 47, 57-59 (2015); *cf.* Weresh, *supra* note 13, at 146-49.

[30] *See 2018 ALWD/LWI Survey*, *supra* note 3, at 79, Question 10.2 (indicating that a majority of schools grant some form of voting rights to their full-time LRW faculty with long-term contract or better status).

[31] *See id.* at 82-83, Questions 10.8 & 10.9#2 (indicating that an overwhelming majority of schools require or permit their full-time LRW faculty to engage in committee service and to vote on matters before that committee, regardless of status).

[32] *See id.* at 84-89, Questions 10.12 & 10.14-10.16.

[33] Maranville, Robbins & Tiscione, *supra* note 24, at 438.

[34] *But see infra* Parts B.5 and C of this chapter, explaining that it may be preferable to select materials for fellows, part-time faculty, or adjunct faculty due to time constraints and to ensure consistent student experiences.

faculty includes the right to engage in a chosen area of research, even if controversial, and to speak one's mind without fear of reprisal.[35]

The interplay of security of position, participation in governance, and academic freedom is important.[36] LRW faculty with less security of position than their colleagues often feel silenced even when given an opportunity to speak.

2. *Suggested Student/Faculty Ratio*

As LRW programs have matured and curricula have developed, faculty have come to expect students to perform at a consistently higher level of competence. At the same time, the number of students entering law school with academic support needs, such as English proficiency problems and learning or other types of disabilities, is on the rise.

The ideal student/faculty ratio for required LRW courses in the first-year or upper-level curriculum will vary, but a reasonable target teaching load for full-time faculty teaching solely LRW and no other courses is 30-35 students, regardless of how many sections the faculty member teaches.[37] Thus, a typical full-time faculty member who teaches two sections of first-year LRW would expect no more than 15 to 18 students in each section.

A number of factors will affect whether this ratio should be even lower at a particular school, including whether the professor is also teaching a casebook class; whether the professor is simultaneously teaching another writing class; how legal research is taught and by whom; and whether LRW faculty are expected to spend extensive time with high-need students.

---

[35] Maranville, Robbins & Tiscione, *supra* note 24, at 435-36.

[36] *See generally* Richard Neumann Jr., *Academic Freedom, Job Security, and Costs*, 66 J. Legal Educ. 595 (2017).

[37] *See 2018 ALWD/LWI Survey*, *supra* note 3, at 91, Question 10.18 (indicating that the average number of students per term for each full-time LRW professor is somewhere between 24.6 and 34.8).

The student/faculty ratio should ensure that faculty have adequate time to engage in the following activities:

- develop high-quality teaching materials that successfully communicate course content to students;[38]
- prepare for class, present new material, reinforce reading assignments, and conduct in-class, small-group exercises;
- develop assignments, critique and grade papers, conduct individual conferences, and answer student questions outside class; and
- provide guidance to inexperienced LRW professors.

Experience demonstrates that greater student loads inhibit professional development, all but preclude scholarship, and cause faculty "burn-out," all of which ultimately compromise student learning outcomes.

3. Reasonable Teaching and Service Loads

Law schools should be careful not to overburden LRW faculty with teaching and service obligations. Most LRW faculty participate in committee service.[39] Increasingly, though, LRW faculty are asked to provide additional service. LRW faculty now teach additional orientation or enrichment courses and assist with bar exam preparation. Many are expected to handle academic support needs (whether compensated as part of their regular contract or as an overload), including serving as associate deans of academic support. Some LRW faculty serve as associate deans for academic affairs. These decanal appointments, in particular, are almost impossible to balance with the demands of a full LRW teaching load.

---

[38] *See generally LWI Monograph Series*, *supra* note 23, Vols. 2 & 3.

[39] *See 2018 ALWD/LWI Survey*, *supra* note 3, at 82, Question 10.8 (some are required and others are expected to perform service).

Together with the fact that 72 percent of LRW faculty are untenured and female,[40] the ability (too often exercised) to exploit LRW faculty has led to criticism that they often bear a disproportionate teaching and service burden.[41] This burden can be exacerbated when LRW faculty participate in and present at regional and national LRW conferences or take on roles in one of the national LRW organizations. Serving one of these organizations as president or planning a regional or national conference brings valued publicity to an LRW program and its law school, but those leadership responsibilities consume significant time. In instances where valued service becomes overwhelming, some course relief would be appropriate.

4. *Lack of Diversity Among LRW Faculty*

Law faculties in general need to be more diverse, but LRW faculties are the least diverse of all.[42] Just as most LRW faculty are women, most LRW faculty of color tend to be women. In

---

[40] *See* Ass'n of Legal Writing Dirs. & Legal Writing Inst., *Report of the 2015 Survey* 69, Question 71(b) (2016) [hereinafter *2015 ALWD/LWI Survey*], https://www.alwd.org/images/resources/2015%20Survey%20Report%20(AY%202014-2015).pdf.

[41] *See, e.g.*, Maureen J. Arrigo, *Hierarchy Maintained: Status and Gender Issues in Legal Writing Programs*, 70 Temp. L. Rev. 117, 165-66 (1997); Peter Brandon Bayer, *A Plea for Rationality and Decency: The Disparate Treatment of Legal Writing Faculties as a Violation of Both Equal Protection and Professional Ethics*, 39 Duq. L. Rev. 329, 366-68 (2001); Robert Steinbuch, *Finding Female Faculty: Empirically Assessing the State of Women in the Legal Academy*, 36 Women's Rts. L. Rep. 375, 377-86 (2015).

[42] *Compare, e.g.,* Section of Legal Educ. & Admissions to the Bar, *Law School Faculty & Staff by Ethnicity and Gender, Data from 2013 Annual Questionnaire*, ABA: Am. Bar. Ass'n (the most recent data available indicating that minorities comprise 14 and 23 percent of traditional tenured male and female faculty, respectively), https://www.americanbar.org/content/dam/aba/administrative/legal_education_and_admissions_to_the_bar/statistics/2013_law_school_staff_gender_ethnicity.xlsx, *with 2015 ALWD/LWI Survey*, *supra* note 40, at 69, Question 71(b) (indicating that 11.4 percent of legal writing faculty are minorities); *see also infra*

combination with the lesser rights and privileges afforded LRW faculty, the intersectional challenges that female faculty of color face[43] may account for this disparity in minority representation. Law schools should adopt hiring practices and select faculty status models with the explicit goal of increasing race and gender diversity among faculty teaching skills-focused courses.

5. *Role of an LRW Director or Coordinator*

When LRW courses independent of casebook courses were introduced in the 1970s and 1980s, they were almost always part of programs led by a director. Those early courses were typically taught by either short-term "instructors" who were expected to teach for just a few years, or by upper-level students. Thus, a director was needed to develop course materials and to hire, train, and evaluate those who taught in the program. With the development of the LRW discipline and the move to mostly full-time faculty, the need for an LRW director in many schools has significantly diminished. The current trend favors autonomous models (i.e., without a director).[44]

When all LRW faculty are tenured or have security of position reasonably similar to tenure, an autonomous model is likely the best practice. Ideally, LRW faculty will collaborate to ensure that course goals are met and that students in different sections learn similar skills and have comparable educational experiences. Even in autonomous models, the LRW faculty may prefer to delegate certain recurring or administrative functions to a coordinator. The coordinator's role is not supervisory; it is administrative. The coordinator

---

Chapter VI, Part B.1.d (discussing the relative lack of diversity among LRW faculty and the intersectional impact of status disparities based on one's teaching field).

[43] *See generally* Meera E. Deo, *Intersectional Barriers to Tenure*, 51 U.C. Davis L. Rev. 101 (2018); Teri McMurtry-Chubb, *Writing at the Master's Table: Reflections on Theft, Criminality, and Otherness in the Legal Writing Profession*, 2 Drexel L. Rev. 41 (2009).

[44] *See supra* note 10 and accompanying text; *see also infra* Chapter VI, Part A.1 (discussing autonomous programs).

can streamline administrative work with other parts of the law school (e.g., associate dean, registrar, or librarians), organize regular events related to LRW (e.g., a visit to a state supreme court to observe oral arguments), and facilitate outreach to other schools. Often, the coordinator is similar to a department chair, serving as an administrator for a period of time and then passing the role on to another colleague.

Schools that still rely on adjunct professors, part-time professors, fellows, or short-term professors who rotate through a program quickly will likely need to hire an LRW director. The director recruits, interviews, and hires faculty, perhaps in consultation with a committee. With adjunct, part-time, and new faculty, the director's role generally includes preparing materials that everyone in the program may use. As faculty gain experience, they may be willing and able to take over this work themselves, but the director must still be available to support their efforts. The director also trains, mentors, supports, and evaluates all LRW colleagues. Another key component of a director's responsibility is ensuring that the first-year course content and curricular offerings beyond the first year are consistent with best practices.

The best directors see themselves as advocates for their LRW faculty on issues such as class size, salaries, professional development opportunities, and office location. Tensions can arise in this model if the director's approach is out of step with the needs of the rest of the LRW faculty. A director should expect to encounter resistance if insisting that experienced colleagues use a common syllabus or assignments that do not match their pedagogical approaches. On the other hand, a director would be remiss in expecting adjuncts or fellows to develop all their own course materials.

6. Methods of Hiring LRW Faculty

a. Hiring Full-Time Faculty

Full-time LRW faculty can be hired using the typical advertising avenues for full-time faculty—the AALS Faculty Recruiting Conference Bulletin, law school placement offices, bar association publications, and legal newspapers. Additional avenues, however, are available. A number of legal writing organizations circulate vacancy announcements, including the Association of Legal Writing Directors; the Legal Writing Institute; and the AALS Section on Legal Writing, Reasoning, and Research. Hiring announcements can thus be communicated in places that are particularly accessible to LRW professors:

- The official listserv of the Legal Writing Institute (LWI), LRWPROF-L, to which most LRW professors subscribe. A school wanting to post a job opening should contact the listserv manager or ask someone who is already a list subscriber to post the announcement. Job announcements can also be posted on the LWI website.
- The official listserv of the Association of Legal Writing Directors (ALWD), DIRCON. Most schools have at least one or more ALWD delegates who subscribe to the list. Here, too, a school wanting to post a job opening should ask someone who is already a subscriber to the list or contact the listserv manager for assistance.

All job announcements for LRW faculty openings posted on the LWI or ALWD listservs should include the disclosure form included below, with each item completed.

Job Posting Disclosure Form

1. The position advertised:

__ a. is a tenure-track appointment.

__ b. may lead to successive long-term contracts of five or more years.

__ c. may lead only to successive short-term contracts of one to four years.

__ d. has an upper-limit on the number of years a teacher may be appointed.

__ e. is part of a fellowship program for one or two years.

__ f. is a part-time appointment, or a year-to-year adjunct appointment.

2. The professor hired:
__ a. will be permitted to vote in faculty meetings.
__ b. will not be permitted to vote in faculty meetings.

3. The school anticipates paying an annual academic year base salary in the range checked below. (A base salary does not include stipends for coaching moot court teams, teaching other courses, or teaching in summer school; a base salary does not include conference travel or other professional development funds.)
__ over $120,000
__ $110,000 - $119,999
__ $100,000 - $109,999
__ $90,000 - $99,999
__ $80,000 - $89,999
__ $70,000 - $79,999
__ $60,000 - $69,999
__ $50,000 - $59,999
__ less than $50,000
__ this is an adjunct appointment paying less than $10,000

4. The number of students enrolled in each semester of the courses taught by the legal research & writing professor will be:
__ a. 30 or fewer
__ b. 31 – 35
__ c. 36 – 40
__ d. 41 – 45
__ e. 46 – 50
__ f. 51 – 55
__ g. 56 – 60
__ h. more than 60

Because the LRW discipline is largely occupied by women, law schools should pay particular attention to salaries provided to LRW faculty to avoid perceptions of gender discrimination.[45] In addition, a school seeking new faculty, including a director, should consider seeking help from officers and board members of ALWD and LWI; the officers of the AALS Section on Legal Writing, Reasoning, and Research; LRW faculty who teach in well-regarded programs; and other leaders in the discipline.

The hiring process for full-time LRW faculty ideally should mirror the hiring process for any other tenure-track professor, and many schools now begin that process at the AALS faculty recruitment conference in Washington, D.C., held each fall, typically in October. Even if the position carries only ABA Standard 405(c) status, following the usual hiring process will give all faculty more confidence in the result because they are familiar and comfortable with this conventional method of hiring. In particular, all applicants should meet with the dean and faculty members (including those teaching LRW) and should give a presentation similar to those given by applicants for tenure-track positions. Whether the "job talk" should focus on pedagogy or scholarship depends on the culture of a particular school.

b. Considerations for Hiring a Director

The prior section on hiring full-time LRW faculty also pertains to hiring a program director. Regardless of the program model, schools should hire directors through the same process used for hiring other tenure-track faculty. Schools should pay particular attention to salaries provided to directors who are women, as statistics

---

[45] *See, e.g.*, J. Lyn Entrikin, Lucy Jewel, Craig T. Smith, Susan Salmon, Kristen K. Tiscione & Melissa H. Weresh, *Treating Professionals Professionally: Requiring Security of Position for All Skills-Focused Faculty Under ABA Accreditation Standard 405(c) and Eliminating 405(d)*, 98 Or. L. Rev. 1, 27-34 (2020); Tiscione & Vorenberg, *supra* note 29, at 49-52; Ass'n of Legal Writing Dirs. & Legal Writing Inst., *Report of the 2014 Survey*, App. A, at 102-03 (2014) (indicating that the salary range for female directors was $71,101-$85,312 and for men was $78,894–$100,009), https://www.lwionline.org/sites/default/files/2014-Survey-Report-Final.pdf [hereinafter *2014 ALWD/LWI Survey*].

show that men are often paid more than similarly qualified women, particularly in the director role.[46]

A candidate for director should have the same qualifications as other tenure-track faculty, along with administrative, managerial, and leadership skills; experience teaching LRW courses; and a genuine career commitment to teaching LRW. In view of the different groups—faculty, administrators, and students—with whom a director works, interpersonal skills are very important. A director also needs excellent judgment and administrative skills. In addition, a director needs a theoretical conception of LRW and its pedagogy. Finally, an ideal director should have the ability to bring esteem to the law school by taking a leadership position in the national LRW community and contributing to the discipline.

c. *Considerations for Hiring Part-time or Adjunct Faculty*

Many attorneys who aspire to join the legal academy on a part-time basis believe that teaching LRW will be enjoyable, easy, and not unduly time-consuming. After a few weeks, these attorneys often find that teaching the course is not only extremely rewarding, but also both challenging and time-consuming. Qualifications as a strong writer with a successful practice do not always translate into an ability to explain to a novice how to write a successful legal argument. Nor do they suggest an ability to provide comments showing a student how and why to improve an early draft. Thus, the director or committee charged with hiring part-time or adjunct faculty must identify candidates who combine an interest in teaching, strong writing skills, and sufficient time (and a sufficiently flexible work schedule) to devote to curricular and student needs, including time for marking papers and meeting individually with students. Especially in a program that provides syllabi, materials, and writing assignments, part-time or adjunct faculty must be willing to conform when necessary to program requirements.

---

[46] *See, e.g.*, *2014 ALWD/LWI Survey*, *supra* note 45, App. A, at 102-03.

Schools that hire adjunct faculty require applicants to have, on average, around three years of law practice experience.[47] Most schools require adjuncts and part-time candidates to attend a personal interview and provide a writing sample, while some also require letters of reference and transcripts.[48] A few also require a candidate to provide a sample critique of a student memo or brief.[49]

Local and state bar organizations can post ads seeking applicants for part-time or adjunct positions. In addition, outreach to local attorneys who have judged oral arguments or mentored first-year students might help expand the pool of qualified candidates. Graduates of the school's LRW program may be especially suited as part-time or adjunct faculty, especially graduates who served as teaching assistants in the program or as research assistants to LRW faculty members. Past teaching experience, even in another field, can indicate that a candidate is more likely to become a successful LRW teacher.

The rest of this chapter describes each of the faculty staffing models currently in use, along with their pedagogical and curricular advantages and disadvantages, financial challenges, and the role of the director or coordinator (if any). For detailed historical and current data on each of these models, see the annual ALWD/LWI Survey reports, which are available on both organizations' websites.

---

[47] *2018 ALWD/LWI Survey*, *supra* note 3, at 180, Question 16.8 (showing that the minimum years of law practice experience required to teach in the first-year LRW program ranges from one to five, with a mean of 3.3 years). Of the schools that reportedly hired part-time faculty to teach LRW courses, only one law school reported requiring some practice experience as a condition for teaching the course. *Id.* at 169, Question 15.12.

[48] *Id.* at 181, Question 16.9 (regarding adjunct faculty); *id.* at 166, Question 15.6 (regarding part-time faculty). As the survey responses show, candidates for part-time positions are more likely to be asked for letters and transcripts.

[49] *Id.* at 181, Question 16.9 (showing that 4 of 30 schools require adjuncts to provide a sample critique); *id.* at 166, Question 15.6 (indicating that 5 of 22 require candidates for part-time positions to provide a sample critique).

B. Full-Time Professors

1. Tenure-Track or Tenured Professors

Many LRW faculty members have traditional "unitary" tenure, enjoying the same security of position and status as other tenured faculty teaching casebook courses, after meeting the same tenure standards that apply to all full-time faculty.[50] In some schools, LRW faculty earn "programmatic tenure." While the terms of this tenure vary by institution, the security of position held by these faculty members is typically indistinguishable from the security held by other tenured faculty.[51] In other words, tenure status can be terminated only for cause,[52] financial exigency,[53] or programmatic

---

[50]According to the 2018 ALWD/LWI annual survey, 66 law schools employed LRW faculty under a tenure model. *Id.* at 52, Question 8.2. Fifty-one of these programs indicated that the tenure was unitary, and fifteen schools indicated that the tenure model was programmatic. *Id.*

[51]*See id.* at viii. Indeed, "credible arguments suggest that legal writing should be a fully tenure-track position." Catherine Martin Christopher, *Putting Legal Writing on the Tenure Track: One School's Experience*, 31 COLUM. J. GENDER & L. 65, 71 (2015).

[52]According to the AAUP Recommended Institutional Regulations on Academic Freedom and Tenure, "[a]dequate cause for a dismissal will be related, directly and substantially, to the fitness of faculty members in their professional capacities as teachers or researchers. Dismissal will not be used to restrain faculty members in their exercise of academic freedom or other rights of American citizens." AAUP, *Recommended Institutional Regulations on Academic Freedom and Tenure* 5(a) (2018), https://www.aaup.org/report/recommended-institutional-regulations-academic-freedom-and-tenure. Because of the strong security of position afforded tenured faculty, the AAUP guidelines provide significant substantive and procedural protections to a faculty member, subject to termination for cause. A unitary tenure system for LRW faculty typically implies commensurate perquisites related to governance, status, and compensation.

[53]The AAUP regulations define financial exigency as a "demonstrably bona fide financial exigency, i.e., a severe financial crisis that fundamentally compromises the academic integrity of the institution as a whole and that cannot be alleviated by less drastic means." *Id.* 4(c)(1).

reductions.[54] Notwithstanding equity with regard to security of position, programmatic tenured positions may differ in other ways. Promotion and retention standards for faculty with programmatic tenure may differ from the standards applicable to casebook faculty, often allowing for a broader range or amount of scholarship necessary to attain tenure.[55] Some faculty members with programmatic tenure do not enjoy the same title, governance rights,[56] or compensation as tenured casebook professors.

LRW faculty who are on tenure track typically teach primarily LRW courses or a combination of LRW and non-LRW courses.[57] Pedagogical, curricular, and financial implications associated with these models are explored below.

---

[54] It is unlikely that a tenured LRW professor could be terminated under this provision. *See* Weresh, *supra* note 21. Weresh argued,

> Because the ABA standards require law schools to provide legal writing instruction in the first year, the standards appear to prohibit a "bona fide formal discontinuance of a program or department of instruction" involving first year legal writing. For example, if a law school had a legal writing *program* staffed by legal writing professors with security of position "reasonably similar to tenure," it could not terminate those faculty members for programmatic discontinuance and then replace the required first year instruction with new faculty. For law schools that provide first year legal writing instruction with faculty who are not part of a formal program, the programmatic reductions mechanism would be inapplicable.

Id. at 550-51 (citations omitted).

[55] Clinical faculty at some institutions are also on a programmatic tenure track. The variation in scholarship requirements for clinical and LRW faculty often reflects the workload associated with these positions, which involves substantial student contact hours and time spent reviewing student work.

[56] In some institutions, professors with programmatic tenure enjoy the full range of voting rights, except that they are not eligible to vote on the promotion of professors on the casebook tenure track.

[57] *See 2018 ALWD/LWI Survey*, *supra* note 3, at 90, Question 10.17 (indicating that 77 percent of LRW faculty with traditional tenure regularly or periodically teach non-legal writing courses as part of their normal course load, as do 60 percent of LRW faculty with programmatic tenure).

a. *Tenure-Track Professors Who Primarily Teach LRW Courses*

i. Pedagogical and Curricular Implications

Full-time, tenured professors who have devoted their careers to the LRW discipline are recognized throughout the legal academy as the best suited to teach first-year law students. ABA Standard 403(b) requires full-time faculty to provide "substantially" all instruction given to first-year students.[58] Although many good or even excellent LRW programs follow other employment models, schools that hire tenured or tenure-track professors specifically to teach LRW recognize LRW as an integral part of the law school curriculum and accept writing professors as an integral part of the school's faculty.

This commitment significantly benefits the students, who are taught by faculty with relevant experience, professionally committed to teaching LRW, and familiar with the scholarship and pedagogy of the discipline. Moreover, these professors are available to students on a full-time basis and can respond to students' needs, whether academic or professional. It is common for the LRW professor, who meets with students in small classes, to be the faculty member who knows each student best and can provide job references and academic advice.

---

[58] ABA Standard 403(b). Notably, in 2017 the ABA considered but ultimately did not recommend changes to this standard. Summarizing its reasoning for retaining the standard, the Section of Legal Education and Admissions to the Bar explained, "[The first] year is important in creating a sense of academic community among students and the faculty. The role of full-time faculty in creating that community is critical and the interaction between law students and full-time faculty that should take place during that year is significant in providing a foundation for future learning." Am. Bar Ass'n Section of Legal Educ. & Admissions to the Bar, Memorandum from Gregory G. Murphy, Council Chairperson & Barry A. Currier, Managing Dir. of Legal Accreditation & Legal Educ., to Interested Persons & Entities, *ABA Standards for Approval of Law Schools: Matters for Notice and Comment* 3 (Mar. 24, 2017), https://www.americanbar.org/content/dam/aba/administrative/legal_education_and_admissions_to_the_bar/council_reports_and_resolutions/20170324_notice_and_comment_memo.pdf.

In addition, tenure-track LRW professors may be uniquely qualified to contribute to the law school curriculum in a wide variety of ways. For example, they have the skills needed to advise a law journal editorial board, coach a moot court competition team, help faculty who teach casebook courses integrate analytical writing assignments,[59] teach seminar faculty how to give effective formative feedback on student writing, teach an upper-level writing course,[60] assist junior faculty in improving their scholarly writing, and contribute to the law schools' efforts to comply with ABA Standards relating to student learning outcomes and assessment.[61]

ii. Financial Implications

The cost of this model per professor is indistinguishable from the costs incurred by employing tenure-track professors to teach any law school course, but the cost per student often appears higher because of the need for small classes in LRW. Whether the cost actually *is* higher depends on how the rest of the curriculum is staffed. A

---

[59] *See supra* Chapter I, Part D; *see also* Andrea McArdle, *Writing Across the Curriculum: Professional Communication and the Writing That Supports It*, 15 Legal Writing 241 (2009); Carol McCrehan Parker, *Writing Is Everybody's Business: Theoretical and Practical Justifications for Teaching Writing across the Law School Curriculum*, 12 Legal Writing 175, 176 (2006); Pamela Lysaght & Cristina D. Lockwood, *Writing-Across-the-Law-School Curriculum: Theoretical Justifications, Curricular Implications*, 2 J. ALWD 73 (2004).

[60] LRW faculty report teaching many upper-level writing courses, particularly those involving advocacy, drafting (including contract, pre-trial, and litigation), judicial opinion writing, and scholarly writing. *See 2018 ALWD/LWI Survey*, *supra* note 3, at 48-49, Question 7.7.

[61] LRW faculty are pioneers in developing institutional and course-level learning outcomes and assessment materials such as rubrics to facilitate student learning. *See, e.g.*, Lori E. Shaw & Victoria L. VanZandt, Student Learning Outcomes and Law School Assessment: A Practical Guide to Measuring Institutional Effectiveness (2015). *See generally supra* Chapter I, Part B.2.b.i, and Chapter IV for more detailed information on formative assessment and related ABA Standards.

casebook faculty member who teaches a large section of one course but small sections of other highly specialized courses may have the same or higher "cost per student" ratio as a tenure-track LRW professor who consistently teaches 30-35 students per semester.

As is true for all professors hired on the tenure track, the law school makes a long-term, career commitment to these professors in return for their satisfying certain criteria, including teaching, service, and scholarship. For this reason, the overall cost of this model is likely to be higher than the cost of models that do not include a long-term, career commitment to the LRW professor, but the benefit to students and the school is substantial.

iii. Other Considerations

Hiring LRW professors on a tenure track deserves thoughtful consideration, particularly because their teaching load requires substantial interaction with students outside class and a significant amount of time evaluating and responding to student papers.[62]

---

[62] *See generally* Jan M. Levine, *Voices in the Wilderness: Tenured and Tenure-Track Directors and Teachers in Legal Research and Writing Programs*, 45 J. Legal Educ. 530 (1995); *see also* Ann C. McGinley, *Employment Law Considerations for Law Schools Hiring Legal Writing Professors*, 66 J. Legal Educ. 585 (2017). McGinley addresses the risk of liability for gender-based discrimination under Title VII with regard to the employment of predominantly female professors under ABA Standard 405(c), which requires security of position "reasonably similar to tenure." She asserted,

> A sticky problem for law schools that decide to use 405(c) contracts instead of tenure-track appointments for legal writing teachers is the predominance of female faculty members who teach writing . . . Law schools have potential legal liability for gender-based employment discrimination under Title VII of the Civil Rights Act of 1964 and Title IX of the Education Amendments of 1972 where legal writing faculty members in the law school are predominantly female.

McGinley, *supra,* at 589 (citations omitted).

For example, the administration and faculty must determine whether the tenure requirements for LRW professors should be the same as those for other tenure-track professors, especially in terms of quantity of scholarship. The labor-intensive requirements of teaching LRW can make publishing, for example, more difficult for LRW professors. The differential workload is not insurmountable assuming that LRW faculty enjoy the same type of scholarship resources as other members of the faculty (e.g., research assistants and research leave). Given a realistic student/faculty ratio, LRW faculty can satisfy reasonable publication requirements.[63]

Schools may also consider whether scholarship on LRW doctrine or its pedagogy is acceptable for satisfying tenure standards. Once a school decides to grant tenure-track status to LRW professors, it would be inconsistent to discount or reject scholarship in the discipline when considering eligibility for tenure and thus discourage LRW faculty from becoming experts in their own discipline. Such an anomalous standard would undermine the significance of granting tenure-track status to LRW professors and burden them far more than other tenure-track professors.[64] Indeed, at most schools,

---

[63] In fact, at the majority of schools that afford LRW faculty traditional or unitary tenure, the scholarship standards for promotion are the same as those applicable to casebook faculty. *2018 ALWD/LWI Survey*, *supra* note 3, at 124-25, Question 11.37.

[64] Mary Beth Beazley, *Finishing the Job of Legal Education Reform,* 51 WAKE FOREST L. REV. 275 (2016). Beazley observed,

> When legal writing faculty are discouraged from writing in their teaching area, . . . the field suffers in at least two ways. First, legal writing is a young field; it needs substantive scholarship to help increase and generate knowledge about the theory and practice of legal writing, and the ways in which each impact legal education, law, and public policy. Second, legal writing faculty who are told not to write about legal writing learn that the field is not respected or secure, and they are discouraged from continuing to teach in the field. When young scholars leave legal writing for more secure or more respected positions, legal writing loses expertise that is crucial to our law students, and thus to the future of the legal profession.

articles about pedagogy qualify as scholarship for promotion and retention purposes.[65]

Faculties might consider the so-called "burn-out" factor sometimes articulated as a problem in hiring tenure-track LRW professors. Because teaching LRW is so labor-intensive, some fear that the professors eventually will want to switch to teaching *solely* casebook courses. The true causes of burn-out, however, are more likely the often overwhelming student/faculty ratios, the lack of opportunity for a sabbatical or other temporary relief from the course's demands, and the tensions that accompany insecure employment status. When LRW professors are given reasonable student/faculty ratios, allowing them to do their jobs well, they are no more likely to burn out than any other tenure-track faculty.

Indeed, faculty candidates who are attracted to teaching LRW usually thrive on the opportunity to work closely and intensively with students, as long as the workload is manageable and the rewards appropriate. Sabbaticals and research leave are as necessary and beneficial for teachers of LRW as they are for any other teachers. When LRW professors have tenure-track status and are accorded the usual benefits and resources of a tenure-track position, the traditional reasons for burn-out are no longer factors.

b. Tenure-Track Professors Who Teach Both LRW and Non-LRW or Casebook Courses[66]

i. Pedagogical and Curricular Implications

All law professors can develop their teaching skills and professional confidence more completely when assigned to teach a range of courses over their teaching careers. Indeed, many schools recognize

---

Id. at 296.

[65] *2018 ALWD/LWI Survey*, *supra* note 3, at 119-23, Questions 11.35-11.36.

[66] "Casebook courses" in this chapter refers to traditional casebook courses such as Constitutional Law, Contracts, and Corporations, as well as upper-level writing seminars.

the value LRW professors bring to other courses in the law school.[67] Some LRW professors may wish to teach courses that address the legal doctrines they employ as the subject of their LRW assignments or their scholarship.[68] Others may be particularly well-suited to teach other skills and simulation courses. LRW professors can also bring new pedagogical ideas to casebook classes, particularly with innovative teaching techniques and small-group work.[69]

Hiring tenure-eligible faculty to teach LRW and enabling them to teach other courses as well conveys several important messages to students and faculty. First, LRW is as important as casebook courses, and students should work just as hard to master the material. Second, those who teach LRW are not mere grammarians and are just as "intellectual" as other faculty. Finally, hiring professors to teach both writing and casebook courses comports with the recommendation of the *MacCrate Report* to incorporate skills training throughout the law school curriculum.[70] Professors who demonstrate expertise in both LRW and casebook doctrine reinforce the idea that an effective lawyer needs both theoretical knowledge and the practical skills required in the "real world" of practice. Faculty with this breadth of expertise also serve as valuable role models for students.[71]

---

[67] Many law schools allow or expect LRW faculty to teach additional courses. *See 2018 ALWD/LWI Survey*, *supra* note 3, at 90, Question 10.17.

[68] *See* Susan E. Thrower, *Teaching Legal Writing Through Subject-Matter Specialties: A Reconception of Writing across the Curriculum*, 13 LEGAL WRITING 3 (2007); Susan P. Liemer, *Many Birds, One Stone: Teaching the Law You Love, in Legal Writing Class*, 53 J. LEGAL EDUC. 284 (2003).

[69] LRW faculty on Standard 405(c) programmatic tenure track regularly teach classes outside the LRW curriculum. *See 2018 ALWD/LWI Survey*, *supra* note 3, at 90, Question 10.17.

[70] *See generally* MACCRATE REPORT, *supra* note 20.

[71] *See, e.g.*, Bryan G. Garth & Joanne Martin, *Law Schools and the Construction of Competence*, 43 J. LEGAL EDUC. 469, 490 (1993); Stuart A. Handmaker,

In the past, a handful of schools used casebook professors to teach LRW as part of a first-year, small-section casebook course, but this model no longer appears to be in regular use.[72] Under this model, tenure-track or tenured professors who taught a first-year casebook course were also responsible for teaching LRW to the students in that course. Typically, the writing assignments were in the subject area of the particular course. Some faculty might have rotated in and out of teaching the course, while others might have taught the course as part of their typical teaching package.

In either situation, whether in the past or currently, having one or more casebook faculty members with expertise in teaching LRW can greatly support a writing program. A school wishing to use this model might want to hire tenure-track professors who are willing and able to teach both first-year casebook courses and legal writing, as well as a tenured director or coordinator who can provide the vision, training, and coordination necessary to make the model work.

ii. Financial Implications and Other Considerations

A large and growing number of professors who have committed their careers to teaching LRW are also well qualified to teach casebook courses. The cost of this model per professor is much the same as the costs of employing tenure-track professors to teach any law school course and should be lower than the cost of hiring tenure-track faculty to teach only LRW since the overall cost per student may be less. The key to hiring for these positions is to stress the equality of teaching load across the faculty (based on actual

---

The Law School Product from the Buyer's Point of View, 29 VAL. U. L. REV. 897, 903-05 (1995); Justice Elizabeth Lacy, et al., *Law School Curriculum, Training Law Students, and the Vitality of the Profession: The Judicial Perspective*, 1 J. ALWD 297 (2002).

[72] *See 2018 ALWD/LWI Survey*, *supra* note 3, at 9-10, Questions 4.4 & 4.10 (noting that only two schools use a staffing model not listed).

hours required rather than credit hours assigned), the importance of educating students about theory as well as practice, and the equality of all faculty. Hiring committees should actively seek candidates with interests in both LRW and casebook teaching from the beginning of the hiring process. The initial recruitment notice should specify that candidates should have interests and skills in both.

While law schools often take chances with faculty candidates having no teaching experience whatsoever, schools looking to hire tenure-eligible LRW professors should give significant weight to a candidate's experience in teaching LRW, demonstrated success in the LRW classroom, and publication of scholarship in the discipline. In interviews, candidates should be told that the quality of their teaching and scholarship in both areas will weigh equally for promotion and tenure if that is the case.

Ultimately, whether tenured and tenure-track faculty should teach courses in addition to LRW depends on institutional and curricular considerations. But if an LRW faculty member is asked or is eligible to teach additional courses, adjustments should certainly be made to the professor's student/faculty ratio in the LRW program.

2. *Standard 405(c) Professors*

a. ABA Standard 405(c)

Under ABA Standard 405(c), full-time clinical faculty are employed with "a form of security of position reasonably similar to tenure and non-compensatory perquisites reasonably similar to those provided other full-time faculty members."[73] Security of position "reasonably similar to tenure" is defined as "a separate tenure track or a program of renewable long-term contracts."[74] Moreover, a long-term contract is defined as "at least a five-year contract that is

---

[73] ABA Standard 405(c).

[74] ABA Standard 405, Interpretation 405-6.

presumptively renewable or other arrangement sufficient to ensure academic freedom."[75]

While Standard 405(c) nominally applies to clinical faculty, many law schools have developed 405(c)-compliant contracts for LRW faculty.[76] Many of those LRW faculty also teach non-LRW courses as part of their normal course load.[77]

b. Pedagogical and Curricular Implications

Professors seeking Standard 405(c) contracts must be effective teachers and meet the school's service requirements. They also likely must meet additional requirements that inure to the benefit of the law school, such as scholarship or other identifiable contributions to LRW as a discipline or academic endeavor.[78]

Professors with long-term contracts are able to make a commitment to teaching LRW, develop expertise in the discipline, and make broader contributions to the law school curriculum. They can also contribute to faculty governance by serving on law school committees and doing other service work. In addition, long-term contract professors can add to the law school's scholarly output. In general, the long-term contract professor's commitment to the law school can approach that of the tenure-track professor.

---

[75] *Id. But see infra* Part B.3 of this chapter, discussing faculty with long-term contracts but without the protection of ABA Standard 405(c).

[76] *See supra* text accompanying note 8.

[77] *See 2018 ALWD/LWI Survey*, *supra* note 3, at 90, Question 10.17 (indicating that 41 percent of Standard 405(c) LRW faculty regularly or periodically teach non-LRW courses).

[78] ABA Standard 405(c) provides that a school "may require these faculty members to meet standards and obligations reasonably similar to those required of other full-time faculty members."

c. Financial Implications

The cost of this model may be less than the cost of models using tenure-track professors if the LRW professors begin at a lower salary level or are not eligible for research support such as stipends or research assistants. Still, costs will increase as professors attain seniority; professors who are granted long-term contracts usually are entitled to higher salaries, research leave, and stipends. Unlike schools with traditional tenure-track or tenured LRW faculty, which benefit from the scholarship and service done in the institution's name, law schools with contract-status faculty cannot expect comparable benefits from faculty scholarship and service.[79]

d. Law School Culture

With long-term contract professors, questions of governance will arise that must be answered prospectively. Professors who have earned Standard 405(c) contract status should be entitled to attend faculty meetings, vote on most if not all matters, and receive financial support for conferences and research assistance. Because long-term LRW faculty can make valuable contributions to faculty governance[80] and scholarly productivity, limitations on full participation should be cautiously considered. Further, these decisions should be clearly communicated to faculty candidates for the positions.

Because it is inappropriate to expect professors to meet tenure requirements if they are not entitled to the full status and security of

---

[79]Notably, service is required or expected at 99 percent of schools with LRW faculty on 405(c) contracts. *2018 ALWD/LWI Survey*, *supra* note 3, at 82, Question 10.8. At some schools, the scholarship standards for promotion and retention are the same or substantially similar to those for casebook faculty. *Id.* at 111-13, Questions 11.27-11.29.

[80]The majority of schools with LRW faculty on Standard 405(c) contracts provide them voting rights on all matters except tenure or promotion decisions pertaining to traditional casebook faculty. *2018 ALWD/LWI Survey*, *supra* note 3, at 79, Question 10.2.

position afforded tenured faculty, a school might reduce the number or scope of scholarly works required; require either scholarly production or professional contributions, but not both; or in some other way reduce scholarship or service expectations below those required for tenure. At schools that provide LRW faculty equity in most aspects of employment associated with tenured faculty such as salary, governance rights, and security of position, requiring LRW faculty to meet similar scholarship and service standards might be reasonable.

Tensions may arise between professors with tenure-track status and those without it because differences in status often result in a two-tier system of rights and privileges. However, many law school faculties are not composed solely of tenured and tenure-track professors. Some law schools have clinical professors, for example, who are hired and reappointed on the basis of different standards and who have a different academic status from casebook, tenure-track professors. Clinical professors may have tenure on a separate track from that created for casebook faculty, may have long-term contracts under ABA Standard 405(c), or may have short-term contracts. Like LRW professors, they may not have the salary, benefits, or status of tenured casebook professors, but they too play a critical role in students' education.

Therefore, law school administrators and faculty members should make considerable efforts to address the legitimate concerns of non-tenure-track professors and to ease any tensions between non-tenure-track and tenure-track professors. Of course, these issues are best addressed in advance of hiring. Fundamentally, a law school should not expect tenure-track work from LRW faculty unless it also provides tenure-track rewards.

3. *Professors with Long-Term Contracts That Do Not Qualify as Standard 405(c) Contracts*

Some full-time professors have terms of employment that do not meet the express requirements of ABA Standard 405(c) but provide some sense of security and the right to vote on many matters.[81] For example, some professors might have long-term contracts with terms five years or longer, but that are not presumptively renewable. Other professors might receive a three-year contract that might be the longest term the school provides to anyone. These same professors might be able to vote on all matters, or they might have limited voting rights (e.g., all matters except promotion of tenure-track colleagues). In each of these examples, the status exceeds the bare minimum required by ABA Standard 405(d), but nevertheless segregates LRW faculty into a limited position within the law school.

Depending on the conditions, the advantages and disadvantages of these models fall between those associated with the Standard 405(c) model (which provides security of position reasonably similar to tenure) and the short-term contract, non-voting model (discussed in the next section). The professors might experience long-term security and make a long-term commitment to teaching under one administration. But without the protection of Standard 405(c), this perceived security may last only until the next dean arrives or financial difficulties strike.

a. Pedagogical and Curricular Implications

The quality of instruction under this model might be very high, depending on the qualifications and teaching experience of the LRW professors, their commitment to the discipline (despite the school's lower commitment to them), the resources available, and the student/faculty ratio. The student/faculty ratio should reflect whether the law school's scholarship and service expectations are closer to those for a Standard 405(c) position or a short-term position. If the

---

[81] *See id.* ABA Standard 405(c) requires "a form of security of position reasonably similar to tenure, and non-compensatory perquisites reasonably similar to those provided other full-time faculty members." Interpretation 405-6 explains that job security includes long-term contracts of at least five years that are presumptively renewable "or other arrangement sufficient to ensure academic freedom." ABA Standard 405(c), Interpretation 405-6.

professor has no service or scholarship requirements, then higher ratios than those recommended in Part A.2 of this chapter[82] might be feasible without negative effects on student learning.

b. Financial Implications

The cost to the school for this model may be less than for LRW faculty with Standard 405(c) contracts but higher than the cost of short-term contract professors. The primary variables affecting the cost of this model include whether initial salaries are on par with salaries for other full-time teachers and the extent to which professors participate in annual or other salary increases. Faculty who start at lower salaries and receive the same percentage increases as higher-paid colleagues will obviously see the pay gap increase over time.

The costs of this intermediate model should be similar to the costs of Standard 405(c) positions regarding professional funding for travel to conferences, research assistants, and teaching assistants. Other costs include non-salary benefits, such as health insurance and retirement accounts.

Because these positions lack security of position reasonably similar to tenure, turnover may be more likely under this model than with a Standard 405(c) model, adding transactional costs in recruiting, hiring, and training new faculty. Further, if the school employs a director, that person's salary and benefits may offset other savings in LRW faculty salaries.

c. Law School Culture

The level of support the law school provides LRW faculty employed with this status will impact the program's success. Schools that embrace LRW professors as full colleagues can hope for high levels of service and even scholarly production. However, the nebulous position of these professors within the faculty as a whole might reduce morale, especially if casebook colleagues with

---

[82] *See supra* note 37 and accompanying text.

greater job security and more rights do not perform at high levels. For instance, morale is likely to suffer if some casebook colleagues have stopped publishing, and at the same time LRW faculty are producing scholarship while lacking job security, opportunities to serve on important committees, and comparable salaries or other perquisites such as research and scholarship support. Student learning can be negatively affected because students are aware of status hierarchies within the law school and may be less inclined to put forth their best efforts for a teacher who has second-level status.

d. Other Considerations

Whether to hire a director, and the role of a director, depends upon the expectations of the LRW professors and the objectives of the law school. In a school with long-term professors (despite contract terms less than five years or not presumptively renewable) and full participation in faculty governance, an autonomous model might be appropriate. Long-term contract professors might have the requisite expertise and experience to develop and maintain LRW courses over time and to ensure that students engage in the required rigorous writing experience. Alternatively, if a school provides three-year contracts but little participation in faculty governance and no voting rights, and if the culture of the school is not welcoming or inclusive of LRW faculty, then a director might be advisable or necessary to ensure the ongoing quality of teaching as well as to advocate for equal and fair treatment of LRW faculty.

4. Professors with Short-Term Contracts Providing Little or No Job Security or Voting Rights

Some schools use full-time LRW faculty with short-term contracts that are not presumptively renewable, providing little or no job security.[83] At the same time, these faculty may have little or no voice

---

[83] *2018 ALWD/LWI Survey, supra* note 3, at 11, Question 4.11 (indicating that 52 schools—roughly 29 percent of 184 schools, with two schools apparently

in faculty governance because they cannot participate in or chair faculty committees or vote at faculty meetings.[84] Often, a director of LRW is hired to provide continuity; ensure quality instruction; and to hire, train, and evaluate LRW professors.

a. Pedagogical and Curricular Implications

Most law schools realize that it is not in the students' best interest to be taught by a faculty member on a short-term contract, which usually lasts "four years or less, whether the contract is presumptively renewable or not."[85] Faculty on short-term contracts whose contracts are not renewed may not have adequate time to develop expertise in LRW pedagogy. In addition, faculty on short-term contracts are typically unable to contribute to faculty governance and are often ineligible for resources to support scholarship. At the same time, they often must worry about finding their next teaching job. In contrast, faculty whose short-term contracts are consistently renewed will undoubtedly develop the requisite expertise, but will most likely be perennially underpaid and prevented from participating in faculty governance.[86]

The pedagogical and curricular advantages of the short-term contract model include the energy and current practice experience brought by new faculty members and, if the faculty remain relatively inexperienced, the ability of school administrators and faculty to rely on program decisions made by an experienced LRW director. However, these advantages are often outweighed by the disadvantage that short-term contract faculty cannot develop expertise as teachers or scholars, unlike faculty with the job security of long-term contracts

---

double-counted—employ exclusively LRW faculty with short-term contracts in a first-year or combined first-year and upper-level program).

[84] *See id.* at 79, Question 10.2.

[85] *Id.* at vii.

[86] *Id.* at 79, Question 10.2 (indicating that 15 schools give short-term contract LRW faculty no voting rights).

or tenure. As a result, the quality of their teaching will not always approach that of more experienced, secure LRW faculty.

Short-term contracts disadvantage the school in other ways, too. Faculty on short-term contracts are much less likely to make service contributions to the law school or develop scholarship agendas. With the necessarily high turnover rate, other LRW faculty, including the director, are forced to recruit, interview, hire, and train new LRW faculty frequently, taking time away from their own teaching and scholarship. In turn, faculty, administrators, and librarians all must get to know new colleagues.

Finally, high turnover, coupled with no voting rights, negatively affects morale among LRW faculty. It can contribute to an often unconscious but insidious attitude among the rest of the faculty and administration that LRW faculty are fungible and easily-ignored temporary residents rather than valued academic colleagues. Even when LRW faculty remain at a school under a series of renewable short-term contracts, they can be viewed by other faculty, administrators, students, and staff as essentially second-class faculty citizens. This culture can have negative implications for student learning as well.

b. Financial Implications

The cost of this model may be less than the cost of models that employ tenure-track or long-term contract professors, if the short-term LRW professors begin at a lower salary level with fewer benefits, and less scholarship and faculty development support. Costs increase the longer LRW professors stay on, even with short-term renewable contracts. However, higher turnover leads to recurring transaction costs for recruiting, hiring, and training replacements.[87]

---

[87] *See* Susan P. Liemer & Jan M. Levine, *Legal Research and Writing: What Schools are Doing, and Who is Doing the Teaching (Three Years Later)*, 9 SCRIBES J. LEGAL WRITING 113 (2003-2004).

c. *Law School Culture*

Schools that do not offer LRW faculty long-term contracts must address issues concerning equal and fair treatment and governance rights. Deans and faculties need to decide in advance who can be members of faculty committees, who can attend and speak at faculty meetings, who can vote at faculty meetings on various types of issues, who can vote on appointments (including appointment of new legal writing faculty), who can attend conferences at the school's expense, and who is eligible for research support and at what level. These decisions should be clearly communicated to candidates for the positions. Understandably, tensions and conflict may arise between faculty with security of position and those without. Short-term contract faculty who lack voting rights, access to scholarship support, and professional development funding naturally feel excluded and undervalued.[88] Students are attuned to faculty dynamics and may be inclined to put forth less effort in courses taught by less-valued members of the law school faculty.

d. *Role of the Director or Coordinator*

In general, a director or coordinator under this model has significant responsibility. If LRW faculty teach for only a few years and move on to other careers, a director must regularly hire, train, mentor, and evaluate colleagues to ensure that the quality of teaching reaches the program's expectations. When it does not, the director will need to develop strategies for improvement and, in some cases, recommend against renewing a professor's contract.

To ease this administrative and management workload, schools should strongly consider making short-term contracts presumptively renewable, which will improve the quality of teaching, reduce the burden on the director, and increase LRW faculty members' opportunities to become involved with other academic responsibilities

---

[88] *Cf.* Melissa H. Weresh, *supra* note 13, at 146-47.

within the law school and the LRW discipline. If LRW professors tend to stay for a number of years despite having short-term contracts and little voice in faculty governance, the director might transition into a coordinator position with less emphasis on hiring and supervising and more emphasis on administering the program and encouraging professional development.

The person serving as director or coordinator should not be held responsible for the performance of colleagues who were hired by others, or who do not agree with the director's approach to pedagogy and collaboration. These challenges are especially difficult if the director lacks security of position.

5. Teaching Fellows and Visiting Assistant Professors

Teaching fellows are full-time employees who teach LRW while engaging in scholarship that will prepare them for tenure-track or similar faculty positions.[89] While the title "visiting assistant professor" (VAP) is more often used to describe other teaching positions of this nature, that term is making its way into LRW hiring. Whatever title is used, the person is typically hired for no more than a few years. Previously, some schools offered an LL.M. degree for fellows, adding coursework to the package of teaching and scholarship, but that approach has fallen by the wayside.[90]

Only a handful of schools report using full-time fellows to teach LRW, either as the primary program model or as part of a hybrid

---

[89] *2018 ALWD/LWI Survey*, *supra* note 3, at ix.

[90] *See id.* at 9-10, Questions 4.4 & 4.10 (reporting no graduate students involved in teaching legal writing); *2015 ALWD/LWI Survey*, *supra* note 40, at 5, Question 10 (reporting no program using primarily graduate students); *2015 ALWD/LWI Survey, supra,* at 6, Question 11 (reporting two programs that included graduate students in a hybrid program).

program.[91] This trend comports with the letter of the ABA Standards, which require full-time faculty to teach substantially all first-year courses,[92] but perhaps not with the spirit of that standard. Other first-year courses are unlikely to be assigned to temporary teachers, and LRW education arguably requires more specialized knowledge of varying pedagogies than do casebook courses.

While few law schools base their LRW program models on these limited-duration positions, a school faced with an immediate teaching need or budgetary constraints might consider using fellows or VAPs to teach LRW courses. If the fellows have no formal academic responsibilities other than teaching LRW and do not receive scholarship support, then in reality, they are short-term contract LRW professors, not "fellows." Similarly, if fellows are not successful in moving to permanent academic positions within a few years, the school should rethink the feasibility of this model.[93] The rest of this section uses the term "fellow" to include VAPs because employing them has similar benefits and challenges.

a. Pedagogical and Curricular Implications

Most entry-level fellows are bright and highly motivated. They can bring energy to the faculty and offer students a perspective that is very close to real-world law practice. Nearly all fellows, however, are under considerable career pressure to devote time to their own

---

[91] In 2018, two schools reported having a fellows-based program for the first-year course, while an additional five schools employed teaching fellows as part of a hybrid program. *2018 ALWD/LWI Survey*, *supra* note 3, at 9-10, Questions 4.4 & 4.10; *see also id.* at 155-64, Questions 14.2-14.16 (providing additional data on teaching fellows in all writing curricula).

[92] ABA Standard 403(a).

[93] *See* Liemer & Levine, *supra* note 87, at 133 (arguing that schools should have to prove to the ABA that teaching fellows are successful in securing tenure-track positions).

preparation and search for permanent academic employment. Some may view teaching LRW as transitional and thus not immerse themselves in the pedagogy of the discipline. They may not have the time to do so, even if they wish to.[94] Some fellows do not teach LRW long enough to develop real expertise, and their intellectual focus may lie elsewhere. Some may even see teaching LRW as an unwelcome condition of their current academic appointment.

Because fellows are usually novice teachers who must devote time to their own research and job searches, each should have no more than 15 to 30 LRW students;[95] the higher numbers are only possible if the fellows receive extensive support in preparing course materials and have few other duties. Regardless of teaching load, fellows need training in best practices for law teaching and in LRW pedagogy, particularly regarding selecting and preparing course materials, holding student conferences, and evaluating student papers. Otherwise, the LRW students may not receive adequate individual attention, and they may receive only minimal levels of instruction and feedback. The situation might be different at a school that focuses on preparing fellows for careers in LRW teaching, or a school where a small number of fellows work alongside long-term LRW colleagues who can train and supervise the fellows, perhaps encouraging them to pursue careers teaching LRW.

b. Financial Implications

The cost of staffing a program with fellows may be lower than the cost of hiring long-term LRW faculty, and may even be less than

---

[94] *See* Ilhyung Lee, *The Rookie Season*, 39 SANTA CLARA L. REV. 473 (1999); Jan M. Levine, *Leveling the Hill of Sisyphus: Becoming a Professor of Legal Writing*, 26 FLA. ST. U. L. REV. 1067, 1092-94 (1999).

[95] In 2018, teaching fellows averaged fewer than 30 total students per semester. *See 2018 ALWD/LWI Survey*, *supra* note 3, at 156, Question 14.5.

hiring dedicated LRW professors on short-term contracts.[96] Fellows expect to be rewarded through mentorship and time to write, and they are not typically assigned any service obligations.

As with all short-term positions, increased transaction costs are associated with the recurring need to recruit new fellows, screen them, and admit some to the LRW program. Because the school commits to mentoring fellows both in pedagogy and in scholarship, the school must allocate experienced faculty to train and supervise fellows as they develop into LRW teachers and scholars. This model therefore requires investment in an LRW director, whose role is explained below.

c. *Law School Culture*

The success of fellows depends in large part on who is selected, the training and mentorship they receive, and the consistency of courses they teach. Fellows who are selected and trained to teach LRW and who have a genuine interest in writing as a distinct discipline will likely fare better. Their pay should begin long enough before the semester starts to allow their immersion in the course materials and pedagogy. Fellows who embrace materials created by an experienced director or full-time colleagues may do well in the classroom over the few years they teach LRW. Fellows who try to create their own materials while also embarking on scholarly pursuits may find themselves overwhelmed and perform neither task well.

---

[96]If the fellows are pursuing graduate degrees, they may be treated by the university as students, and thus ineligible for faculty personnel benefits such as health insurance. In these situations, costs are hard to quantify because compensation may be folded into fellowships having other, far different demands. Moreover, if the parent college or university has formal rules for graduate students who also teach, such as collective bargaining agreements and teaching load limitations, it might not be feasible for a law school to use fellows to teach LRW.

Student dissatisfaction may be a significant issue in this program model because fellows are often brand-new teachers focused on research, publication, and preparing to enter the full-time teaching market. The first semester of teaching and the semester the fellows are on the job market are likely to generate lower student course evaluations. The fellows' attention is understandably diverted, and classes may need to be rescheduled for interviews. Student dissatisfaction also may negatively affect morale among the fellows, LRW faculty, and the rest of the faculty. Morale problems may arise due to tension between LRW faculty committed to long-term teaching and fellows who view the position as temporary.

The service performed by fellows that is required, expected, or allowed can have a significant impact on the success of individual fellows, the program, and the students. Typically fellows are required only to teach and produce scholarship. An unstated expectation of service, however, places additional pressure on the fellows, decreasing time available for teaching and scholarship. Even with no expectation of service, a fellow may volunteer to undertake extra obligations, whether due to genuine interest or as a way to gain favor. A director should caution fellows about the allure of service that does not enhance their job prospects and should be willing to intervene if service negatively affects teaching.

d. Role of the Director

This model cannot provide minimally acceptable LRW instruction without a full-time director who is a committed LRW professional enjoying full faculty status. The director's role necessarily includes recruiting a pool of qualified applicants, hiring the best candidates, developing course materials (e.g., syllabi and assignments), mentoring in teaching and LRW pedagogy (including how to give effective written feedback and how to hold effective student conferences), securing scholarship mentors for fellows writing in other casebook disciplines, reviewing course evaluations, and serving as a job reference.[97] One critical tool for a committed director is involvement in post-fellowship placement, which may encourage fellows to perform better as LRW teachers. Professional development funding to engage with the national legal writing community is crucial to enable the director to collaborate with peers at other law schools who are engaged in similar responsibilities.[98] Assigning the director's role to a faculty member who does not teach LRW, or who has no special interest or experience in LRW, is unlikely to yield optimal results.

C. Part-time and Adjunct Professors

In 2018, only 8 schools reported relying exclusively on part-time and adjunct faculty to teach the traditional first-year LRW course.[99] The trend away from this staffing model is not surprising given that ABA Standards require that "full-time faculty shall teach substantially all of the first one-third of each student's coursework."[100] Few

---

[97]Furthermore, if fellows are also LL.M. students, the school must have some method for resolving the inherent conflict between the needs of the LRW program and the focus of the LL.M. program, which may be administered and supervised by another faculty member or faculty committee.

[98]Of those schools with directors, 13 percent report having more than one director for the first-year program, and 12 percent report having more than one director for upper-level courses. *2018 ALWD/LWI Survey*, *supra* note 3, at 60, Question 9.2.

[99]*2018 ALWD/LWI Survey*, *supra* note 3, at 9, Question 4.4 (roughly 4 percent). Roughly 33 schools employ some part-time and adjunct faculty with full-time faculty teaching the traditional first-year course, and 15 employ some adjuncts with full-time faculty in a combined first-year and upper-level program. The number of schools using solely part-time or adjunct faculty has steadily declined for a number of years. *See, e.g.*, *2006 ALWD/LWI Survey*, *supra* note 3, at 6, Question 10 (indicating that 27 schools—15 percent—relied exclusively on part-time and adjunct faculty to teach first-year LRW).

[100]ABA Standard 403(a).

practicing attorneys and judges are able to successfully balance their demanding careers with the challenges of teaching first-year LRW students.

This chapter treats part-time and adjunct faculty together because of the similar advantages, disadvantages, and implications of models based on the two faculty categories.[101] Once common, purely adjunct LRW programs are now rare. Anecdotally, they made a reappearance during the recent economic downturn as schools struggled with shrinking budgets, but few schools now use adjuncts or part-time faculty as a primary staffing model, especially in the first-year LRW program.[102] As for upper-level LRW, one school reports using primarily part-time faculty, and 14 rely primarily on adjuncts.[103] Among hybrid programs (discussed in detail below in Part D), part-time and especially adjunct faculty are frequently used to flesh out the LRW faculty.[104] This practice can raise pedagogical challenges as some students learn from experienced professors while classmates learn from busy practitioners. However, over half

---

[101] A part-time professor is "[a] faculty member, regardless of other status, who is hired to perform duties less than what is considered a normal full teaching or administrative load at the school. As distinguished from Adjunct faculty, a Part-[t]ime faculty member is typically obligated to work a set number of hours in a given time period (e.g., per week or per semester)." *2018 ALWD/LWI Survey*, *supra* note 3, at viii. In contrast, an adjunct is "[a] faculty member hired to teach one or more courses, who may or may not have substantial outside employment. As distinguished from Part-[t]ime faculty, an Adjunct faculty member is typically obligated to teach one or more specific courses but does not typically have an obligation to work a set number of hours in a given time period (e.g., per week or per semester)." *Id.* at vi.

[102] *See supra* note 99 and accompanying text.

[103] *2018 ALWD/LWI Survey*, *supra* note 3, at 9, Question 4.4.

[104] *See supra* note 99.

of all schools use part-time or adjunct faculty to teach at least one LRW course.[105]

Given the number of schools relying at least in part on adjuncts, a careful consideration of the advantages and disadvantages of this model is important. As explained below, this model must have a committed director, or at least a coordinator, to be successful.

1. Pedagogical and Curricular Implications

Whether part-time or adjunct, the people hired under this model are usually practicing attorneys, legislators, or judges with at least two or three years of practice experience. Part-time and adjunct-taught programs have worked best in large metropolitan areas, where attorneys are plentiful,[106] but most schools have found that the disadvantages of using either outweigh the advantages.

The major advantage of this model is that students are taught by someone with current experience in the practice of law, adding credibility to the professor's opinions and allowing the professor to share real-life situations relevant to the lesson or assignment. For some first-year students, the part-time or adjunct faculty member is the first practicing attorney they meet, providing that professor the opportunity to serve as a valuable role model. Another advantage of this model is that students are taught in smaller classes. Extremely small sections, however, may lack the critical mass needed to support in-class discussion or to demonstrate the breadth of ability in the student body.

The obvious disadvantage of part-time or adjunct programs is that part-time or adjunct faculty members have not made LRW pedagogy the focus of their professional lives, unlike career LRW professors.

---

[105] *2018 ALWD/LWI Survey*, *supra* note 3, at 58, Question 8.3 (indicating that 13 percent of schools use part-time faculty and 60 percent use adjuncts to teach one or more LRW courses).

[106] *See, e.g.*, Levine, *supra* note 94, at 1089-92.

Few law schools allow adjuncts to teach other first-year courses[107] or to regularly teach required courses. A professional commitment to the field is as important for LRW as it is for any other subject.

The major problem with part-time and adjunct-taught programs is that these faculty most often have other employment and owe their primary allegiance and devotion to that employer, meaning the LRW course is a lesser commitment in that faculty member's life. If an adjunct professor has a case go to trial unexpectedly, the class may need to be rescheduled or a substitute teacher found. Moreover, part-time and adjunct professors are not as available to students as are full-time professors. They may be unable to schedule regular office hours at the law school, in which case much of the students' contact with the professor may be by e-mail. A related concern is scheduling conferences within the confines of the part-time or adjunct faculty member's availability and the students' other courses.

A related disadvantage is the need for a director.[108] The director's workload and the extensive support likely needed by busy practitioners may feel stifling, both to the part-time or adjunct faculty member and to the director. Part-time or adjunct professors have limited time for training sessions, even in their first year. The director must prepare extensive materials and rely on the part-time or adjunct professors to read them carefully. The teaching materials might include teaching techniques and theory; techniques for formative assessment and grading papers; ideas for developing assignments; optional exercises in citation, grammar, and research; or week-by-week lesson plans.

---

[107] *See* ABA Standard 403(a) (requiring substantially all first-year courses to be taught by full-time faculty members).

[108] *See 2018 ALWD/LWI Survey*, *supra* note 3, at 179, Question 16.6. To evaluate the effectiveness of the part-time or adjunct professor and to ensure consistency of instruction, most directors conduct class observations and review students' course evaluations. Some also review samples of papers that the adjunct professor has graded and returned to students. *See id.* at 182, Question 16.10.

The need for uniform teaching materials highlights an inherent disadvantage in part-time and adjunct-based LRW programs. Students in part-time or adjunct-based programs are particularly sensitive to differences in treatment. Directors often respond by keeping adjunct syllabi[109] and textbooks[110] as uniform as possible and by creating at least the major writing assignments.[111] The resulting uniformity necessarily stifles adjuncts' academic freedom and may require them to use a course design that is not a good fit with their particular teaching style. Experienced directors working with experienced part-time or adjunct faculty may encourage more flexibility in creating lesson plans and assignments. In any event, directors must seek to ensure that first-year students have comparable experiences and learn the same essential skills.

2. *Financial Implications*

The major attraction of this model is its relatively low cost. Practicing attorneys are motivated to teach for a variety of reasons, but money is rarely an important factor. Teaching LRW courses, however, often requires more of the professor's time outside the classroom than teaching casebook courses, and part-time or adjunct faculty may have trouble balancing competing obligations. The school employing this staffing model should consider paying these professors a higher salary than it pays part-time or adjunct casebook faculty, recognizing the additional time and energy required

---

[109] *See id.* at 171, Question 15.16; *id.* at 184, Question 16.12 (indicating that adjuncts at 20 of 29 schools must use a syllabus provided to them; at 6 of 29 schools, adjuncts have the option of using a provided syllabus or creating their own).

[110] *See id.* at 174, Questions 15.18-15.20; *id.* at 187, Question 16.14 (indicating that these faculty who teach in the first-year program at 23 of 29 schools have no autonomy in selecting textbooks).

[111] *See id.* at 172, Question 15.17; *id.* at 185, Question 16.13 (indicating that adjuncts at roughly 13 schools must use major assignments provided to them, and at 11 schools, they are or may be expected to create their own major assignments).

for assessing student work and meeting with individual students for conferences.[112]

Attorneys, judges, and others teaching in these adjunct positions need classes small enough to manage comfortably with a full-time law practice or other commitments, but large enough to allow adequate comparison of students' papers. A reasonable teaching load might range from 10-20 students per semester. LRW adjuncts should be provided teaching assistants whenever possible.[113]

The director's time devoted to recruiting, hiring, training, and preparing materials for adjuncts often represents a hidden cost of this program model. If the director's primary work is supervising adjuncts rather than teaching LRW students, the salary of that single professor-administrator can add significantly to the model's cost.

3. *Law School Culture*

Part-time and adjunct faculty likely have no service or scholarly obligations to the law school and do not vote at faculty meetings. Whether they may attend faculty meetings should be clarified before hiring. A part-time or adjunct professor with strong views may become frustrated if those views are not welcomed.

Part-time or adjunct faculty are more likely to fit into the law school's culture if perceived as respected practitioners[114] who are hired through a formal process that includes a personal interview, a writing sample, and other indicia of excellence.[115] Schools should

---

[112] *See id.* at 165, Question 15.2; *id.* at 177, Question 16.2 (suggesting that at least 69 percent of adjuncts teaching LRW receive the same or higher salary as adjuncts teaching other courses).

[113] *See infra* Part D.3 of this chapter.

[114] The minimum or average number of years of practice experience for part-time and adjunct faculty teaching the first-year course is 3. *2018 ALWD/LWI Survey*, *supra* note 3, at 175, Question 15.21; *id.* at 180, Question 16.8.

[115] *See id.* at 181, Question 16.9.

give their LRW adjuncts a title such as "adjunct professor," which costs nothing and results in three benefits: The adjuncts work harder and feel better about their positions, the students respect the adjuncts more and treat them better, and better candidates apply for future positions. Schools also can enhance the part-time or adjunct professor's experience through small gestures such as inviting them to attend faculty colloquia or to serve as guest speakers in their areas of practice.

4. Role of a Director

A successful LRW program based on a part-time or adjunct model requires a talented director with security of position and the support of the law school administration. The director's role in these programs is more substantial than in other types of programs. In many adjunct-based programs, the director prepares all curricular materials, from major writing assignments to the class-by-class syllabus.[116] While some programs allow or even require part-time or adjunct faculty to create course materials,[117] many practitioners lack the time and experience to create a highly structured course for their students. Directors thus often spend considerable time reviewing and improving adjunct-created assignments.

Administratively, the director usually has more professors to supervise and evaluate in this model than in others. A high-quality administrative assistant or an assistant director is essential to assist the director with answering routine inquiries from part-time or adjunct faculty, producing materials, scheduling rooms, rescheduling classes, distributing assignments, and dealing with the other high-volume logistical aspects of an LRW program associated with a large number of professors.

---

[116] *Id.* at 184, Question 16.12 (indicating that 20 of 29 schools do so).

[117] *See supra* note 111 and accompanying text.

Another disadvantage of this model is that the director must hire some new professors almost every year. The rest of the casebook professors may not want to be involved in the hiring, so the politics of that process may be simplified. However, the main burden of recruiting, locating, interviewing, evaluating, choosing, hiring, and training part-time and adjunct faculty falls on the director and the director's assistant. Occasionally, a director might have to make a tricky political judgment (or consult with the dean) about turning down, terminating, or not rehiring a prominent law school graduate, judge, or spouse of a faculty member. Because of the credentials of the attorneys who are attracted to adjunct teaching, these political difficulties arise more often in adjunct-taught programs, but they are by no means common.

D. Hybrid Models

As the percentage of schools with full-time LRW faculty has increased, the percentage with hybrid programs has decreased.[118] Hybrid programs take one of two basic forms and generally involve faculty on different kinds of contracts teaching in the same program or school. The first type likely requires a director and uses a combination of full-time and part-time or adjunct faculty, who remain on those tracks, designated below as "Type 1—Full-time and Part-time Faculty."[119] The second type, which may or may not require a director or coordinator, uses a combination of full-time faculty who are on, or who become eligible for, different long-term contracts, designated below as "Type 2—Full-time Faculty on Different Tracks." As status and employment conditions for LRW faculty have improved

---

[118] *Compare 2018 ALWD/LWI Survey*, *supra* note 3, at 9, Question 4.4 (indicating that 23 percent of schools use a hybrid program in the first year) *with 2006 ALWD/LWI Survey*, *supra* note 3, at 6, Question 10 (indicating that 30 percent of schools used a hybrid program in the first year).

[119] Only a few schools still use upper-level students as part of a hybrid program to provide substantial written feedback or to help teach the first-year course. *See 2018 ALWD/LWI Survey*, *supra* note 3, at 10, Question 4.10.

over the years, the variations among Type 2 hybrid programs have increased, with some faculty provided the opportunity to move from (or remain on) different types of short- and long-term contracts, including tenure.

1. Type 1 Hybrid: A Combination of Full-time and Part-time Faculty

a. Pedagogical and Curricular Implications

The advantages of this hybrid model include the interplay among faculty members who are experienced and those who may be inexperienced or part-time faculty. Less experienced faculty may be able to rely on existing curricular choices and advice from full-time, long-term faculty. However, as with models using short-term contracts or part-time faculty,[120] these advantages may be outweighed by the disadvantage of part-time or adjunct faculty focusing on other jobs or careers. In turn, such faculty are often unable to develop as teachers and scholars, remain readily available to students, or make larger contributions to the law school. The quality of their teaching is thus not likely to approach that of more experienced full-time faculty.

The more varied the contract status of faculty teaching LRW, the more likely it is that pedagogical concerns will arise. When faculty with widely varying expertise and commitment to the discipline of LRW teach in the same program, students may have valid reasons to complain about inconsistencies among sections. For example, experienced full-time faculty are likely better able to design assignments and understand the typical strengths and weaknesses of a school's students. This difference in teaching ability and experience is exacerbated when all LRW students are asked to be active learners and produce comparable written assignments. Full-time faculty are also more accessible to students and more likely to have time to meet with them individually than are adjunct faculty.

---

[120] *See supra* Parts B.3 and C of this chapter.

One way to mitigate this problem is for a director or coordinator (or cohort of experienced faculty) to provide adequate guidance and support to less experienced faculty teaching the course. When this role is particularly burdensome, faculty providing guidance and support should be compensated appropriately. Allowing less-experienced faculty to make some choices about assignments and teaching methods or exercises that play to their strengths will help ease tensions that may arise. The goal of consistency, as opposed to uniformity, can encourage students to accept differences among LRW sections in the same way that they learn to accept differences among other first-year courses. Variations among sections in an LRW course may be more apparent and vexing for students if the program's design creates an expectation of uniformity.

b. Financial Implications

The cost of this model is generally much less than the cost of models using all full-time faculty, since part-time and adjunct compensation tends to be significantly lower. However, a predictably higher turnover rate, together with the greater number of faculty members required to staff the program, creates recurring transaction costs for recruiting, hiring, and training replacements, and other related administrative costs. Moreover, the disadvantages associated with instruction inferior to that provided by full-time faculty, particularly in an ABA-required first-year course, should be carefully considered.

c. Law School Culture

When faculty members with different terms of employment appear to be doing the same work for different levels of compensation and benefits, or under different conditions, resentment and conflict will naturally occur. These tensions may be lessened somewhat by encouraging all LRW faculty to become (or remain) involved in the discipline of LRW and the broader academic endeavors of the law school. Discussing openly the different performance expectations for different types of faculty positions may help to reduce or minimize resentment about different levels of compensation and benefits.

If the finances and politics of the law school allow, the school should consider involving everyone who teaches LRW in the life of the law school. For example, part-time or adjunct faculty might be invited to faculty events or retreats where they can interact with full-time faculty and share their views. Treating all LRW faculty with respect and support in ways that are relatively simple (e.g., using the title "adjunct professor") can go a long way in alleviating political concerns.

d. Role of the Director

Supervising an LRW program with faculty members who vary in status, expertise, and experience places a significant burden on a director. Even if the director is charged only with overseeing the adjunct portion of the program, full-time teachers must follow the director's lead, or students could have very different experiences depending on whether their professor is full-time or an adjunct. Although consistency, as opposed to uniformity, across sections is a desirable pedagogical goal, it may exacerbate supervisory challenges.

In addition, the predictably high rate of turnover among part-time or adjunct faculty forces other faculty, including the director, to frequently recruit, interview, hire, and train new writing faculty, taking time away from teaching and scholarship. Finally, high turnover, coupled with no voting rights, negatively affects morale among legal writing faculty. High turnover can also contribute to an attitude among the rest of the faculty and administration that legal writing faculty are fungible and unimportant temporary residents within the law school community.

2. *Type 2 Hybrid: Full-time Faculty on Different Tracks*

This kind of hybrid program, which may or may not require a director or coordinator, uses full-time faculty who are on or eligible for different types of long-term employment tracks. A school might adopt this model during a program transition from Standard 405(c) contracts to tenure. Some new faculty might have short-term contracts while others have Standard 405(c) status and still others have already achieved tenure status.

a. Pedagogical and Curricular Implications

When all faculty are full-time, issues that typically arise under the first type of hybrid program are mitigated. Short-term contract faculty can consult with more experienced faculty on everything from syllabus design to grading strategies. Consistency among sections is thus easier to achieve, reducing student dissatisfaction. So too, all full-time faculty members, regardless of contract status, are equally available to students.

Another advantage of this hybrid model is that feedback can be provided to inexperienced teachers early in their careers, before they are reviewed for long-term contracts. With this model, faculty have the potential to develop as scholars and teachers, invest in the school's long-range goals, and contribute more broadly to the school in terms of service. Pedagogical issues that stem from varied contract status arise less often in this type of hybrid LRW program, in which all faculty teach full time, and the experience required to move from a short-term to a long-term contract is the same for everyone.

b. Financial Implications

The cost of this model may be less than the cost of models using tenure-track professors—if the LRW professors begin at a lower salary level, do not receive all faculty personnel benefits, or lack scholarship support. Still, costs will increase as professors attain seniority. Faculty members who are granted long-term contracts or tenure usually are entitled to higher salaries, research stipends, and benefits, including retirement benefits.

c. Law School Culture and Programmatic Politics

If all faculty start on short-term contracts with the potential for better status and security of position as they gain more experience, the potential for resentment and conflict among faculty is reduced significantly. For example, faculty still on short-term contracts may have limited governance rights and lower personnel benefits but can look forward to acquiring those perquisites based on performance. LRW faculty working towards long-term contracts in this type of hybrid program model should be entitled to equal respect as well as scholarship support and professional development funding to maximize their potential for success.

If short-term contract faculty may elect at some point to apply either for long-term contracts or tenure, tensions may arise when the LRW program relies on a mix of short-term contract, long-term contract, and tenured faculty, all with differing security of position, status, and titles. In that case, each LRW faculty member should be afforded the same rights and privileges as other faculty members who have the same rank or title.

d. Role of the Director

Due to a predictably low rate of turnover and the likelihood that LRW faculty will develop into seasoned and expert teachers and scholars, this type of hybrid program, once established, probably does not need a director. Some schools instead appoint a rotating coordinator who assists with administrative tasks but who does not function in a supervisory or evaluative role.

3. Teaching Assistants

Regardless of the staffing model a school chooses, 69 percent of schools use student teaching assistants to assist LRW faculty.[121] These second- or third-year students are usually assigned to work with individual LRW faculty to assist in class preparation and review of student papers; some may hold conferences with students on individual assignments. As schools have come to recognize that

---

[121] *See 2018 ALWD/LWI Survey*, *supra* note 3, at 192, Question 17.2. Teaching assistants are different from student teachers or research assistants, who may help with class preparation but do not interact with students.

LRW courses should be taught by experts in the discipline, teaching assistants teach in the classroom rarely, if at all.[122] Nor should they assign grades.[123] They can best be used in this context to give formative feedback on research and citation exercises that have correct and incorrect answers (as opposed to assignments that require more subjective feedback), and to help students talk through their developing analysis.

In all LRW program models, teaching assistants can increase the opportunities for students to obtain formative feedback and answers to their myriad questions. Often, first-year law students are initially less reluctant to approach a peer for assistance than a professor, and these selected and trained peers are especially effective at helping them avoid problems and misconceptions at the outset of the school year. Teaching assistants generally engage well in the course material and are motivated to improve their own writing, to serve as mentors to novice writers, and to provide support to new law students. The duties of teaching assistants vary widely from school to school, depending on the professors' ability to train and supervise them closely.

If teaching assistants are assigned to individual professors, the LRW faculty may decide what duties can be safely delegated to their teaching assistants based on the nature of the course and the teaching assistants' qualifications. Professors might want to collaborate on this decision so that all LRW students receive comparable help from teaching assistants. Teaching assistants who performed well in their own LRW courses or who have been teachers or undergraduate

---

[122] *See id.* at 193, Question 17.5 (indicating that teaching assistants do not teach at all or only minimally in 80 percent of schools that use them).

[123] *See* Patricia Grande Montana, *A Contemporary Model for Using Teaching Assistants in Legal Writing Programs*, 42 MITCHELL HAMLINE L. REV. 185, 211 (2016) ("Importantly, the teaching assistants should not grade the students in any way, nor should they suggest or recommend grades.")

writing tutors often make good candidates. If teaching assistants are assigned to a program generally, the director must determine their responsibilities. To avoid inconsistencies with an individual professor's expectations, these responsibilities should rarely include subjective judgments or advice that might contradict that offered by the professor.

LRW students should be encouraged to reach out to faculty as well as teaching assistants, even if the near-peer teaching assistant seems less judgmental or threatening. For this reason, LRW faculty should make a point to be equally available to meet with students. Caution is always advisable, for the use of student teaching assistants creates temptations and risks. Professors should not shift to teaching assistants those responsibilities that only professors can competently fulfill.

a. Assignment Preparation

When appropriate, the professor can use a teaching assistant to help research and draft LRW assignments. Sometimes the teaching assistant may have a good idea for an assignment based on a problem encountered as a summer law clerk or judicial intern, an issue in a recent case studied in an upper-level course, or a legal dispute in an advanced moot court experience. Or teaching assistants may be able to create realistic fact patterns for an area of law selected by the professor as appropriate for the pedagogical goals of each assignment.

When a problem is developed by the professor, the student assistant can research the chosen problem; discover any ambiguities needing clarification; and prepare a list of cases, statutes, and other sources the students should be expected to find and analyze. The teaching assistant might write a sample answer (e.g., an email, memorandum, or brief). This type of vetting is beneficial to the professor as it will likely highlight problems or ambiguities in the assignment. Having the teaching assistant prepare a model answer also gives the professor another opportunity to provide feedback to students. The model answer can be given to the class for comparative purposes,[124] or it can serve as a bench brief for a moot court assignment.

b. Research Training

Teaching assistants can be a valuable supplementary resource in the research training phase of the course. Although developing research strategies is a sophisticated skill that few upper-level students are prepared to teach without supervision, teaching assistants can help first-year students by responding to research questions regarding a particular assignment, or by discussing their own research methods and strategies more generally. Often, teaching assistants can help students with their research questions simply by reflecting on and guiding them in the research process.

Teaching assistants can also provide valuable support in the classroom for small group discussions or exercises, brief library visits, or online research demonstrations. For example, faculty and teaching assistants can rotate among student groups working on in-class research exercises, making sure all students receive some form of individual attention. If exercises have right and wrong answers, the teaching assistants can even check them.

c. Formative Feedback on Written Assignments

Teaching assistants can offer valuable, if limited, feedback on students' written work. The less substantive the teaching assistant's feedback, the less likely it is to cause tension between professor and teaching assistant or confusion between teaching assistant and student. A well-trained teaching assistant can review papers for depth of research, basic grammar and style errors, and citation format. If

---

[124] *But see* Elizabeth Ruiz Frost, *Feedback Distortion: The Shortcomings of Model Answers as Formative Feedback*, 65 J. LEGAL EDUC. 938 (2016).

expected to give more substantive feedback, such as drafting initial comments on student writing or conferencing with students, teaching assistants must be well trained and work under direct faculty supervision.[125] Comments provided by teaching assistants should always be reviewed carefully by the professor before returning them to students. In that situation, professors must explain to students that they are getting the benefit of two readers instead of one. Often, perceived differences in feedback between professor and teaching assistant are different ways of saying the same thing, which can be very beneficial to students who understand the commenting process.

d. Answering Questions

Teaching assistants should understand that they cannot expect to know the answers to every student's questions. If the teaching assistant knows the answer to a question, she should give it. If not, she should refer the student to the professor. Written responses to student writing or written answers to course-related questions should be approved by the professor before sending them to students, except on routine matters. When possible, professors should have written policies for teaching assistants to guide them in exercising discretion.

Teaching assistants should establish a schedule of times when they are available to meet with students and answer questions, to prevent first-year students from consuming too much time and expecting help at all hours. Students should be instructed to consult the teaching assistant for questions dealing with particular areas, such as citation form, research issues, or general questions.

---

[125] *See 2018 ALWD/LWI Survey*, *supra* note 3, at 197, Question 17.13 (indicating that schools spend an average of 12 hours training new teaching assistants).

e. Conducting Practice Arguments

If a first-year LRW course includes an appellate brief and formal oral argument, teaching assistants can conduct practice arguments to help students sharpen their oral communication skills. They also can help students focus on the important arguments and, if necessary, reorganize, deepen, or sharpen their analysis and reasoning.

f. Providing Student Support

The first year of law school is challenging for many students. The LRW class can be especially traumatic because it typically is the only class in which the students receive frequent critical feedback and grades. Although students may feel more comfortable speaking to their LRW professor than their casebook professors, the teaching assistant may provide an even better source of psychological support and free up some of the professor's time otherwise spent providing that support. However, teaching assistants should receive guidance on issues that indicate serious concerns and know the law school's resources for students experiencing those issues.

g. Choosing and Compensating Teaching Assistants

Professors should establish minimum qualifications for teaching assistants. Obvious criteria include high performance in all courses, especially in LRW and other research or writing courses. Good interpersonal skills are essential. Law review or moot court experience is desirable but often not possible with busy second-year students. Teaching or tutoring experience, especially in writing, is an important plus as well. Other key factors include motivation, maturity, dependability, a sincere desire to help others, promptness, punctuality, respect for confidentiality, and a keen sense of responsibility.

Student teaching assistants may be compensated with hourly wages, tuition waivers, academic credit (graded or pass/fail), or a combination.[126] In determining the amount of academic credit, the

---

[126] *See id.* at 196, Question 17.10.

LRW faculty should consider the amount and type of work the teaching assistant is expected to do, and compare it to the amount and type of work required in a one-, two-, or three-credit course or seminar. Thus, for example, if the teaching assistant is responsible for researching and writing a sample memorandum of law, reading all student papers for grammar and citation, critiquing the students' research, and meeting with students three or four hours a week, the work might be equivalent to a two-credit seminar or clinical experience.

E. Considerations in Hiring a Director

As noted in earlier discussions of programmatic models, law schools that hire LRW faculty on tenure track or Standard 405(c) track most likely do not need an LRW director once the program has become well-established. Those schools might choose to appoint a coordinator (similar to a department head), but that role does not include hiring, training, or evaluating colleagues, or designing course materials for colleagues to use.

This section explains the role of a director in an LRW program employing (a) professors with short-term contracts and little job security or voting rights; (b) teaching fellows or visiting assistant professors; (c) part-time or adjunct professors; or (d) a mix of some of these in a hybrid program. It also addresses briefly the process for hiring a director and what to look for in applicants.

Selecting an LRW director is a significant hiring decision. In supervising a course that all students are required to take,[127] the LRW director fulfills a vital function in the curriculum. The responsibility to hire, train, mentor, and evaluate colleagues means that the director may function as both an Appointments Committee and a Personnel Committee. The job requires not just expertise in the subject matter, but also leadership, supervisory skills, a vision of how a quality program works, and sufficient political savvy to gain

[127] *See* ABA Standard 303(a)(2).

faculty support for needed enhancements to the existing program.[128] This level of responsibility requires a long-term commitment by the director to the school and vice versa.[129]

The most important question in structuring the director position is whether the incumbent will be eligible for tenure. A tenure-track directorship is a sound investment and one that many law schools have already made.[130] Many highly qualified candidates will not consider a position that is not tenure-track, especially if those candidates already have tenure at their current schools. At the very least, the director position should carry Standard 405(c) long-term contract status.[131]

The status, security, and voting rights that accompany tenure and tenure-like positions are essential for a director's success, the program's success, and optimal student learning. The director may need to make unpopular decisions, especially in the first few years as the curriculum is updated, existing LRW faculty adjust to new expectations, and the director draws faculty attention and school resources to LRW concerns. Faculty colleagues who teach in other areas must view the LRW director as an equal. Status as a faculty peer helps the director advocate not only for curricular changes that benefit students, but also for status, salary, workload, academic freedom, and even class schedules and office locations that benefit LRW faculty.

---

[128] *See* Jan M. Levine, *You Can't Please Everyone, So You'd Better Please Yourself: Directing (or Teaching in) a First-Year Legal Writing Program*, 29 VAL. U. L. REV. 611 (1995).

[129] In 2018, the vast majority of LRW directors had some form of tenure or long-term contract status. *2018 ALWD/LWI Survey*, *supra* note 3, at 63, Question 9.5#2.

[130] *See id.* (indicating that 49 schools have directors of first-year or combined programs who are tenured or on tenure track).

[131] *See id.* (indicating that 52 schools' directors of first-year or combined programs have Standard 405(c) contract status, and an additional 18 have long-term contracts).

The second most important question is whether the director will be expected to closely supervise faculty in the program (the "close supervision model"), or whether the director can assume a more general management style (the "general management" model).

The close supervision model is appropriate for directors of programs that rely on adjuncts, part-time faculty, teaching fellows, and visiting assistant professors. These teachers do not make a long-term commitment to LRW pedagogy and have other major commitments. For those reasons, they might not be interested in, and often cannot manage, investing the time needed to develop effective materials, and they often need guidance in providing effective feedback. Directing these teachers requires ongoing interaction to the point of creating a common syllabus, designing or approving all assignments, and reviewing a portion of the graded papers. This extent of oversight is important in providing students consistent, high-quality instruction.

The general management model is more appropriate for programs with full-time professors who are committed to LRW, even if their contracts are short-term and their status precludes participation in some facets of faculty governance. For these professors, the director should offer training and materials, especially for new teachers, and, upon request, review their syllabi and assignments. But the director must ultimately respect the academic freedom of these colleagues.

In both the close supervision and general management approaches, the director should use persuasion and consensus to support individual professors and help them develop professionally. Professors may want to brainstorm new teaching ideas, or they may need help dealing with challenging students; a successful director will prioritize those conversations. Beyond regular meetings of the LRW faculty, the director should contact each professor individually on a regular basis. One-on-one meetings encourage professors to discuss concerns that might not seem serious enough for a specific phone call or email request for help. For professors who hope to move to full-time or long-term academic positions, the director should provide information about relevant conferences, connect them with mentors in scholarship areas of interest, offer to read article drafts, and make specific recommendations to encourage engagement in the national legal writing community.

Another goal for both supervising and managing directors is strategic planning for the long-term benefit of the students' education and the program's advancement, even when those decisions prove unpopular with individual LRW colleagues. While it may be difficult, and even politically unpopular, for example, to recommend nonrenewal of a colleague's contract or to advocate for hiring additional faculty to reduce class size, the director's role is to create and sustain a program that exemplifies best practices. In a general management model, LRW professors may also contribute to the broader strategic planning for the law school.

When a school chooses between a close supervision director model and a general management model, the school makes an important decision, but only a temporary one. Closely supervising directors should become managing directors as their programs mature. Sometimes that happens because the school has decided at the outset to transition from adjunct professors to full-time, permanent professors; sometimes it happens because as LRW colleagues become seasoned experts, the supervising director realizes that the management role warrants changing. A director hired under the managing model might have the ultimate goal of moving to an autonomous program for which no director is needed, freeing up time to focus on teaching or scholarship, rather than administration.[132]

For either approach, once LRW faculty no longer need direction, and hiring and evaluation responsibilities are shifted to the law school's faculty committees, the continuation of a director and

---

[132] Such a transition can be difficult for a director, who can nevertheless continue to provide leadership to colleagues in much the same way that a department head might in other disciplines.

the attendant hierarchy can have negative consequences for experienced, long-term LRW professors. In their place, the former director might adopt the coordinator role, which could rotate every few years. Alternatively, any remaining responsibilities of the director could be divided among all LRW faculty.

An LRW coordinator is a first-among-equals colleague who assumes organizational and administrative work that would be unnecessarily repetitive if performed by all LRW professors. The LRW faculty as a whole should determine which responsibilities the coordinator will assume, how the coordinator will ensure consensus from the group, how often the position should rotate, and how to select the next coordinator. If the LRW faculty expects the coordinator to handle many time-consuming activities, the group should approach the administration with a recommendation for compensating the coordinator with a stipend, reduced service obligations, or a reduced teaching load.

Typical responsibilities assumed by a coordinator include organizing periodic meetings of LRW faculty; planning program-wide activities (e.g., oral arguments); arranging external events (e.g., annual visits of the state supreme court); envisioning the national outreach of the program; meeting with donors interested in supporting LRW education; taking the lead in hiring, training, and overseeing student teaching assistants or research assistants; managing a central budget for the LRW program; and supervising administrative assistants or a program manager who attends to some of these administrative details.

In a program based on either the director or the coordinator model, the director or coordinator typically teaches courses in the program as well. The experience of teaching LRW courses ensures that the director is keeping current in the pedagogy of the discipline, appreciates the specific challenges that LRW professors are facing (e.g., class size, student ability levels, and time commitments), and knows the impact that outside events have on the curriculum (e.g., supreme court visits to the law school or oral argument scheduling).

The director might also teach other courses, whether upper-level writing courses or casebook courses, that complement the director's practice experience or scholarly interests. Doing so will fully integrate the director into the faculty as a whole and ensure curricular cohesion.

The law school should take into account the administrative workload of the director and provide course relief, especially pre-tenure or pre-promotion, to allow time for scholarship. The school should also consider the burden of administrative requirements in determining the quantity of scholarship required, or the length of time for completing the scholarship.[133] The law school should respect the director's expertise in selecting the subject matter of her scholarship, whether legal writing or a more traditional area of law.[134]

A director should actively participate in the national legal writing community through work in professional organizations,[135] participation in academic conferences, or comparable activities. The director must remain aware of current developments in teaching theory relating to classroom activities and one-on-one instruction, and propose changes—or evaluate changes proposed by others—to improve the program and the student experience. Thus, the law school must provide professional development support to the director, such as research stipends, research assistants, and travel funds, on the same terms that apply to other faculty. Particularly in schools with adjunct-based programs, the director may have no professional peers onsite and will benefit from collaborating with and learning from directors at other schools.

---

[133] *See* Levine, *supra* note 62, at 546-48.

[134] *See* Liemer, *supra* note 24, at 1019-29.

[135] Some directors may maintain practice connections through state or local bar associations to enhance their scholarship and outreach to the general legal community.

F. Transitioning Between Program Models

LRW is one of just two subject areas that are required components of the curriculum at ABA-accredited law schools.[136] Given the emphasis on writing in the ABA Standards, studies of best practices in legal education, and the expectations of legal employers,[137] law schools should provide students with the best possible experience in LRW. Often that means transitioning at some point from one program model to another that offers LRW professors more security of position and more autonomy.[138]

Most schools have established first-year LRW courses that are taught by full-time faculty: Some afford tenure; some offer positions that comply with ABA Standard 405(c); still others provide long-term contracts and participation in faculty governance that reflect a long-term commitment to LRW faculty but do not fully comply with Standard 405(c).[139] These schools recognize that providing LRW faculty with security of position and faculty governance rights has many advantages.[140] The institution benefits from service and scholarship by these faculty members. Students benefit from a demonstrated commitment to LRW as a professional requirement and the message of equality among faculty. This commitment

---

[136] ABA Standard 303(a)(2) requires a law school curriculum to include a faculty-supervised writing experience in the first year and an additional experience in the second or third year. Standard 303 also requires a course in professional responsibility. ABA Standard 303(a)(1).

[137] *See, e.g.*, MacCrate Report, *supra* note 20.

[138] *See* Entrikin et al., *supra* note 45 (advocating that all LRW faculty should be afforded security of position at least equivalent to ABA Standard 405(c) and that Standard 405(d) should be eliminated). Other ways to enhance an LRW program include increasing the number of credits allocated to required courses and offering more elective courses.

[139] *See supra* Part B.3 of this chapter.

[140] *See generally supra* Part B of this chapter.

to equality is particularly powerful given that LRW faculty are predominantly women.[141]

But a number of schools still provide short-term contracts for LRW faculty, or they employ part-time or adjunct professors.[142] Any school that does not yet provide LRW faculty with the opportunity for tenure may consider enhancing its LRW program and the value of its instruction by changing models. As a school's LRW program matures, and its faculty members become better established in teaching and make scholarly and service contributions, their rank and status in the law school should increase and become more secure.

The benefits associated with each transition are explored more fully below. The transitions are described here in a graduated manner, using an incremental approach that moves from part-time faculty to full-time faculty to more secure positions to tenure. Each section addresses the considerations for a target staffing model. A school may, of course, decide to transition immediately from a part-time program to one that affords Standard 405(c) status, or from short-term faculty to tenure-track faculty. Such sweeping transitions implicate considerations from multiple target models, but the most relevant will be those related to the chosen target model. Thus, for a school contemplating a transition from a short-term contract model to a long-term Standard 405(c) contract model, the most relevant considerations associated with the transition are discussed below in Part F.3 of this chapter, but the considerations in Part F.2 might also be useful.

Schools are cautioned against revisiting the LRW program model too frequently. A new model needs time to develop, faculty need time to adjust to new positions, and first-year students may

---

[141] *See supra* text accompanying note 40.

[142] *See supra* note 83 and accompanying text. Part-time and adjunct LRW faculty may be problematic in light of ABA Standard 403(a), which requires that "full-time faculty shall teach substantially all of the first one-third of each student's coursework."

need to modify their expectations from what upper-class students experienced. A few challenges in the early years after a transition are not necessarily an indication that the transition is a failure. But they might suggest the need for fine-tuning, such as smaller class sizes, additional faculty support, or clarified expectations.

1. Part-time or Adjunct Professors to Full-Time Professors

Many schools have transitioned from a model using part-time or adjunct faculty to one using full-time faculty, as demonstrated by the low number of schools still functioning under a part-time or adjunct model.[143] This type of transition comports with ABA Standards, requiring that full-time faculty provide substantially all instruction in the first year.[144] It also represents a commitment to the required first-year writing experience, recognizing that full-time faculty are more responsive to student needs than part-time faculty. Full-time faculty members are also much more likely to be productive scholars and to engage in service to the institution.

a. When to Transition from a Part-time or Adjunct-Based Program

A transition from a part-time or adjunct model is most likely to occur when students, alumni, or employers pressure the school to improve the students' preparation for practice or the school's specialty ranking in LRW. The transition might also result from a law school's assessment of its learning outcomes related to LRW.

In preparing for this transition, experts at the law school should be consulted: the faculty who teach LRW; librarians who teach legal research; and others knowledgeable in the fields of writing, research, and law practice. These experts can compare the school's

---

[143] *See supra* Part C of this chapter.

[144] ABA Standard 403(a).

program with national models and best practices.[145] A school might also rely on data to demonstrate the need for a change and to determine what change will best meet the school's goals. For example, in addition to assessment of student learning outcomes, a survey instrument for students, alumni, and employers could gauge how well graduates have mastered essential skills and how they fare in securing employment and beginning to practice. Additional student surveys could ask how much time students devote to the required LRW course; whether they saw inconsistencies between course content and outcomes among sections; whether their part-time or adjunct professors were sufficiently available for office hours and conferences; and whether they perceived that classmates took the course seriously. Alternatively, focus groups from each of the three constituencies could meet with school leaders and writing experts to discuss the current program. Finally, an outside specialist could be brought in to review the program and to propose steps for moving away from a part-time or adjunct model.

b. Financial Challenges

Perhaps the greatest challenge in the transition from a part-time or adjunct-based model to a full-time model—regardless of the status of the full-time professors—is cost.[146] On a purely monetary basis, the part-time or adjunct model is less expensive, as it would be for teaching any other course.[147] The data gathered can

---

[145]For example, the majority of first-year LRW programs employ full-time faculty members. *2018 ALWD/LWI Survey*, *supra* note 3, at 9, Question 4.4.

[146]A vexing question concerns the status and salary to offer the new full-time professors. Some schools favor hiring full-time LRW faculty on par with tenure-track hires. These schools object to bringing in "second-class" citizens at lower salaries. Other schools might take incremental steps toward parity, hiring faculty at lower salaries or status with a commitment to improve them as more resources become available.

[147]On the other hand, an adjunct model is more appropriate for casebook courses taught primarily through lecture and an exam than for skills-focused courses that require assessing and grading multiple papers and conferencing with students.

show whether the school is receiving an adequate return on its low investment in the current program, or whether the program is merely cost-efficient but not educationally effective.

Resources for the transition to a full-time model may become available due to faculty retirement or a major gift, though often writing instruction will be competing with other worthy causes. Accepting the added costs of progressing beyond a part-time or adjunct model allows a school to support promotional and admissions statements about the value of legal writing instruction. Devoting additional resources to LRW allows a school to anticipate or respond to questions about the strengthened program of legal education during an accreditation visit, especially if data identify concerns about declining student profiles, graduate practice-readiness, or student satisfaction. In addition, prospective students are increasingly aware of the importance of LRW instruction. A strong LRW program can therefore enhance student recruitment efforts.

c. Transition Steps for Success

Once the school has decided to convert to a full-time model, the following steps can foster success.

First, the faculty search should be designed to attract well-qualified candidates, demonstrate the school's commitment to the success of the new model, and allow existing faculty to become vested in the new LRW faculty and view them as colleagues. At some schools, these goals can be accomplished through a committee specifically focused on hiring LRW faculty. In the best case, the search should follow the same norms and procedures for filling any other faculty position.

A thoughtful, national search encourages the law school faculty to become vested in both the new program model and the faculty hired to teach in it. A hasty search for local candidates (even if it produces the same new colleagues as a national search would) can result in colleagues who lack the support of the faculty and consequently lack confidence in their own new positions.

Second, before hiring, the school should decide the length of each short-term contract, the standards for contract renewal, the extent to which LRW faculty will participate in law school committees and faculty meetings, and any limits on LRW faculty members' voting rights.

Third, the new full-time LRW faculty should be involved in deciding as many issues concerning the conversion as possible (e.g., balancing consistency with academic freedom; selecting books; deciding when and how often class will meet; and determining course goals and content). If the school expects to hire experienced professors who will arrive with time-tested curricula, their positions might begin in mid-summer. Otherwise, the new professors should be selected well before the summer and put on the payroll at least by mid-May. A minimum of three months of planning allows time to become familiar with LRW pedagogy, select textbooks, finalize syllabi, and prepare major writing assignments. The summer also allows the new full-time colleagues to get together to share pedagogical approaches and develop a collaborative environment. Obviously, the academic freedom to develop their own courses should be on par with that of other faculty.[148]

Fourth, new faculty should receive stipends for travel to summer conferences so they can be immersed in the LRW discipline, work with national mentors and colleagues, stay on the cutting edge of LRW pedagogy, and represent the school at the national level.

d. Evaluating a Program After Transition

Converting from a part-time or adjunct model to a full-time model may take time. Changes might happen slowly as new faculty members develop expertise in the classroom and as students adjust to increased contact hours and higher expectations. Despite efforts to prepare, points of conflict will inevitably arise.

One positive change that might initially result in conflict is that students will need to manage their time more effectively. For

---

[148] *See generally* ABA Standard 405.

example, if students previously prioritized casebook over LRW assignments, casebook faculty might be disturbed to note a shift toward LRW as students spend more time on the LRW course. To help with the transition, faculty from all first-year courses could coordinate due dates and exams to ensure that students have sufficient time to devote to both. The school should commit to the full-time model for at least three years before evaluating its success, to give it adequate time to become established.

e. Evolution of the Director's Role

Once a school hires full-time faculty to teach LRW, the director's role should change markedly. Full-time LRW professors can be expected to create their own syllabi and course materials, though novice professors will still benefit from samples provided by the director and may lean on the director for guidance in developing writing assignments. Because full-time professors should have professional development funding to attend conferences that immerse them in the pedagogy and theory of the LRW discipline, the director should be relieved of that aspect of mentorship. Some mechanism should be put in place to encourage new faculty to take advantage of these professional development opportunities.

As a result of the transition, the director might be able to assume more teaching responsibilities, which could be a welcome alternative to administrative obligations; devote more time to scholarship (especially if the director is on tenure track); or assume new administrative positions within the law school while continuing to teach a reduced load. If, however, the full-time LRW faculty have only short-term contracts, the director may need to continue in the supervisory role for a few years, actively mentoring new hires, providing programmatic structure and administrative support, evaluating LRW professors, and leading any ongoing hiring efforts. Similarly, if the transition leaves short-term faculty with little participation in faculty governance, the director must continue to advocate on behalf of the LRW faculty to create optimal educational experiences for students.

If the transition is to a program with long-term contracts, a director might simultaneously transition to a coordinator role to organize program-wide events; synchronize work with librarians and other internal offices; and lead the LRW faculty in strategic planning, developing upper-level writing courses, creating CLE programs, or initiating donor relations.

2. *Transitioning to Long-term Contracts*

a. *When to Transition to Long-term Contracts*

Law schools with part-time or adjunct-based LRW programs may choose to move directly to long-term contracts to avoid the inherent challenges of a program with short-term positions: frequent turnover, structural hierarchies within faculties, and student dissatisfaction. Law schools with faculty on short-term, renewable, or presumptively renewable contracts should make the transition to long-term contracts when at least some LRW faculty members are experienced teachers with a demonstrated commitment to building the LRW discipline and contributing to the law school community. When LRW faculty demonstrate this commitment, it is beneficial to the law school to afford those faculty security of position and governance rights to encourage and enhance their service, scholarship, and teaching endeavors.

A law school can expect LRW faculty with improved security of position to experience a newfound potential to develop and grow as teachers, and to bring new energy and expertise to the program, all of which will redound to the students' benefit. Failure to make a timely transition, on the other hand, can result in reduced faculty morale that affects student learning, and may even result in the loss of talented professors who move to schools offering better positions.

b. *Financial Implications*

Costs associated with a transition from short-term to long-term contracts include increased salaries over time as LRW faculty remain at the school, as well as administrative and financial support for scholarship and professional development. The predictably lower rate of faculty turnover, however, reduces transaction costs for the school in recruiting, hiring, and training replacement faculty. If a director transitions from administrative work to teaching, the school might realize overall savings for the program.

c. *Transition Steps for Success*

The first transition issue is what contract status to give long-term faculty: a path to either a long-term, non-presumptively renewable contract, or a presumptively renewable contract for at least five years that complies with ABA Standard 405(c).[149] The school must also decide what criteria to adopt for hiring, promotion, and retention of faculty, including teaching, scholarship, and service. The qualifications for hiring, promoting, and retaining long-term contract faculty may differ significantly from those used for short-term faculty because scholarship is likely to be expected or required. For long-term contract faculty without Standard 405(c) status, a school might expect or require scholarship but at a lower quantity to reflect the distinction in status or salary. When setting contract terms and establishing criteria, the law school should also confirm that long-term LRW faculty will participate fully in faculty governance, or establish any limits on that participation (e.g., ineligibility to vote on promotion to a rank the LRW professor has not already achieved).

Second, the school should ensure that the long-term LRW faculty have the academic freedom to design their own courses, choose their own textbooks, and set class deadlines. Consistency, not uniformity, should be the goal. Writing faculty as a group should be encouraged to identify those curricular matters in which consistency is most important, such as the number of major assignments, opportunities for revision, type and depth of research instruction, conference requirements, and duration of the course. With this level

---

[149] For transitioning to Standard 405(c) contracts, see *supra* Part F.3 of this chapter.

of coordination, students will more readily accept differences in implementation among LRW professors, as they do for professors who teach other first-year courses.

Schools also need to decide whether to conduct a national search, and whether to require or allow current LRW faculty to apply. If allowed by law school and university rules, LRW faculty on short-term contracts should be permitted to convert to long-term contracts based on the review process established in the new LRW faculty standards. These experienced faculty can help shape the program for the future and train new hires. Requiring the law school's current faculty members to reapply for jobs they have had for several years might be perceived as insulting, and could result in the school losing the very professors whose commitment and success have been instrumental in the conversion decision.

d. Evaluating a Program After Transition

If thought out carefully in advance, a school's transition to long-term contracts should be fairly smooth, as long as experienced faculty remain in the program and salaries are reasonable. Particularly important steps include clarifying any modifications to salary or criteria for promotion. A preliminary review could be set up after two or three years to consider unforeseen questions, such as whether long-term faculty are eligible to serve on the school's ABA Self-Study Committee or to apply for endowed positions. As with any major change in a law school's organizational structure, a few vocal detractors can make an otherwise smooth transition unnecessarily difficult.

The quality of the LRW program after transition can be evaluated by traditional means similar to those for other programs, including student evaluations and assessment of learning outcomes. Graduating students can be surveyed to reflect on the nature and quality of the new LRW program. Sometimes students' views of a demanding first-year course evolve as they meet the challenges of their first legal employment. Of course, additional studies could be done with the assistance of career counselors and employers.

e. Evolution of the Director's Role

As LRW faculty transition from short- to long-term contracts, the burden on the director to train and mentor colleagues is generally reduced. But if the long-term faculty cannot fully participate in faculty governance, the pressure on the director to advocate on their behalf and to enhance the curriculum could be even greater. Depending on the director's ongoing role in evaluating LRW faculty members for promotion, the director could have an even heavier workload after transition than before.

In the long run, long-term faculty with academic freedom to design and teach their courses in ways that play to their strengths require less oversight. In recognition of all these changes, the LRW faculty might prefer at some point to move from a director to a coordinator, whose primary functions would be assisting with administrative tasks, planning special events, and ensuring sufficient consistency among sections so that students have comparable experiences.

3. Transitioning to Standard 405(c) Security of Position

Law schools employing LRW faculty on long-term contracts that comport with ABA Standard 405(c) must provide contracts with terms of five or more years[150] that are presumptively renewable and that include "non-compensatory perquisites reasonably similar to those provided other full-time faculty members." Previously, schools had an incentive to ensure security of position "reasonably similar to tenure" because a faculty member whose contract complied with Standard 405(c) criteria could be counted as 1.0 full-time-equivalent faculty member in calculating the student/faculty ratios that were an important consideration in the ABA Standards.[151]

---

[150] ABA Standard 405, Interpretation 405-6 allows for short-term contracts for probationary periods.

[151] *See* Melissa H. Weresh, *Form and Substance: Standards for Promotion and Retention of Legal Writing Faculty on Clinical Tenure Track*, 37 Golden

While the ABA Standards no longer consider student/faculty ratios, providing faculty with security of position reasonably similar to tenure demonstrates a commitment to LRW as a core component of legal education and provides the type of security that reduces turnover. At the same time, it allows schools to require LRW faculty with Standard 405(c) contracts "to meet standards and obligations reasonably similar to those required of other full-time faculty members," which may include scholarship or service requirements.

a. When to Transition

A school should transition to a model with faculty whose contracts comply with Standard 405(c) when it wants to recognize the importance of LRW education and to integrate LRW faculty fully in the work and mission of the school. A law school's transition to this model reflects a commitment by the institution to enhance the status and security of position of its LRW faculty members. As a result, the transition is likely to occur in an established program populated by long-term faculty, or by professors holding short-term contracts who have been employed successfully at the school for a number of years. For a school in one of those situations, the transition to a

---

GATE U. L. REV. 281, 291 (2007) (explaining that under former ABA Standard 402, full-time, long-term faculty were counted as 1.0 faculty member, while LRW faculty whose contracts did not comply with Standard 405(c) were counted as 0.7 of a faculty member in calculating student/faculty ratios). Moreover, in calculating student/faculty ratios, previous ABA Standards classified full-time legal writing faculty and clinicians who lacked Standard 405(c) long-term contracts as "additional teaching resources" along with adjunct faculty, who "counted" as 0.2 full-time-equivalent faculty member. And law schools could only count "additional teaching resources" in the student/faculty ratio up to 20 percent of a law school's full-time faculty resources. *See* AM. BAR ASS'N, STANDARDS AND RULES OF PROCEDURE FOR APPROVAL OF LAW SCHOOLS (2011-2012), Interpretation 402-1. The student/faculty ratio was an important consideration in determining whether a law school complied with the former ABA Standards. *See id.* Interpretation 402-2 ("Student/faculty ratios are considered in determining a law school's compliance with the Standards."). The ratios therefore offered an incentive to law schools to provide security of position to legal writing faculty and clinicians at least akin to Standard 405(c) contracts.

Standard 405(c) model seems modest. Even so, it should result in LRW faculty enjoying more secure positions and participating more fully in faculty governance.

Because ABA Standard 405(c) requires security of position reasonably similar to tenure, protections associated with these positions should be similar to those afforded tenured faculty. Safeguarding security of position for tenured faculty is often tied to the AAUP Recommended Institutional Regulations on Academic Freedom and Tenure. The AAUP recommendations authorize dismissal of a tenured faculty member only for cause, except in cases of financial exigency or discontinuance of a program or department for educational reasons.[152]

b. Financial Implications

No obligatory financial consequences are associated with this type of transition, as it simply incorporates the "reasonably similar to tenure" focus of ABA Standard 405(c).[153] Faculty involved in the transition should be part of negotiations regarding the timing and amount of any salary adjustment contemplated. Morale could be affected if the transition to Standard 405(c) status includes additional obligations for scholarship and service without appropriate compensation.

c. Evaluating a Program After Transition

This type of transition is unlikely to have any significant program impact because it simply enhances the security of position for long-standing faculty members. A move from a part-time or short-term contract model to a Standard 405(c) long-term contract model may warrant evaluation, but only in the fourth year, after the transition is fully realized. The change might also have an impact on

---

[152]Weresh, *supra* note 21, at 544.

[153]Neumann Jr., *supra* note 36 (demonstrating that enhanced job security imposes no additional costs on an institution).

the faculty as a whole if the transition changes how LRW faculty participate in faculty governance, especially if they are permitted to vote on additional matters.

d. Evolution of the Director's Role

Some schools contemplating this transition will have already moved away from a directed program to either a coordinated program or an autonomous program, so it may not involve a director. In those schools with a director, a simultaneous transition to a coordinator role might be appropriate because the LRW faculty's strengthened security of position empowers them to advocate for needed curricular advancements or employment perquisites reasonably similar to those enjoyed by other full-time faculty.[154] In a coordinated program in which experienced faculty have short-term or long-term contracts, the transition is unlikely to impact the coordinator's role at all because it merely enhances the security of position afforded to LRW faculty. In these long-term employment models, the coordinator's role vis-à-vis faculty colleagues is typically limited to coordination, administration, and mentorship of junior faculty.

4. Transitioning to Tenure

The ultimate transition for an LRW program is to afford LRW faculty some form of tenure. With this transition, a school must decide whether to afford unitary tenure, with criteria for promotion and retention indistinguishable from those applicable to other tenure-track faculty, or a form of programmatic tenure that is unique to LRW faculty or all skills faculty. Significant benefits accrue to law schools that provide full security of position to LRW faculty. This form of employment demonstrates a full commitment to LRW instruction and practice-readiness for students. It also encourages LRW faculty members' full participation in governance, service, and scholarship. As a result, law schools that afford LRW faculty

---

[154] *See* ABA Standard 405(c).

the opportunity for tenure benefit from the contributions of LRW faculty colleagues and significantly boost faculty morale.

a. When to Transition

The transition to a program offering tenure is influenced by many institutional considerations. The most important is likely the performance of LRW faculty in terms of teaching, service, and scholarship. Programs that have successfully managed this transition report that a solid record of service and scholarship by LRW faculty facilitated the change. If LRW faculty members have not made contributions similar to those of casebook faculty, resistance should be expected to affording comparable status.

The support of key administrative faculty, including the dean, is an essential feature of this type of transition. Some schools have reported that losing experienced and valued LRW faculty to institutions that do provide tenure prompts the transition. Finally, the timing of the transition should consider that more and more programs have adopted the tenure model for LRW faculty.[155]

At the same time, LRW faculty may be reticent to put their current jobs on the line by taking on additional service or scholarship requirements while continuing to teach time-intensive courses. As a result, many schools making this transition permit existing faculty to apply for tenure without fear of losing their jobs. If a national search is undertaken, the hiring process should consider the existing faculty's expertise and often superior qualifications. A current faculty member who is not awarded tenure should remain on a long-term contract; it would be inconsistent to terminate faculty after several years as if they were unqualified to teach there in the first place.

---

[155] A list of law schools that provide unitary and programmatic tenure for LRW faculty is maintained on the website of the Legal Writing Institute, https://www.lwionline.org/sites/default/files/media-documents/School-Tenure%20Status%20List.April2019.pdf (last visited Dec. 17, 2019).

Two legal writing organizations, the Association of Legal Writing Directors (ALWD) and the Legal Writing Institute (LWI), have committees that focus on the status and employment conditions for LRW faculty. The ALWD ABA Task Force "monitors potential changes in the ABA standards that impact the legal writing academy; testifies before committees related to the review of ABA standards; [and] prepares position letters on behalf of ALWD and LWI."[156] The LWI Professional Status Committee "gather[s] information about status issues and challenges facing its members at their respective institutions, act[s] as a resource for them, and assist[s] the LWI Board in addressing these issues and their effect on its members."[157] Members of these committees can serve as valuable resources as a law school considers the timing of the transition to a tenure model.

b. *Financial Implications*

While some institutions are resistant to this form of transition for fear that it will require additional resources, no obligatory financial consequences result from affording LRW faculty full security of position. Tenure does not protect faculty salary or other benefits and does not prevent an institution from downsizing if it experiences serious financial strain.[158] As Professor Richard Neumann Jr. explains,

> [d]espite myths to the contrary, no form of job security inherently raises the cost of education to any significant degree. Nothing in academic employment law prevents discharge, suspension, or salary reduction for a bad teacher, a bad scholar, a disruptive colleague, or an insubordinate faculty

---

[156] *ABA Engagement,* ASS'N OF LEGAL WRITING DIRS., https://www.alwd.org/aba-engagement (last visited Dec. 17, 2019).

[157] *The Professional Status Committee and Status-Related Advocacy*, LEGAL WRITING INST., https://www.lwionline.org/resources/status-related-advocacy (last visited Dec. 17, 2019).

[158] Neumann Jr., *supra* note 36, at 599-602.

member. Job security does not protect salary or other workplace benefits. And it does not prevent faculty downsizing.[159]

Thus, transitioning from long-term contracts to tenure does not necessarily have any financial impact. However, if LRW faculty have been paid considerably less than tenure-track faculty, then a school should offer comparable salaries for comparable work responsibilities, including scholarship and service expectations for LRW faculty.

c. *Transition Steps for Success*

When a law school elects to transition to a tenure-track model for LRW faculty, it must first determine whether to offer programmatic tenure or unitary tenure. Two significant benefits associated with unitary tenure are administrative ease and equity. First, the institution does not need to draft new tenure criteria, which can be administratively difficult and might require approval not only by the law faculty but also by a parent university or board of trustees. When LRW faculty members are afforded unitary tenure, the institution does not require additional promotion and retention criteria, but simply applies those that exist for all other tenure-track faculty. Second, offering unitary tenure to LRW faculty eliminates the caste or hierarchy system associated with different tiers of faculty. Adoption of unitary tenure sends a strong message of equality to students and faculty alike.

Institutional reasons, however, might justify a decision to offer programmatic tenure to LRW faculty. Programmatic tenure provides security of position comparable to that for other tenured faculty, but the criteria for promotion may differ. Nonetheless, the security of position for both unitary and programmatic tenure typically reflects the AAUP tenure recommendations, securing the faculty member's position against dismissal except for cause, financial exigency, or programmatic reductions.

---

[159] *Id.* at 605.

Institutions transitioning to tenure must determine scholarship obligations for LRW faculty. Some institutions do not credit scholarship related to the LRW discipline, preferring scholarship related to traditional casebook areas of law. This attitude could be characterized as shortsighted because LRW is a substantive doctrine in its own right,[160] and scholarship associated with pedagogy is critically valuable in reforming legal education.[161] If programmatic tenure is

---

[160]Linda H. Edwards, *Legal Writing: A Doctrinal Course*, 1 SAVANNAH L. REV. 1 (2014).

> In addition to teaching the legal doctrine governing particular issues, legal writing courses teach legal doctrines specific to the course. These include: (1) the meaning and application of standards of appellate review; (2) complicated questions of civil and appellate procedure; (3) ethical requirements that apply to predictive and persuasive writing; (4) principles of statutory construction; and (5) a wealth of other legal methods topics. All of these legal topics are taught in the typical first-year Legal Writing course, and for some of them, the Legal Writing course is the only place the topics typically appear in the law school curriculum.
>
> The remainder of a first-year Legal Writing course clearly meets the broader, older, and first-listed definition of "doctrine": a body or system of teachings relating to a particular subject. In addition to matters of citation and style, these courses teach a very specific body of information about such matters as: (1) the core forms of legal reasoning; (2) sources and methods of legal research; (3) particular organizational paradigms for analysis and argument; (4) particular formats for analogies and counter analogies; (5) the components of particular documents, including the substantive requirements for those components; (6) informal rules and principles of persuasion applicable to fact statements; and (7) customs and principles of persuasion for engaging in counterargument. Most of these vital subjects appear nowhere else in the typical law school curriculum. Together, they certainly constitute a body of teachings relating to the subject of legal writing.

Id. at 5–6 (footnotes and citations omitted).

[161]Terrill Pollman & Linda H. Edwards, *Scholarship by Legal Writing Professors: New Voices in the Legal Academy*, 11 LEGAL WRITING 3 (2005). Pollman and Edwards argue that articles addressing pedagogy "can serve important

selected, scholarship obligations often allow for different kinds of scholarship or fewer publications. For example, scholarship criteria for programmatic tenure might be crafted to allow amicus briefs and non-traditional legal scholarship to qualify. Allowing a different quantity of scholarship to reflect the teaching obligations associated with LRW, or other distinctions in status or salary, are also possibilities with programmatic tenure.

In any move to tenure, the school must anticipate additional logistical considerations associated with the transition. Some schools employ a national search, asking existing faculty to reapply for their positions. This approach can lead to both positive and negative consequences. On the positive side, seasoned LRW faculty have the opportunity to showcase their achievements and solidify their entitlement to this ultimate form of job security. On the other hand, requiring faculty to apply for positions they have presumably held for many years—and performed so well that the school elected to move to a tenured LRW program—might be perceived by current faculty as disrespectful of their contributions.

Institutions must also determine the process for transitioning incumbent faculty. One issue is whether a faculty member must proceed to the tenure track or may elect to remain in a long-term contract position. Another question is how to account for years in service, and whether a long-term professor may proceed directly to a tenure review or must instead proceed through the entire tenure process. For faculty with long-term experience in teaching, service,

---

scholarly values by directly improving our ability to make good lawyers, thereby improving the law and the legal process," and that these articles should be evaluated consistent with other scholarship based upon "the intellectual rigor the article required, the comprehensiveness of the research on which it is based, its contribution to the scholarly conversation on its topic, and its potential to advance the study and practice of law." *Id.* at 41. If articles about pedagogy do not count toward promotion, the authors stress that institutions "should not say that one of the primary reasons for spending massive institutional and personal resources on scholarship is to enhance our teaching." *Id.* at 41–42.

and scholarship, it makes little sense to require them to begin at the inception of the tenure process. This is particularly true when these faculty have been employed under long-term contract standards with teaching, service, and scholarship obligations similar to those associated with tenure. Under those circumstances, fairness dictates that faculty members' prior contributions should count toward tenure.

d. Evaluating a Program After Transition

If LRW faculty members who are employed under criteria applicable to long-term contracts have teaching, service, and scholarship obligations similar to those applicable to tenured faculty, few significant programmatic changes are likely to result when the program transitions from long-term contracts to tenure. Faculty are evaluated individually as they are considered for promotion and tenure. If a school transitions from part-time or short-term contracts to a tenure program model, however, some considerations addressed in prior sections might be relevant.

e. Evolution of the Director's Role

A tenure-style LRW program has no role for a traditional director. If the previous program model included a director, that person might continue as a coordinator, especially during the first few years following transition. For larger programs, a coordinator may still be helpful in mentoring junior faculty, and if the program is highly coordinated, in administering program details.

VI. ENSURING QUALITY INSTRUCTION

A. Administration of Programs

Many people in legal education assume that every law school has an LRW director who closely supervises the faculty who teach LRW. That may once have been true, but it is no longer an appropriate generalization. For many reasons,[1] the future organizational trend will likely be away from a director who closely supervises the writing faculty. Indeed, as more LRW professors are hired on the tenure track or on long-term contracts, the need for close supervision disappears. Future law school planning will therefore likely favor coordinated programs in which the professors are largely autonomous.

In both autonomous programs and those with a director, some level of coordination is still needed. Administrative tasks and programmatic concerns require ongoing oversight and some supervision, such as developing consistent learning outcomes; liaising between administration, faculty, and students; serving as the "face" of the LRW program; and providing other special services.

Presently, some programs have directors who act as both coordinators and supervisors, while some programs do not regularly need a person in a supervisory role but do need regular coordination of tasks. This chapter will address the various ways in which LRW programs can meet these challenges.

1. Autonomous Programs

In autonomous programs, coordinating administrative tasks is often more efficiently carried out by one person than by a collective. Therefore, some schools have adopted a rotating chair or coordinator model to address these duties, while others have incorporated

---

[1] See Chapter V for details on faculty status and governance issues.

them into an associate dean role. To the extent that the remaining sections of this chapter refer to administrative matters handled by the director, the person in one of these alternative roles can often address those matters effectively.

In autonomous programs, direct supervision of full-time faculty is not needed. When a new faculty member joins an autonomous program, the existing members of the department can use their group and individual experience, as well as the techniques described below, to mentor their new colleague.

2. *Programs with a Director*

The director—whether a career director, a director with a short-term or rotating appointment, or an associate dean—commonly takes responsibility for four administrative tasks: (a) acting as a liaison between administration, faculty, and students; (b) providing programmatic oversight; (c) serving as the face of the program; and (d) creating and providing other student services. The director's supervisory tasks are addressed in Parts B and C of this chapter.

a. Liaison Among Administration, Faculty, and Students

The director of an LRW program must often play the role of politician. This is true in the sense that she[2] serves many different constituencies. She is not only a member of the faculty; she is also an administrator. She is responsible to the students for ensuring that they receive a high-quality legal education, but she is also a representative of and an advocate for the faculty who teach in the LRW program.

---

[2]Women comprise 73% of full-time faculty who teach LRW. Lorraine K. Bannai, *Challenged X3: The Stories of Women of Color Who Teach Legal Writing*, 29 BERKELEY J. GENDER L. & JUST. 275, 278 (2014). In recognition of this fact and for simplicity, the pronouns "she" and "her" will be used to refer to directors throughout this chapter.

Development and training of the faculty who teach in the LRW program, including scholarship, are addressed later in this chapter. This part focuses on how directors deal with two particular groups outside the legal writing faculty: non-LRW faculty and students.

i. Dealing with Non-LRW Faculty

While a variety of issues might arise when dealing with non-LRW faculty, scheduling conflicts or challenges are particularly likely. As all legal educators begin to incorporate more and more frequent formative assessments,[3] the chances increase that students will have multiple assignments due or exams scheduled during the same week, or even on the same day. Even without actual conflicts in scheduling due dates or exams, it is not uncommon for faculty who teach in lecture-based courses to complain that their students were either absent or not adequately prepared to participate in class on the day or two before a legal writing assignment is due. Nor is it unusual for students who are unprepared for another class to blame their lack of preparation on the time spent completing the assignments for their LRW course. Non-LRW faculty have therefore been known to point the finger at the LRW program when students fail to perform up to their expectations.

To avoid or minimize this type of resentment from non-LRW faculty, it is good practice for LRW faculty to share information about major assignment deadlines, midterms, and other formative assessments. The law school may even have a policy mandating information sharing among all faculty who teach a given section of the first-year class. With or without such a policy, the director may initiate the information-sharing effort by distributing the LRW class syllabi, or a list of major writing assignments and their due dates, to the non-LRW faculty who teach the same students. In return, non-LRW faculty can share information about midterms and any significant dates in their lecture-based courses. Final exam dates, or at least

---

[3]For a discussion of formative assessment, see Chapter IV.

the overall timeframe for final exams, are likely to be readily available to all. A shared calendar may prevent major conflicts, such as another first-year course professor scheduling a midterm exam or a make-up class on the same day that a major LRW assignment is due.

Of course, even with everyone's genuine best efforts, it may not be possible to avoid scheduling conflicts altogether. If a major conflict is unavoidable, LRW faculty and non-LRW faculty may have to negotiate a compromise. If the LRW faculty member is not tenured, the director should step in to assist in the negotiations.[4] Because the LRW course typically has a busier schedule of assignments during the semester, it is sometimes less difficult to reschedule the exam date in a lecture-based course.

If a compromise solution is impossible, students should be made aware at the start of the semester to allow them to plan accordingly. Effective time management is an important lawyering skill, and a scheduling conflict is a good opportunity to remind students of the need to develop this skill.[5]

ii. Dealing with Students

A significant portion of the director's time is devoted to dealing with student complaints about writing professors or course content. These situations represent some of the most delicate parts of the

---

[4]The reality is that the legal academy is a hierarchical institution. Because of her status, a tenured faculty member has more power and authority than a non-tenured faculty member. One of the many reasons the director of an LRW program should have tenure (or eligibility for tenure) is to enable the director to assist a non-tenured colleague in this type of situation. See Chapter V for more details on professional status. *See also* Kristen Konrad Tiscione, *"Best Practices": A Giant Step Toward Ensuring Compliance with ABA Standard 405(c), A Small, Yet Important Step Toward Addressing Gender Discrimination in the Legal Academy*, 66 J. LEGAL EDUC. 566 (2017).

[5]*See* Camille Lamar, *Timing Is Everything: Teaching Essential Time Management Skills for "Real World" Legal Writing*, 22 PERSPS. 125 (Spring 2014), https://info.legalsolutions.thomsonreuters.com/pdf/perspec/2014-spring/2014-spring-6.pdf.

director's job and require sensitivity and respect for both the student and the LRW professor. Although a director should be willing to hear student grievances, allowing students to come immediately to the director with any and all grievances risks encouraging frivolous complaints.

Most law schools have a pre-existing set of policies that determine the process a student must use to initiate a complaint. The law school should not permit multiple pathways for student complaints, and the director should ensure that the school does not permit or encourage students to bypass the director to complain to a dean. Instead, the director should be the second step for a complaining student, after discussing the issue with the student's own LRW professor. When dealing with a complaint, the director might first encourage the student to attempt to resolve difficulties directly with the LRW professor unless the student has a valid reason for not doing so. The director may wish to adopt a requirement that the student first exhaust internal administrative remedies, a policy common to many schools' grievance policies.

Whenever possible, the director might require the student to write out the nature of the specific complaint and submit any relevant documentation. Students should be directed to state alleged facts, not conclusions. This requirement may avoid general complaints such as "the professor doesn't tell us what she wants," or "I did everything my professor told me to but I still got a bad grade." The requirement to focus on facts also enables the director to point out pages in the textbook where the specific issue is discussed, or to give the student another source to read that might clarify the student's specific problem.

Once presented with the student's allegations, and before taking any action, the director should attempt to determine whether the professor's actions in dealing with the complaint were unreasonable. Most student complaints necessitate some fact-finding; one cannot merely accept a student's allegations as true without asking the professor for information. The director should therefore advise the student at the outset of the complaint process that she may not be able to maintain the student's anonymity. It is difficult for the director to ask the professor for specific information without revealing that a specific student has made a complaint. Of course, if the student is required to exhaust internal remedies, the professor likely already knows about the student's complaint. However, the professor might be upset to learn that the student is not satisfied with the professor's handling of the matter and has gone to the director.

Even if the student's anonymity cannot be maintained, the director should confront the problem directly, inform the professor of the complaint, and ask for the professor's perspective on the issue. If there is a real problem, the director must work with the professor in mediating the best solution possible. If the student's complaint lacks substance, the director still has to work with the student to ameliorate any bad feelings and to convince the student there will be no adverse repercussions for raising the issue in the first place.

A special problem is presented by a grade appeal. Grade appeals in LRW courses should be treated in exactly the same manner as they are in other courses. If not, the law school sends the message that LRW courses are different and that different rules apply. In fact, the director can reasonably decide not to review individual grades at all, but rather limit oversight to ensuring that the distribution of grades is consistent across all sections of the LRW program.[6] It is impossible, in any case, for a director to review all papers in the class to evaluate one student's grade in context. Furthermore, reviewing grades assigned by LRW professors would greatly diminish their stature in the eyes of the students and other faculty. It may a good idea, however, to be available to consult with LRW professors who identify problematic papers, particularly those at the low end of the grading scale, to offer a "second opinion" before grades are assigned.

If grade appeals in LRW classes are allowed, the policy should include a readily understandable standard of review. A director might

---

[6] *See* Part B of this chapter for information regarding teacher training and quality control.

refuse to change a grade unless it arises from arbitrary and capricious grading, an abuse of discretion, or credible bias against a group of which the student is a member. If the director finds a reasonable basis for believing the grade awarded is not appropriate, the director should not change the grade without reviewing a representative sample of excellent, average, and poor papers on that same assignment. If the director disagrees with the particular grades awarded, the LRW professor might be urged to adjust all grades for that paper, to make adjustments on the weight of the assignment, or to make appropriate adjustments at the time of awarding the final course grade.

Occasionally a student asks to change LRW professors, either during a semester or between semesters. Apart from a scheduling conflict verified by the dean of students, this request should never be granted without a very substantial reason such as demonstrated discriminatory treatment or harassment. A student should not be allowed to transfer sections merely based on a vague claim such as "the learning chemistry isn't there," or "I can't learn from this professor, and I'm paying a lot of tuition money." While the director may have to mediate the student-professor relationship or refer the student for additional help (for example, from the writing center), the morale problems that would result from letting students switch sections just because they do not like the assigned professor would be severe, with the effect of encouraging students to "shop" for LRW professors. If first-year students are not permitted to select their professors for other law school courses, they should not be permitted to do so for LRW courses.

Special concerns are raised by complaints of faculty bias or discrimination against a student or group of students based on characteristics protected by law, such as race, gender, sexual orientation, gender identity, or religion. By its very nature, explicit bias that negatively impacts the student experience is easier to identify than implicit bias. Moreover, law professors who aim direct threats or derogatory comments against students in a target group are fortunately a dying breed, and non-discrimination policies are generally effective to deter or remedy express threats. But not infrequently, law professors and others in authority act in ways that manifest implicit or unconscious bias.[7]

The best approach to address bias and discrimination is prevention through education and awareness. Law schools often conduct anti-bias and anti-harassment trainings for faculty and staff to minimize the negative and unfair results of implicit bias. As discussed below, trainings on implicit bias, specifically regarding the evaluation of student writing assignments, should be a regular part of full-time and adjunct faculty orientation and training.[8]

Unfortunately, however, it is not possible to completely eradicate bias or its effects. When faced with a student complaint of bias, the director should maintain uniform policies and procedures as described above. As with other student complaints, not all claims of bias have merit, but they must be handled with the same diplomacy, attention, and care as all other complaints. This approach is particularly important because even if the director cannot take action (e.g., change a grade or transfer the student into a different section), the student who has raised the complaint certainly feels strongly that she has been treated differently than other students.

If the law school has a dean of diversity, equity, and inclusion, it may be useful to consult that person during the complaint process.

---

[7]To oversimplify for the sake of brevity, implicit bias is "the automatic association of stereotypes or attitudes with particular social groups." Rachel D. Godsil, *Breaking the Cycle: Implicit Bias, Racial Anxiety, and Stereotype Threat*, 24 POVERTY & RACE 1, 1 (Jan./Feb. 2015), http://prrac.org/newsletters/janfeb2015.pdf. On a daily basis, each of us constantly makes decisions and judgments without recognizing that unconscious negative associations with people in groups that are different from us, as well as positive associations with people in groups who share characteristics with us, both disadvantage the former and benefit the latter. *See* Nicole E. Negowetti, *Implicit Bias and the Legal Profession's "Diversity Crisis": A Call for Self-Reflection*, 15 NEV. L.J. 930 (2015); *see also* IMPLICIT RACIAL BIAS ACROSS THE LAW (Justin D. Levinson & Robert J. Smith eds., 2012).

[8]*See* Part B.1.a.i of this chapter.

When dealing with complaints of bias, it is critical to inform the student that anonymity cannot be guaranteed. The professor who is the subject of the complaint must have an opportunity to understand the situation and to provide her point of view. The director should also take every precaution to assure that the student does not experience any repercussions for having raised the issue in the first place. Sometimes it might be appropriate for a professor to undertake anti-bias training. If repeated complaints arise about an adjunct, the director or academic dean should consider not inviting that person back to teach.

b. Coordinating Curriculum, Learning Goals, and Outcomes

i. Uniformity in Learning Goals, If Not Teaching Strategies

Any LRW program, whether supervised by a director or not, should have a uniform set of learning goals and outcomes.[9] A program that is united by common learning goals allows the faculty who teach in the program to exercise greater autonomy in the classroom. Once a set of learning goals has been developed, agreed upon, and committed to, each LRW professor should be given discretion to utilize whatever teaching strategies she thinks best, given her particular student population and other relevant variables.[10]

The responsibility for developing a uniform set of learning goals and outcomes rests with the director, the entire full-time faculty, and the administration of the law school, all working in cooperation.

---

[9] *See* Anthony Niedwiecki, *Prepared for Practice? Developing a Comprehensive Assessment Plan for a Law School Professional Skills Program*, 50 U. S.F. L. Rev. 245 (2015).

[10] Of course, new law teachers need proper mentorship and guidance to develop the expertise to make these decisions. See Part B of this chapter for more on teacher training and quality control.

Each of these stakeholders is important to the process because developing specific learning outcomes for the LRW program requires an extensive understanding of the general learning outcomes for the entire law school.[11]

As daunting as this task may sound, it need not be overwhelming. Law schools regularly engage in curricular mapping (and remapping) projects for accreditation purposes. Ideally, the learning goals and outcomes for the LRW program will take the entire law school's curricular map into consideration. LRW and other skills-based and experiential learning classes should not be siloed off from the rest of the law school curriculum. To the extent possible and practical, analytical thinking and organizational skills that are the focus of LRW courses should be reflected throughout the law school curriculum. As LRW programs become more academically robust (more than two required courses), and as LRW faculty become integrated as full citizens of their law schools by teaching traditional casebook and seminar courses in addition to skills courses, these overlaps and synergies will develop organically. But in the meantime, it is critical to attend to these matters deliberately and strategically.

One good reason for the LRW program to be concerned with law school curricular mapping is to discourage students from perceiving LRW courses as separate and discrete subjects without a connection to other courses. Students benefit from understanding that the strategic organization and analysis learned in LRW class will help them with issue-spotting and problem-solving skills assessed on midterm and final exams in lecture-based courses.[12]

---

[11] *See* Anthony Niedwiecki, *Law Schools and Learning Outcomes: Developing a Coherent, Cohesive, and Comprehensive Law School Curriculum*, 64 Clev. St. Rev. 661 (2016).

[12] *See* Sherri Lee Keene, *Legal Writing Professors Without Borders: Exploring the Benefits of Integrated Teaching of Legal Writing, Doctrine, and More*, 29 Second Draft 36 (Fall 2016); Anthony Niedwiecki, *Lawyers and Learning: A Metacognitive Approach to Legal Education*, 13 Widener L. Rev. 33 (2006).

While taking into consideration the general curriculum, the specific learning goals and outcomes of the LRW program should be the collective work product of the director, the full-time LRW faculty, and even the adjunct faculty who teach in the program. Although adjunct faculty may be less aware than full-time faculty about the pedagogical goals of the institution, those who teach specialized writing, research, or rhetoric courses will likely have important insights to share.[13]

The learning goals and outcomes of the LRW program should establish which skills each student should be able to demonstrate by the time she has completed the course requirements. The learning goals and outcomes should also determine the level of mastery each student should achieve for each skill identified.[14] For example, client counseling is an important lawyering skill. LRW students might be introduced to this skill during a simulated client interview in their very first semester. But client counseling is not likely to play a significant role in the overall assessment of a student during her first year. Stated otherwise, a first-year law student would not be expected to gain mastery over the skill of client counseling, but might be expected to have an introductory grasp of the skill. Mastery of client counseling skills might come later in a student's law school career through clinical courses or externships. By contrast, a first-year law student would likely be expected to master the skill of proper and accurate citation to legal authority in office memos and persuasive briefs by the end of the year.

---

[13]Adjunct faculty engage in part-time teaching because their full-time occupation is in law practice. *See* Chapter V for a more detailed discussion of LRW programs that employ adjunct faculty. Any law professor who has taught full-time (in a non-clinical setting) for longer than two or three years simply does not have the same daily contact with the practice of law. Therefore, adjunct faculty can provide invaluable insight in developing LRW program goals.

[14]Niedwiecki, *supra* note 9, at 260-61 (identifying four levels of competence—introductory, competent, mastery, and advanced).

Whatever the desired learning outcomes, the process of creating and developing the LRW program's curricular map should be a transparent, collaborative, and recurring one. LRW faculty should be encouraged to reflect regularly on the learning goals and outcomes of their individual classes and how to best promote and reinforce those skills throughout the law school curriculum.

ii. Innovation in Response to Market and Accreditation Demands

Apart from serving as an important reminder about the desired learning outcomes, a periodic, scheduled curricular review will likely reveal opportunities to innovate in response to the evolving needs of the professional legal services market. During the last fifteen years, for example, changing expectations of law firms and their clients have instigated reform in the law school classroom. Because clients are no longer willing to pay junior associates top-dollar salaries for on-the-job training, law firms expect law school graduates to be "practice-ready" at the entry level. In addition, due to the substantial revisions to the ABA Accreditation Standards over approximately the same time period, law schools are now required to ensure that each student earns a minimum of six credit hours in experiential learning. These developments mark a sea change in legal education as compared to just a generation ago.

As a result, LRW professors—who teach practice-ready, experiential skills—have been at the forefront of innovations in legal education. In some schools, these innovations have included expanding the required LRW curriculum, including developing new upper-level courses.[15] In others, LRW professors have made concerted efforts at bridging gaps between LRW courses and experiential

---

[15] *See, e.g.*, Kim D. Chanbonpin & Sarah Dávila-Ruhaak, *Lawyering Skills and Clinical Cooperation: Teaching Spanish for Lawyers at John Marshall*, 29 SECOND DRAFT 29 (Fall 2016) (describing the development of a new curricular offering in the LRW program).

learning or client-focused courses.[16] At yet other schools, LRW faculty have developed additional class modules, short workshops, or co-curricular programs.[17]

c. Public Relations Responsibilities

As an administrator, the director is often called on to serve as the public "face" of the LRW program. As such, she interacts with alumni, the practicing bench and bar, and media to promote the strengths of the LRW program. Many of the innovative curricular updates mentioned earlier in this chapter came about as a result of consultation with practitioners about the current needs of the legal market. For example, many schools employ surveys or focus groups of alumni and employers to ascertain what they mean by the term "practice-ready." And although it is rarely part of the official job description, public relations and marketing are real burdens that many directors shoulder beyond their many other responsibilities.

LRW programs must have a presence at the national level, too. While the law school community is often loath to admit it, both the published rankings of top law schools and the auxiliary rankings of specialty programs matter. Every dean declares that the numerical ranking system is flawed and does not provide sufficient details for a potential law student to adequately evaluate the strengths and

---

[16] *See, e.g.*, JoAnne Sweeney, *Teaching Professionalism and How to "Act Professionally" by Coordinating Legal Writing with Professional Development*, 29 SECOND DRAFT 20 (Fall 2016) (explaining how the author worked in cooperation with the Dean of Professional Development to incorporate professionalism values and skills exercises in her first-year LRW courses); Nantiya Ruan, *Student, Esquire?: The Practice of Law in the Collaborative Classroom*, 20 CLINICAL L. REV. 429 (2014) (describing possibilities for collaboration between law teachers and non-profit lawyers to provide live-client experiences to first-year law students).

[17] *See, e.g.*, Chantal Morton, *Legal Writing Specialists and Our Contribution to Experiential Learning Outcomes*, 29 SECOND DRAFT 41 (Fall 2016) (detailing a series of workshops on persuasive writing, networking, negotiation, and teamwork).

weaknesses of her law school. But the same dean will often tout her law school's overall ranking as well as its rankings in specialty categories. *The U.S. News & World Report* has included LRW as a specialty ranking category since 2005. LRW program rankings are based on the votes of LRW directors or others identified by the law schools as working in that field.[18]

Because the specialty program rankings impact the law school's reputation and recruitment efforts, the director is often responsible for producing or collaborating to produce marketing materials that showcase the accomplishments of the faculty and students in the program. Beyond serving as a mere marketing tool, a report that regularly compiles the achievements of LRW students and faculty can be an effective way to boost esteem and morale. Full-time faculty each engaged in their own individual projects may not always be aware of the good work that their colleagues are doing. These informational materials, too, are useful in advocating for equitable LRW faculty status in relation to other faculty in the law school.

The director may consider creating a media guide for her LRW faculty that lists their diverse areas of expertise. Working in cooperation with the public relations or marketing department of the law school or university, the director can assure that when media inquiries arrive at the law school, the public relations staff know whom to contact to provide knowledgeable and prompt responses. The media guide can also be published on the program's landing page on the law school's website.

Finally, many LRW programs rely on adjunct faculty to teach upper-level or specialty writing courses. It is important for the director to keep a constant eye out for good candidates to serve as adjunct faculty. One way is to remain active in local bar associations and to attend alumni events. Some schools have partnered with affinity

---

[18] *See* Robert Morse, Kenneth Hines & Elizabeth Martin, *Methodology: 2020 Best Law Schools Rankings*, U.S. News & World Rep. (Mar. 28, 2019), https://www.usnews.com/education/best-graduate-schools/articles/law-schools-methodology.

groups and other organizations to host programming intended to facilitate relationships with potential adjunct faculty, particularly candidates who would add diversity to the LRW program.[19]

d. Other Special Services

LRW courses are the foundation of a law student's education and socialization into the discourse community of the law.[20] The first-year LRW curriculum introduces the student to legal methodology, the hierarchy of authority, analysis and critical thinking skills, and effective written communication. In other words, in LRW the student learns to become a lawyer and to communicate with lawyers. Of course, analytical skills are exercised in non-writing courses, but LRW courses provide students repeated practice as well as recurring feedback and assessment. Moreover, the LRW classroom is likely much more intimate in size than other first-year classes.

The special dynamics of the LRW classroom, while of fundamental value, can also mean that students experience a peculiar vulnerability as compared to their experiences in lecture-based courses. Some students experience crises of self-confidence as they receive feedback designed to reshape their thinking and writing; others struggle with early grades that seem to signal a personal shift from the top of their undergraduate classes to the middle or lower end of the law school class. Under the circumstances, the director and LRW faculty might take a defensive posture to avoid acknowledging potential student angst—or they can take affirmative steps to acknowledge student needs and to provide support.

---

[19]The Society of American Law Teachers (SALT) frequently partners with law schools to host "Breaking In" programs that help identify potential full-time and adjunct faculty among minority groups that historically have been underrepresented in the legal academy.

[20]*See* Teri McMurtry-Chubb, *Toward a Disciplinary Pedagogy for Legal Education*, 1 SAVANNAH L. REV. 71 (2014).

To the latter end, some LRW programs have engaged in community-building projects to ameliorate the stresses of law school. The following list provides a few examples of LRW-program-sponsored events:

- Providing a photographer at orientation to take professional headshots for students to use in social media profiles (e.g., LinkedIn, Twitter)
- Providing program-branded Snapchat filters on campus
- Providing "Instagram" photo frames during oral arguments
- Offering program-branded swag (e.g., pens or t-shirts declaring, "I survived oral arguments!")
- Holding award ceremonies for the best first-year memo or appellate brief
- Opening wellness rooms during final exam periods, with guided yoga and meditation sessions[21]
- Providing access to therapy pets during final exams

To the extent of any crossover or overlap with services provided by a law school's student services office or student organizations, these ideas also present opportunities for LRW faculty to collaborate with others in the law school and to break down the walls that often separate constituencies.

B. Faculty Training and Development

While most law schools have an associate dean who is responsible for faculty development, the LRW director also plays an important complementary role when it comes to encouraging, supporting, and providing mentorship for LRW faculty colleagues. The director often has more access to information and resources originating both within and outside the institution and can focus, in particular, on resources relating to LRW faculty and programs.

---

[21] See Part C.2.b of Chapter X for a more extensive discussion of ideas for innovative wellness programs.

The quality and quantity of faculty development support that a director can offer her LRW colleagues depends on their status and experience. While experienced full-time faculty may need advice about developing scholarly agendas and balancing teaching, scholarship, and service responsibilities, adjunct faculty will need supervision that focuses on teaching concerns.

1. Full-Time Faculty Development

Tenured or tenure-track faculty have three main responsibilities at a law school. They must be good teachers, they must be good scholars, and they must be good institutional citizens. New faculty need training for the first; all law faculty demonstrate the last quality through service to the law school. The second, the production of legal scholarship, has not always been required of full-time LRW faculty on long-term Standard 405(c) contracts. But because a growing number of schools have provided opportunities for LRW faculty to obtain equality of status through tenure, scholarship plays an increasingly important role for an increasing number of full-time professors.

The remaining parts of this chapter focus on each of the three responsibilities of an LRW professor. This part focuses on teaching and service obligations; scholarship is addressed below in Part C of this chapter.

a. Teaching in the Classroom and Beyond

The director should be responsible for training new professors (whether full-time, part-time, or adjunct), and training sessions can be provided individually, in groups, or some combination. Training for new law teachers is offered at the annual Association of American Law Schools' Workshop for New Law School Teachers[22] and,

---

[22] *See AALS Workshop for New Law School Teachers*, AM. ASS'N OF LAW SCHOOLS, https://www.aals.org/about/publications/newsletters/spring2019/nlt/ (last visited Jan. 17, 2020). The AALS workshop focuses on new or recently hired full-time faculty. The most recent was held in June 2019. *See 2019 Workshop for New*

specifically for LRW professors, at biennial conferences sponsored in alternating years by the Legal Writing Institute (LWI)[23] and the Association of Legal Writing Directors (ALWD).[24] In addition, regional LRW conferences are regularly held in the Rocky Mountain, Central States, Southeastern, and Western regions, and consortia of LRW professors hold regular workshops in New England and the Great Lakes area.[25] Each year in December, LWI works with partner schools to host low-cost One-Day Workshops around the country.[26] The One-Day Workshops are excellent venues for LRW teachers at all experience levels to learn new teaching techniques and to share their own.

New LRW professors can learn more quickly if the director has prepared an introductory manual explaining all the details about the program and the law school that a new professor would need to know.[27] In general, training should be incremental: new professors cannot absorb everything they need to know in one or two sessions. Of particular value are materials about writing pedagogy, learning

---

Law School Teachers, AM. ASS'N OF LAW SCHOOLS, https://www.aals.org/events/nlt2019/ (last visited Dec. 20, 2019).

[23] *See Conferences of All Types*, LEGAL WRITING INST., https://www.lwionline.org/conferences [hereinafter *LWI Conferences*] (last visited Dec. 20, 2019). New LRW professors benefit from participating in the Critiquing Workshop, typically held concurrently with the LWI Biennial Conference.

[24] *See About the Biennial Conference*, ASS'N OF LEGAL WRITING DIRS., https://www.alwd.org/about-conference (last visited Dec. 20, 2019). ALWD's biennial conference usually takes place in odd years, while LWI's takes place in even years.

[25] See *LWI Conferences*, *supra* note 23, for more information on regional legal writing conferences.

[26] *See id.* for more information on One-Day Workshops. The most recent workshops were held in December 2019. *See One-Day Workshops*, LEGAL WRITING INST., https://www.lwionline.org/one-day-workshops (last visited Dec. 20, 2019).

[27] This training manual should include information regarding administrative resources, law school policies, and other relevant information.

theory, collaborative learning techniques, and psychological pressures on students at various times of the year.[28]

In addition, new professors should learn about the variety of classroom teaching techniques: lecture, Socratic method, collaborative group work, work in pairs, videos, role-playing, peer editing, and in-class individual writing work. They should also understand the situations in which each technique is particularly effective.[29]

New professors need training in developing writing assignments, including written guidance on the parameters of each assignment (e.g., teaching goals, level of difficulty, subject matter limitations, format, deadlines, and word or page length).[30] In general, LRW assignments increase in complexity over the academic year, with initial assignments focusing on material that will be building blocks for later assignments. The director can suggest how to vary subjects, jurisdictions, research tools, and practice settings over multiple assignments. As suggested by the discussion below in Part B.1.a.ii of this chapter, new faculty should also be encouraged to consider the diverse views, identities, and life experiences of their students when crafting assignments. Finally, new professors should be encouraged to present facts for assignments using actual or simulated documents such as depositions and interrogatories, rather than canned fact summaries.

---

[28]The LWI Monograph Series is a valuable resource for new teachers. *See The Monograph Series*, LEGAL WRITING INST., https://www.lwionline.org/publications/monograph-series (last visited Dec. 20, 2019) [hereinafter *LWI Monograph Series*]. Volume 2, *The New Teacher's Deskbook*, can be accessed for free at https://www.lwionline.org/publications/monograph-series/volume-two (last visited Dec. 20, 2019).

[29]For more information on peer editing, see Cassandra Hill, *Peer Editing: A Comprehensive Pedagogical Approach to Maximize Assessment Opportunities, Integrate Collaborative Learning, and Achieve Desired Outcomes*, 13 NEV. L.J. 667 (2011).

[30]LWI's Teaching Bank is a good resource for sharing LRW assignments. LWI members may access the Teaching Bank at https://www.lwionline.org/resources (last visited Dec. 20, 2019).

i. Grading and Conferences

New LRW professors also need guidance in learning how to grade and effectively comment on student papers.[31] New professors are frequently surprised by the relatively poor quality of new law students' writing and may need to adjust their expectations accordingly.[32] Law students must be taught to write effectively, not merely to draft for another lawyer's editing. Therefore, the editing and general feedback that supervisors in the practice of law commonly provide is not appropriate for law teaching. New professors should learn to diagnose problems in students' writing and analysis, make specific suggestions on methods of improvement rather than editing, and maintain a positive and professional tone.[33] Students benefit if the professor identifies both some strengths revealed by the writing as well as some weaknesses to work on to improve future assignments.[34]

---

[31] *See LWI Monograph Series, supra* note 28, Vol. 1, *The Art of Critiquing Student Work*, https://www.lwionline.org/publications/monograph-series/volume-one (last visited Dec. 20, 2019). For more information on grading and assessment, see Chapter III.

[32] Sherri Keene, *Are We There Yet? Aligning the Expectations and Realities of Gaining Competency in Legal Writing*, 53 DUQ. L. REV. 99, 101-02 (2015) (suggesting that the standard one-year LRW curriculum at most law schools is insufficient to prepare students for the practice of law).

[33] *See* Anne Enquist, *Critiquing Law Students' Writing: What the Students Say is Effective*, 2 LEGAL WRITING 145, 155 (1996); Susan P. Liemer, *The Quest for Scholarship: The Legal Writing Professor's Paradox*, 80 OR. L. REV. 1007, 1016 (2001).

[34] Mary Algero, Associate Dean of Faculty Development and Academic Affairs at Loyola University New Orleans College of Law, has an entertaining story illustrating the importance of providing positive feedback along with the negative or more critical. After returning memos to her students, a teaching assistant pulled her aside in confidence. "Professor Algero," he told her, "these memos are like their babies. When all they see is criticism, it's like you're telling them they have ugly babies."

Although all new LRW professors can benefit from written guidance on marking papers, such guidance is particularly helpful for part-time, adjunct, and short-term faculty. A general teaching manual for the course could have a section on guidelines for the law school's grading system, information on teaching theory underlying the marking of papers, suggestions for commenting on various types of errors, techniques for commenting on papers to be rewritten, suggestions on how to write a memo to the class on common errors, information on the relationship between paper marking and individual conferences, and examples of critiqued student work. A grading rubric for each assignment would complement the general guidance provided in the teaching manual by listing the learning outcomes identified for the assignment, criteria on which the papers will be evaluated, and associated point values for each grading guideline.[35]

As an exercise, new professors can be asked to mark a sample student paper and assign a letter grade. The director can then have an orientation or training session during which more experienced professors present their comments and compare their paper corrections with those of the newer professors. The grades of the entire group could be compared, so newer professors get a sense of the mean. The director can review and comment on the work of the new professors, giving them specific suggestions for improvement, and then all of the papers can be collected and distributed to the new professors for future reference.

New professors should be warned against overreliance on the grading rubric. While schema for review are helpful to a new professor, they should not be used when the results are not consistent with a professional assessment of a paper's relative and holistic quality, and they should not reduce the critique to an accounting of technical and stylistic errors. Grading rubrics on individual assignments also fail to account for an individual student's progress and improvement

[35] Jessica Clark & Christy DeSanctis, *Toward a Unified Grading Vocabulary: Using Rubrics in Legal Writing Courses*, 63 J. Legal Educ. 3, 7-8 (2013).

throughout the semester, an important consideration when assigning the final course grade.

To learn how to conduct effective student conferences, new professors can read relevant materials and watch either a video or a demonstration of a student conference. To prepare for a conference in which the professor will explain her critique of a student paper, the professor should return the papers in advance of the conference (at least a day ahead) so students can read and consider the comments before the conference.[36] If the meeting occurs before an assignment deadline, professors may want to have the student bring a portion of the draft to the conference to discourage procrastination and to encourage the student to concentrate on an area that needs improvement.[37]

A training session on student feedback and conferences may also be a good place to raise issues about diversity and implicit bias.[38] A now-notorious 2014 study found that when presented with identical research memos, supervising attorneys who were told that the work product was submitted by an African American litigation associate were more critical and awarded lower scores as compared to the same memo submitted by a Caucasian associate.[39] The study

---

[36] *But see* Mark E. Wojcik, *Results of an Informal Student Survey on the 'Live Grading' Experience* (July 15, 2008), https://ssrn.com/abstract=1161176.

[37] Cassandra Hill, *The Elephant in the Law School Assessment Room: The Role of Student Responsibility and Motivating Our Students to Learn*, 56 How. L.J. 447 (2013).

[38] *See* Leslie Culver, *White Doors, Black Footsteps: Leveraging "White Privilege" to Benefit Law Students of Color*, 21 J. Gender, Race & Justice 37 (2017) (suggesting that heightened White Privilege Awareness and active leveraging on this privilege by Caucasian law professors on behalf of students of color is effective as a corrective to implicit racial bias).

[39] Arin N. Reeves, *Written in Black & White: Exploring Confirmation Bias in Racialized Perceptions of Writing Skills*, Nextions (Yellow Paper Series No. 2014-0404), http://nextions.com/wp-content/uploads/2017/05/written-in-black-and-white-yellow-paper-series.pdf (last visited Dec. 20, 2019).

demonstrated the ways that implicit bias and confirmation bias work hand-in-hand to exacerbate negative impacts on people of color generally and African American individuals in particular.

Likewise, an egalitarian-minded law professor might unconsciously rely on implicit racial biases when grading. Human beings process large quantities of information through schemas—cognitive shortcuts that help us quickly organize specific examples into broad categories. Through categorical thinking, we place people into social groups. Race and gender are two examples of social groups. By processing information about individuals in this way, the stereotypes and attitudes that we associate—either negatively or positively—are activated automatically. Implicit bias is the phenomenon that occurs during this sorting process.[40] Confirmation bias exacerbates implicit bias because people seek out and are more disposed to credit information that confirms their existing biases. Because these processes operate mostly on an unconscious level, the best way to neutralize implicit bias and its negative impact is to thoughtfully and actively confront it.[41]

ii. An Interlude on Diversity

Our student population is more diverse in various ways than ever before. Although race and class equity still have a long way to go when it comes to accessing legal education, it is not uncommon now for women to have a majority of spots in entering law school classes. For years now, the LRW community has tried to be more thoughtful about how to reflect the diversity of lived experience in

---

[40] *See* Jerry Kang et al., *Are Ideal Litigators White? Measuring the Myth of Colorblindness*, 7 J. EMPIRICAL L. STUD. 886 (2010).

[41] *See, e.g.*, Cynthia Lee, *Making Race Salient: Trayvon Martin and Implicit Bias in a Not Yet Post-Racial Society*, 91 N.C. L. REV. 1555 (2013) (citing social science research demonstrating that identifying implicit biases and racial stereotypes encourages people to suppress what would otherwise be automatic responses and instead to act in a more egalitarian manner).

the writing assignments we give our students.[42] It is also becoming increasingly more common for students to identify themselves as transgender, gender queer, gender neutral, or genderless. Gender identity expressions such as those listed here may seem odd or unusual to law professors, but they are unremarkable for our students. And law faculty must keep pace.[43]

A current topic of perhaps special concern for LRW faculty and students is the use of the gender-neutral "them" or "they" as a singular pronoun. Promoting the use of more inclusive, gender-neutral language is not a new idea,[44] but for law teachers, who tend to be fastidious about accurate use of language, substituting the plural pronoun for singular nouns can seem jarring and confusing. The world and the language we use to describe it, however, are always changing.[45] Of course, the individual LRW professor should feel

---

[42] *See, e.g.*, Charles R. Calleros, *In the Spirit of Regina Austin's Contextual Analysis: Exploring Racial Context in Legal Method, Writing Assignments and Scholarship*, 34 J. MARSHALL L. REV. 281 (2000); Lorraine Bannai & Anne Enquist, *(Un)Examined Assumptions and (Un)Intended Messages: Teaching Students to Recognize Bias in Legal Analysis and Language*, 27 SEATTLE U. L. REV. 1 (2003); Tonya Kowalski, *The Forgotten Sovereigns*, 36 FLA. ST. U. L. REV. 765 (2009); Samantha A. Moppett, *Acknowledging America's First Sovereign: Incorporating Tribal Justice Systems into the Legal Research and Writing Curriculum*, 35 OKLA. CITY U. L. REV. 267 (2010); Julie Spanbauer & Katerina P. Lewinbuk, *Embracing Diversity through a Multicultural Approach to Legal Education*, 1 CHARLOTTE L. REV. 223 (2009).

[43] Gabriel Arkles, *Improving Law School for Trans and Gender Nonconforming Students: Suggestions for Faculty* (Northeastern Univ. Sch. of Law Res. Paper No. 221-2015, July 12, 2014), https://papers.ssrn.com/sol3/papers.cfm?abstract_id=2585707.

[44] *See, e.g.*, Judith D. Fischer, *Framing Gender: Federal Appellate Judges' Choices about Gender-Neutral Language*, 43 U. S.F. L. REV. 473 (2009).

[45] Joyce R. Rosenberg, *A Singular Understanding of "They"* (Mar. 1, 2016), https://papers.ssrn.com/sol3/papers.cfm?abstract_id=2755582 (noting that the *Merriam-Webster Dictionary* and *The Washington Post* now authorize use of the singular "they").

empowered to make her own decisions and demands about acceptable usage in the classroom, but being aware of the reasons that students might be making these choices is an important contextual point to consider.

iii. Dealing with Student Complaints

New LRW professors must also learn how to deal with dissatisfied students. As discussed above, the professor, not the director, should be the first point of contact in the student complaint process. Therefore, the professor must learn how to listen non-defensively to student complaints, how to take into account the interests of other students in the class, how to fashion a solution to the problem, and when to refer the student to the director.

Students feel more vulnerable in a legal writing course with less distance between student and professor, and they receive constant criticism of their work as well as grades several times during the semester. And although the focus of a lecture course is a body of subject-specific doctrine (which first-year students think they can memorize), an LRW course combines a variety of subject-specific doctrines (including LRW doctrine) with a wide variety of skills, including analytical skills, about which neophyte law students lack confidence. The LRW class is also more likely to be taught by a female professor[46]—a situation that may unfairly cause students

---

[46] *See* Bannai, *supra* note 2; Teri McMurtry-Chubb, *Writing at the Master's Table: Reflections on Theft, Criminality, and Otherness in the Legal Writing Profession*, 2 DREXEL L. REV. 41 (2009); Jo Anne Durako, *A Woman's Place: Employment Patterns in Legal Writing*, 6 EMPLOYEE RIGHTS & EMP. POL'Y J. 134 (2002); Jo Anne Durako, *Second-Class Citizens in the Pink Ghetto: Gender Bias in Legal Writing*, 50 J. LEGAL EDUC. 562 (2000); Pamela Edwards, *Teaching Legal Writing as Women's Work: Life on the Fringes of the Academy*, 4 CARDOZO WOMEN'S L.J. 75 (1997).

to feel less compunction about complaining.[47] Professors of color and others who are marked by difference are even more likely to encounter this phenomenon.[48]

The director should train new professors about a range of techniques for handling difficult students. A professor may refuse to talk with a student until the student can voice complaints civilly; the professor might also ask the student questions to elicit sources of stress or resentment outside the LRW course, or refer the student to a counselor if available and appropriate. Finally, the professor should set explicit boundaries on what conduct is or is not acceptable and, if necessary, involve the director or dean of students.[49] The LRW professor must have confidence that the director and deans will support reasonable steps to deal with abusive students.

Faculty should be instructed to report any concerns that their personal safety may be at risk. Likewise, directors and deans should take seriously any report by an LRW professor of a student's threatening statements or behavior. LRW professors are more likely to be the object of a disturbed student's aggression because they work more closely with students than many other law professors, they often give students their first feedback and grades they receive in law school, and they critique students' very personal efforts at written expression.

iv. Mentoring Legal Writing Faculty

To continue the training process, the director might consider having a formal mentoring system for new LRW professors. One method would be to assign a more experienced professor to work closely with a new professor, to share materials and sample assignments, and even

---

[47] *See, e.g.*, PRESUMED INCOMPETENT: THE INTERSECTIONS OF RACE AND CLASS FOR WOMEN IN ACADEMIA (Gabriela Gutiérrez y Muhs et al. eds., 2012).

[48] *See id.; see also supra* note 46 (citing sources).

[49] For information on plagiarism, see Lurene Contento, *Plagiarism: What Every Legal Writer Should Know*, 7 KAZANCI PEER-REVIEWED L.J. (2011).

to sit in on a student conference or two. The overall goal should be to encourage the best possible LRW instruction, and the prime purpose of the mentor system should be training LRW professors.

The director should attempt to mentor the professors as much as possible. Having lunch or coffee with each professor allows the director to learn about the concerns and frustrations of the professor in an informal setting, without pressure. The director might offer advice on how to handle problems, construct assignments, and deal with troublesome students.

Another aspect of mentoring is to provide LRW professors with information on how to pursue opportunities for professional advancement. The director should consider holding informal seminars, including other members of the law school faculty, to discuss all aspects of law school teaching. Topics might include the various kinds of scholarship and methods of getting published, teaching methods, networking, and guest teaching a lecture class.

b. Balancing Service Obligations

It is not uncommon for LRW faculty to take on excessive workloads. In addition to the time spent teaching in the classroom, LRW professors spend countless hours during the semester grading, holding office hours, and conferencing with students.[50] Whether required by institutional obligations or driven by personal interest, LRW faculty also engage in research and scholarship. Further, academic institutions require that all faculty provide service to maintain good standing as citizens of the school.

Standard service to the law school includes active participation on faculty committees. LRW faculty, however, are often asked to participate in other projects such as long-range strategic planning, open houses, student orientation, coaching moot court or trial

---

[50] *See, e.g.*, McMurtry-Chubb, *supra* note 46, at 48 (providing an accounting of hours spent preparing for class, teaching in the classroom, and meeting with students outside the classroom).

advocacy teams, or judging student advocacy competitions. Perhaps more than other faculty members, LRW faculty tend to say yes to all these requests for help because of their genuine connection with students, their desire to provide support where needed, and the institutional pressure on LRW professors to earn reputations as good citizens. These heightened service pressures are further exacerbated by professional status vulnerability.

Single-minded attention to service, however, presents significant danger to the development of a new faculty member's career. Taking this tendency into consideration, the director should take care to provide support and advice about maintaining a healthy balance in all aspects of a new professor's professional identity. As the saying goes, no one was ever denied tenure for lack of service. Faculty members lose tenure or retention bids because of shortcomings related to teaching or scholarship, not for failing to do enough service. Simple advice a director could give new LRW faculty is to say yes to say no. In other words, it is always easier to decline a request because of a pre-existing obligation. A new faculty member should focus time and energy on service responsibilities that have special meaning so that the professor, when asked to provide support for other projects that are not as important or meaningful, can politely decline with a rational explanation for doing so.

c. *Open Communication and Team-building*

Directors should schedule periodic meetings (formal or informal) with the LRW faculty at least once each semester to review the semester's work and to plan for the immediate and long-range future. Many directors hold regular program meetings, which can be as informal as eating lunch in the director's office or as formal as agenda-based faculty meetings. For programs using mostly adjunct professors, weekly e-mail reminders and updates from the director are a more realistic approach, perhaps coupled with group meetings near the beginning and end of the semester to address concerns such as scheduling and grading.

Particularly in programs with full-time faculty, meetings should be open-ended, and LRW faculty should be encouraged to put anything on the agenda. Meetings offer a good opportunity for the director to find out what additional help the LRW faculty think they need in such areas as library support, audio-visual equipment, computer training, or administrative support, or to find out what general concerns the faculty might have about their roles in the law school.

In addition to holding agenda-focused program meetings, directors can build community by organizing extracurricular events. The director can establish an atmosphere of mutual respect, camaraderie, and high group morale by engaging her faculty in team-building events such as brunches, retreats, and informal group outings. One director who teaches at a South Florida school hosts biannual LRW faculty brunches in her home and occasionally organizes group outings to the beach or theme parks. In casual settings like these, faculty can be encouraged to get to know each other on a personal level. Not unlike the old-fashioned round of golf, participants will likely gain intangible benefits from socializing with their peers outside the law school.

d. People of Color in LRW

Of those who are privileged to teach LRW on a full-time basis, very few are people of color.[51] Of that small number, most are women.[52] Recruitment and retention of legal writing faculty of color should be a matter of special concern to directors. Strategies for hiring a diverse faculty are addressed below in Part B.4 of this chapter.

People of color, as well as others who are and have been historically marginalized (for example, LGBTQIA folks or people with

---

[51] *See, e.g.*, Teri A. McMurtry-Chubb, *On Writing Wrongs: Legal Writing Professors of Color and the Curious Case of 405(c)*, 66 J. Legal Educ. 575 (2017); Bannai, *supra* note 2; McMurtry-Chubb, *supra* note 46.

[52] *See* Bannai, *supra* note 2; McMurtry-Chubb, *supra* note 46.

disabilities), bring particular ways of viewing and thinking about the world into the law school classroom. To the extent that faculty of color are absent from law school classrooms, our students lose an opportunity to learn about the law and legal processes from someone who has experienced life and the workings of the legal system from this marginalized position. As others have noted, law as an institution historically has been structured around the perspectives of elite white men and their particular analytical processes.[53] Student lawyers who learn from this monolithic frame of reference therefore replicate systems of analysis and reasoning that reinforce the existing power structure.[54] Our students are lawyers in training who need to know how to interact with a diverse array of clients. Learning how to view and solve problems from a variety of different perspectives is an invaluable lawyering skill.

Directors must also realize, however, that in addition to getting faculty of color into the classroom, they must strive to retain them. Establishing rapport through team-building events and interactions is one way to provide this support. But because of their marginalized position in general society, faculty of color face special challenges in the classroom that can negatively impact professional development.[55] Students as well as faculty colleagues, whether consciously or unconsciously, subject faculty of color to stereotypes based on

---

[53] McMurtry-Chubb, *supra* note 46, at 54 (citing WENDY LEO MOORE, REPRODUCING RACISM: WHITE SPACE, ELITE LAW SCHOOLS AND RACIAL INEQUALITY (2008)).

[54] *See* Kathryn M. Stanchi, *Resistance is Futile: How Legal Writing Pedagogy Contributes to the Law's Marginalization of Outsider Voices*, 103 DICK. L. REV. 7 (1998) (exploring the ways in which LRW pedagogy, as one example among other law school courses, tends to mute the voices of outsider students).

[55] *Cf.* Bannai, *supra* note 2, at 278 (addressing the triple threat that women of color face who teach LRW). Professor Bannai's article also contains poignant narratives from women of color.

race and gender. Presumptions of incompetence because of one's race or color are compounded for faculty of color who are women.[56]

Teaching evaluations play a significant role in the retention and promotion bids of law faculty. Faculty who make promotion decisions should be aware of the wealth of social science research concluding that anonymous student evaluations are unreliable measures of teaching effectiveness, especially for women and people of color. The director may have to remind her colleagues about these facts during retention and promotion reviews.

At the same time directors work to overcome the effects of marginalization, they can provide guidance to faculty members about how to draw the sting from negative teaching evaluations. One way is to ask students to engage in self-assessments of their own work, or to provide several teaching evaluations throughout the semester (and before grades are assessed). This strategy is discussed in more detail in Part B.3.c of this chapter.

2. *Contingent Faculty Training and Supervision*

In contrast to a program staffed by full-time LRW faculty, close supervision is essential in a program taught by contingent faculty (including adjuncts, graduate teaching fellows, visiting assistant professors, or upper-level law students).

Even a teaching assistant who comes in to work with LRW students on citation skills, for instance, should first be carefully screened by faculty and engaged in a meaningful conversation about active teaching methods, the honor code, and professionalism. Every representative of the LRW program in the classroom can reflect positively or negatively on the program, and a proactive approach to some key issues can go a long way. Despite the extra work required to supervise teaching assistants, law students receive several benefits from

---

[56] *See generally* PRESUMED INCOMPETENT, *supra* note 47.

"near-peer" mentoring.[57] These benefits include increased access, approachability, and emotional support. Teaching assistants also benefit from the mentoring relationship.

3. *Quality Control*

a. *Uniformity in Curriculum*

The type of uniformity that would be inappropriate in LRW programs staffed by full-time faculty makes sense, and may even be preferable, in a program or in individual courses staffed by adjunct faculty or other faculty on short-term appointments. Among other things, the LRW director takes the major role in hiring, prepares the course syllabi, designs or approves all assignments, reviews at least a sample of graded papers, and makes nearly all the major decisions affecting the program as a whole such as selecting textbooks and determining the number and types of assignments.[58]

In a program staffed by contingent faculty, all sections typically use the same texts and a master syllabus, as well as similar assignments, page limits, deadlines, student conference schedules, and grading formulae.[59] Directors typically require substantial uniformity across sections to ensure that all students receive a basic,

---

[57] *See generally* Laura S. Tenenbaum et al., *An Innovative Near-Peer Mentoring Model for Undergraduate and Secondary Students: STEM Focus*, 39 INNOV. HIGHER EDUC. 375 (Mar. 2014), https://apps.dtic.mil/dtic/tr/fulltext/u2/a622882.pdf (discussing the benefits of near-peer mentoring among college-level science students).

[58] *See* Jan M. Levine, *Response: "You Can't Please Everyone, So You'd Better Please Yourself": Directing (Or Teaching in) a First-Year Legal Writing Program*, 29 VAL. U. L. REV. 611, 618-20 (1995).

[59] For information concerning consistency among LRW sections, see Part D of the ALWD/LWI Survey. *See* Ass'n of Legal Writing Dirs. & Legal Writing Inst., *Report of the 2017-2018 Institutional Survey* 14-18 (2019), https://www.lwionline.org/sites/default/files/Final%20ALWD%20LWI%202017-18%20Institutional%20Survey%20Report.pdf.

competent level of instruction and to avoid the students' perception of unfairness.

The director should distribute draft copies of course syllabi and assignments to the LRW faculty and encourage edits and suggestions. The syllabus and policies will certainly be stronger for the additional input. When creating the syllabus, the director must juggle many scheduling concerns including those of the students, faculty, librarians, teaching assistants, outside speakers, guest judges for oral argument, and even representatives of the electronic research vendors. The director should be candid with LRW faculty when the many factors that go into an effective syllabus preclude incorporating their suggestions.

In programs staffed primarily by contingent faculty, the director typically creates all writing assignments or, time permitting, might delegate that responsibility to experienced LRW teachers. If adjunct professors develop their own assignments, the director can head off a variety of problems by requiring professors to submit assignments to the director for review well before they are finalized and distributed to students.

In reviewing assignments prepared by adjunct professors, the director should first determine whether the assignment is within the parameters set for the course. Second, the director should determine if the assignment is too hard or too easy when compared to those given by the other professors and, if necessary, make suggestions for modifying the assignment. Third, the director should determine whether two or more sections are using similar assignments, which might present potential plagiarism problems or excessive student demand for library materials. Similarly, the director should determine whether the assignment is similar to one used in recent semesters, posing a risk that students might have access to upper-class students' work.

To ensure fairness to students, a director should try to keep grading criteria and standards as consistent as possible. Much can be done before the semester begins by meeting with the professors and setting clear parameters on critiquing and grading. Potential problems can also be avoided or alleviated by having the professors critique and grade sample papers, and then discussing the process and explaining any disparities. The director can also assist the professors in determining fair deadlines for all LRW assignments, as well as a consistent approach for handling violations of program or course rules.

Even if an individual LRW professor's path to assigning final grades may differ, the final results should be the same across all sections, just as for other law school courses. At some law schools, LRW courses are graded on the same curve as all other first-year courses. If not, the director may consider suggesting a median grade-point average for each multi-section course to prevent a wide disparity in grades across sections. While good reasons often justify grades that fall outside the median GPA, it might be wise to require a written explanation if the section average falls outside that band.

During the semester, as each set of papers is graded, the director of a program staffed primarily by contingent faculty can ask each professor to turn in copies of three faculty-critiqued papers ranging from strong to weak. The director can then discuss with individual professors any grades or critiques that seem significantly different from those critiqued by other LRW professors. In any LRW program, professors should be encouraged to share examples of their assignments and discuss their process of assessing student work, so they can improve their teaching by learning from one another.

b. Classroom Visits

The director should also visit LRW classes and give both positive and critical feedback to the professors. As a courtesy to the professor, the visit should be scheduled in advance. If the program employs a number of adjuncts, it may be necessary to record classes for review. Video recording has an additional benefit of permitting the professor to review her own teaching, thus providing the faculty member with an opportunity for self-observation and reflection.

LRW professors should also be encouraged to observe the director's own classes. New teachers may benefit from watching experienced teachers in the classroom even more than they gain from having an experienced professor observe their own first steps.

Regardless of program structure, the director's assessment of the quality of a professor's classroom instruction plays an important, even dominant, role in the overall evaluation of the professor. The following is an assessment rubric that could be used in almost all circumstances:

Are the students getting significant value from being in class? Classroom activities should supplement and build on readings and activities required outside class. Repeating information from the text without doing more is usually an ineffective use of class time.

Does the professor have clear goals for the class session? A professor should articulate goals for each class session and demonstrate the ability to meet these goals effectively.

Does the professor have an effective classroom style? No one style is preferable over others, as long as the teaching style engages students and teaches them what they need. In assessing teacher effectiveness, student evaluations should not be given undue weight, but neither should they be discounted entirely.

Are the professor's teaching techniques effective for the subject or skill taught? A technique's effectiveness cannot be evaluated without considering how and when it is used. For example, a video may be ineffective to introduce a new skill but very effective to reinforce or supplement an introductory lecture.

Is the professor comfortable using the technique? Not all teaching techniques work for all professors. For example, a novice professor may not be comfortable with a technique that cedes too much control to students, or one that results in unpredictable responses that must be addressed immediately in class. Professors should be adept at more than one teaching technique and continue to add more as their careers progress.

Can the professor vary the teaching technique? A professor should have the flexibility to change teaching approaches and techniques if students are not learning. For example, a professor who observes that a class is struggling to work in groups because the task is ill-defined must either switch to another technique or clarify the task. A professor who allows students time to think through a new skill reflectively may also need to use an approach that engages more active learners.

Is the technique appropriate for the time available? In planning a class session, a professor must estimate how long an activity will require. For example, professors may wish to leave time to debrief the students, to reinforce what they were supposed to have learned, and to allow them to ask questions.

Do the students understand what is taught and why the teaching technique is used? In general, the most effective teaching is transparent: students should understand what they are doing, why they are doing it, and what they are supposed to learn from it. While the excitement of an "ah ha!" moment should not be underrated, faculty must not regularly allow students to walk away from the classroom with no idea what they have been doing.

Does the professor "check in" with the students to be sure they understand the material? Professors may wish to take the time to debrief students at the end of each class and get feedback that allows them to determine whether the goals planned for the class period have been met. If those objectives have not been achieved by the end of the class, it may be possible to administer an e-mail quiz, or the professor may re-visit the topic at the start of the next class.

The director should provide both written and oral commentary to the professor to document that notice was given of any deficiencies that could lead to a decision not to retain the professor. If written teaching assessments are required by the law school, documents and procedures should parallel those used for evaluating other faculty.

Visiting assistant professors (VAPs) and student teachers raise some other issues. Like "capped" faculty, student teachers will leave the program within one or two years, reducing the need for an elaborate evaluation process. The director might find it useful to require student evaluations, however, as a means of gaining a better understanding of the characteristics that make for successful VAPs or student teachers.

c. Evaluation Processes

Directors should regularly review contingent LRW faculty for teaching effectiveness according to clear standards and criteria. Because the circumstances and work obligations of adjuncts can change from year to year, an annual review ensures that the professor still has sufficient time and interest in teaching LRW. For a relatively new LRW professor, review should also be annual unless the director has reason to believe that the individual's teaching is not consistent with program standards, which may warrant more frequent review.

Along with teaching, faculty should be evaluated on their compliance with program rules and policies. A program taught mainly by contingent faculty requires professors to follow a set curriculum with standardized objectives, assignments, and due dates. This approach ensures that adjunct faculty with significant professional responsibilities to clients or to other employers will have the necessary time to devote to teaching legal writing.

Teaching assessments should encompass classroom visits, as discussed above. In addition, directors should require each professor to submit examples of critiqued assignments to evaluate written feedback given to students.

The greatest challenge in evaluating faculty is the proper use of student evaluations. Student teaching evaluations of legal writing professors are necessary and appropriate,[60] but they should

---

[60] *See* David D. Walter, *Student Evaluations—A Tool for Advancing Law Teacher Professionalism and Respect for Students*, 6 LEGAL WRITING 177 (2000).

not be given undue weight in the retention or promotion process.[61] Because of the unique teaching methods and goals of an LRW course, including the need to provide students with critique, feedback, and grades throughout the semester, the director may want to consider using midterm student evaluations of teaching in addition to end-of-semester evaluations, or otherwise varying the way evaluations are administered.

Any student teaching evaluation should address the professor's effectiveness in holding conferences, in giving constructive criticism through written and oral comments on student papers, in clarifying ambiguities in assignments, and in being available to students outside class. Questions that solicit the students' views on the books required, the exercises used, and the problems assigned are unlikely to be useful because students simply do not have enough knowledge about the available alternatives to make informed comments on these points. Evaluation forms should be developed with input from all LRW faculty and should be available to them at the start of the course.

If a law school or university-wide evaluation form is required, LRW faculty may wish to design an additional form if permitted. Any such evaluations may be further supplemented by other opportunities for student feedback regarding individual adjuncts. For example, supplemental feedback might be solicited by interviewing students in the class, or by requesting feedback through e-mail.

Individual law schools may weigh evaluation forms differently, and faculty should understand how much consideration their institutions give student evaluations for purposes of reappointment or

---

[61] An ever-expanding body of academic literature demonstrates that gender and racial biases negatively impact teaching evaluations, which are therefore not reliable measures of teaching effectiveness. *See, e.g.*, Michelle Falkoff, *Why We Must Stop Relying on Student Ratings of Teaching*, CHRON. HIGHER EDUC., Apr. 25, 2018 (citing a litany of such studies, including one by the American Association of University Professors).

retention. At some universities, teaching evaluations become part of the public record and must be included in a tenure or promotion file. Accordingly, new evaluation forms should be drafted with full awareness of public records laws and university policies.

The timing of evaluations is important.[62] Typically, course evaluations in lecture-based courses are distributed before the final exam—often before students have received any substantial feedback from the professor. Distributing student evaluations for LRW courses before the final project is graded, however, may present a misleading picture of the course or the professor. At that point in the course, especially in the first semester, LRW students may have already received low grades or strong criticism that they perceive as inconsistent with the feedback they received as undergraduates and not commensurate with the amount of work they have invested.[63] In addition, LRW grades are usually the only ones students have received at this point. While students may have been repeatedly warned that these early grades do not necessarily reflect how they are doing in law school, or even how they ultimately will do in the LRW course, students tend to disbelieve these warnings and may resent the course, the professor, or both. The focus of LRW students and faculty alike on completing the next assignment may prevent students from realizing that they are acquiring important legal skills as they proceed through the semester.

In light of these considerations, the director may decide to distribute student evaluations on a different schedule, or to follow up on targeted activities. For example, evaluations could be distributed before the final writing assignment or after a particularly engaging exercise, such as a simulated client interview or oral argument, or in

---

[62] *See* Judith D. Fischer, *How to Improve Student Ratings in Legal Writing Courses: Views from the Trenches*, 34 U. BALT. L. REV. 199 (2004).

[63] *See* Barbara Glesner Fines, *The Impact of Expectations on Teaching and Learning*, 38 GONZ. L. REV. 89, 126-127 (2002).

the very last class of the semester. Another alternative is to lead the class in a discussion of LRW doctrine, perhaps even having students complete a simple in-class or out-of-class assignment requiring them to articulate the stages of the writing process and to identify tasks appropriate to each one, or to identify elements of legal analysis or ways to use authority effectively. Also useful are efforts to encourage students to engage in metacognitive learning practices, such as self-assessments of their work that specifically guide them to consider their own time and effort relative to the weight of any assignment. Students who complete exercises of this type are better able to give an accurate assessment of what they have learned during the semester, regardless of any grades they receive.

Evaluations may be most useful when distributed at the time students turn in their final semester assignment, and again at the end of the full year. Some schools have found it very helpful to ask students to assess the LRW course when they return to law school for their second year after a summer clerkship. Other programs employ short evaluations at several points during the semester, hoping to get more insight into what is working and what is not before the semester is over.

The form used should allow students to add suggestions for improvement for both the course and the professor. Many of the suggestions, of course, will have to be disregarded, such as "cut down the number of assignments" or "have the papers graded and returned in two days." But a student may offer an excellent idea or raise a problem only a student's perspective could reveal.

The director should read all the evaluations. The evaluations should not be given to an LRW professor until all grades have been submitted for that section. In the short term, the director should discuss any troubling issues raised by the evaluations with the individual professor. For the long term, the director should compile summaries of narrative comments and numerical statistics for retention and promotion purposes.

4. Hiring and Diversity Concerns

An important aspect of an LRW director's job is hiring, for much of the success of the program depends on the teaching faculty who have direct contact with students. Because the director is the person who oversees the big picture of the LRW program, she must play an active role in hiring. Ideally, the hiring process for full-time LRW faculty is the same as that employed for other faculty appointments. Although the director should be a strong voice on the faculty appointments committee, she does not act alone in her decision-making. If the program hires adjunct faculty to staff courses, the process should similarly mimic the adjunct-hiring process for non-writing courses.

A hiring decision should never go forward if the director strenuously objects. Others involved in the hiring process should recognize that a director's strong objection to a proposed hire merits deference. An experienced director understands the LRW program much better than anyone else at the school and is uniquely qualified to evaluate an applicant's ability and "fit." Further, the director's authority would be undermined if she were forced to accept an applicant over a strenuous objection. Faculties and administrators usually hold the director responsible for the work of those teaching in the program, and therefore should not saddle a director with professors the director feels are not competent, not qualified, or not team players.

A hiring decision for LRW faculty, as for all law school faculty, should be based solely on criteria measuring who can do the best job in the interests of the students, the profession, and future clients. Potentially problematic hires such as law school or university donors, judges, and faculty spouses should be evaluated using the same criteria that apply to other applicants.

Hiring goals should be determined before recruitment begins. Identifying the desired qualities and accomplishments of a faculty candidate lends a sense of fairness and transparency to a process that can otherwise fairly be criticized as byzantine. Questions to be answered before recruitment include the following:

- What kind of person is the school trying to hire?
- What academic credentials are essential?
- How long ago should the candidate have graduated from law school?
- What kind of legal experience is desirable and how much?
- How much weight should be given to law review or moot court background?
- What personal and professional qualities will the school look for?
- By what criteria will the school judge an applicant's own writing skills?

Methods of recruitment may vary according to the status of the position. Recruitment for full-time LRW faculty should use the traditional mechanisms including the *AALS Placement Bulletin*, the AALS Faculty Recruiting Conference, or advertisements in the *Chronicle of Higher Education*, as well as vacancy announcements circulated on the LWI and ALWD listservs.

On the other hand, contingent LRW faculty are usually hired primarily from a local pool of candidates, particularly at law schools in major metropolitan areas. Few candidates from outside the local area would be willing to relocate for short-term or part-time positions. For local hiring, publishing hiring announcements in placement bulletins, local or regional law-oriented newspapers, and newsletters and listservs of local bar associations, including affinity bar associations, is usually effective. The Society of American Law Teachers (SALT)[64] and LatCrit[65] regularly organize events to assist and train practitioners who are interested in law teaching.

---

[64] Society of American Law Teachers, https://www.saltlaw.org/ (last visited Dec. 20, 2019).

[65] Latina and Latino Critical Legal Theory, Inc., http://latcrit.org/index/ (last visited Dec. 20, 2019).

Recruiting a pool of candidates that is racially and ethnically diverse is not an easy task. The legal academy is still largely white and male. White women law professors are outnumbered by men at a rate of nearly two to one.[66] In the LRW community, women faculty make up the majority, and only a small minority are women of color.[67] Concerns about diversity on the law school faculty should include not only race, ethnicity, and gender, but also sexual orientation, gender identity, class, academic pedigree, and work experience. Distributing job placement advertisements widely using both conventional channels and informal methods can increase the likelihood that faculty candidates will represent a diverse pool.

Advertisements should request writing samples (preferably documents written solely by the applicant) in addition to a résumé and reference list. The hiring committee can review all applications, or the director can screen and circulate the strongest ones to the hiring committee. On-site interviews by faculty are critical, and student interviews of candidates can be very revealing of personality traits and commitment to teaching.

As a further screening device, some schools consider performance on a practical test. These law schools send selected applicants instructions for marking a paper, as well as grading criteria focusing on organization and analysis. Applicants then come to the school for a timed grading exercise in a quiet room, during which they can critique a short, representative student paper. Some schools may also ask applicants to conduct a short writing conference with a hypothetical student. Other schools incorporate a similar process in the interviewing schedule on the theory that a discussion afterward with the applicant can be more revealing than comments the

---

[66] Meera E. Deo, *Looking Forward to Diversity in Legal Academia*, 29 BERKELEY J. GENDER L. & JUST. 352, 357 (2014).

[67] *See, e.g.*, Bannai, *supra* note 2; McMurtry-Chubb, *supra* note 46; McMurtry-Chubb, *supra* note 51.

applicant writes on a student paper. Experienced teachers can submit examples of their own critiques of student papers.

Applicants selected for interviews can be sent a letter describing the interview process, a copy of the school's course catalog or a link to access the school's online catalog, and a detailed description of the LRW program and courses. Interviewers may then judge applicant interest in the program by noting how carefully the applicant has read the supplied materials. Particularly when hiring for adjunct or short-term positions, schools may wish to send applicants citations to or reprints of pertinent articles about critiquing and conferencing. Motivation to learn new teaching methods is highest at this point, and interview preparation is often a "teachable moment" for applicants.

At the interview, questions about the candidates' own writing experiences can be revealing. For example, candidates might be asked to explain how they learned to write, to describe some legal writing that impressed them or distressed them, or to describe their own writing process. In addition, practical considerations should be stressed, such as the time demands of grading papers, the importance of holding student conferences, and the need to be available to respond to student questions.[68]

Candidates for tenure-track positions normally make a presentation (a "job talk"). At schools with full-time, long-term positions, the entire faculty should have the opportunity to interview the finalists and participate in the appointment decision or recommendation to the dean and director. This approach helps build faculty confidence in the LRW program and breaks down barriers between the LRW professors and the rest of the faculty. Of course, references should be carefully checked.

---

[68] *See* Maureen Arrigo-Ward, *How to Please Most of the People Most of the Time: Directing (or Teaching in) a First-Year Legal Writing Program*, 29 VAL. U. L. REV. 557, 564-70 (1995).

C. Scholarship

1. Status and Scholarship

One of the greatest gains in the LRW field over the past decade has been the increased professionalization of programs across the nation. While LRW programs and LRW faculty still face daunting hierarchies and status inequity issues in the legal academy, huge strides have occurred in increased professional regard for both the discipline and those teaching in the field. These changes are reflected programmatically through the expanded number of required LRW semesters and credit hours. They are also reflected individually through the elevation of LRW faculty to various leadership roles in law schools as well as national academic organizations.

Numerous former LRW faculty currently serve as law school deans, and others have been promoted to vice dean or associate dean posts. Several LRW directors serve concurrent leadership roles as both director of the LRW program and associate dean. These leadership models have been especially effective in diminishing the traditional status issues of LRW faculty because these leaders are able to effectively exercise their administrative responsibilities while honoring their commitment to the LRW program.[69] Such positional changes can favorably influence the institutional culture of the law school faculty in connection with LRW faculty.

---

[69]While these professional gains have been mostly positive, LRW professors who serve double-duty as administrators should be mindful that they can be exploited in their new posts. Without security of position, LRW professors remain vulnerable to being overworked and underpaid. The "impostor syndrome" can also impair a person's ability to ask for fair treatment in course load, compensation, and other benefits. An LRW director entrusted with a leadership role provides a tangible and valuable benefit to the law school. The director's compensation, faculty status, and security of position should reflect that value; therefore, newly-minted senior administrators who come up through the LRW pipeline should not be reluctant to ask for appropriate recognition and compensation. Simply receiving the "Associate Dean" title, along with the increased workload, is not sufficient.

The support and diversification of LRW scholarship has also been a key component warranting improved academic status. This shift signals a huge departure from previous generations of law professors, who sometimes questioned whether LRW professors should be engaged in legal scholarship at all.[70] Today's LRW scholars recognize that scholarship both fuels and follows the increasing professional status of LRW professors. As LRW professors gain more status within the academy, they are more widely recognized for the significant scholarship contributions they make. And scholarly contributions by LRW professors are also key to raising the status of the discipline. LRW professors have also authored significant LRW and other textbooks. They have written highly regarded law review articles about LRW as well as other areas of expertise. In addition to their contributions to the LRW discipline, LRW professors are nationally recognized expert authors in gender studies, health law, and other legal subjects.[71]

Recent emphasis on formative assessment in the ABA Standards has created another powerful platform for LRW professors to highlight their long-time expertise in teaching and assessment. Because feedback and formative assessment are the cornerstones of effective writing instruction, LRW professors are well-practiced in thinking about and implementing formative assessment strategies.

---

[70] Linda L. Berger, Linda H. Edwards & Terrill Pollman, *The Past, Presence, and Future of Legal Writing Scholarship: Rhetoric, Voice, and Community*, 15 LEGAL WRITING 537, 537 (2010).

[71] *See, e.g.*, Bridget J. Crawford, Kathryn M. Stanchi, & Linda L. Berger, *Feminist Judging Matters: How Feminist Theory and Methods Affect the Process of Judgment,* 47 U. BALT. L. REV. 167, 168 (2018) (feminist jurisprudence); Christine Coughlin, *Legal Methods for Medical Professionals: Implementing a Medical School Rotation in the Law School to Promote Greater Cooperation and Understanding Between the Professions,* 21 ANNALS HEALTH L. 257, 261 (2012) (health law); *see also* Terrill Pollman & Linda H. Edwards, *Scholarship by Legal Writing Professors: New Voices in the Legal Academy*, 11 LEGAL WRITING 4, 55 (2005).

For example, ABA Standard 314[72] requires law schools to provide formative assessment. Other "hot" topics include active teaching, rubrics, and metacognition. All of these issues raised by the revised ABA Standards have created space for the rise of the LRW scholar, who can write with experience and expertise about these topics.[73] The developments have also broadened the role of the LRW professor, who can share expertise on teaching and assessment with non-LRW faculty members who are committed to making strides in their teaching methods.

2. *Discipline Building and Rebranding*

Several LRW professors have been deliberate about building the discipline of LRW through legal scholarship. The discipline-building approach is rooted in the exploration of rhetoric. As LRW scholars have noted, "[t]he study and practice of law as rhetoric is a thread that can run through the fabric of a professional life, weaving

---

[72] Section of Legal Educ. & Admissions to the Bar, *ABA Standards and Rules of Procedure for Approval of Law Schools (2017-2018)*, ABA: AM. BAR. ASS'N, Standard 314, https://www.americanbar.org/content/dam/aba/publications/misc/legal_education/Standards/2017-2018ABAStandardsforApprovalofLawSchools/2017_2018_aba_standards_rules_approval_law_schools_final.authcheckdam.pdf.

[73] LRW professors have dominated the field in many of these scholarly subjects. Indeed, as one scholar has observed, "[l]egal research and writing courses are . . . some of the most pedagogically sound educational experiences in the law school." Catherine Martin Christopher, *Putting Legal Writing on the Tenure Track: One School's Experience*, 31 COLUM. J. GENDER & L. 65, 72 (2015). A small sample of LRW professors who have emerged as leaders in learning and assessment include Sophie Sparrow (rubrics), *see* Sophie M. Sparrow, *Describing the Ball: Improve Teaching by Using Rubrics—Explicit Grading Criteria,* 2004 MICH. ST. L. REV. 1, 27-28 (2004); Anthony Niedwiecki (metacognition), *see* Niedwiecki, *supra* note 12, at 35; and Olympia Duhart (formative assessment), *see* Olympia Duhart, *The F Word: The Top Five Complaints (and Solutions) About Formative Assessment*, 67 J. LEGAL EDUC. 531 (2018).

together the legal writing professor's work in scholarship, teaching, and professional service."[74]

Though a strong preference remains in many academic circles for theory-based scholarship, legal scholarship has evolved well beyond its traditional emphasis solely on theory and doctrine.[75] Legal scholarship rooted in pedagogy and teaching students how to write has made consistent, steady movement. New disciplines have also moved legal scholarship toward interpretation of legal texts. Specifically, scholarship applying theories "derived from linguistics, classical and contemporary rhetoric, social science, and cognitive science"[76] has explored "how and why particular texts were rhetorically effective."[77] Writing about rhetoric and pedagogy has also been very effective in discipline-building because it is often interdisciplinary in nature, intersecting in important ways with feminist theory, linguistics, cognitive science, critical race theory, and narrative reasoning and persuasion—legal storytelling.[78] The Applied Legal Storytelling movement has been particularly robust as reflected in its biennial conferences along with several published articles and textbooks.[79]

---

[74] Berger at al., *supra* note 70, at 537.

[75] Indeed, scholars have effectively made the case for "engaged scholarship." *See* Sonia K. Katyal, *Encouraging Engaged Scholarship: Perspectives from an Associate Dean for Research*, 31 TOURO L. REV. 53, 53 (2015). Given the recent criticism directed at the value and cost of traditional legal scholarship, others have defended legal scholarship more generally. *See, e.g.*, Tamara R. Piety, *In Praise of Legal Scholarship*, 25 WM. & MARY BILL RTS. J. 801, 801 (2017).

[76] Berger at al., *supra* note 70, at 530.

[77] *Id.*

[78] *See* Pollman & Edwards, *supra* note 71, at 19.

[79] The Seventh Applied Legal Storytelling Conference was held in the summer of 2019 at the University of Colorado Law School. *Seventh Applied Legal Storytelling Conference*, LEGAL WRITING INST., https://www.lwionline.org/conferences/seventh-applied-legal-storytelling-conference (last visited Dec. 20, 2019) [hereinafter *Seventh Applied Legal Storytelling Conference*]. For other sources on Applied Legal Storytelling, see Christopher Rideout, *Applied Legal Storytelling: A*

Despite all of the excitement about and growth in the development of scholarship avenues for the LRW community, the fine art of discipline-branding remains a challenge for many experts in the field. Professor J. Lyn Entrikin recently noted,

> We all teach *legal reasoning and analysis,* an absolute prerequisite before any student can successfully communicate in a legal community. Neither legal "writing" nor legal "communication" reflects the essence of what students must learn first and foremost—understanding the hierarchy of legal authority, recognizing the law applicable to a specific legal problem, and predicting a solution. All of these are *thinking and reasoning* skills.[80]

The ongoing struggle to effectively brand the discipline presents some constant battles. It is clear that discipline-building through scholarship remains a critical goal—no matter which lens is used to pursue the goal. Support for scholarship among members of the LRW community has emerged through publications, presentations, workshops, and conferences. Other efforts to support scholarship include publication platforms for shorter practical pieces (some as short as 500 words) and for extensive, heavily annotated articles. The advent of digital publications has created multiple opportunities to showcase writing by LRW faculty.

3. *Training Scholars*

To facilitate the development of LRW scholarship, increasing efforts have been made to create space and time for that scholarship.

Bibliography, 12 LEGAL COMM. & RHETORIC: J. ALWD 247 (2015); RUTH ANNE ROBBINS, STEVE JOHANSEN & KEN CHESTEK, YOUR CLIENT'S STORY: PERSUASIVE LEGAL WRITING (2013); CAMILLE LAMAR CAMPBELL & OLYMPIA DUHART, PERSUASIVE LEGAL WRITING: A STORYTELLING APPROACH (2017).

[80]Email from J. Lyn Entrikin, Charles Baum Distinguished Professor of Law, William H. Bowen School of Law, University of Arkansas Little Rock, to LRW Professors Listserv (LRWPROF-L) (Aug. 18, 2018, 11:11 a.m.) (on file with author).

For many LRW professors, the intensive demands of teaching the course require a dedicated effort to carve out time to pursue writing goals. Through institutional sponsorships and volunteer hours, the number of writing retreats—opportunities to meet in small groups to dedicate time to writing in a collegial and supportive setting—has steadily grown.

The numerous publications and writing conferences, workshops, and retreats available to support scholarship among LRW professors include the following:

a. Publications

- *Legal Communication & Rhetoric: Journal of the Association of Legal Writing Directors (J. ALWD)*
  Legal Communication & Rhetoric: J. ALWD is a peer-reviewed journal that focuses on "the substance and practice of professional legal writing."[81] *J. ALWD* is a publication of the Association of Legal Writing Directors. "Its mission is to advance the study of professional legal writing and lawyering and to become an active resource and a forum for conversation between the legal practitioner and the legal writing scholar."[82]
- *Legal Writing Institute, The Monograph Series*
  The Monograph Series provides a disciplinary knowledge base for teachers and scholars in legal communication by collecting and reprinting foundational articles in the LRW discipline.[83] Each of the electronic volumes focuses on a specific topic that is central to teaching and studying professional legal communication.

---

[81] *Legal Communication & Rhetoric: JALWD*, ASS'N OF LEGAL WRITING DIRS., https://alwd.org/aboutlcr (last visited Dec. 20, 2019).

[82] *Id.*

[83] *See supra* note 28.

- *The Second Draft*

  "The Second Draft is a twice-a-year online publication. Its goal is to provide an environment for sharing ideas and insights about teaching legal research and writing. The Second Draft publishes essays, book reviews, and shorter articles of interest to legal writing professionals."[84] Issue themes have included technology and teaching methodologies.[85] *The Second Draft* is published by the Legal Writing Institute.

- *The Scribes Journal of Legal Writing*

  The *Scribes Journal* is published by Scribes, the American Society of Legal Writers. It is dedicated to publishing "clear, succinct, and forceful" legal writing.[86] The organization's goal is to foster an interest in writing about the history, philosophy, and language of the law and those who make, interpret, and enforce it.[87]

- *Legal Skills Prof Blog*

  This blog – founded in 2010 – is part of the Law Prof Blog Network.[88] The Legal Skills Prof Blog features posts and articles addressing the teaching of practical legal skills in law school.

- *Perspectives: Teaching Legal Research & Writing*

  This electronic journal is published by Thomson Reuters two times a year for LRW professors and law librarians. The

---

[84] *The Second Draft,* LEGAL WRITING INST., http://www.lwionline.org/publications/second-draft (last visited Dec. 20, 2019).

[85] *Id.*

[86] *The Scribes Journal of Legal Writing*, SCRIBES: AM. SOC'Y OF LEGAL WRITERS, http://www.scribes.org/the-journal-of-legal-writing (last visited Dec. 20, 2019).

[87] *History: The History of Scribes*, SCRIBES: AM. SOC'Y OF LEGAL WRITERS, https://www.scribes.org/history (last visited Dec. 20, 2019).

[88] *Legal Skills Prof Blog*, http://lawprofessors.typepad.com/legal_skills (last visited Dec. 20, 2019).

journal provides a forum for discussing all aspects of teaching LRW, including research and writing materials, tools, theories, techniques, and pedagogies.[89]

- *Professional Newsletters*

  These include the newsletter for the Section on Legal Writing, Reasoning, and Research of the Association of American Law Schools, which features articles and other news.[90] *The Scrivener* is another high-profile newsletter focused on legal writing. Published three times a year in digital format,[91] the newsletter focuses on "anything to do with legal writing," which includes long articles, book chapters, short pieces, interviews, book reviews, and sometimes even poetry.[92]

b. Writing Support: Conferences, Workshops and Retreats

- *Biennial Conference on Applied Legal Storytelling*

  This conference is held every two years with the support of the Legal Writing Institute.[93] The focus is applied legal storytelling, "defined broadly to allow people creativity in the way they think and present on the topic. Among the broadest categories are the uses of storytelling in law practice, legal education, and legal scholarship; the ways in which fiction-writing techniques or narrative theory can inform

---

[89] THOMSON REUTERS, Legal Solutions, *Perspectives: Teaching Legal Research and Writing*, http://info.legalsolutions.thomsonreuters.com/signup/newsletters/perspectives/ (last visited Dec. 20, 2019).

[90] *Section on Legal Writing, Reasoning, and Research*, ASS'N OF AM. L. SCHS., http://www.aals.org/wp-content/uploads/2017/06/AALS-LWRR-Newsletter-Summer-2017.pdf (last visited Dec. 20, 2019).

[91] *The Scrivener*, SCRIBES: AM. SOC'Y OF LEGAL WRITERS, https://www.scribes.org/the-scrivener (last visited Dec. 20, 2019).

[92] Mark Wojcik, *Scribblings from the President*, SCRIVENER (Summer 2018), http://docs.wixstatic.com/ugd/3eec74_fe258ad6b4d746819104dd8736577ca4.pdf.

[93] *See* Seventh Applied Legal Storytelling Conference, *supra* note 79.

legal storytelling; stories in the law, or law as stories; legal storytelling and metaphor; legal storytelling and cognitive science; and ethical considerations in legal storytelling."[94]

- *LWI Writers' Workshop (*renamed *Sirico Scholars' Workshop)*[95]
  The Legal Writing Institute (LWI) is a nonprofit organization with nearly 3,000 members dedicated to improving legal communication. LWI holds an annual writer's workshop that eligible members of the organization may attend. Workshop participants present their projects and receive feedback in discussion groups guided by seasoned LRW scholars.

- *ALWD Scholars Workshop and Forum*[96]
  The Scholars Forum offers scholars an environment to present their ideas and works-in-progress to a group of LRW faculty. The Workshop involves an exchange of substantially completed drafts for peer review. Participants circulate drafts of their papers and are expected to read and provide feedback on other participants' papers.

- *Writing as Resistance: LRW Professor of Color Scholarship Workshop*
  This writing workshop made its debut in July 2018 in Wisconsin. The workshop was designed to respond to the challenges in "status, perception and integration" that LRW faculty of color face. The first workshop was organized by professors and generously supported by the University of

---

[94]Rideout, *supra* note 79.

[95]For information about the most recent workshop in July 2019, see https://www.lwionline.org/conferences/sirico-scholars-workshop (last visited Dec. 20, 2019). The workshop was recently renamed in honor of the late Professor Lou Sirico, a long-time mentor and friend to the legal writing community who regularly volunteered to lead the LWI Writers' Workshop as a senior scholar. *Id.*

[96]For discussion of this event and other ALWD events, see https://www.alwd.org/events/otherevents (last visited Dec. 20, 2019).

Denver Sturm College of Law.[97] The organizers[98] announced on the website, "We resist any notion to otherwise disregard or invalidate our contribution. Instead, we support one another to amplify our voices through scholarship, including legal writing's substance and practice."[99]

- *We Write: LWI Scholarship Retreat Program*[100]

  This scholarship retreat offers a fixed space and dedicated time for LRW professors to devote to focused and intensive scholarly writing, away from regular professional and personal commitments. The retreat is designed to help participants develop effective scholarly writing habits. The retreat consists of a four-day, three-night workshop that meets when law school is on break, typically early December, early May, and late July.

Conference organizers have also created more accessible platforms to present scholarship. For example, LRW faculty with less experience writing or presenting their scholarship are encouraged to consider participating in a poster presentation at a conference. More and more LRW conferences, including the LWI Biennial Conference, have begun to incorporate this mode of sharing knowledge into their conference offerings. As Professor Samantha

---

97 *Writing as Resistance*, UNIV. OF DENVER STURM COLL. OF LAW, https://www.law.du.edu/writing-as-resistance (last visited Dec. 20, 2019) [hereinafter *Writing as Resistance*].

98 Professor Nantiya Ruan, Professor of the Practice of Law at the University of Denver Sturm College of Law, was instrumental in establishing the first *Writing as Resistance* workshop in 2018. The inaugural steering committee included Leslie Culver, Olympia Duhart, Brenda Gibson, Latisha Nixon-Jones, and Saleema Snow. Other faculty volunteers from around the country also made the workshop a reality.

99 *See Writing as Resistance*, *supra* note 97.

100 *See We Write Retreats*, LEGAL WRITING INST., https://www.lwionline.org/conferences/we-write-retreats (last visited Dec. 20, 2019).

Moppett explains, "unlike an oral presentation, [a poster presentation] encourages informal, one-on-one communication between the audience and the presenter."[101]

c. School-Based Efforts

In addition to the expansive support of an active LRW writing community on the national stage, several law schools are working to create supportive scholarship environments for their own faculty. At the institutional level, LRW directors have become more creative in their efforts to support scholarship among their LRW colleagues.

One law school[102] organized a "Writing Lockdown" for both faculty and students to have dedicated time on campus for scholarly productivity. Under the "Writing Lockdown" model, students and faculty members are invited to spend time in the dean's conference room to complete writing projects. Food is provided. Another school organized a "Write In" for professors, offering dedicated writing time away from home and work responsibilities.[103] At the "Write In," professors spend several hours together in a large room with plenty of food and quiet to focus on their writing. After a brief (five-minute) declaration of writing goals for the session, participants sit down and write. Short breaks are scheduled for stretch-

---

[101] Samantha A. Moppett, *Think It, Draft It, Post It: Creating Legal Poster Presentations*, 18 LEGAL WRITING 339 (2012). Professor Moppett's excellent article provides a how-to guide for creating poster presentations.

[102] This approach was adopted by Suffolk Law. Professor Kathleen Elliott Vinson has shared her approach to helping students and faculty battle procrastination. *See* Kathleen Elliott Vinson, *Legal Writing Matters: Using a Writing Lockdown to Help Law Students Avoid Procrastination,* SUFFOLK LAW SCH. LEGAL WRITING MATTERS, Aug. 25, 2016, https://sites.suffolk.edu/legalwritingmatters/2016/08/25/legal-writing-matters-using-a-writing-lockdown-to-help-law-students-avoid-procrastination/.

[103] The "Write In" approach was adopted by Nova Southeastern University Shepard Broad College of Law. Professor Olympia Duhart was inspired by Professor Vinson to create a version of the Writing Lockdown dedicated solely to faculty.

ing throughout, with wine and dessert provided at the end. Both models build on a combination of peer pressure and dedicated time to overcome two huge obstacles to completing any writing project—procrastination and interruptions.

The examples of workshops, publication platforms, and scholarship supports listed above are not exhaustive; nevertheless, they illustrate the expansive opportunities available to LRW faculty who seek support for their writing and a platform for their publications.

In conclusion, the demands on LRW faculty have grown tremendously, expanding the responsibilities for ensuring a quality program. Whether shared through an autonomous program or led by a director, running a successful program requires several essential elements. From hiring, to fielding student complaints, to classroom visits and scholarship support, numerous critical components support LRW faculty and ensure quality instruction.

VII. LAW STUDENTS WHO SPEAK ENGLISH AS A SECOND LANGUAGE

A. Introduction

Law schools are admitting greater numbers of ESL students—lawyers and law students who speak English as a second language.[1] These international and recent immigrant students see value in learning about the American legal system and U.S. views on transnational and comparative law. Additionally, in many parts of the world English has become the language of international business and trade, even when neither party to a business negotiation speaks English as a first language.[2] English is also a language of instruction in law schools across Europe, parts of Asia and Africa, and Mexico. The need for "Legal English" is increasingly global.

American law schools have also recognized the value of admitting students from other countries. Within the law school, international students enrich the cultural diversity and educational experience of the classroom and campus.[3] Students who bring knowledge of the civil law system, for example, can provide a rich comparative experience for everyone. Some law schools enter into sister school agreements and other exchange programs with law schools in other countries. And because law students from other

---

[1]This chapter may also contain useful information for teaching students whose native language is English, but not American English. Some of these students may share cultural and legal-language challenges similar to those that confront ESL students.

[2]For example, a lawyer from China who negotiates a contract with a lawyer from Japan, Germany, or Brazil will likely negotiate and draft the contract in English.

[3]*See, e.g.*, Rachel Burke, *The Role of ESL Professionals in the Promotion of Culturally Inclusive Universities*, 34 TESL Rep. 20 (2001) (encouraging universities to actively promote intercultural communication to gain the utmost benefit from enrolling international students).

countries usually do not receive financial aid or scholarships from U.S. sources, they provide an important source of tuition revenue for many institutions.

Law schools that recruit and admit international students must support the unique educational needs of students who speak English as a second (or third) language.[4] Schools must offer courses for non-native speakers of English[5] and provide additional support to international students to ensure their success in law school.

B. International Students

Law students who speak English as a second language may be enrolled in an LL.M. program, a J.D. program, an M.S. program, or a non-degree law school certificate program. Although students from other countries often take the Test of English as a Foreign Language ("TOEFL") before admission to law school, even a high score on the TOEFL does not necessarily guarantee that each student has sufficient practice or confidence in all of the skills necessary to succeed in law school.[6] For example, law students must be proficient in reading court decisions, statutes and regulations, and legal commentary; they must be able to listen actively to their professors' lectures and follow classroom discussion (usually between native speakers of English); they must be able to ask and answer questions about the course material; they must be able to take meaningful notes; they must learn and master cost-effective legal research skills; they must be able to write legal memoranda, motions, briefs, articles, and other class assignments; and they must be able to pass comprehensive

---

[4]*See, e.g.*, Mark E. Wojcik & Diane Penneys Edelman, *Overcoming Challenges in the Global Classroom: Teaching Legal Research and Writing to International Law Students and Law Graduates*, 3 LEGAL WRITING 127 (1997).

[5]Many legal publishers have also begun to recognize the market demand for legal writing textbooks focused on the needs of non-native speakers of English.

[6]*See* Wojcik & Edelman, *supra* note 4, at 129.

examinations. It is unrealistic to expect an ESL student to acquire a level of fluency in academic and professional legal English with only a semester or two of study, especially when mastery of the English language typically takes several years.

Some general observations about ESL students may be valid. For example, despite any difficulties they may have with English communication, these students are highly educated, highly qualified, and highly motivated to succeed. Individual students, however, have different backgrounds, abilities, and expectations when learning legal writing, legal research, and various areas of legal doctrine.

1. LL.M. Students Who Plan to Return to Their Home Countries

Many ESL students come to the United States as recent law graduates seeking advanced training in international and comparative law. Others come because of an interest in specialized LL.M. programs in subjects as varied as banking law, environmental law, international criminal law, international human rights, intellectual property, international business transactions, or taxation. The students in the latter category may be prosecutors, lawyers, or judges whose work in their home country requires professional training in these specialized areas of law.

Although American law students are exposed to multiple semesters of instruction in legal writing and research, some international students may never have had such a course before starting their LL.M. studies. Those students are often at a relative disadvantage in classes with lawyers who may have years of experience in American legal research and scholarly legal writing. In addition, the first law degree in most other countries is an undergraduate degree, so international LL.M. candidates often have no more formal education than the typical first-year American law student.

Research and writing needs and expectations for LL.M. students who plan to return to their home countries when their studies are finished should generally focus on (a) skills needed to complete course requirements, such as research skills for writing a paper; and (b) skills related to the type of work they expect to do when they return to their home countries. These areas of focus mean that otherwise typical writing assignments—such as drafting a complaint or an appellate brief, or even conducting a practice oral argument—may have little relevance to students who do not plan to practice law in the United States after they graduate. Instead, these students are better served by focusing on short assignments, including contract drafting, client letters and other forms of correspondence, shorter legal memoranda, and documents in preparation for an international arbitration or transnational litigation rather than domestic litigation.[7]

2. LL.M. Students Who Plan to Take a State Bar Examination

Many foreign lawyers who pursue an LL.M. degree in the United States plan to take the bar examination in New York, Texas, the District of Columbia, or another jurisdiction that allows foreign lawyers to take the bar exam after undertaking additional study at a U.S. law school.[8] Although some jurisdictions are not as willing to admit foreign-trained lawyers, some have updated their admission rules in light of U.S. treaty obligations under the General Agreement

---

[7]As one LRW professor observed, a lawyer from Germany usually will not need to draft a memorandum on intentional infliction of emotional distress under Connecticut law. A much more useful writing exercise, for example, might ask students to resolve whether an oral contract between a buyer in Germany and a seller in the United States is valid under the U.N. Convention on Contracts for the International Sale of Goods.

[8]For a comprehensive list of requirements and limitations for each jurisdiction in the United States, see Nat'l Conf. of Bar Exam'rs & Am. Bar Ass'n Section of Legal Educ. & Admissions to the Bar, *Comprehensive Guide to Bar Admission Requirements* (2019), http://www.ncbex.org/assets/BarAdmissionGuide/NCBE-CompGuide-2019.pdf.

on Trade in Services (GATS),[9] which is part of the agreement establishing the World Trade Organization. Other jurisdictions may allow non-U.S. lawyers to apply for bar admission after a minimum number of years of practice experience in their home countries.[10] Many jurisdictions also allow foreign-trained lawyers to work as "foreign legal consultants," advising on the laws of their home jurisdiction.[11]

Some LL.M. students who take an American bar exam plan to practice law in the United States. Others plan to return to their home countries with the cachet of having a license to practice law in the United States, even if they have never appeared as counsel in a U.S. courtroom. LL.M. students can study anywhere in the United States, but most will also take a bar review course to prepare them for a bar exam that may not be in the same state where they study law.

3. J.D. Students Who Speak English as a Second Language

The United States is a nation of immigrants, and many law schools have experienced an increase in the number of ESL students enrolled in their J.D. programs. Some of these students may have completed part or all of their undergraduate studies in their home

---

[9] *See* Annex 1B, General Agreement on Trade in Services of the General Agreement on Tariffs and Trade: Multilateral Trade Negotiations Final Act Embodying the Results of the Uruguay Round of Trade Negotiations, 33 I.L.M. 1125, 1168 (1994). *See generally* Laurel S. Terry, *GATS' Applicability to Transnational Lawyering and its Potential Impact on U.S. State Regulation of Lawyers*, 34 VAND. J. TRANSNAT'L L. 989 (2001).

[10] Illinois, for example, allows certain foreign-trained lawyers to take the state bar exam, but only if they have practiced law for at least five of the seven years immediately before filing the application. *See* ILL. SUP. CT. R. 715(b). Most but not all students in an LL.M. program will not have practiced law for five years.

[11] Jurisdictions that permit foreign legal consultants have so far licensed, registered, or certified only small numbers of consultants, but these numbers may increase if the rules ever expand the scope of legal advice that foreign legal consultants may give.

countries. Other students may have completed their undergraduate studies in the United States or in another English-speaking country.

The presence of ESL students in a J.D. program is far from unusual; indeed, in many parts of the United States, it is rare for an LRW professor to teach a class that does not include bilingual students. If a student has been in the United States for some time, the fact that the student speaks English as a second language may not even be known to the admissions office or admissions committee, which may consider only the student's undergraduate institution.

4. *Non-Degree Students*

Some ESL students are visiting scholars or for some other reason do not seek a degree from the U.S. law school. Some students, for example, take classes that will be counted toward law degrees in their home countries, just as U.S. students may travel abroad to take courses that count toward the J.D. degree. These students should be able to access all of the resources that the law school makes available to regular students and other students who might be visiting the law school during a particular semester.

5. *EFL Students*

Some LRW professors have opportunities to teach LRW in other countries. These students are learning English as a Foreign Language (EFL), and they typically do not have the English-language resources that are available to students who study in the United States or another English-speaking country. For example, these students may not have access to an English-language legal dictionary or an English-language law library, nor will they encounter English in their daily conversations outside the classroom. These students typically structure their written work using the only tools at their disposal: "translated" versions of the rhetorical modes of their native (legal) language and a bilingual dictionary.

C. Meeting Student Needs with Special Classes

J.D. students who speak English as a second language are normally enrolled in a regular J.D.-level LRW course. LL.M. students who have previous training as lawyers in other countries may not have had the opportunity to take any formal courses whatsoever in legal writing and American legal research. Students in some LL.M. programs designed specifically for international and comparative law may take a course that introduces U.S. law, legal institutions, and jurisprudence (including common law reasoning), but this kind of introductory course often fails to include any substantial training in legal writing or research.

If a law school has a sufficient number of international students, the school may decide to create a special writing course for students who speak English as a second language. For schools with smaller numbers of international students, it may not be feasible or cost-effective to arrange a special writing course for these students, even if they can find a qualified professor to teach it. Although law schools vary on the number they consider sufficient, a special section of LRW for non-native speakers of English can be held with as few as three students. At the other end of the spectrum, a special section should have no more than fifteen ESL students.

A special writing course may be offered in the first semester, or short courses may be offered during the summer before the first semester. Offering a special legal writing course before the student undertakes doctrinal course work will allow the student to learn all the material more effectively. When schools offer special courses for their international students, they greatly appreciate the opportunity to improve their written communication and research skills, as well as to practice listening and speaking skills that will facilitate more meaningful classroom participation. The students recognize that to be successful in their other courses, they must improve their ability to read English-language court decisions and statutes, which are generally far more detailed than most statutes in civil law jurisdictions.

Law schools may recommend or even require that incoming ESL students attend a summer program in Legal English, Introduction to American Law, or another legal writing course that might be offered by a private institution or another law school. If a suitable law-related program cannot be found, an Intensive English Program (IEP) devoted to business or professional training may be an effective supplement, although it will not fulfill all the needs that a law-specific program could serve.[12]

If a law school cannot offer a separate class, it might provide ESL students with additional help in a supportive writing center, or with a tutor who has some background and training in teaching ESL students. Working with students who speak English as a second language involves a substantial commitment of time and effort, but if law schools admit these students, they must be willing to provide the academic support and training they need to succeed. A foreign law student or lawyer is not like a foreign science graduate student. Language is the quintessential tool of law.

In addition to special classes, the law school should provide opportunities for international students to meet with LRW professors and with writing center professionals who can assist them. Some international students may be reluctant to visit an LRW professor to review written work for any of several reasons. For example, a student may come from an academic culture that offers no opportunity to meet individually with a professor. Alternatively, the student might fear that the professor will be critical of a student's failure to understand a certain legal point. One remedy to cure the reluctance of students to visit faculty members about their written work is to make attendance mandatory for periodic conferences.[13] Another proven remedy is to provide access to a student teaching

---

[12] Some universities may also have ESL programs that can provide additional resources for law students.

[13] *See* Wojcik & Edelman, *supra* note 4, at 133.

assistant who can help the international student gain confidence and encourage the student to meet with the LRW professor.

D. Identifying Resources

Most LRW professors do not have training in ESL instruction, just as most ESL teachers have no training in law. A handful of instructors, however, have training in both fields. A law school would do well to locate an individual who has training in both law and ESL education, and law school writing centers should seek out individuals who have ESL training and experience.

Some law schools may be fortunate enough to have an ESL training program on their own university campus. Although the professors and students in that program likely have had little exposure to legal education, law school faculty should investigate how the university's ESL faculty might assist them in developing courses[14] and materials[15] for ESP (known variously as "English for Special Purposes" or "English for Specific Purposes") or EAP ("English for Academic Purposes"). There may be opportunities for collaborative work that might be published for the benefit of students, other LRW professors, and other ESL professors.

Schools should also search for undiscovered resources within their own institutions. A law school may find one or more students who have come to law school after working as ESL teachers. These students might be willing to use their previous training and experience to tutor international students. Relying on student assistance is not a complete solution, however, because these students often

---

[14] *See, e.g.*, JANICE YALDEN, PRINCIPLES OF COURSE DESIGN FOR LANGUAGE TEACHING (1996).

[15] *See, e.g.*, MATERIALS DEVELOPMENT IN LANGUAGE TEACHING (Brian Tomlinson ed., 2d ed. 2011); J. DONALD BOWEN, HAROLD MADSEN & ANN HILFERTY, TESOL TECHNIQUES AND PROCEDURES 65 (1985).

have exams and assignment deadlines just when the ESL students are most in need of assistance.

As they investigate and identify a range of resources to assist international students, schools should recognize that work with international students can involve a good deal of time and labor. First, it is important to provide quality assistance without burning out those who provide the assistance. Second, schools should acknowledge that international students may learn more quickly and more effectively when a range of resources is made available to them. Exclusive dependence upon and exposure to the language and teaching style of a single instructor may lead a student to learn only that one instructor's speech and teaching habits. Like native learners, second-language learners need as many language samples as possible to learn linguistic themes and appropriate variations. Third, faculty should understand that some international students may be reluctant to approach their LRW professors for assistance. Some students may come from an academic culture that discourages students from questioning their professors; other students may prefer to ask questions of fellow students.

E. Materials and Methods

A few years ago, only a handful of texts were available to teach lawyers and law students who spoke English as a second language.[16] Today, several suitable texts are available for teaching these students legal writing, legal research, and introductory principles of American law. Some texts are introductory, focusing on increasing a student's legal vocabulary and introducing various aspects of

---

[16]For example, some teaching materials about government that were used to study for the U.S. Citizenship examination could have been used for teaching lawyers and law students who spoke English as a second language.

legal discourse.[17] Other texts are designed for graduate students who are already lawyers in their home countries, but who have not yet had a legal writing course in English.[18] Still other writing texts are designed for native English speakers but wisely include materials specific to ESL students. Even legal dictionaries have been designed for lawyers who speak English as a second language.[19] Even more legal writing and research texts for ESL students are likely to be published in the coming years.

LRW professors in the United States who create additional course teaching materials such as fact patterns and specific writing assignments should be aware of culture-specific, non-legal jargon or references and be prepared to provide students with appropriate explanations.

Outside the United States, a growing number of texts specialize in English for law. Although some of these texts are excellent,[20] some are riddled with typographical and grammatical errors that

---

[17] *See* DEBRA S. LEE, CHARLES HALL & SUSAN M. BARONE, AMERICAN LEGAL ENGLISH (2d ed. 2007); ANN SINSHEIMER & TERESA BROSTOFF, LEGAL ENGLISH: AN INTRODUCTION TO THE LEGAL LANGUAGE AND CULTURE OF THE UNITED STATES (2d ed. 2003); MARK E. WOJCIK, INTRODUCTION TO LEGAL ENGLISH (2d ed. 2011).

[18] *See, e.g.*, KAREN LUNDQUIST, LEGAL WRITING AND LEGAL SKILLS FOR FOREIGN LL.M. STUDENTS (2017); ANN M. PICCARD, U.S. LEGAL WRITING FOR INTERNATIONAL LAWYERS AND LAW STUDENTS (2017); ALISON RILEY, LEGAL ENGLISH AND THE COMMON LAW (2015) (including a Legal Grammar Handbook by Patricia Sours); ALISON RILEY & PATRICIA SOURS, COMMON LAW LEGAL ENGLISH AND GRAMMAR: A CONTEXTUAL APPROACH (2014); JOHN B. THORNTON, U.S. LEGAL REASONING, WRITING, AND PRACTICE FOR INTERNATIONAL LAWYERS (2014).

[19] *See* CHRISTINE ROSSINI, ENGLISH AS A LEGAL LANGUAGE (1998).

[20] *See, e.g.*, MARIA FRADDOSIO, ENGLISH FOR LAWYERS: CORSO DI INGLESE GIURIDICO (4th ed. 2013).

students may model as correct.[21] LRW professors should ask their ESL students about the specific legal English texts they may have previously used and, if possible, ask to review them.

Special writing courses for international students should train them to use materials they are likely to encounter in their other studies. If students are expected to read lengthy court decisions in their course work, they should have some training in how to read judicial opinions. If students are expected to read law review articles and treatises, they should have some training in reading those scholarly works. If students are expected to interpret complex statutes, they should have some training in how to read statutes and regulations. Although civil law lawyers from Europe and South America will have had extensive training in statutory construction, this may not be true for lawyers from common law jurisdictions or from the People's Republic of China. Even lawyers with previous training in reading statutes are often surprised at the unusual length and specificity of some federal and state statutes and regulations.

F. Assessing ESL Students' Communication Skills

Students who speak English as a second language must be evaluated to assess and assist their progress in improving written and oral communication skills in English. As law students, they should also be evaluated to assess their mastery of substantive materials and concepts. ESL teachers engage in constant debate about testing methodologies and alternatives.[22] Law faculty generally have long debated whether ESL students should be subject to the same evaluation standards as native English speakers. Students, for their part,

---

[21] For example, mistakes in just the title of one textbook from China reflect the large number of other mistakes and questionable materials throughout the text.

[22] *See, e.g.,* James D. Brown & Thom Hudson, *The Alternatives in Language Assessment,* 32 TESOL Q. 653 (1998).

are anxious about evaluation and assessment[23]—particularly in a law school setting in which anxiety over the single, final examination used for many courses may impair a student's ability to do well.

In the realm of oral language assessment, some theories of language instruction previously assumed that the acquisition of language was more or less a linear process, and that a standardized objective test (such as an oral examination) could effectively measure an individual's language proficiency as a single point along the road to language fluency.[24] Language evaluation has since evolved to recognize that the essential measure is not how well a person performs on an artificial language test, but how well that person can communicate with others.[25]

Assessing the written work of ESL students in a legal writing class can be labor-intensive and complex, especially if the course uses a traditional LRW curriculum that includes longer assignments. It is easier to assess ESL students on shorter assignments; students may also learn better from engaging in shorter, more frequent writing assignments than a single long writing assignment. Shorter and more frequent assignments, followed by quick, relevant feedback, will help students acquire the vocabulary and high-frequency grammatical and rhetorical structures that constitute "the language of law." Appropriate feedback should be given at each stage of the

---

[23] *See, e.g.*, Kassim Shaaban, *Persistent Issues in Assessment of English as a Foreign Language*, 34(1) TESL Rep. 1, 3 (2001).

[24] *See* Nic Underhill, Testing Spoken Language: A Handbook of Oral Testing Techniques 5 (1987).

[25] *Id.* In the United Kingdom, the Test of Legal English Skills (TOLES) was "developed to meet the demand from law firms, companies, legal institutions, lawyers and law students for an accurate method of assessing an individual's legal English." The test has not been used in the United States, although an American version of this examination may be developed sometime in the future. *See generally* Toles Legal, https://www.toleslegal.com/ (last visited Dec. 18, 2019).

writing process, taking care to avoid shorthand abbreviations or cultural references that might confuse non-native speakers of English.[26] Feedback should allow students to distinguish between errors and "rhetorical preferences" in legal writing.[27]

The assessment of an ESL student's written work in doctrinal courses is also important. An ongoing debate among law faculty focuses on whether the work done by international students should be assessed using the same standards that apply to native speakers of English. The issue is particularly difficult when grading is anonymous. Some professors, for example, may overlook mistakes in grammar when grading an examination in a doctrinal course. Other professors may refuse to overlook grammatical and spelling mistakes, or may overlook mistakes only if an international student intends to practice law in the student's home country rather than in the United States.[28]

Additionally, a professor who comments anonymously that a student "needs work on grammar" may not recognize that the problems on a final examination may reflect "academic culture shock" rather than grammatical deficiencies.[29] On the other hand, anonymous grading has often surprised professors when they learn that the highest grades were earned by students who speak English as a second language. Like students who are native English speakers, ESL students are not a monolithic group.

---

[26]Wojcik & Edelman, *supra* note 4, at 131; *see also* Luanga A. Kasanga, *Responding to Feedback in Revision in Multiple-Draft Writing,* 34(2) TESL REP. 1 (2001). For example, assignments should avoid using terms from American sports unless those terms are explained.

[27]*See* LAUREL CURRIE OATES, ANNE ENQUIST & KELLY KUNSCH, THE LEGAL WRITING HANDBOOK: ANALYSIS, RESEARCH, AND WRITING 913 (3d ed. 2002).

[28]Wojcik & Edelman, *supra* note 4, at 131 n.14.

[29]*Id.* at 132.

Plagiarism is a significant issue that may arise with research papers written by any student.[30] With international students, the issue of plagiarism is sometimes explained in cultural terms. For example, a defender of an international student charged with plagiarism may say that a foreign academic culture devalues original thought and instead values the ability to repeat what has been taught in class. For this reason, law schools should provide international students with clear written guidelines on how to avoid plagiarism by providing proper attribution to the original source.

G. Commitment

If law schools continue to recruit and admit international students—and they will—those schools and their faculties must also be willing to commit the resources necessary for their international students to succeed. Part of that commitment involves providing special classes and resources for international students. Another part of that commitment involves providing financial and other support to enable faculty members and writing center professionals to obtain adequate training in ESL education.

Professional organizations such as TESOL (Teachers of English to Speakers of Other Languages, Inc.) and its state affiliates offer regional training programs, annual conferences, publications, listservs, and other resources for ESL teachers. An annual Global Legal Skills Conference, held in various locations around the world, has brought together LRW professors and ESL experts to discuss teaching methodologies and materials. Organizations such as the Legal Writing Institute offer biennial conferences that often include sessions on skills training for international students. Regional ESL programs for legal education are also starting to appear in the United

[30] It may be easier to detect plagiarism in the work of international students than in the work of native English speakers. For example, a research paper may have dramatic shifts in writing style or use of language. For general information addressing the issue of plagiarism in LRW courses, see Chapter II, Part A.3.f.v.

States and in other countries. And ESL academic journals such as *English for Specific Purposes* may publish occasional articles on legal education for second-language learners.

It may be unrealistic to expect LRW professors to return to school to obtain a Master's Degree or doctorate in teaching English to non-native speakers. However, ESL training courses are available that can help LRW professors expand their teaching abilities. LRW professors who take training courses in teaching English as a second language will find that much of the training also improves their ability to teach native speakers of English.

VIII. SERVING STUDENTS WITH SPECIAL NEEDS

Law schools have a special responsibility to support law students who request educational accommodations for disabilities. This chapter explains the legal basis for these obligations, identifies relevant ABA accreditation standards, and provides information for LRW faculty on how to provide suitable accommodations for those students when requested.

A. Legal Considerations in Accommodating Students with Disabilities

Federal and state statutes, and sometimes local law, obligate law schools to accommodate students with disabilities under certain circumstances.[1]

Long before Congress enacted the Americans with Disabilities Act (ADA) in 1990,[2] § 504 of the federal Rehabilitation Act of 1973[3] guaranteed equal access for persons with disabilities to programs and services "receiving [f]ederal financial assistance."[4] Section 504, which remains in effect, expressly applies to "all of the operations of . . . a college, university, or other postsecondary institution, or a public system of higher education"[5] that receives federal financial assistance, including law schools that accept federal financial aid for their students.

---

[1]Governing laws at the state and local level vary considerably and are beyond the scope of this *Sourcebook*. Faculty should consult with law school disability services offices to identify additional protections that state or local law may provide to students in public and private postsecondary education settings.

[2]*See infra* Part A.1 of this chapter.

[3]*See* 29 U.S.C. § 701 note.

[4]Rehabilitation Act of 1973, § 504, *codified at* 29 U.S.C. § 794.

[5]29 U.S.C. § 794(b)(2)(A).

With the enactment of the ADA in 1990, Congress expanded protections for persons with disabilities well beyond entities that receive federal funding, including most private commercial and educational institutions open to the public,[6] with the exception of "religious organizations or entities controlled by religious organizations."[7]

1. Americans with Disabilities Act (ADA)

The ADA of 1990,[8] as amended by the ADA Amendments Act of 2008,[9] prohibits discrimination against otherwise qualified individuals on the basis of disability.[10] The ADA applies to employment,[11] state and local government services (including public transportation),[12] public accommodations (including commercial facilities

---

[6]*E.g.*, Berardelli v. Allied Servs. Inst. of Rehab. Med., 900 F.3d 104, 115 (3d Cir. 2018) ("Congress designed the ADA to fit hand in glove with the [Rehabilitation Act of 1973], leaving intact the 'scope of protection . . . under the [Rehabilitation Act],' . . . but extending its reach beyond federally funded programs to three 'major areas of public life,' . . . including employment . . .; public entities, . . .; and public accommodations . . . .").

[7]42 U.S.C. § 12187.

[8]42 U.S.C. §§ 12101 *et seq.*

[9]ADA Amendments Act of 2008 (ADAAA), Pub. L. No. 110-325, 122 Stat. 3553 (effective Jan. 1, 2009).

[10]*See* 42 U.S.C. § 12131(2).

> The term "qualified individual with a disability" means an individual with a disability who, with or without reasonable modifications to rules, policies, or practices, the removal of architectural, communication, or transportation barriers, or the provision of auxiliary aids and services, meets the essential eligibility requirements for the receipt of services or the participation in programs or activities provided by a public entity.

Id.

[11]ADA Title I, *codified at* 42 U.S.C. §§ 12111 *et seq.*

[12]ADA Title II, *codified at* §§ 12131 *et seq.*

operated by private entities),[13] and telecommunications services.[14] Independent of the ADA, as noted above, § 504 of the Rehabilitation Act of 1973,[15] as amended, guarantees individuals with disabilities equal access to programs and services that receive federal funds, including student loan funds.[16] Section 504 expressly applies to postsecondary institutions, including law schools.[17]

In the context of postsecondary education, the term "qualified" means that the student meets the academic and technical standards required for participation in the class, program, or activity;[18] however, the student also has a physical or mental impairment, or both, that substantially limits a major life activity (e.g., seeing, hearing, walking, breathing, performing manual tasks, learning, caring for oneself, and working) and therefore requires a reasonable accommodation to have equal access.[19] Major life activities may also include school-related tasks such as learning, reading, concentrating, thinking, and communicating.[20]

---

[13] ADA Title III, *codified at* §§ 12181 *et seq.*

[14] ADA Title IV, 47 U.S.C. § 225 (relating to telecommunications services for hearing-impaired and speech-impaired individuals).

[15] *See* 29 U.S.C. § 701 note.

[16] Rehabilitation Act of 1973, § 504, *codified at* 29 U.S.C. § 794.

[17] 29 U.S.C. § 794(b)(2)(A).

[18] *See, e.g.*, Laura Rothstein, *Forty Years of Disability Policy in Legal Education and the Legal Profession: What Has Changed and What Are the New Issues?*, 22 Am. U. J. Gender Soc. Pol'y & L. 519, 554 (2014) (explaining that a "qualified" student with a disability must nevertheless meet essential requirements of the program, with or without accommodations).

[19] *Id.* at 545-53 (discussing the definition of "disability" in the context of legal education and the legal profession).

[20] *See infra* notes 31-32 and accompanying text (referring to ABA Standard 207 and Interpretation 207-1 as relevant when determining whether a law student with a disability is "qualified").

2. Campus or Law School Disability Offices

Each law school articulates its own processes and procedures for students to request accommodations for disabilities.[21] Most, if not all, law schools use a university or law school disability office to help assess whether a student has a qualified disability, and if so, to develop the reasonable accommodations necessary for the student. Students with disabilities who know their rights and responsibilities are much better equipped to succeed in law school, so disability offices work closely with students to help them understand their rights and responsibilities. An LRW professor should work closely with the law school's disability office to ensure that any proposed accommodations neither undermine mastery of the essential skills of the course nor fail to prepare the student for law practice.

Another federal statute that guides disability offices is the Family Educational Rights and Privacy Act (FERPA).[22] Faculty and disability services personnel are not permitted to discuss specific student circumstances or student records without the express permission of the student. However, FERPA permits school personnel to disclose education records without the consent of the student in some limited circumstances, including when necessary to inform faculty of any accommodation a student may need.

Federal law provides that every school must develop and administer grievance procedures to ensure that students may raise concerns fully and fairly, and requires disability offices to provide for the prompt and equitable resolution of complaints.[23]

---

[21] *See, e.g.,* Halpern v. Wake Forest Univ. Health Scis., 669 F.3d 454, 463 (4th Cir. 2012) ("[S]ister [federal] circuits have overwhelmingly extended some level of deference to schools' professional judgments regarding students' qualifications when addressing disability discrimination claims.").

[22] 20 U.S.C. § 1232g; 34 C.F.R. pt. 99.

[23] *See* 34 C.F.R. § 104.4.

A student who is dissatisfied with the outcome of the school's grievance procedures, or who wishes to pursue alternative procedures, may file a complaint against the school with the Department of Education's Office of Civil Rights (OCR) or directly in court.[24]

3. *Requested Accommodations That Would Impose Undue Hardship*

An obligation to provide a "reasonable accommodation" to a law student does not require the law school to provide an accommodation that would impose an "undue hardship."[25] An undue hardship means significant difficulty or expense, considering the available resources and circumstances of the particular student in light of the cost or difficulty of providing the specific accommodation. Undue hardship refers not only to financial difficulty, but also to requested accommodations that are unduly extensive, substantial, or disruptive to the institution.[26]

---

[24] For details about the OCR complaint process, see U.S. DEP'T OF EDUC., *How to File a Discrimination Complaint with the Office for Civil Rights*, https://www2.ed.gov/about/offices/list/ocr/docs/howto.pdf (last visited Dec. 18, 2019).

[25] *E.g.*, Dean v. Univ. at Buffalo Sch. of Med. & Biomed. Scis., 804 F.3d 178, 186–87 (2d Cir. 2015) ("In the education context, the ADA and the Rehabilitation Act require a covered institution to offer reasonable accommodations for a student's known disability unless the accommodation would impose an 'undue hardship' on the operation of its program . . . ."). A law school can assert "undue hardship" by showing that a requested accommodation would "(a) impose undue hardship on the operation of the defendant's service, program, or activity, or (b) require a fundamental or substantial modification to the nature of its academic program or standards." *Id.* at 190; *see also* Kaltenberger v. Ohio Coll. of Podiatric Med., 162 F.3d 432, 436 (6th Cir. 1998) (noting that a college need not make "fundamental" or "substantial" modifications to accommodate students with disabilities, but "may be required to make 'reasonable' ones").

[26] *See* LaToya Jones Burrell, *So What's Next? Life After the Americans with Disabilities Amendment Act of 2008 for the Learning Disabled Law Student*, 41 S.U. L. REV. 59, 79 (2013) (interpreting "undue hardship" of the sort that warrants an exception from the obligation to provide a requested accommodation).

B. Relevant ABA Accreditation Standards

Consistent with federal statutes, specifically Title VII, Part D of the Higher Education Opportunity Act of 2008, as amended,[27] the ABA Standards prohibit law schools from discriminating against applicants or students on the basis of disability.[28] Law schools must also ensure equal educational opportunity without discrimination or segregation based on disability.[29]

Moreover, the ABA Standards expressly require law schools to "demonstrate by concrete action a commitment to diversity and inclusion by providing full opportunities for the study of law and entry into the profession by members of underrepresented groups."[30] With respect to students with disabilities, Standard 207 specifically requires law schools to "[a]ssur[e] equality of opportunity for qualified individuals with disabilities [by] provid[ing] such students . . . with reasonable accommodations consistent with applicable law."[31] Further, Standard 207 requires law schools to maintain "written policies and procedures for assessing and handling requests for reasonable accommodations made by qualified individuals with disabilities."[32]

---

[27] 20 U.S.C. §§ 1140 *et seq.* As noted in Chapter I, the Council of the ABA Section of Legal Education and Admissions to the Bar is the designated accrediting agency for postsecondary legal education under federal law. *See* Binno v. Am. Bar Ass'n, 826 F.3d 338, 342 & n.1 (6th Cir. 2016) (explaining that while the ABA is certified by the Department of Education as the accrediting agency for legal education, "the actual accrediting agent is the Council of the ABA's Section [of] Legal Education and Admission[s] to the Bar").

[28] Section of Legal Educ. & Admissions to the Bar, *ABA Standards and Rules of Procedure for Approval of Law Schools (2019-2020)*, ABA: Am. Bar. Ass'n, Standard 205(a) [hereinafter ABA Standards], https://www.americanbar.org/content/dam/aba/administrative/legal_education_and_admissions_to_the_bar/standards/2019-2020/2019-2020-aba-standards-and-rules-of-procedure.pdf.

[29] ABA Standard 205(b).

[30] ABA Standard 206(a).

[31] ABA Standard 207(a).

[32] ABA Standard 207(b). Interpretation 207-1 expressly requires law schools to individually evaluate each applicant and student with disabilities to ensure they

Once a qualified student with a disability is admitted to a law school, a professor need not offer accommodations unless (1) the student requests an accommodation, and (2) the requested accommodation is a reasonable one.[33] A recent federal court decision illustrates the point. In 2018, the Eleventh Circuit rejected a former law student's ADA claim against a law school after his LRW professor turned down his belated request to extend the appellate brief deadline.[34] The eye injury on which the student based his ADA claim had happened three weeks before the student made the extension request, which the court held was unreasonable given the complications the requested extension would have created for the course schedule.

---

meet relevant academic standards. *Id.* The Interpretation also clarifies the term "qualified" for purposes of the accreditation standards.

> The use of the term "qualified" in the Standard requires a careful and thorough consideration of each applicant and each student's qualifications in light of reasonable accommodations. Reasonable accommodations are those that are consistent with the fundamental nature of the school's program of legal education, that can be provided without undue financial or administrative burden, and that can be provided while maintaining academic and other essential performance standards.

Id.

[33] *See, e.g.,* Kaltenberger v. Ohio Coll. of Podiatric Med., 162 F.3d 432, 437 (6th Cir. 1998) (holding that defendant college was not obligated to provide a student with an accommodation until plaintiff had provided a proper diagnosis of ADHD and requested a specific accommodation).

[34] Cooney v. Barry Sch. of Law, 720 Fed. App'x 571, 573-74 (11th Cir.), *cert. denied*, 139 S. Ct. 174 (2018), *rev'g in part and aff'g in part* No. 6:14-cv-106-Orl-22krs, 2016 WL 7130941 (M.D. Fla. Mar. 9, 2016). Although the Eleventh Circuit rejected the trial court's principal holding that the student's eye injury did not qualify as a disability, the appellate court affirmed on the alternative ground that the "plaintiff's belated request for additional time to turn in his brief was [not] a reasonable request for accommodation." 720 Fed. App'x at 574.

C. Types of Disabilities Common in Law Schools

The ADA defines a disability to include physical and psychological conditions that substantially limit one or more major life activities.[35] Examples of major life activities include hearing, walking, speaking, working, and studying, among many others.[36] Common physical disabilities that LRW professors may encounter in their classes include a student's inability to walk or perform physical functions, mobility problems, deafness or hearing loss, blindness or visual impairments, and chronic diseases.

Psychological conditions that may be considered disabilities include cognitive disabilities such as autism, attention deficit disorder, dyslexia, and various learning disabilities. Learning disabilities involve difficulty in one or more, but not uniformly in all, basic psychological processes: input (auditory and visual perception); integration (sequencing, abstraction, and organization); memory (working, short-term, and long-term memory); output (expressive language); and fine or gross motor skills.

Learning disabilities vary from individual to individual and may present in a variety of ways. Learning disabilities may manifest as difficulties with any of the following: processing information by visual and auditory means, which may impact a student's ability to read, spell, write, and understand or use language; prioritizing,

[35] 42 U.S.C. § 12102(1)(A). An individual also has a "disability" if the person has "(B) a record of such [a physical or mental] impairment" or "(C) [is] regarded as having such an impairment." *Id.* § 12102(1)(B), (C). The "regarded as having" term is more specifically defined in § 12102(3).

[36] Under the ADA, the statutory term "person with a disability" generally means any person who (1) has a physical or psychological condition that substantially limits one or more life activities (including walking, seeing, hearing, speaking, breathing, learning, and working); (2) has a record of such impairment; or (3) is regarded as having such an impairment. 42 U.S.C. § 12102(1).

organizing, doing mathematics, and following instructions; storing or retrieving information from short- or long-term memory; using spoken language; or struggling with handwriting.

The legal definition of "disability" also includes cognitive disabilities, meaning deficits or difficulties with memory; problem-solving; attention; reading, linguistic, and verbal comprehension; math comprehension; or visual comprehension. Other psychological conditions that may constitute a disability include anxiety disorders, depression, mania, manic-depression, schizophrenia, recovery from alcoholism or other substance abuse, or obsessive-compulsive disorders. Cognitive impairments and psychological conditions may be especially challenging for students under the unusual stress of law school.

1. Temporary or Mitigated Disabilities

Treatable impairments of mental or physical faculties that may impede a student from functioning normally while under treatment are also classified as disabilities. While a normal pregnancy is not itself considered a disability under the ADA, pregnancy-related complications may qualify under certain circumstances.[37]

2. Past Accommodations in Other Education Programs

Although a law school is not bound by any accommodations provided to a disabled student in earlier years of education, a previous diagnosis and accommodations may be relevant to determining the specific type and form of educational accommodations offered to a law student. As law schools receive requests for exam modifications and determine the specific type of accommodations to provide

---

[37] *See* Darian v. Univ. of Mass. Bos., 980 F. Supp. 77, 87 (D. Mass. 1997).

each student, the amount, form, and extent of exam modifications the student was provided in high school or undergraduate studies might serve as a baseline for initial discussions with disability services offices. The success of past accommodations, changes in the nature and extent of the student's disability, and the format of previous exams are all relevant factors when considering a request for exam modification.

The school-administered evaluation of a student's need for accommodations may be deficient if the law school fails to fully appraise a particular student's longstanding disability history. Prior to ruling on the proposed accommodation, the law school should consider past educational accommodations, any changes in the student's disability, and other related factors. In all cases, whether the school requests an independent evaluation or administers its own, a student with disabilities should be permitted to offer the student's own expert evaluations for the law school to consider in deciding whether to offer an academic accommodation.

D. Alignment with Bar Exam Accommodations

Law schools should align accommodations for disabilities with those offered to bar applicants in the various states.[38] State boards

---

[38] Just because an applicant secures accommodations from bar examiners in one state does not necessarily obligate bar examiners in another state to provide the same or similar accommodations. *See, e.g.,* Ware v. Wyoming Bd. of Law Exam'rs, 973 F. Supp. 1339, 1357 (D. Wyo. 1997) ("[T]he fact that a person has been granted a particular accommodation in the past [on another state's bar exam] does not mean that such accommodations are presumably reasonable. Each testing agency has an independent duty under the ADA to determine reasonableness on a case-by-case basis."), *aff'd,* 161 F.3d 19 (10th Cir. 1998) (tbl.); Cox v. Alabama State Bar, 330 F. Supp. 2d 1265, 1268 (M.D. Ala. 2004) ("Although information regarding past accommodations may be probative in determining whether a current request constitutes a reasonable accommodation, such accommodations are

of bar examiners must provide reasonable accommodations to avoid discriminating against bar applicants with disabilities who are otherwise qualified to sit for the bar examination.[39] Required accommodations may include "modifications in policies, practices, or procedures when the modifications are necessary to avoid discrimination on the basis of disability" and not unduly burdensome on the school.[40] Some examples include additional bathroom breaks, separate rooms for exams, books in Braille, and note takers in class. Reasonable modifications may also include increasing the time permitted for completing an assignment or examination.[41]

---

not per se reasonable in every new testing situation."); *In re* Henry, 2013 S.D. 93, ¶ 16, 841 N.W.2d 471, 475–76 (2013) ("[W]e do not take the decision to admit Henry to the bar in Iowa [after undergoing a psychological evaluation] as definitive in South Dakota"); *cf. In re* Durbano, 2019 UT 34, ¶ 37, 449 P.3d 24, 30 (2019) (denying a request to waive Utah's bar exam requirement based in part on the disabled applicant's 16-year membership in another state's bar).

[39] *See* 42 U.S.C. § 12189 ("Any person that offers examinations or courses related to applications, licensing, certification, or credentialing for secondary or postsecondary education, professional, or trade purposes shall offer such examinations or courses in a place and manner accessible to persons with disabilities or offer alternative accessible arrangements for such individuals."); 28 C.F.R. § 36.309(a) (same); *see, e.g.,* Enyart v. National Conference of Bar Exam'rs, 823 F. Supp. 2d 995, 999 (N.D. Cal. 2011) (requiring accommodations requested by legally blind applicant); Jones v. National Conference of Bar Exam'rs, 801 F. Supp. 2d 270, 284–85 (D. Vt. 2011) ("Defendant must grant accommodations to Plaintiff that 'best ensure' that her knowledge of the law governing a lawyer's ethical and professional obligations is tested by the MPRE rather than the extent to which Plaintiff is able to overcome her uncontested [visual and learning] disabilities . . . .").

[40] 28 C.F.R. § 35.130(b)(7)(i).

[41] 28 C.F.R. § 36.309(b)(2) ("Required modifications to an examination may include changes in the length of time permitted for completion of the examination and adaptation of the manner in which the examination is given.").

E. Disability Issues in the LRW Classroom

In the context of an LRW course, professors may be asked to provide a variety of specific accommodations. In most cases, exam-taking accommodations, such as a request for additional time, do not apply to written assignments in LRW courses. If the course requires a final exam or quizzes, however, additional time may be necessary. Regardless, other reasonable accommodations may be suitable under certain circumstances in the LRW class.[42] In determining whether an accommodation is reasonable, disability offices may need to determine the skills necessary to practice law. LRW professors are well-suited to help make this determination as well as to prevent over-accommodating students, which may put them at a disadvantage in law practice where similar accommodations may not be possible.

Because of potential problems with perceived unfairness, professors and students should keep any accommodations confidential. However, it may be more readily apparent in an LRW classroom that a student is receiving an accommodation because of the large number of written assignments in the course.[43]

One difference from other law courses is that LRW courses are usually designed with a series of incremental assignments, with later assignments building on earlier ones. Students with disabilities may be at a disadvantage if accommodations allowing additional time for completing assignments cause the student to lose step with the rest of the class.

---

[42] *See generally* Suzanne Rowe, *Reasonable Accommodations for Unreasonable Requests: The Americans with Disabilities Act in Law School Writing Courses*, 12 LEGAL WRITING 3, 37 (2006), a helpful and comprehensive source of information on how to accommodate students in the LRW classroom. Many of the recommendations outlined in this chapter are taken from Professor Rowe's article.

[43] *Cf.* Rowe, *supra* note 42, at 36-37 & n.225 (noting that fairness should be considered from the perspective of all students, with or without disabilities).

Instead, the LRW professor might consider giving a student a moderate accommodation that helps the student without giving her a substantial advantage compared to other students in the course. For example, the instructions and materials for a major writing assignment might be provided to the student a day or two in advance of the date they are available to other students.[44]

A number of other accommodations may be necessary in the LRW class because of the experiential nature of the course.

1. Proofreading Assistance

Essential to excellent legal writing are good proofreading skills—"the more mechanical aspects of a written document, [including] spelling, grammar, and format."[45] Some professors do not allow students to receive proofreading help from anyone except the LRW professor because proofreading is an essential aspect of good legal writing. This course rule may need to be relaxed if accommodations are warranted for a particular student.

All students, regardless of disability, should use grammar check and spell check to assist with editing writing assignments. Students may also want to use other electronic tools that can be helpful when proofreading in law practice. For example, students can use the "find" feature to locate common errors they might otherwise miss during regular proofreading.[46] Professors may also want to encourage students to change the typeface size, which will change the way they read their work and will help them identify mistakes or typos.

---

[44] *Id.*

[45] *Id.* at 46.

[46] *Id.* at 46-47. Professor Rowe uses the example of searching for the misspelling of the word "statute," which is often spelled "statue" by students. *Id.*

Reasonable accommodations for proofreading might include the sort of routine tasks a legal secretary would perform in a law practice setting. As Professor Suzanne Rowe explains,

> [a]n assistant could proofread the written assignment for just the types of problems created by the student's learning disability. Depending on the severity of the disability, the assistant could simply mark the line on which an error appeared, or mark the error itself, without providing the correction. Before the assistant is allowed to review the student's assignment, the assistant should meet with the LRW professor or disability coordinator to ensure that the assistant is providing no more help than is warranted. A few extra days may be needed for the assistant to review the work and the student to make corrections. The student may need to agree not to make substantive changes past the due date for the legal writing assignment.[47]

2. *Writing Assignment Deadlines*

Students with learning disabilities often request more time to complete writing assignments. Depending on the nature of the disability, additional time may be warranted if the nature of the disability realistically precludes a student from working at the same pace as classmates without disabilities. Extended time may be particularly appropriate for students who have difficulties with processing language in both reading and writing. Working closely with the disability office, the professor may find it reasonable to provide students with these kinds of disabilities more time to complete writing assignments. For a student who has a learning disability, a professor might consider giving the student an extra day to allow more time for proofreading.

---

[47] *Id.*

Any substantial extensions in deadlines for writing assignments, however, may have a negative effect on both students and the professor.[48]

> In addition to the pedagogical sacrifice made when a student does not follow the course progression, allowing extra time for assignments may place an extra burden on the LRW teacher, who must comment on and return papers quickly, and in some instances hold an individual conference with each student.[49]

Further, providing additional time for assignments may cause other concerns, as Professor Rowe explains.

> Unlimited time to complete a writing assignment would never be a reasonable accommodation. That accommodation would never be available in law practice and would place undue administrative burdens on the school. Moreover, if a student does not learn of her disability until after the assignment is submitted (or after the deadline passed), the teacher should not have to make retroactive accommodations.[50]

---

[48] *See, e.g.*, Cooney v. Barry Sch. of Law, 720 Fed. App'x 571, 573-74 (11th Cir.), *cert. denied*, 139 S. Ct. 174 (2018), *rev'g in part and aff'g in part* No. 6:14-cv-106-Orl-22krs, 2016 WL 7130941 (M.D. Fla. Mar. 9, 2016) (rejecting argument that a law school violated the ADA because a legal writing professor turned down a student's request to extend the deadline for an appellate brief assignment).

[49] Rowe, *supra* note 42, at 38-39 & n.235 ("The initial Sourcebook suggests line-by-line comments aimed at teaching students 'how to make writing and analytical decisions.' The Sourcebook also notes that '[m]uch of the best learning happens in individual conferences.'").

[50] *Id.* at 40-41 (discussing and citing M. Kay Runyan & Joseph Smith, *Identifying and Accommodating Learning Disabled Law Students*, 41 J. LEGAL EDUC. 317 (1991) (discussing the possible need for students to complete law school in more than three years)); Zukle v. Regents of the Univ. of Cal., 166 F.3d 1041, 1049 (9th Cir. 1999) (deferring to medical school's decision regarding interrupted course of study for learning-disabled student).

3. *Class Participation*

Some students are overwhelmed with anxiety by the prospect of being called on in class. If a student's learning disability limits the ability to participate or speak in class, accommodations may be necessary.[51] The accommodation might include limiting the timing or duration of the student's participation, not requiring the student to read aloud, or using small group exercises in place of large class discussions.

Because many law students feel anxiety at some point in law school, a bona fide learning disability needs to be distinguished from general anxiety or a diagnosed anxiety disability. A student with a learning disability should not be excused from participation simply because she shares an anxiety common to all law students. It is also important to consider that, unlike other law courses, the LRW classroom may be a better setting for students with anxiety disabilities because of the smaller class size and the multiple opportunities to meet individually with the professor outside class.

4. *Legal Research*

Students with either physical or mental disabilities may need accommodations to do legal research, including both print and online research. Legal research instruction may also require that students do library exercises, complete research journals or logs, develop lists of primary and secondary authority, and summarize or brief key cases. Because of either a physical disability or a learning disability, students may need accommodations for any of these assignments and also at various stages of conducting independent research on a major assignment.[52]

---

[51] *See generally* Heidi K. Brown, *The "Silent but Gifted" Law Student: Transforming Anxious Public Speakers into Well-Rounded Advocates*, 18 LEGAL WRITING 291 (2012).

[52] Rowe, *supra* note 42, at 42-44.

Conducting legal research is a required component of most first-year LRW courses, and legal research cannot be separated from legal analysis.[53] Therefore, professors should avoid any accommodation that prevents a student from learning how to analyze the law. For example, they should not allow librarians or student assistants to conduct the research for students with learning disabilities. Locating cases in a digest and using West headnotes are more than mechanical tasks; both require deciding, from among a variety of topics and key numbers, which ones are most likely to lead to the most helpful cases. Legal research also often requires a student to skim multiple case summaries in a digest or online research tool.

All of these tasks require and teach essential legal analysis skills.

> Reading and analyzing authorities is the most critical part of legal research. No student should be able to have classmates, research assistants, librarians, or professors read and brief authorities for them, as this would fundamentally alter the course. To accommodate for learning disabilities in reading, a student may need more time, but the student cannot skip this critical step in legal research.[54]

When accommodating a student in developing research logs or bibliography tables, the nature of the accommodation provided depends on whether the disability makes it difficult for the student to do an administrative task or whether it goes to the heart of legal analysis. When a research assignment is primarily bibliographic as opposed to analytical, the LRW professor should consider ways to accommodate a disability that will also help the student eventually practice law. For example, students could dictate their research into

---

[53] *See supra* Chapter II.

[54] Rowe, *supra* note 42, at 43.

a recording app on their phone or other device. Some of the apps may even transcribe the recording for the student. These accommodations are available to practicing lawyers and do not diminish the comprehensive legal analysis required for an assignment, so they are likely appropriate accommodations.

As a general rule, students should be exposed to various methods of conducting legal research even if their disabilities might restrict them to certain types of research in practice. If an accommodation goes to the heart of legal analysis, the professor should look for other accommodations that require the student to perform legal analysis. Some tools that may be helpful include programs that read printed or online materials aloud. Whether an administrative assistant could permissibly help a practicing lawyer with an accommodation is generally a good guide to determine if an accommodation touches upon legal analysis or is purely administrative.

F. Particular Physical Disabilities in the LRW Classroom

1. *Visual Disabilities*

To succeed in law school, students who are blind or visually impaired have particularized needs for a wide variety of academic accommodations. The accommodations a specific student finds most effective depend on the student's degree of remaining vision, if any, and on the learning methods that work best for that student.

Specialized software, devices, and other forms of technology have removed many of the traditional barriers once faced by students with visual impairments in law school. The technology is constantly changing and improving, but some effective tools currently available to students in an LRW classroom include screen readers that verbalize online text, screen magnifiers, adaptive keyboards, and optical character recognition products that read aloud the text of a book.

Many textbooks may be available in Braille, and some law schools might be willing to pay for books to be converted to Braille. Converting text to Braille for most of the material used in an LRW classroom may not be a viable option, however, because of the large amount of material. For these materials, technology options should be explored.

Students with visual disabilities should work closely with Lexis and Westlaw representatives to design techniques to use screen readers effectively and efficiently. Typical Lexis and Westlaw seminars are designed from a visual perspective. Students with visual disabilities who use screen readers can access the web, but the process is different from that used by students who do not have visual disabilities. For that reason, it is a good idea to provide blind and low-vision students with their Lexis and Westlaw passwords well before instruction begins.

a. Feedback on Written Assignments

Students with visual disabilities have difficulty accessing handwritten feedback on briefs and memoranda. Verbal or electronic feedback is most helpful, and many easy-to-use technological tools are available to help the professor and student embed typed or recorded oral comments into a document. Working with students in individual conferences may also be helpful because it allows the student to ask questions about the professor's feedback.

b. Citation

Citation work presents unique access challenges for students with visual disabilities, especially because of the detail and precision required for legal citation. Students with visual impairments should have access to an electronic copy of the *Bluebook*, the *ALWD Citation Guide*, or similar citation manual. Institutions should consider subsidizing the purchase of online citation manual subscriptions for students needing accommodations. Again, software products that read documents could prove useful to students with visual disabilities when creating or reading citations.

c. Exams

Students with visual disabilities will likely be given similar accommodations for all law school exams. LRW exams might differ from other exams by including citation and legal research, so students may need additional accommodations similar to the ones they receive for other LRW assignments. Because students with visual disabilities may require more time to navigate textbooks and access exam questions, extended time is likely a reasonable accommodation. Many students with visual disabilities must prepare their exams electronically, but some exam software may not be compatible with access technology. These students may need to prepare the exam with a traditional word processor rather than exam software.

If a student will use a reader application or software program for an exam, the law school should enable the student to practice for the final by taking an old exam using the reader or program. For students with some vision, lighting can be an important consideration during exams. The student should have the opportunity to inspect the location of each exam in advance.

2. *Deafness or Hearing Impairments*

Listening is an important skill for all law students. As with visual impairments, technology is helping hearing-impaired and deaf students overcome barriers to learning. A variety of auxiliary aids and services are suitable accommodations under the ADA for a student who is deaf or hard of hearing. Some typical accommodations include on-site or video interpreter services, note takers, computer-aided transcription services, closed captions, amplifiers, technology that transcribes the spoken word, technology that operates with hearing aids, and any other tools that allow students to participate in class or complete their work. If technology is not a viable option, law schools should provide sign language interpreters in class or during the student's individual conferences with LRW professors.

3. Functional Disabilities

Faculty can make simple adjustments as needed to their teaching styles to address a wide range of functional disabilities. Many LRW faculty already use a number of these approaches. For example, an LRW professor might provide students with written learning objectives for each class, outline key points throughout and at the end of class, provide several examples to illustrate points made in class, select textbooks that organize the material easily for the students, and provide tools to help students better organize their material.

G. Conclusion

When alerted to students with disabilities in the classroom, the LRW professor should work closely with the law school or greater campus disability office, or both, to facilitate accommodations for students with disability needs. At the same time, the professor should avoid accommodations that place an undue burden on the course and the professor's teaching and grading obligations, and be wary of over-accommodating in ways that ill-prepare students for the practice of law.

IX. LEGAL WRITING SPECIALISTS AND WRITING CENTERS

Legal writing specialists (LWSs) have been an essential fixture at law schools for decades.[1] Currently, at least 58 law schools employ LWSs in either a full-time or part-time capacity, with a total of 79 LWSs among them.[2] Law schools hire LWSs to provide additional writing support beyond what students receive in their law school courses. LWSs meet with students, typically in person in one-on-one sessions in which the LWS and the student discuss the student's writing needs. These sessions engage students in ways that a classroom or other teaching setting cannot.[3] LWSs introduce writing strategies, allow time for students to practice those strategies, and give students immediate feedback. During advising sessions,

---

[1]*See* Jessie Grearson & Anne Enquist, *A History of Writing Advisors at Law Schools: Looking at Our Past, Looking at Our Future*, 5 LEGAL WRITING 55, 62-65 (1999). The 1997 survey conducted by the authors, which is the subject of their article, identified 37 LWSs employed by law schools across the country.

[2]Ass'n of Legal Writing Dirs. & Legal Writing Inst., *Report of the 2017-2018 Institutional Survey* 99-203, Questions 18.3 & 18.4 (2019), https://www.lwionline.org/sites/default/files/Final%20ALWD%20LWI%202017-18%20Institutional%20Survey%20Report.pdf [hereinafter *2017-2018 ALWD/LWI Survey*]. Nearly all current LWSs are members of the Association of Legal Writing Specialists (ALWS), which sponsors a listserv and provides authors for the column titled *From the Writing Specialist* published in *The Second Draft.* For information about membership, writing specialists, or writing centers, please contact Lurene Contento at lurene.contento@gmail.com or any ALWS member. For information about *The Second Draft*, see https://www.lwionline.org/publications/second-draft (last visited Dec. 18, 2019).

[3]Muriel Harris, *Talking in the Middle: Why Writers Need Writing Tutors*, 57 COLLEGE ENGLISH 27, 31-36 (1995). Muriel Harris, Professor Emeritus of English at Purdue University, started Purdue's iconic Writing Lab in the 1970s. Her article discusses the unique advantages of a tutoring/advising relationship. While the article focuses on tutors at the university level, the same benefits apply when law students consult with professional LWSs.

LWSs encourage students to think about their writing and to discover answers on their own. LWSs provide students with tools to become self-aware and self-sufficient writers, as well as critical self-editors.

LWSs understand the process of writing and excel at focusing on the elements common to all good writing, such as logically developing ideas, clearly expressing those ideas, and integrating and synthesizing complex resources.[4] LWSs also understand the rules of legal discourse and the unique conventions of legal writing. Most importantly, LWSs excel at communicating how students can incorporate these elements, rules, and conventions into their own written work.

Beyond meeting with students, LWSs have an array of roles and responsibilities both inside and outside their home institutions. And LWSs come from a variety of educational backgrounds and experiences. A law school wishing to add writing support for its students has many choices and must carefully consider the school's reasons for providing additional writing support and the resources currently available to do so.

While LWSs have been around for decades, the need for their services is likely to grow. Many entering law students have had insufficient opportunities to think or write critically.[5] And because legal writing differs in significant ways from other genres of writing, even students with some writing experience can find the transition to legal writing difficult. Currently, too, law schools are enrolling more

---

[4] ERIC EASTON ET AL., ABA COMMC'NS SKILLS COMM., SOURCEBOOK ON LEGAL WRITING PROGRAMS 71-72 (2d ed. 2006) [hereinafter SOURCEBOOK 2d ed.].

[5] *See* Aida M. Alaka, *The Grammar Wars Come to Law School*, 59 J. LEGAL EDUC. 343, 344 (2010) (suggesting that trends in K-12 education since the 1980s have contributed to poor writing skills that have become "endemic" in America); *see also* RICHARD ARUM & JOSIPA ROKSA, ACADEMICALLY ADRIFT: LIMITED LEARNING ON COLLEGE CAMPUSES (2011) (finding, based on data-driven analysis, that college students have insufficient educational opportunities to improve writing and critical thinking skills).

international students, who bring another unique set of writing challenges if English is not their first language.[6] For these reasons, more law schools will likely hire LWSs in the future.

A. Role of the Legal Writing Specialist

A legal writing specialist's primary role is to help students become better legal writers—mainly through one-on-one advising sessions and group workshops. LWSs work with all types of students on various genres of writing and on many different writing-related issues. But LWSs also provide students with other services, work with LRW directors and faculty, and play an expanding number of roles within their home institutions and in the wider legal writing community.

The LWS's role is frequently misunderstood at institutions that do not have an LWS and by faculty who do not work closely with the LWS. Faculty and administrators may think that LWSs work only with first-year students and address only remedial writing issues like grammar and punctuation. While LWSs do address grammar and punctuation, they also address myriad other issues that students encounter throughout the writing process. Depending on the student and the project, the LWS may discuss pre-writing techniques, organizational paradigms, logical transitions, effective use of persuasion, proper citation, and editing techniques, among many other topics.

Additionally, LWSs work with students at all levels of writing proficiency engaged in many genres of writing. Legal writing specialists work closely with first-year students, but they also serve other cohorts including upper-level J.D. students, LL.M. or other Master's degree students, and international students at all levels. LWSs can help students with interoffice memoranda, trial and appellate briefs, email memos, seminar or journal articles, writing for clinics or externships, cover letters, resumes, writing samples, and more.

---

[6] *See generally supra* Chapter VII.

1. One-on-One Student Conferences

Typically, an LWS's main responsibility is holding one-on-one conferences with students. During these conferences, which are generally held in person, the student and LWS engage in a dialogue about the student's writing. The student receives personalized advice on writing-related issues that either the LWS, the student, or the student's professors have identified. A typical conference may last from a few minutes to an hour or more, depending on both participants' schedules and the student's needs. An advising session can cover a range of legal writing issues or may focus on a single issue in a specific writing project. Often, the LWS will have read the student's work before the meeting and will have targeted certain issues to discuss. But in other instances, the issues are determined through the dialogue that occurs during the advising session.

Sessions with an LWS are highly collaborative. Through dialogue between the LWS and the student, the LWS can better assess the student's needs and offer writing advice tailored specifically to that student. The in-person nature of the session allows the LWS to ensure that a student understands the advice and, if necessary, adjust delivery of the advice accordingly. The student also has an immediate opportunity to practice new strategies that the LWS may introduce and to receive immediate feedback. Perhaps most importantly, the LWS encourages students to ask questions, to think about their writing and their writing process, and to develop their own solutions with the LWS's help.

A session with an LWS is also a safe space for students to express concerns about their writing. Because LWSs do not grade or judge students' work, students feel safe disclosing their writing weaknesses or even their fears about writing—topics that students may not feel comfortable addressing with their professors. The LWS has the opportunity not only to help guide the student's writing, but also to encourage and reassure the student. Meeting with an LWS can help students feel more comfortable when writing and more confident as writers.[7]

The work done by an LWS varies by institution.[8] At many institutions, working with the LWS is voluntary. Students self-select to work with the LWS and may choose to meet only once or routinely over the course of a semester or longer. At other institutions, certain students may be required to work with the writing specialist while others may need a professor's referral to do so. Some institutions may also restrict the type of work that students can bring to an LWS. While LWSs frequently work with students on written coursework, some institutions allow an LWS to review a draft only after the student has submitted it for a grade; at other law schools, the LWS may review drafts before they are submitted.[9] Students generally benefit more when the LWS reviews a working draft because they receive help when they need it, and because students are generally more invested in improving a work in progress than a completed assignment already submitted for a grade.

Phone or Skype-type sessions and online advising are also possibilities, but many of the benefits of a face-to-face dialogue are lost with those alternatives.[10] However, as video conferencing platforms continue to improve and to more closely approximate live, in-person sessions, the drawbacks will be fewer. Online advising with

---

[7] *See* Harris, *supra* note 3, at 35-37 (finding that students frequently report feelings of confidence after an advising session).

[8] *See 2017-2018 ALWD/LWI Survey*, *supra* note 2, at 205-06, Questions 18.6 & 18.7.

[9] *See id.* at 206, Question 18.7 (reporting that well over 50 percent of responding schools allow the LWS to review drafts before students submit them for a grade).

[10] *See* Lurene Contento, *Why Online Resources Won't Replace Writing Specialists – At Least Anytime Soon!*, 29 SECOND DRAFT 23 (Spring 2016).

no video component has an additional disadvantage. Students may wrongly assume that they are simply submitting a draft for review, and that the LWS will act as a proofreader or editor rather than as a writing advisor and counselor.

2. *Student Workshops and Other Institutional and Academic Activities*

LWSs are frequently responsible for developing and presenting group workshops for students.[11] Typical topics for first-year workshops include using persuasive techniques, avoiding plagiarism, organizing legal memoranda, or using proper citation form. LWSs can also develop workshops to address the specific needs of international students, as well as workshops for upper-level students on topics such as writing moot court briefs or law review articles, or writing for externship or clinical positions. At some institutions, the LWS may offer workshops focusing on skills other than legal writing such as networking, negotiation, or professionalism.[12]

Other student-focused responsibilities might include developing and administering diagnostic writing assessments, working with students on reading strategies, creating hard copy or digital resources for students, and working with career services or academic support departments to develop materials and programming.[13] LWSs can also serve as advisors for student-edited journals, supervise students' scholarly writing, and supervise independent study projects.

Despite the varied ways that they work with students, LWSs do not edit, proofread, or cite-check students' work. LWSs also

---

[11] *2017-2018 ALWD/LWI Survey*, *supra* note 2, at 206, Question 18.7.

[12] Chantal Morton, *Legal Writing Specialists and Our Contribution to Experiential Learning Opportunities*, 29 SECOND DRAFT 41 (Fall 2016).

[13] *See 2017-2018 ALWD/LWI Survey*, *supra* note 2, at 205-06, Questions 18.6 & 18.7. LWSs engage in many other activities in addition to those listed in the *Survey*.

generally do not advise students on substantive issues of law. The role of the LWS is to reinforce and support what students are learning in their courses and to offer advice and guidance on specific writing projects, specific writing concerns, or legal writing generally.

a. Collaboration with LRW Directors and Faculty

Collaboration between an LWS and the school's LRW program is essential. This collaboration helps the LWS understand both programmatic goals and the preferences of individual faculty members who teach in the program. The more the LWS understands these goals and preferences, the better the LWS can support them, and the more seamless and consistent student advising becomes. Any concern that an LWS will advise a student to write in a way that is contrary to a professor's expectations is largely alleviated when the LWS works closely with the LRW program. LWSs should be invited to attend departmental meetings and should be encouraged to work with individual faculty members to learn their preferences and expectations.

LWSs can also collaborate with faculty members to help design materials for LRW courses. Because LWSs work so closely with students, and because many LWSs have expertise in education or teaching methodologies, LWSs are in a unique position to notice common problems in students' writing and to suggest solutions for those problems.

LWSs are also an excellent resource to help develop training programs for adjunct faculty or full-time faculty new to LRW. Because the core of an LWS's job is conferencing with students, LWSs can be particularly helpful in training others on conferencing and critiquing methods. A long-term LWS can also provide institutional continuity in LRW programs staffed mainly with adjuncts or faculty on short-term contracts.[14]

---

[14] SOURCEBOOK 2d ed., *supra* note 4, at 121.

b. Other Responsibilities Within the Home Institution

Many LWSs engage in far more activities than meeting with students and collaborating with or training faculty. They can act as directors of writing centers or LRW programs; collaborate with academic support programs; serve on faculty committees; share expertise with administrators; and collaborate with career services, clinics, and externship programs.[15] LWSs also teach first-year LRW courses, upper-level LRW courses, and courses for international or ESL students.[16] An LWS with faculty status may also teach courses outside the LRW program.[17]

c. External Roles

Many LWSs engage in service outside their home institutions, for example, as board or committee members for national organizations, as editors for legal writing publications, or as conference organizers.[18] LWSs also present frequently at conferences both in the U.S. and abroad, and they offer legal writing training for practitioners both locally and internationally.[19] And while many LWSs do not have publication requirements, some publish widely on a range

---

[15] *See* Anne Enquist, *The Role of Writing Specialists in the First 25 Years of the Legal Writing Institute*, 24 SECOND DRAFT 18 (Spring 2010); Contento, *supra* note 10, at 23-24; *2017-2018 ALWD/LWI Survey*, *supra* note 2, at 205-06, Questions 18.6 & 18.7.

[16] Enquist, *supra* note 15, at 19; Contento, *supra* note 10, at 24; *2017-2018 ALWD/LWI Survey, supra* note 2, at 206, Question 18.7.

[17] For example, LWSs with faculty status have taught law practice management at Touro Law Center, and client counseling and negotiation at The John Marshall Law School.

[18] Contento, *supra* note 10, at 23-24; Enquist, *supra* note 15, at 18.

[19] Lurene Contento, *Way Beyond Grammar: What Today's Legal Writing Specialist Can Do for You*, SCRIVENER, Summer 2015, at 1-2*; see also* Contento, *supra* note 10, at 23-24; Enquist, *supra* note 15, at 18.

of topics.[20] Because of their commitment to the wider legal community, LWSs have received numerous awards including the Burton Award (recognizing outstanding contributions to legal writing education), the AALS Section on Legal Writing, Research, and Reasoning (LWRR) Award (recognizing significant lifetime contributions to the LRW discipline), and the Deborah Hecht Memorial Writing Award (created specifically to honor articles authored by LWSs).[21]

B. Writing Support Models

Law schools have several models from which to choose when offering their students additional writing support, including university-based writing centers or university professors, law school writing centers staffed with student tutors, and in-house writing centers staffed by professional LWSs.

1. University-Based Writing Support for Affiliated Law Schools

Law schools that are affiliated with a university can provide law students with writing support at the university level. In 2018, 110 out of 182 responding law schools reported that they allow their students to use an affiliated university-based writing center or specialist.[22] Because this model relies on services that already exist at the

---

[20] *See* Grearson & Enquist, *supra* note 1, at 86-92 (Appendix B). Appendix B lists an impressive number of LWS works published before 1999. The number of LWSs and the quantity of their publications have both grown considerably since that time. A list of ALWS member publications current through June 2018 is on file with the author, Lurene Contento.

[21] For example, Burton Award recipients include Anne Enquist; recipients of the AALS LWRR Section Award include Anne Enquist, Elizabeth Fajans, Terri LeClercq, and Mary Barnard Ray; and recipients of the Hecht Award include Ann Nowak, Stephanie Juliano, Jeremy Francis, and Lurene Contento.

[22] *2017-2018 ALWD/LWI Survey*, *supra* note 2, at 207, Question 18.9.

university, it is the least costly model, but it may also be the least effective.[23]

University-based writing centers are generally staffed by upper-level or graduate student tutors who are supervised by a full-time director.[24] Some universities require tutors to complete a training course before meeting with students.[25] Peer tutors who are drawn from such graduate programs as English, education, or linguistics may already have some experience teaching or conferencing with students, but other peer tutors may have little previous experience or training. Additionally, university-based writing centers typically serve the needs of students across many disciplines, so writing advice is often general in nature rather than tailored to a specific discipline like law and legal writing.[26]

Because peer tutors regularly rotate in and out of university-based writing centers and must schedule tutoring sessions around their studies, students seeking writing help may find it difficult to meet regularly with the same tutor or to get consistent advice from different tutors.[27] Additionally, some university writing centers are geographically distant from the law school, making it less likely that law students will use their services. Further, law students may perceive that working with peer tutors in an undergraduate writing center is "beneath them."[28] Perhaps because of these drawbacks, LRW faculty at a majority of the responding law schools report that

---

[23] SOURCEBOOK 2d ed., *supra* note 4, at 122.

[24] Kristen E. Murray, *Peer Tutoring and the Law School Writing Center: Theory and Practice*, 17 LEGAL WRITING 161, 166-67 (2011).

[25] The University of Illinois at Chicago and Purdue University are just two universities with required tutor-training courses.

[26] *See* SOURCEBOOK 2d ed., *supra* note 4, at 122.

[27] *Id.*

[28] *Id.*

they rarely or never recommend that law students use an affiliated university-based writing center.[29]

In the alternative, a university-affiliated law school might consider seeking a joint appointment or borrowing faculty from, for example, the university's English or linguistics departments.[30] This model is slightly more expensive than referring law students to a university writing center, but it can offer students more continuity and may give the faculty member time to develop expertise in legal analysis.[31] However, the joint faculty member's time and intellectual focus would necessarily be divided between the university and the law school, and faculty members whose promotion and advancement are considered at the university level may feel compelled to devote more effort to university students.[32]

2. *Law School Writing Centers Staffed by Student Tutors*

A law school can also provide its own in-house writing center staffed by student tutors. Under this model, tutors are generally upper-level law students who are trained by a faculty member, a staff member, a dedicated writing center director, or by other students under the supervision of a staff or faculty member.[33] Costs of this model depend on who is doing the training; how many peer tutors are needed to meet students' needs; and whether the tutors are paid, unpaid, or earn credit for working in the writing center. To be effective, law student tutors must be rigorously trained and

---

[29] *See 2017-2018 ALWD/LWI Survey*, *supra* note 2, at 207, Question 18.10 (reporting that 60 percent of 110 responding law schools' LRW faculty rarely or never refer students to university-based writing centers).

[30] SOURCEBOOK 2d ed., *supra* note 4, at 122.

[31] *Id.*

[32] *Id.*

[33] *See* Murray, *supra* note 24, at 186-88.

supervised. The substantial workload associated with properly training and supervising student tutors is also a recurring one as students graduate and must be replaced.[34] In 2015, 24 law schools reported having writing centers staffed by student tutors.[35]

Like tutors at university-based writing centers, law student tutors may have little or no experience teaching writing or conferencing with students. Most probably have less experience in those areas than university-based tutors who come from graduate programs such as education or linguistics, or tutors who have taken a pre-tutoring training course. However, upper-level law students have gained some experience with legal writing through their earlier LRW coursework, so they can tailor their advice more specifically to legal analysis.

Upper-level law students, however, are not experts in legal analysis, and their writing advice may be heavily influenced by their earlier LRW courses. Their LRW experience as students can be a benefit if, like a TA, a student tutor works solely with students who are currently taking LRW from the tutor's former professor. But tutors may provide incorrect or misleading advice if they wrongly ascribe one LRW professor's preferences or expectations to legal writing generally.[36]

Under this model, continuity and consistency can also be constrained by the structure and rigors of law studies. Upper-level students may work in the writing center for only a semester or two, leaving them little time to develop expertise and offering little continuity to students seeking help. And the rigors of law studies may

---

[34] *See id.*

[35] Ass'n of Legal Writing Dirs. & Legal Writing Inst., *Report of the 2015 Survey* 23, Question 31(a) (2016) [hereinafter *2015 ALWD/LWI Survey*], https://www.alwd.org/images/resources/2015%20Survey%20Report%20(AY%202014-2015).pdf. More recent surveys do not provide statistics for student tutors working in law school writing centers.

[36] *See* SOURCEBOOK 2d ed., *supra* note 4, at 124.

limit student tutors' available time for training or for offering sufficient tutoring sessions to meet student needs. As with a university-based writing center, law students in need of writing help may find it difficult to work consistently with the same tutor or to receive consistent writing advice from different tutors.

Law students may also question the advice of student tutors who are only slightly ahead of them in their legal studies. Further, upper-level students writing seminar or journal articles may question the value of advice from student tutors who have not yet engaged in those kinds of writing themselves, and LL.M. students may not see the value in working with tutors who have not yet received a J.D. themselves. On the other hand, first-year law students may appreciate tutoring by students who recently faced similar challenges in their first-year law studies.[37]

3. *Law School Writing Centers Staffed with Professional Writing Specialists*

Staffing a law school writing center with one or more professional legal writing specialists avoids the drawbacks of the two models described above. LWSs provide students with consistent writing advice, delivered by experienced professionals who understand legal analysis and who are dedicated to working with law students. In 2017, 58 law schools employed a total of 79 full-time and part-time LWSs.[38] Costs of this model are discussed below.

LWSs understand the conventions of legal writing, so they can offer advice targeted to legal analysis as well as to general writing skills. Long-term LWSs have the opportunity to build on their experience and gain insights into an institution's writing program and

---

[37] *See* Murray, *supra* note 24, at 179-80 & n.98 (citing Ted Becker & Rachel Croskery-Roberts, *Avoiding Common Problems in Using Teaching Assistants: Hard Lessons Learned from Peer Teaching Theory and Experience*, 13 LEGAL WRITING 269, 277-78 (2007)).

[38] *2017-2018 ALWD/LWI Survey*, *supra* note 2, at 202-03, Question 18.5.

students. A long-term LWS also brings continuity to writing support for students at the school. And LWSs who work closely with LRW programs can offer more consistent advice than can student tutors.

Because LWSs work exclusively at the law school, no conflicts arise with commitments to other university departments. Nor do time conflicts exist for the LWS whose main function is working with law students. Full-time or multiple part-time LWSs can offer sufficient conferencing sessions to meet the needs of the institution.[39] Further, professional LWSs have the expertise to work with upper-level students as well as first-year students. LWSs can address the needs of the full student body and offer advice on a full range of writing projects.[40] Additionally, law students seeking writing help are much less likely to question the value of advice from a professional LWS, especially one who is part of the school's LRW community.

C. Considerations When Hiring a Legal Writing Specialist

Before hiring an LWS, administrators should carefully consider the institution's needs, goals, and resources. For example, if the goal is to offer numerous one-on-one conferences, the school should consider hiring more than one LWS. If the LWS is expected to teach LRW courses, then a full-time LWS with faculty status may be the most appropriate choice. Alternatively, the law school may wish to hire an LWS with a linguistics or TESOL (Teachers of English to Speakers of Other Languages) background, especially if the LWS will work primarily with students whose first language is not English.

---

[39] For example, four part-time LWSs at one law school held over 1700 one-on-one appointments during a single academic year. (Statistics are on file with the author, Lurene Contento.)

[40] *See 2017-2018 ALWD/LWI Survey*, *supra* note 2, at 205, Question 18.6.

1. Costs

Costs of this model depend on the number of LWSs, their backgrounds and experience, whether they are full time or part time, their status, and their expected roles and responsibilities. No current published data give a complete view of LWS salaries. In 2015, salaries for full-time LWSs reportedly ranged from $23,500 to $121,000, with an average full-time salary of $71,750.[41] The average part-time LWS salary was reported as $20,333.[42] However, these numbers can be misleading because LWSs' status and responsibilities vary so widely. For example, a full-time LWS may also hold a faculty position or have administrative duties, compensation for which may be rolled into the LWS salary reported by past survey respondents.

2. Education and Experience

Most LWSs hold at least one advanced degree. The majority hold a J.D. degree.[43] Many writing specialists who hold J.D. degrees have practiced law and are familiar with the traditions of legal discourse, the expectations of the legal discourse community, and the preferred rhetorical styles for different genres of legal writing. They are adept at advising students on questions of legal analysis as well as addressing general writing questions.

Other LWSs may hold MATs (Master of Arts in Teaching), M.F.A.s, or M.A.s or Ph.D.s in English, linguistics, education, or

---

[41] *2015 ALWD/LWI Survey*, *supra* note 35, at 20-21, Question 29. More recent surveys do not report LWS salary information.

[42] *Id.*

[43] *2017-2018 ALWD/LWI Survey*, *supra* note 2, at 204-05, Questions 18.5 & 18.6. This information has been consistent over the last several years. *See 2015 ALWD/LWI Survey*, *supra* note 35, at 20, Question 29; *see also* related information in the 2014, 2013, and 2012 surveys. (The survey questions were reorganized after the 2015 survey, resulting in some different question numbering.) For links to all surveys, see *Survey*, Ass'n of Legal Writing Dirs., https://www.alwd.org/resources/survey (last visited Dec. 18, 2019).

TESOL.[44] LWSs with these advanced degrees may have greater familiarity with teaching methodology and learning theory. They may also have prior teaching experience, such as teaching composition at the undergraduate level.[45] However, if an LWS holds a Ph.D. in English, the law school should consider the subject matter of the doctoral studies. Studies in composition or rhetoric may be more applicable to the work of an LWS than studies in, for example, medieval literature.[46]

To be most effective, an LWS may need to engage in cross-discipline training. An LWS with a J.D. may need training in learning theory or teaching methodologies. An LWS without a J.D. must learn the conventions of legal discourse and analysis to work most effectively with law students. But no matter the degree, a successful LWS must have excellent communication skills, must understand the metalanguage necessary to communicate *how* to write, and must be dedicated to working with students.

3. Status and Contract Issues

Administrators must also consider whether to employ the LWS full time or part time, and what status the LWS will hold. Hiring a full-time LWS benefits the institution in several ways. A full-time LWS can take on other institutional duties beyond meeting with students, such as teaching an LRW course or training other writing support staff. A full-time LWS who is fully immersed in the culture of the institution is more likely to seek additional professional

---

[44] *2017-2018 ALWD/LWI Survey*, *supra* note 2, at 204, Question 18.5; *see also* Grearson & Enquist, *supra* note 1, at 65-66 (listing degrees held by LWSs in the late 1990s).

[45] SOURCEBOOK 2d ed., *supra* note 4, at 119-20.

[46] Grearson & Enquist, *supra* note 1, at 76 n.28.

opportunities in the law school and beyond.[47] Outside opportunities such as presenting at conferences or publishing can help raise the visibility of the school's LRW program. Additionally, students may feel more comfortable meeting with an LWS who is an integral part of the law school community.[48] Full-time LWSs with multiple responsibilities also tend to enjoy greater job satisfaction and avoid the risk of burnout than part-time LWSs whose sole duties focus on conferencing with students.[49] But additional responsibilities also reduce the number of hours the LWS can devote to individual conferences with students.

The law school should also consider contract terms and status issues. Offering LWSs longer contracts benefits the institution by avoiding the "revolving door" turnover problem that results in loss of interdisciplinary knowledge and expertise.[50] And while part-time LWSs are generally staff positions, full-time LWSs can be hired as faculty with tenure-track positions or with short- or long-term renewable contracts. An institution offering better status, longer contracts, a variety of roles within the law school, and opportunities for professional development will attract better-qualified candidates.[51]

4. Alignment Within the Institution

The law school must also decide administrative and organizational questions when hiring an LWS. If the LWS's primary role is to support students enrolled in LRW courses, the LWS is generally best aligned with the LRW program or faculty to offer a better

---

[47] *See* Kim Baker, *Filling up the Candy Jar; Advantages of a Full-Time Writing Specialist*, 19 SECOND DRAFT 13 (Dec. 2004); *see also* Grearson & Enquist, *supra* note 1, at 76-77.

[48] Baker, *supra* note 47, at 13.

[49] Grearson & Enquist, *supra* note 1, at 76-77.

[50] *Id.* at 79-81.

[51] *Id.* at 76-78.

opportunity for the LWS to become familiar with the program and the individual preferences of LRW faculty.[52] This greater familiarity allows the LWS to tailor advice to students more appropriately. An alignment with the LRW program also allows LRW directors and faculty to more easily collaborate with the LWS and take advantage of the LWS's expertise. However, an LWS who is hired to work primarily with international students may be better aligned with the law school department charged with overseeing LL.M. or international programs.

---

[52] *See* Murray, *supra* note 24, at 182.

X. INNOVATIONS INSIDE AND OUTSIDE THE LRW CLASSROOM

This chapter explores innovative activities to enrich the traditional LRW curriculum. These innovations bring the outside world into the LRW classroom and bring legal writing out into the world. In doing so, these innovations help our students become practice-ready, ethical, reflective, and social-justice minded.

The chapter begins by discussing collaborations between LRW and clinical faculty to improve transfer of student learning. It then describes an example of LRW-clinical collaboration: joint teaching projects involving social justice issues. It concludes with an idea for outreach programs that can be implemented outside the LRW classroom to help reinforce and introduce soft skills essential to success in law school and beyond.

A. Working with Clinical Programs to Improve Transfer of Learning

A key innovation that law schools should consider involves collaboration between LRW faculty and clinicians to help students transfer their LRW learning to student practice in clinical courses and beyond in legal practice.[1]

Transfer is "the use of knowledge or a skill acquired in one situation to perform a different task."[2] The recent call for law schools to produce practice-ready lawyers implicitly recognizes the importance

---

[1]For a more comprehensive treatment of this topic, see Mary Nicol Bowman & Lisa Brodoff, *Cracking Student Silos: Linking Legal Writing and Clinical Learning Through Transference*, 25 CLINICAL L. REV. 269 (2019).

[2]Laurel Currie Oates, *I Know I Taught Them How to Do That*, 7 LEGAL WRITING 1, 1 (2001).

of teaching for transfer.[3] This issue has gained new urgency given the downturn in law school applicants and the academic credentials of those who do apply.[4] Therefore, law schools generally, and LRW faculty specifically, need to think about teaching our students not just for their success in our own courses, but also to enable them to take that learning and apply it to later experiences such as law clinics, externships, and legal practice.[5]

LRW and clinical faculty are in some ways natural partners in working together to improve transfer of student learning, but most schools have failed to maximize opportunities to do so, to the detriment of students. LRW and clinical faculties both have well-developed pedagogies to enhance student learning. Additionally, clinical courses often engage students in tasks that are closely related to the skills taught in LRW courses, including performing legal research, analyzing how the law applies to a client's situation, and writing objective or persuasive documents. However, despite the seemingly apparent cross-fertilization, law students in clinical courses often struggle to apply their foundational LRW skills in their clinical course work.[6] These challenges suggest that graduates will also struggle to apply their learning in law practice.

---

[3] *See, e.g.*, Elizabeth Adamo Usman, *Making Legal Education Stick: Using Cognitive Science to Foster Long-Term Learning in the Legal Writing Classroom*, 29 GEO. J. LEG. ETHICS 355, 277 (2016).

[4] *See generally* Jennifer Cooper, *Smarter Law Learning: Using Cognitive Science to Maximize Law Learning*, 44 CAP. U. L. REV. 551 (2016).

[5] *See* Anthony S. Niedwiecki, *Lawyers and Learning: A Metacognitive Approach to Legal Education*, 13 WIDENER L. REV. 33, 41 (2006) (noting that legal practice requires more ongoing learning than do most careers).

[6] *See* Shaun Archer et al., *Reaching Backward and Stretching Forward: Teaching for Transfer in Law School Clinics*, 64 J. LEGAL EDUC. 258, 269 (2014) (discussing common research and writing tasks that students struggle with in clinics); Tonya Kowalski, *Toward A Pedagogy for Teaching Legal Writing in Law School Clinics*, 17 CLINICAL L. REV. 285, 287-89 (2010) (discussing transfer problems the author observed as a clinician and later as an LRW professor).

Educational research and learning theory provide several explanations for this phenomenon. First, students may initially fail to learn the foundational LRW content effectively, often due to problems with their writing process.[7] A significant body of research demonstrates that student cramming in a particular subject is less effective for transfer of learning than studying that subject over a longer time frame.[8] Similarly, research shows that it is more effective to study multiple, related topics for shorter periods of time rather than to focus intensively on a single topic.[9] Thus, students who devote large blocks of time exclusively to LRW assignments are likely doing themselves a disservice compared to students who break LRW work into smaller segments and integrate it with work in other classes.[10]

Second, students struggle to retrieve prior learning because they often mentally "store" the information by course (e.g., LRW) rather than by topic (e.g., legal analysis applied to a client's fact situation).[11] This problem, known as "cue-dependent forgetting," involves "the inability to recall information not because a memory has been lost, but rather because of missing cues, contexts, or stimuli that were present when the memory was encoded."[12] Finally, even when students retrieve prior learning, they may struggle to apply that learning correctly in a new context (e.g. clinic versus LRW class). That struggle may be exacerbated by differing surface-level details (e.g.,

---

[7]Laurel Currie Oates, *Did Harvard Get It Right?*, 59 MERCER L. REV. 675, 689 (2008) ("You cannot transfer what you do not know. If students do not learn the material that is to be transferred, they cannot transfer that information to the new task.").

[8]Archer et al., *supra* note 6, at 264.

[9]*Id.* at 265-66.

[10]*See, e.g.,* Kowalski, *supra* note 6, at 340-41 (discussing student struggles with "cognitive overload" and the benefit of breaking the writing process down into smaller steps to help overcome that challenge).

[11]Oates, *supra* note 2, at 5.

[12]Archer et al., *supra* note 6, at 266.

moving from preparing a motion for summary judgment in a contract dispute for LRW to writing an appellate brief on a procedural issue in a criminal defense clinic).[13]

These typical learning challenges are often exacerbated by the contrast between the traditional lawyer-centered approach of the LRW curriculum and the more client-centered approach in traditional clinical pedagogy.[14] LRW faculty teach beginning 1Ls how to think, read, and write like lawyers, so LRW courses often focus on documents written for other lawyers, such as objective memos addressed to a senior partner or persuasive briefs written to a judge. In clinics, however, the focus is often on producing client-centered advocacy documents, and the professor plays a supporting role while teaching the student to act as the first chair.[15]

When LRW and clinical faculty recognize these barriers to learning transfer, however, they present opportunities for collaboration. Collaboration can take various forms, including developing a common vocabulary for core concepts.[16] LRW and clinical faculty

---

[13]Tonya Kowalski, *True North: Navigating for the Transfer of Learning in Legal Education*, 34 SEATTLE U. L. REV. 51, 61-62 (2010).

[14]Sarah O'Rourke Schrupe, *The Clinical Divide: Overcoming Barriers to Collaboration Between Clinics and Legal Writing Programs*, 14 CLINICAL L. REV. 301, 303 (2007). "The most fundamental barrier to collaboration and integrated learning between LRW programs and clinical programs stems from differences in the development of the two disciplines and the resultant differences in teaching approaches. Using broad generalizations, these differences are defined on the clinical side by a progressive or 'rebellious' approach to lawyering that is at odds with the more traditional or 'regnant' approach that is adopted in many first-year LRW classes." *Id.*

[15]See Susan L. Brooks, *Meeting the Professional Identity Challenge in Legal Education Through a Relationship-Centered Experiential Curriculum*, 41 U. BALT. L. REV. 395, 412-13 (2012).

[16]*See* Kowalski, *supra* note 6, at 363-71 (providing a detailed discussion of the variations in LRW vocabulary and an explanation of the underlying core features of LRW teaching, regardless of the specific vocabulary used).

can minimize cue-dependent forgetting by guest teaching in each other's classes.

LRW faculty can also focus on "stretching forward" to help students anticipate future applications of the foundational material taught.[17] For example, when teaching students how to draft an issue statement based on a question the supervising attorney has asked the student to research, LRW faculty can note that in a clinic or legal practice, students will need to identify the question for themselves. LRW faculty can also explain how to adapt the structure of a traditional memo for other types of documents such as client advice or demand letters,[18] and they can mention that students will often write these other documents in clinical courses and law practice. Doing so can help students store and retrieve the material within a broader rather than course-specific framework.[19]

LRW faculty should also look for opportunities to add some client-centered activities to traditional LRW assignments, such as writing a client advice letter based on a memo students have already written, or conducting client interviews to gather the facts for traditional assignments. LRW faculty can also incorporate reflection, a key piece of clinical pedagogy, by asking students to reflect on how they will apply LRW learning to future clinical work or to projects they will likely encounter in law practice.[20]

LRW faculty can also work with clinicians to help them engage students in "reaching back" to their prior learning.[21] For example,

---

[17] *See* Archer et al., *supra* note 6, at 280.

[18] *See id.*

[19] *See* Oates, *supra* note 2, at 5 ("*[U]nless told to do otherwise*, our students will store new information about contracts with the other information that they have learned in contracts. . . .") (emphasis added).

[20] *See* Schrupe, *supra* note 14, at 310 (noting the emphasis on reflection in clinical education, consistent with adult learning theory).

[21] Archer et al., *supra* note 6, at 276-79.

LRW faculty should encourage clinicians to have students write a short reflection identifying things they learned in LRW that they think will apply in the law clinic. Doing so cues students to retrieve prior learning and provides clinicians with information to help students transfer that learning effectively, mindful of the change in context or surface-level details of projects. LRW faculty can also share with clinicians material taught in LRW courses that might work well in clinical courses; for example, clinicians may not know about email memos, which many LRW faculty teach and work well for clinical projects.[22] LRW faculty can also provide clinicians with foundational LRW course documents or handouts that clinicians can use to create connections between the two courses.[23]

These collaborations that focus on transference can be valuable for student learning in their own right, and they can also lay important groundwork for joint teaching projects around social justice issues, as discussed in the next section.

B. Introducing Real Client Work to Introduce Social Justice Issues and to Teach Valuable Lawyering Skills

Another key innovation brings real client work into the LRW classroom. Too often, the first year of law school exclusively focuses on traditional doctrinal courses that teach using the "case method" based on excerpts from appellate decisions. As a result, most first-year law students lack any real experience with the most critical feature of legal practice: the client. This lack of practical experience and perspective prompted the Carnegie Foundation's

---

[22] *See* Bowman & Brodoff, *supra* note 1, at 313-15.

[23] *See id.* at 316-17.

highly publicized 2007 critique of law schools' failure to adequately prepare students for the practice of law.[24]

LRW faculty can reconnect theory with practice by bringing real client work into the first-year classroom. For example, first-year students can interview clients, conduct factual investigations, draft pleadings, and write memoranda and briefs based on real-life issues (as opposed to canned problems). Such innovative projects—which this section identifies as Real Client in the First Year (RCFY) projects—often involve partnerships between LRW, doctrinal, and clinical faculty on the one hand, and community partners on the other.[25]

RCFY projects can vary in focus, structure, and process,[26] but they share at least two hallmarks. First, they occur in the law student's first year. Second, they focus on actual work for real clients.

The RCFY project at Seattle University School of Law is one example. The Seattle project is pursued in the LRW classroom, where students receive an assignment requested by a community partner such as a legal aid organization seeking research on a potential impact litigation issue, or an assessment of the viability of a proposed legislative proposal. Or perhaps the school's clinical program needs research on a recurring issue troubling the clinic. Or students

---

[24] William M. Sullivan et al., Educating Lawyers: Preparation for the Practice of Law 188 (Carnegie Found. for Advancement of Teaching 2007); *see also* Roy Stuckey et al., Best Practices for Legal Education: A Vision and a Road Map (2007).

[25] *See generally* Sara Rankin et al., *We Have a Dream: Integrating Skills Courses and Public Interest Work in the First Year of Law School (and Beyond)*, 17 Chap. L. Rev. 89 (2013) (explaining RCFY projects and detailing ways faculty can get started).

[26] *See* Eduardo R.C. Capulong et al., The New 1L: First-Year Lawyering with Clients (2015) (surveying concrete examples of RCFY projects at different schools across the country).

might be asked to assist in drafting an amicus brief or an advice letter on a pending issue.

Although these projects take time and effort, they generate a host of benefits for students, faculty, and law schools alike.[27] One of the primary benefits for students is sparking motivation and engagement. When they move on from a canned problem to an RCFY assignment, students know their work will have a real impact on a real-world issue. LRW faculty who develop RCFY assignments have seen students at the top and bottom of the class, and everywhere in between, throw themselves into these projects because they can actually make a difference.

Increased motivation and engagement also usually lead to an improved work product. Through RCFY, students often absorb, apply, and learn more productively. They are challenged to integrate their understanding of the law with practice, exercising lawyering skills in the context of "real-world messiness" and the associated complexity. More realistic experiences in the classroom better prepare students for practice, which necessarily requires them to grapple with indeterminacy, fluidity, and flexibility: a sort of "street smartness" that only real-world legal experience can offer.

RCFY projects also lead to increased team-building and collaborative skills. The students develop a keen sense of community inside and outside the classroom. The projects challenge students to think about their roles in social justice and public service.[28] The real-life dynamics not only engage students in complex legal research and analysis, but also challenge them in nuanced ways about social justice, morality, and the ethical challenges of lawyering.

---

[27] *See generally* CAPULONG ET AL., *supra* note 26 (highlighting benefits); Rankin et al., *supra* note 25 (same).

[28] *See, e.g.*, Sara Rankin, *The Fully Formed Lawyer: Why Law Schools Should Require Public Service to Better Prepare Students for Private Practice*, 17 CHAP. L. REV. 17 (2013) (explaining links between public service work in law school and practice-readiness).

For example, one of Seattle University's RCFY classes involved a collaboration between LRW students and the administrative law clinic. A client had been denied Medicaid coverage for gender reassignment surgery. The LRW students analyzed whether the client had legal grounds to challenge that denial. For some students, this project required them to adopt a perspective they had never considered before. The RCFY project placed the whole class squarely at the intersection of health care policy, marginalized communities, and their own perspectives on life. The students engaged in deep levels of reflection uncommon in law school, let alone the first year.

But RCFY projects can also result in unanticipated benefits such as generating student interest in clinical programs or in particular areas for continued study or specialization. First-year students who have RCFY experience often show improved readiness for participation in clinics or advanced specialty courses as well.

RCFY experience also enhances student marketability for externships, summer jobs, and post-graduation positions. Potential employers commonly ask about RCFY projects, and students often reflect increased confidence in their lawyering skills.

Faculty and institutions can also benefit from RCFY projects, which help to break down institutional silos. RCFY projects often stem from collaborations across doctrinal, clinical, LRW, and even library faculty. These collaborations spark new ideas, creativity, and energy, thus building professorial capacity in terms of substantive and pedagogical experience. These projects can also fuel new scholarship. As a result, RCFY-engaged faculty often report enhanced faculty motivation, engagement, and satisfaction.

So how can LRW faculty investigate or evaluate potential RCFY options? Diverse options exist,[29] but interested faculty can consider connecting with local street activists, community organizers, or service providers to identify needs and interests that could serve as a

---

[29] *See generally* Rankin et al., *supra* note 25.

focus for an RCFY project. Faculty can also bring guest speakers into class, support an independent study, hire a research assistant, or bring news articles or contemporary issues into class. Finally, interested faculty can participate in related conferences or events, which often feature ways to get involved in RCFY efforts.

C. Creating Outreach Programs to Support Students and Promote Interconnections

For some schools and programs with limited class time, instructors and administrators may be concerned that incorporating "real-world" situations into the classroom will take away from the already-sound curricular goals of the LRW program. If resources are limited, adding more coverage to an already-packed syllabus can be daunting.

One way to give students exposure to real-world situations is to create an outreach program to accomplish some of these goals in a setting outside the classroom. An outreach program brings in speakers and develops activities that introduce students to real-world legal players such as lawyers, judges, and even upper-level students in ways that promote student engagement and motivation without using class time. As a side benefit, an outreach program can target student deficiencies and encourage solutions to correct those shortcomings. Additionally, it can create a culture of support; recent research suggests that law students who feel supported report significant professional gains.[30]

---

[30]Carole Silver, Louis Rocconi, Heather Haeger & Lindsay Watkins, *Gaining from the System: Lessons from the Law School Survey of Student Engagement About Student Development in Law School*, 10 U. St. Thomas L.J. 286, 306 (2012).

1. Structure of an Outreach Committee

Most law schools have limited resources to devote to new programs. As a result, an outreach committee would likely include volunteers from the LRW department. However, LRW faculty could also look to library faculty, career development offices, or student services staff to help. Most invited speakers will probably volunteer their services, alleviating the need for an honorarium. To fill the speaker roles, the committee can look to alumni and upper-class students.

Some schools may offer the faculty a stipend for organizing an outreach program, but if not, faculty could ask for a service or teaching load reduction. If neither is available, the faculty may be able to count the outreach committee service toward tenure, contract, or annual review requirements.

2. Possible Outreach Programs

Because most LRW students have lots of competition for their time, limiting sessions to two each semester is ideal. Depending on the school's population and needs, some suggested programs in the fall are Time Management, Writing and Wellness, and a Citation Workshop. Suggested programs for the spring semester include a Professionalism Field Trip; Oral Argument Tips; and Cover Letters, Writing Samples, and Summer Internships.

a. Time Management

Many law students struggle with how to manage their time as they begin law school.[31] Therefore, a program helping students develop those skills can be particularly well-received by the student body as well as the faculty. This program could cover calendaring programs, note-taking strategies, or editing tips. Bringing

---

[31] *See generally* Christine P. Bartholomew, *Time: An Empirical Analysis of Law Student Time Management Deficiencies*, 81 U. CIN. L. REV. 897 (2013).

in successful alumni or upper-class students to discuss these topics can create student buy-in. If that is not possible, current faculty, especially those well-versed in academic support, could lead the discussion.

b. Writing and Wellness

Forty percent of law students suffer from depression and anxiety by the time they graduate, although they enter with relatively normal rates of depression.[32] A program that discusses wellness and its correlation with success can help students find ways to combat this pervasive problem. For example, the program might bring in a yoga instructor who discusses the benefits of yoga and demonstrates chair yoga poses students can do while studying. The program could also feature a personal trainer to discuss how working out increases brain activity. Another speaker might be a nutritionist who could discuss how feeding the body also feeds the brain, and who could give tips on healthy meals and snacks for law students on a budget or in a time crunch.

c. Citation Workshop

The final suggestion for the fall semester is an interactive session that brings in law review editors to teach citation. The editors could set up a Kahoot! or Poll Everywhere interactive quiz and award prizes to the winners. The benefit of this kind of initiative is multi-faceted. First, LRW students gain a view into an honors organization that they may want to join; second, the law review gains a recruiting opportunity with a captive audience to explain to students the advantages of

---

[32]Dave Nee Foundation, *Lawyers & Depression*, http://www.daveneefoundation.org/scholarship/lawyers-and-depression/ (last visited Dec. 19, 2019). According to the Dave Nee Foundation, about 8-9% of law students suffer from depression at the time they enter law school, but that number increases to 27% after one semester, 34% after two semesters, and disturbingly, 40% after three years. Further, the risk of depression follows students into practice: lawyers are the most frequently depressed occupational group in the United States. *Id.*

law review membership. Further, the initiative shows students that good citation is important outside the LRW classroom.

d. *Professionalism Field Trip*

In most LRW programs, students begin learning persuasive writing techniques in the spring semester. As part of this education, it is important to teach them to be ethical advocates. Judges are especially well-suited to teach LRW students the principles of ethical advocacy.

In this program, students might take a field trip to a nearby courthouse. Most law schools are located within a reasonable distance of a courthouse, and most courthouses have some sort of meeting room, such as a jury assembly room or a ceremonial courtroom, that will hold a large group of visitors. Holding the session at a courthouse makes it more convenient for judges, thus ensuring participation from the bench.

Four judges is an ideal number to participate, and each might begin the program by giving a couple of tips on good legal writing.[33] Then students can break off into four groups, each one led by a different judge. Each group might be given a different hypothetical involving an ethical dilemma. The judge can then discuss the best way to handle the ethical issues. Next, the four groups can come back together, and each individual group can report its conclusions so that all participants benefit from the small-group discussions. The program could end with a question-and-answer session with the judges.

e. *Oral Argument Tips*

Also in the spring semester, most LRW programs hold some sort of mandatory oral argument experience for the students. Many

---

[33] Most of the judges will probably repeat things that LRW professors have already told students in class, reinforcing those points.

students are nervous about learning this skill and are unsure how it fits into the practice of law. The LRW faculty might bring in an appellate court judge to help alleviate the students' fears about what an oral argument entails. Teaming up with the school's moot court program, the session could feature a mock oral argument as well as a discussion with the judge about tips for effective oral argument. It would be helpful to give students the opportunity to ask the judge questions and to mingle with the judge afterward, perhaps at an informal reception.

f. Cover Letters, Writing Samples, and Summer Internships

As the spring semester ends and LRW students begin to look for summer jobs, professors are often asked to help with writing samples and cover letters. Designing a program that addresses these topics could save classroom and faculty time for more substantive matters. This effort also creates an opportunity for the LRW program to collaborate with a school's career services office and encourages students to consult that valuable resource.

3. Benefits and Drawbacks

The evident benefit of these outreach efforts is that they do not take up valuable class time that can be better spent working on writing skills, and they reinforce some of the soft skills that are taught in the classroom. But they offer other, less obvious, benefits. Many of these initiatives engage the first-year LRW students with upper-class students, alumni, attorneys, and judges. This engagement creates mentoring connections, including job prospects. The outreach activities can also introduce 1Ls to the extra-curricular opportunities available and get them out of the law school and into the legal community. For example, many law students have never visited a courthouse. Allowing them to do so in a safe environment with their peers can alleviate some of the fears inherent in the first year of law school.

The initiatives also help build relationships between the bench, the bar, and the law school. They show students that judges are human and approachable. This sense of professional identity increases the likelihood that students will pursue judicial internships and clerkships after law school, and the events help create connections between LRW students and judges.

The outreach efforts benefit LRW faculty as well. They promote collaboration with other parts of the law school and the larger university of which students may not be aware, such as the career services office, a fitness facility, or nutrition services. Moreover, the co-curricular aspects of these initiatives strengthen the credibility of the LRW faculty: the students will hear upper-class students, attorneys, and even judges repeat many of the points their LRW professors have already made in class and in comments on their papers. They further provide leadership opportunities for LRW professors and a chance to develop program-planning and relationship-building skills.

Of course, these outreach programs have some drawbacks as well, the most obvious of which is cost. Though some of these initiatives can be carried out cost-effectively, providing lunch or a reception afterward garners more participation. Seeking sponsors for these events can help offset cost. Certainly, creating and supporting these programs can tax an already overworked LRW faculty. A school's willingness to give service credit or service relief to the planners can help combat that problem.

Finally, outreach initiatives will likely compete with numerous other activities and speakers sponsored by student organizations and other law school departments. Coordinating with others to make the calendar work for all, however, promotes a collaborative and non-competitive culture within the school. Overall, while innovative programs require time and effort, many benefits are to be had for all involved.

INDEX